2010 33RD ANNUAL EDITION

SONGWRITER'S MARKET®

From the Editors of Writer's Digest Books

WRITER'S DIGEST BOOKS
CINCINNATI, OH

Publisher & Editorial Director, Writing Communities: Jane Friedman
Managing Editor, Writer's Digest Market Books: Alice Pope

Writer's Market Web site: www.writersmarket.com
Writer's Digest Web site: www.writersdigest.com

Distributed in Canada by Fraser Direct
100 Armstrong Avenue
Georgetown, ON, Canada L7G 5S4
Tel: (905) 877-4411

Distributed in the U.K. and Europe by David & Charles
Brunel House, Newton Abbot, Devon, TQ12 4PU, England
Tel: (+44) 1626 323200, Fax: (+44) 1626 323319
E-mail: postmaster@davidandcharles.co.uk

Distributed in Australia by Capricorn Link
P.O. Box 704, Windsor, NSW 2756 Australia Tel: (02) 4577-3555

ISSN: 0161-5971
ISBN-13: 978-1-58297-585-6
ISBN-10: 1-58297-585-X

Cover design by Claudean Wheeler
Production coordinated by Greg Nock

Contents

MARKETS

RESOURCES

INDEXES

How To Use Songwriter's Market

Before you dive into the *Songwriter's Market* listings and start submitting songs willy-nilly, it's a good idea to take the time to read the following information. By educating yourself on how to best use this book, you'll be better prepared when you actually do send off your tape or CD.

THE LISTINGS

Beyond the articles, there are 11 sections in the book, from Music Publishers and Record Companies to Contests & Awards. Each section begins with an introduction detailing how the different types of companies function—what part of the music industry they work in, how they make money, and what you need to think about when approaching them with your music.

These listings are the heart of *Songwriter's Market*. They are the names, addresses and contact information of music biz companies looking for songs and artists, as well as descriptions of the types of music they are looking for.

So how do I use *Songwriter's Market*?

The quick answer is that you should use the indexes to find companies who are interested in your type of music, then read the listings for details on how they want the music submitted. For support and help of all sorts, join a songwriting or other music industry association. Read everything you can about songwriting. Talk to other songwriters. That's a good start.

How does *Songwriter's Market* 'work'?

The listings in *Songwriter's Market* are packed with a lot of information. It can be intimidating at first, but they are put together in a structured way to make them easy to work with. Take a few minutes to get used to how the listings are organized, and you'll have it down in no time. For more detailed information about how the listings are put together, skip ahead to "Where Should I Send My Songs?" on page 10.

The following are general rules about how to use the listings:

1. **Read the entire listing** to decide whether to submit your music. Please do not use this book as a mass mailing list. If you blindly mail out demos by the hundreds, you'll waste a lot of money on postage, annoy a lot of people, and your demos will wind up in the trash anyway.

2. **Pay close attention to the "Music" section in each listing.** This will tell you what kind of music the company is looking for. If they want rockabilly only and you write heavy metal, don't submit to that company. That's just common sense.

3. **Pay close attention to submission instructions** shown under "How to Contact" and follow them to the letter. A lot of listings are very particular about how they want submissions packaged. Pay close attention. If you do not follow their instructions, they will probably throw your submission in the garbage. If you are confused about their directions, contact the company for clarification.

4. **If in doubt, contact the company for permission to submit.** This is a good general rule. Many companies don't mind if you send an unsolicited submission, but some will want you to get special prior permission from them. Contacting a company first is also a good way to find out their latest music needs. This is also a chance to briefly make contact on a personal level.

5. **Be courteous, be efficient and always have a purpose** to your personal contact. Do not waste their time. If you call, always have a reason for making contact—permission to submit, checking on guidelines, following up on a demo, etc. These are solid reasons to make personal contact, but once you have their attention, do not wear out your welcome. Always be polite.

6. **Check for a preferred contact.** A lot of listings have a designated contact person shown after a bolded "Contact" in the heading. This is the person you should contact with questions or to whom you should address your submission.

7. **Read the "Tips" section.** This part of the listing provides extra information on how to submit or what it might be like to work with the company. This is just the beginning. For more detailed information about the listings, see Where Should I Send My Songs? on page 10 and the sidebar with the sample listing called A Sample Listing Decoded on page 12.

FREQUENTLY ASKED QUESTIONS
How do these companies get listed in the book anyway?

No company pays to be included—all listings are free. The listings come from a combination of research the editor does on the music industry and questionnaires requested by companies who want to be listed (many of them contact us to be included). All questionnaires are screened for known sharks and to make sure they meet our requirements.

Why aren't other companies I know about listed in the book?

We may have sent them a questionnaire, but they did not return it, were removed for complaints, went out of business, specifically asked not to be listed, could not be contacted for an update, etc.

What's the deal with companies that don't take unsolicited submissions?

In the interest of completeness, the editor will sometimes include listings of crucial music companies and major labels he thinks you should be aware of. We want you to at least have some idea of what their policies are.

A company said in their listing they take unsolicited submissions. My demo came back unopened. What happened?

Some companies' needs change rapidly and may have changed since we contacted them for this edition of the book. This is another reason why it's often a good idea to contact a company before submitting.

So that's it. You now have the power in your fingertips to go out and become the professional songwriter you always wanted to be. Let us know how you're doing. Drop us a line at songmarket@fwmedia.com and tell us about any successes you have had because you used the materials found in this book.

Where Should I Send My Songs?

I t depends a lot on whether you write mainly for yourself as a performer, or if you only write and want someone else to pick up your song for their recording (usually the case in country music, for example). Are you mainly a performing songwriter or a non-performing songwriter? This is important for figuring out what kind of companies to contact, as well as how you contact them. (For more detail, skip to Submission Strategies on page 25.)

What if I'm a non-performing songwriter?

Many well-known songwriters are not performers in their own right. Some are not skilled instrumentalists or singers, but they understand melody, lyrics and harmony and how they go together. They can write great songs, but they need someone else to bring them to life through skilled musicianship. A non-performing songwriter will usually approach music publishers first for access to artists looking for songs, as well as artists' managers, their producers and their record companies. On the flip side, many incredibly talented musicians can't write to save their lives and need someone else to provide them with good songs to perform. (For more details on the different types of companies and the roles they play for performing songwriters, see the section introductions for Music Publishers on page 96, Record Companies on page 146, Record Producers on page 196, and Managers & Booking Agents on page 218. Also see Submission Strategies on page 25.)

What if I am a performing songwriter?

Many famous songwriters are also famous as performers. They are skilled interpreters of their own material, and they also know how to write to suit their own particular talents as musicians. In this case, their intention is also usually to sell themselves as a performer in hopes of recording and releasing an album, or they have an album and want to find gigs and people who can help guide their careers. They will usually approach record companies or record producers first, on the basis of recording an album. For gigs and career guidance, they talk to booking agents and managers.

A smaller number also approach publishers in hopes of getting others to perform their songs, much like non-performing songwriters. Some music publishers in recent years have also taken on the role of developing artists as both songwriters and performers, or are connected to a major record label, so performing songwriters might go to them for these reasons. (For more details on the different types of companies and the roles they play for performing songwriters, see the section introductions for Music Publishers on page 96, Record Companies on page 146, Record Producers on page 196, and Managers & Booking Agents on page 218. Also see Submission Strategies on page 25.)

How do I use *Songwriter's Market* to narrow my search?

Once you've identified whether you are primarily interested in getting others to perform your songs (non-performing songwriter) or you perform your own songs and want a record deal, etc., there are several steps you can then take:

1. **Identify what kind of music company you wish to approach.** Based on whether you're a performing or non-performing songwriter, do you want to approach a music publisher for a publishing deal? Do you want to approach a record producer because you need someone to help you record an album in the studio? Maybe you want to approach a producer in hopes that an act he's producing needs songs to complete their album. Also see Submission Strategies on page 25 and the section introductions for Music Publishers on page 96, Record Companies on page 146, Record Producers on page 196, and Managers & Booking Agents on page 218.

Types of Music Companies

- **Music Publishers**—evaluate songs for commercial potential, find artists to record them, find other uses for the songs such as film or TV, collect income from songs, protect copyrights from infringement
- **Record Companies**—sign artists to their labels; finance recordings, promotion and touring; release songs/albums to radio and TV
- **Record Producers**—work in the studio and record songs (independently or for a record company), may be affiliated with a particular artist, sometimes develop artists for record labels, locate or co-write songs if an artist does not write their own
- **Managers & Booking Agents**—work with artists to manage their careers, find gigs, locate songs to record if the artist does not write their own

Getting Started

2. **Check for companies based on location.** Maybe you need a manager located close by. Maybe you need to find as many Nashville-based companies as you can because you write country and most country publishers are in Nashville. In this case start with the Geographic Index on page 418. You can also tell Canadian and Foreign listings by the icons in the listing (see "A Sample Listing Decoded" on page 12).

3. **Look for companies based on the type of music they want.** Some companies want country. Some record labels want only punk rock. Check the Category Indexes on page 370 for a list of music companies broken down by the type of music they are interested in.

4. **Look for companies based on how open they are to beginners.** Some companies are more open than others to beginning artists and songwriters. Maybe you are a beginner and it would help to approach these companies first. Some music publishers are hoping to find that wild card hit song and don't care if it comes from an unknown writer. Maybe you are just starting out looking for gigs or record deals, and you need a manager willing to help build your band's career from the ground up. Check the Openness to Submissions Index on page 413.

For more information on how to read the listings, see A Sample Listing Decoded below.

A SAMPLE LISTING DECODED
What do the little symbols at the beginning of the listing mean?

Those are called "icons," and they give you quick information about a listing with one glance. Here is a list of the icons and what they mean:

EASY-TO-USE REFERENCE ICONS

TERMS OF AGREEMENT

DETAILED SUBMISSION GUIDELINES

WHAT THEY'RE LOOKING FOR

INSIDER ADVICE

🅽🅞🄿🅨 **METAL BLADE RECORDS** 2828 Cochran St., Suite 302, Simi Valley CA 93065. (805)522-9111. Fax: (805)522-9380. E-mail: metalblade@metalblade.com. Website: www.metalblade.com. Record company. Estab. 1982. Releases 20 LPs, 2 EPs and 20 CDs/year. Pays negotiable royalty to artists on contract.

How to Contact Submit demo CD by mail. Unsolicited submissions are OK. CD with 3 songs. Does not return material. Responds in 3 months.

Music Mostly **heavy metal** and **industrial**; also **hardcore, gothic** and **noise.** Released "Gallery of Suicide," recorded by Cannibal Corpse; "Voo Doo," recorded by King Diamond; and "A Pleasant Shade of Gray," recorded by Fates Warning, all on Metal Blade Records. Other artists include As I Lay Dying, The Red Chord, The Black Dahlia Murder, and Unearth.

Tips "Metal Blade is known throughout the underground for quality metal-oriented acts."

Openness to submissions

☐ means the company is open to beginners' submissions, regardless of past success

◖ means the company is mostly interested in previously published songwriters/ well-established acts*, but will consider beginners

◗ these companies do not want submissions from beginners, only from previously published songwriters/well-established acts*

⊘ companies with this icon only accept material referred by a reputable industry source**

* Well-established acts are those with a following, permanent gigs or previous record deal

** Reputable industry sources include managers, entertainment attorneys, performing rights organizations, etc.

Other icons

⊡ means the listing is Canadian

⊕ means the listing is based overseas (Europe, Britain, Australia, etc.)

Ⓝ indicates a listing is new to this edition

$ is for companies who have won an industry award of some sort

⊡ shows a company places songs in films or television (excluding commercials)

Additional Resources

For More Info

Songwriter's Market lists music publishers, record companies, producers and managers (as well as advertising firms, play producers and classical performing arts organizations) along with specifications on how to submit your material to each. If you can't find a certain person or company you're interested in, there are other sources of information you can try.

The Recording Industry Sourcebook, an annual directory published by Norris-Whitney Communications, lists record companies, music publishers, producers and managers, as well as attorneys, publicity firms, media, manufacturers, distributors and recording studios around the U.S. Trade publications such as *Billboard* or *Variety*, available at most local libraries and bookstores, are great sources for up-to-date information. These periodicals list new companies as well as the artists, labels, producers and publishers for each song on the charts.

CD booklets can also be valuable sources of information, providing the name of the record company, publisher, producer and usually the manager of an artist or group. Use your imagination in your research and be creative—any contacts you make in the industry can only help your career as a songwriter. See Publications of Interest on page 345.

Demo Recordings

What Should I Know?

What is a "demo"?

The demo, shorthand for demonstration recording, is the most important part of your submission package. They are meant to give music industry professionals a way to hear all the elements of your song as clearly as possible so they can decide if it has commercial potential.

Should I send a cassette or a CD?

More and more music industry people want CDs, although the cassette is still commonly accepted. A few companies want demos sent on CD only. It's getting cheaper and easier all the time to burn recordings onto CDR ("CD-Recordable"), so it is worth the investment to buy a burner or borrow one. Other formats such as DAT ("Digital Audio Tape") are rarely requested.

What should I send if I'm seeking management?

Some companies want a video of an act performing their songs. Check with the companies for specific requirements.

How many songs should I send, and in what order and length?

Most music industry people agree that three songs is enough. Most music professionals are short on time, and if you can't catch their attention in three songs, your songs probably don't have hit potential. Also, put three *complete songs* on your demo, not just snippets. Make sure to put your best, most commercial song first. An up-tempo number is usually best. If you send a cassette, *put all the songs on one side of the cassette and cue the tape to the beginning of the first song so no time is wasted fast-forwarding or rewinding.*

Should I sing my own songs on my demo?

If you can't sing well, you may want to find someone who can. There are many places to check for singers and musicians, including songwriters organizations, music stores, and songwriting magazines. Some aspiring professional singers will sing on demos in exchange for a copy they can use as a demo to showcase their singing.

Should I use a professional demo service?

Many songwriters find professional demo services convenient if they don't have time or the resources to put together musicians on their own. For a fee, a demo service will produce your songs in their studio using in-house singers and musicians (this is pretty common in Nashville). Many of these advertise in music magazines, songwriting newsletters and bulletin boards at music stores. Make sure to hear samples of work they've done in the past. Some are mail-order businesses—you send a rough tape of your song or the sheet music, and they produce and record a demo within a month or two. Be sure you find a service that will let you have some control over how the demo is produced, and tell them exactly how you want your song to sound. As with studios, look around for a service that fits your needs and budget. (Some will charge as low as $300 for three songs, while others may go as high as $3,000 and boast a high-quality sound—*shop around and use your best judgment*!)

Should I buy equipment and record demos myself?

If you have the drive and focus to learn good recording technique, yes. If not, it might be easier to have someone else do it. Digital multi-track recorders are now easily available and within reasonable financial reach of many people. For performing songwriters in search of record deals, the actual sound of their recordings can often be an important part of their artistic concept. Having the "means of production" within their grasp can be crucial to artists pursuing the independent route. But, if you don't know how to use the equipment, it may be better to go into a professional studio.

How elaborate and full should the demo production be if I'm a non-performing songwriter?

Many companies in *Songwriter's Market* tell you what they prefer. If in doubt, contact them and ask. In general, country songs and pop ballads can often be demoed with just a vocal plus guitar or piano, although many songwriters in those genres still prefer to get a more complete recording with drums, guitars and other backing instruments. Up-tempo pop, rock and dance demos usually need a more full production.

What kind of production do I need if I'm a performing songwriter?

If you are a band or artist looking for a record deal, you will need a demo that is as fully produced as possible. Many singer/songwriters record their demos as if they were going to be released as an album. That way, if they don't get a deal, they can still release it on their own. Professionally pressed CDs are also now easily within reach of performing songwriters, and many companies offer graphic design services for a professional-looking product.

How Do I Submit My Demo?

You have three basic options for submitting your songs: submitting by mail, submitting in person and submitting over the Internet (the newest and least widely accepted option at this time).

SUBMITTING BY MAIL

Should I call, write or e-mail first to ask for permission or submission requirements?

This is always a good idea, and many companies ask you to contact them first. If you call, be polite, brief and specific. If you send a letter, make sure it is typed and to the point. Include a typed SASE they can use to reply. If you send an e-mail, again be professional and to the point. Proofread your message before you send it, and then be patient. Give them some time to reply. Do not send out mass e-mails or otherwise spam their e-mail account.

What do I send with my demo?

Most companies have specific requirements, but here are some general pointers:

- Read the listing carefully and submit exactly what they ask for, in the exact way they describe. It's also a good idea to call first, just in case they've changed their submission policies.
- Listen to each demo to make sure they sound right and are in the right order (see Demo Recordings: What Should I Know? on page 14).
- If you use cassettes, make sure they are cued up to the beginning of the first song.
- Enclose a brief, typed cover letter to introduce yourself. Tell them what songs you are sending and why you are sending them. If you are pitching your songs to a particular artist, say so in the letter. If you are an artist/songwriter looking for a record deal, you should say so. Be specific.
- Include typed lyric sheets or lead sheets, if requested. Make sure your name, address and phone number are on each sheet.
- Neatly label each tape or CD with your name, address, e-mail and phone

Submission Mailing Pointers

Send your package with bubble wrap or in a **padded envelope** to protect pieces.

Laser Print all text on computer for a professional look.

Include **lyric sheets** with your demo and label each song selection (verse, chorus, etc.)

Keep **cover letter brief** and let the song speak for itself.

Be sure to enclose sufficient **return postage** for all your materials.

If you send a **cassette**, make sure you've cued the tape to the beginning of the first song.

Include **contact information** on every piece.

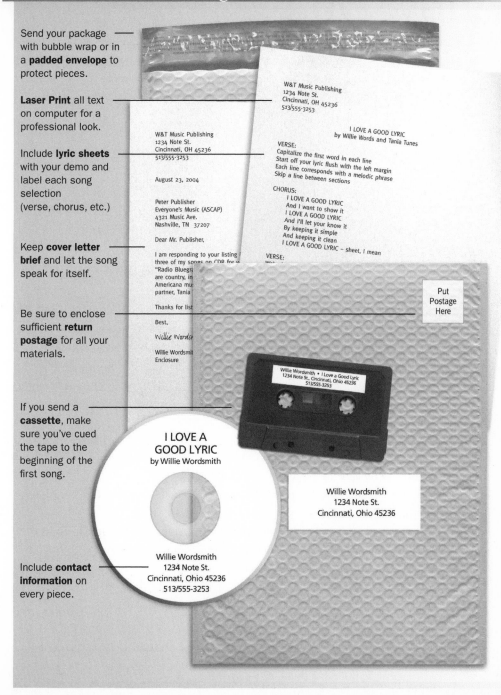

W&T Music Publishing
1234 Note St.
Cincinnati, OH 45236
513/555-3253

I LOVE A GOOD LYRIC
by Willie Words and Tania Tunes

VERSE:
Capitalize the first word in each line
Start off your lyric flush with the left margin
Each line corresponds with a melodic phrase
Skip a line between sections

CHORUS:
I LOVE A GOOD LYRIC
And I want to show it
I LOVE A GOOD LYRIC
And I'll let your know it
By keeping it simple
And keeping it clean
I LOVE A GOOD LYRIC – sheet, I mean

VERSE:

W&T Music Publishing
1234 Note St.
Cincinnati, OH 45236
513/555-3253

August 23, 2004

Peter Publisher
Everyone's Music (ASCAP)
4321 Music Ave.
Nashville, TN 37207

Dear Mr. Publisher,

I am responding to your listing
three of my songs on CDR for
"Radio Bluegra
are country, in
Americana mus
partner, Tania

Thanks for list

Best,

Willie Wordsm

Willie Wordsmit
Enclosure

Put Postage Here

Willie Wordsmith • I Love a Good Lyric
1234 Note St., Cincinnati, Ohio 45236
513/555-3253

Willie Wordsmith
1234 Note St.
Cincinnati, Ohio 45236

I LOVE A GOOD LYRIC
by Willie Wordsmith

Willie Wordsmith
1234 Note St.
Cincinnati, Ohio 45236
513/555-3253

number, along with the names of the songs in the order they appear on the recording.

- Include a SASE with sufficient postage and large enough to return all your materials. **Warning: Many companies do not return materials, so read each listing carefully!**
- If you submit to companies in other countries, include a self-addressed envelope (SAE) and International Reply Coupon (IRC), available at most post offices. Make sure the envelope is large enough to return all of your materials.
- Pack everything neatly. Neatly type or write the company's address and your return address so they are clearly visible. Your package is the first impression a company has of you and your songs, so neatness counts!
- Mail first class. Stamp or write "First Class Mail" on the package and the SASE you enclose.
- Do not use registered or certified mail unless requested! Most companies will not accept or open demos sent by registered or certified mail for fear of lawsuits.
- Keep records of the dates, songs and companies you submit to.

Is it OK to send demos to more than one person or company at a time?

It is usually acceptable to make simultaneous submissions. One exception is when a publisher, artist or other industry professional asks to put your song "on hold."

What does it mean when a song is "on hold"?

This means they intend to record the song and don't want you to give the song to anyone else. This is not a guarantee, though. Your song may eventually be returned to you, even if it's been on hold for months. Or it may be recorded and included on the album. If either of these happens, you are free to pitch your song to other people again.

How can I protect myself from my song being put "on hold" indefinitely?

You can, and should, protect yourself. Establish a deadline for the person who asks for the hold (for example, "You can put my song on hold for [number of] months."), or modify the hold to specify you will still pitch the song to others but won't sign another deal without allowing the person with the song on hold to make you an offer. Once you sign a contract with a publisher, they have exclusive rights to your song and you may not pitch it to other would-be publishers.

SUBMITTING IN PERSON
Is a visit to New York, Nashville or Los Angeles to submit in person a good idea?

A trip to one of the major music hubs can be valuable if you are organized and prepared to make the most of it. You should have specific goals and set up appointments before you go. Some industry professionals are difficult to see and may not feel meeting out-of-town writers is a high priority. Others are more open and even encourage face-to-face meetings. By taking the time to travel, organize and schedule meetings, you can appear more professional than songwriters who submit blindly through the mail.

What should I take?

Take several copies of your demo and typed lyric sheets of each of your songs. More than one company you visit may ask you to leave a copy for them to review. You can expect occasionally to find a person has cancelled an appointment, but want you to leave a copy of your songs so they may listen and contact you later. (Never give someone the only or last copy of your demo if you absolutely want it returned, though.)

Where should I network while visiting?

Coordinate your trip with a music conference or make plans to visit ASCAP, BMI, or SESAC offices while you are there. For example, the South by Southwest Music Conference in Austin and the NSAI Spring Symposium often feature demo listening sessions, where industry professionals listen to demos submitted by songwriters attending the seminar. ASCAP, BMI, and SESAC also sometimes sponsor seminars or allow aspiring songwriters to make appointments with counselors who can give them solid advice.

How do I deal with rejection?

Many good songs have been rejected simply because they were not what the publisher or record company was looking for at that particular point. Do not take it personally. If few people like your songs, it does not mean they are not good. On the other hand, if you have a clear vision for what your particular songs are trying to get across, specific comments can also teach you a lot about whether your concept is coming across as you intended. If you hear the same criticisms of your songs over and over—for instance, the feel of the melody isn't right or the lyrics need work—give the advice serious thought. Listen carefully and use what the reviewers say constructively to improve your songs.

SUBMITTING OVER THE INTERNET
Is it OK to submit over the Internet?

It can be done, but it's not yet widely accepted. There can still be problems with audio file formats. Although e-mail is more common now if you look through the listings in *Songwriter's Market*, not all music companies are necessarily equipped with computers or Internet access sufficient to make the process easy. But it shows a lot of promise for the future. Web-based companies like Tonos.com or TAXI, among many others are making an effort to connect songwriters and industry professionals over the Internet. The Internet is proving important for networking. Garageband. com has extensive bulletin boards and allow members to post audio files of songs for critique. Stay tuned for future developments.

If I want to try submitting over the Internet, what should I do?

First, send an e-mail to confirm whether a music company is equipped to stream or download audio files properly (whether mp3 or real audio, etc.). If they do accept demos online, one strategy becoming common is build a website with audio files that can be streamed or downloaded. Then, when you have permission, send an e-mail with links to that website or to particular songs. All they have to do is click on the link and it launches their Web browser to the appropriate page. Do not try to send mp3s or other files as attachments. They are often too large for the free online e-mail accounts people commonly use, and they may be mistakenly erased as potential viruses.

How Do I Avoid the Rip-Offs?

The music industry has its share of dishonest, greedy people who will try to rip you off by appealing to your ambition, by stroking your ego, or by claiming special powers to make you successful—for a price, of course. Most of them use similar methods, and you can prevent a lot of heartbreak by learning to spot them and stay away.

What is a "song shark"?

"Song sharks," as they're called, prey on beginners—songwriters unfamiliar with how the music industry works and what the ethical standards are. Two general signs of a song shark are:

- Song sharks will take any songs—quality doesn't count.
- They're not concerned with future royalties, since they get their money up front from songwriters who think they're getting a great deal.

What are some of the more blatant rip-offs?

A request for money up front is the most *common element*. Song sharks may ask

If You Write Lyrics, But Not Music

- **You must find a collaborator.** The music business is looking for the complete package: music plus lyrics. If you don't write music, find a collaborator who does. The best way to find a collaborator is through songwriting organizations. Check the Organizations section (page 302) for songwriting groups near you.
- **Don't get ripped-off.** "Music mills" advertise in the back of magazines or solicit you through the mail. For a fee they will set your lyrics or poems to music. The rip-off is that they may use the same melody for hundreds of lyrics and poems, whether it sounds good or not. Publishers recognize one of these melodies as soon as they hear it.

for money in the form of submission fees, an outright offer to publish your song for a fee or an offer to re-record your demo for a sometimes hefty price (with the implication that they will make your song wildly successful if you only pay to have it re-demoed in *their studio*). There are many variations on this theme.

Here is a list of rules that can help you avoid a lot of scams:

- **DO NOT SELL YOUR SONGS OUTRIGHT!** It's unethical for anyone to offer such a proposition. If your song becomes successful after you've sold it outright, you will never get royalties for it.
- **Never pay any sort of "submission fees," "review fees," "service fees," "filing fees," etc.** Reputable companies review material free of charge. If you encounter a company in this book that charges to submit, report them to the editor. If a company charges "only" $15 to submit your song, consider this: if *"only" 100 songwriters pay the $15, this company has made an extra $1,500 just for opening the mail!*
- **Never pay to have your songs published.** A reputable company interested in your songs assumes the responsibility and cost of promoting them, in hopes of realizing a profit once the songs are recorded and released. If they truly believe in your song, they will accept the costs involved.
- **Do not pay a company to pair you with a collaborator.** It's much better to contact a songwriting organization that offers collaboration services to their members.
- **Never pay to have your lyrics or poems set to music.** This is a classic rip-off. "Music mills"—for a price—may use the same melody for hundreds of lyrics and poems, whether it sounds good or not. Publishers recognize one of these melodies as soon as they hear it.
- **Avoid "pay-to-play" CD compilation deals.** It's totally unrealistic to expect this will open doors for you. These are mainly a money-maker for the music company. CDs are cheap to manufacture, so a company that charges $100 to include your recording on a CD is making a killing. They claim they send these CDs to radio stations, producers, etc., but they usually wind up in the trash or as drink coasters. Music industry professionals have no incentive to listen to them. Everybody on the CD paid to be included, so it's not like they were carefully screened for quality.
- **Avoid "songpluggers" who offer to "shop" your song for an upfront fee or retainer.** This practice is not appropriate for *Songwriter's Market* readers, many of whom are beginners and live away from major music centers like Nashville. Professional, established songwriters in Nashville are sometimes known to work on a fee basis with song-pluggers they have gotten to know over many years, *but the practice is controversial even for professionals.* Also, the songpluggers used by established professionals are very selective about their clients and have their own reputation to uphold. Companies who offer

you these services but barely know you or your work are to be avoided. Also, contracting a songplugger by long distance offers little or no accountability—you have no direct way of knowing what they're doing on your behalf.

- **Avoid paying a fee up front to have a publisher make a demo of your song.** Some publishers may take demo expenses out of your future royalties (a negotiable contract point usually meant to avoid endless demo sessions), but avoid paying up front for demo costs. Avoid situations where it is implied or expressed that a company will publish your song in return for you paying up front to use their demo services.

- **No record company should ask you to pay them or an associated company to make a demo.** The job of a record company is to make records and decide which artists to sign *after* listening to demo submissions.

- **Read all contracts carefully before signing.** And don't sign any contract you're unsure about or that you don't fully understand. It is well worth paying an attorney for the time it takes him to review a contract if you can avoid a bad situation that may cost you thousands of dollars.

- **Before entering a songwriting contest, read the rules carefully.** Be sure what you're giving up in the way of entry fees, etc., is not more than what you stand to gain by winning the contest. See the Contests & Awards section on page 285.

- **Verify any situation about an individual or company if you have any doubts at all.** Contact the company's Performing Rights Society—ASCAP, BMI, SESAC, or SOCAN (in Canada). Check with the Better Business Bureau in the company's town, or contact the state attorney general's office. Contact professional organizations you're a member of and inquire about the reputation of the company.

How Do I File a Complaint?

Write to the *Songwriter's Market* editor at: 4700 E. Galbraith Rd., Cincinnati OH 45236. Include:

- A complete description of the situation, as best you can describe it.
- Copies of any materials a company may have sent you that we may keep on file.

If you encounter situations similar to any of the "song shark" scenarios described above, let us know about it.

- **If a record company or other company asks you to pay expenses up front, be careful.** Record producers commonly charge up front to produce an artist's album. Small indie labels sometimes ask a band to help with recording costs (but seek less control than a major label might). It's up to you to decide whether or not it is a good idea. Talk to other artists who have signed similar contracts before you sign one yourself. Research companies to find out if they can deliver on their claims, and what kind of distribution they have. Visit their website, if they have one. Beware of any company that won't let you know what it has done in the past. If a company has had successes and good working relationships with artists, it should be happy to brag about them.

I noticed record producers charge to produce albums. Is this bad?

Not automatically. Just remember what your goals are. If you write songs, but do not sing or perform, you are looking for publishing opportunities with the producer instead of someone who can help you record an album or CD. If you are a performing artist or band, then you might be in the market to hire a producer, in which case you will most likely pay them up front (and possibly give them a share in royalties or publishing, depending on the specific deal you negotiate). For more information see the Record Producers section introduction on page 196 and Royalties: Where Does the Money Come From? on page 28.

Will it help me avoid rip-offs if I join a songwriting organization?

Yes. You will have access to a lot of good advice from a lot of experienced people. You will be able to research and compare notes, which will help you avoid a lot of pitfalls.

What should I know about contracts?

Negotiating a fair contract is important. You must protect yourself, and there are specific things you should look for in a contract (see What About Contracts? on page 38).

Are companies that offer demo services automatically bad?

No, but you are not obligated to make use of their services. Many music companies have their own or related recording studios, and with good recording equipment becoming so cheap and easy to use in recent years, a lot of them are struggling to stay afloat. This doesn't mean a company is necessarily trying to rip you off, but use your best judgment. In some cases, a company will submit a listing to *Songwriter's Market* for the wrong reasons—to pitch their demo services instead of finding songs to sign—in which case you should report them to the *Songwriter's Market* editor.

Submission Strategies

NON-PERFORMING SONGWRITERS

Here's a short list of avenues non-performing songwriters can pursue when submitting songs:

1. Submit to a music publisher. This is the obvious one. Look at the information under "**Music**" in the listing to see examples of a publisher's songs and the artists they've found cuts with. Do you recognize the songs? Have you heard of the artists? Who are the writers? Do they have cuts with artists you would like to get a song to?

2. Submit to a record company. Are the bands and artists on the record company's roster familiar? Do they tend to use outside songs on their albums? When pursuing this angle, it often helps to contact the record company first. Ask if they have a group or artist in development who needs material.

3. Submit to a record producer. Do the producer's credits in the listings show songs written by songwriters other than the artist? Does he produce name artists known for using outside material? Be aware that producers themselves often write with the artists, so your song might also be competing against the producer's songwriting.

4. Submit to an artist's manager. If an artist needs songs, their manager is a prime gateway for your song. Contact the manager and ask if he has an act in need of material.

5. Join a songwriting organization. Songwriting organizations are a good way to make contacts. You'll discover opportunities through the contacts you make that others might not hear about. Some organizations can put you in direct contact with publishers for song critique sessions. You can increase your chances of a hit by co-writing with other songwriters. Your songs will get better because of the feedback from other members.

6. Approach Performing Rights Organizations (PROs). PROs like ASCAP and BMI have writer relations representatives who can sometimes (if they think you're ready) give you a reference to a music company. This is one of the favored routes to success in the Nashville music scene.

Getting Started

PERFORMING SONGWRITERS
This is a bit more complicated, because there are a lot of different avenues available.

Finding a record deal
This is often a performing songwriter's primary goal—to get a record deal and release an album. Here are some possible ways to approach it:

1. Approach a record company for a record deal. This is another obvious one. Independent labels will be a lot more approachable than major labels, who are usually deluged with demos. Independent labels give you more artistic freedom, while major labels will demand more compromise, especially if you do not have a previous track record. A compromise between the two is to approach one of the "fake indie" labels owned by a major. You'll get more of the benefits of an indie, but with more of the resources and connections of a major label.

2. Approach a record producer for a development deal. Some producers sign artists, produce their album and develop them like a record company, and then approach major labels for distribution deals. This has advantages and drawbacks. For example, the producer gives you guidance and connections, but it can also be harder to get paid because you are signed to the producer and not the label.

3. Get a manager with connections. The right manager with the right connections can make all the difference in getting a record deal.

4. Ask a music publisher. Publishers are taking on more and more of a role of developing performing songwriters as artists. Many major publishers are sister companies to record labels and can shop you for a deal when they think you're ready. They do this in hopes of participating in the mechanical royalties from an album release, and these monies can be substantial when it's a major label release.

5. Approach an entertainment attorney. Entertainment attorneys are a must when it comes to negotiating record contracts, and some moonlight by helping artists make connections for record deals (they will get their cut, of course).

6. Approach PROs. ASCAP and BMI can counsel you on your career and possibly make a referral. They also commonly put on performance showcases where A&R ("artist and repertoire") people from record labels attend to check out new artists.

Finding a producer to help with your album
Independently minded performing songwriters often find they need help navigating the studio when it comes time to produce their own album. In this case, the producer often works for an upfront fee from the artist, for a percentage of the royalty when the album is released and sold (referred to as "points," as in "percentage points"), or a combination of both.

Things to keep in mind when submitting a demo to a producer on this basis:

1. Is the producer known for a particular genre or "sound"? Many producers have a signature sound to their studio productions and are often connected to specific genres. Phil Spector had the "Wall of Sound." Bob Rock pioneered a glossy metal sound for Metallica and The Cult. Daniel Lanois and Brian Eno are famous for the atmospheres they created on albums by U2. Look at your favorite CDs to see who produced. Use these as touchstones when approaching producers to see if they are on your wavelength.

2. What role does a particular producer like to take in the studio? The "Tips" section of *Songwriter's Market* Record Producers listings often have notes from the producer about how they like to work with performing songwriters in the studio. Some work closely as a partner with the artist on developing arrangements and coaching performances. Some prefer final authority on creative decisions. Think carefully about what kind of working relationship you want.

Finding a manager

Many performing songwriters eventually find it necessary to find a manager to help with developing their careers and finding gigs. Some things to keep in mind when looking:

1. Does the manager work with artists in my genre of music? A manager who typically works with punk rock bands may not have as many connections useful to an aspiring country singer-songwriter. A manager who mainly works with gospel artists might not know what to do with a hedonistic rock band.

2. How big is the manager's agency? If a manager is working with multiple acts, but has a small (or no) staff, you might not get the attention you want. Some of the listings have information in the heading about the agency's staff size.

3. Does the manager work with acts from my region? You can check the Geographic Index on page 418 to check for management agencies located near your area. Many of the listings also have information in their headings provided by the companies describing whether they work with regional acts only or artists from any region.

4. Does the manager work with name acts? A manager with famous clients could work wonders for your career. Or you could get lost in the shuffle. Use your best judgment when sizing up a potential manager and be clear with yourself about the kind of relationship you would like to have and the level of attention you want for your career.

5. If I'm a beginner, will the manager work with me? Look in the Openness to Submissions Index on page 413 to find companies open to beginners. Some may suggest extensive changes to your music or image. On the other hand, you may have a strong vision of what you want to do and need a manager who will work with you to achieve that vision instead of changing you around. Decide for yourself how much you are willing to compromise in good faith.

Remember that a relationship between you and a manager is a two-way street. You will have to earn each other's trust and be clear about your goals for mutual success.

Royalties

Where Does the Money Come From?

NON-PERFORMING SONGWRITERS
How do songwriters make money?

The quick answer is that songwriters make money through rights available to them through the copyright laws. For more details, keep reading and see the article "What About Copyright?" on page 33.

What specific rights make money for songwriters?

There are two primary ways songwriters earn money on their songs: Performance Royalties and Mechanical Royalties.

What is a performance royalty?

When you hear a song on the radio, on television, in the elevator, in a restaurant, etc. the songwriter receives royalties, called "Performance Royalties." Performing Rights Organizations (ASCAP, BMI and SESAC in the U.S.A.) collect payment from radio stations, television, etc. and distribute those payments to songwriters (see below).

What is a mechanical royalty?

When a record company puts a song onto a CD, cassette, etc. and distributes copies for sale, they owe a royalty payment to the songwriter for each copy they press of the album. It is called a "mechanical royalty" because of the mechanical process used to mass produce a copy of a CD, cassette or sheet music. The payment is small per song (see the "Royalty Provisions" subhead of the Basic Song Contract Pointers sidebar on page 40), but the earnings can add up and reach massive proportions for songs appearing on successful major label albums. ****Note: This royalty is totally different from the artist royalty on the retail price of the album.****

Who collects the money for performance and mechanical royalties?

Performing Rights Organizations collect performance royalties. There are three organizations that collect performance royalties: ASCAP, BMI and SESAC.

These organizations arose many years ago when songwriters and music publishers gathered together to press for their rights and improve their ability to collect fees for the use of their songs. ASCAP, BMI and SESAC collect fees for the use of songs and then pass along the money to their member songwriters and music publishers.

Music Publishing Royalties

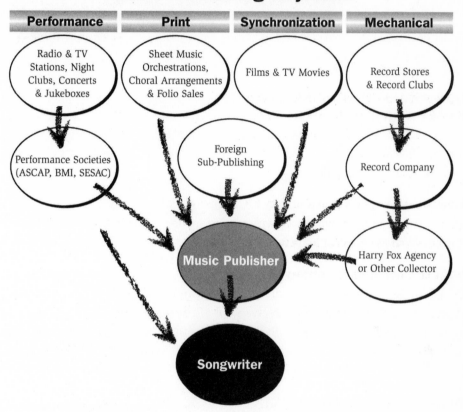

Mechanical rights organizations collect mechanical royalties. There are three organizations that collect mechanical royalties: The Harry Fox Agency (HFA), The American Mechanical Rights Agency (AMRA) and The Songwriters Guild of America (SGA). These three organizations collect mechanical royalties from record companies of all sizes—major labels, mid-size and independents—and pass the royalties along to member music publishers and songwriters.

How do songwriters hook up with this system to earn royalties?

For **Performance Royalties**, individual songwriters **affiliate** with a Performing Rights

Organization of their choice, and register their songs in the PRO database. Each PRO has a slightly different method of calculating payment, different ownership, and different membership structure, so choosing a PRO is an individual choice. Once a songwriter is affiliated and has registered their songs, the PROs then collect fees as described above and issue a check to the songwriter.

For **Mechanical Royalties**, three different things can happen:

1. The songwriter is signed to a publisher that is affiliated with The Harry Fox Agency. The Harry Fox Agency collects the mechanical royalties and passes them along to the publisher. The publisher then passes these along to the songwriter within 30 days. This case usually happens when a songwriter is signed to a major publisher and has a song on a major label album release.

2. The songwriter is not signed to a publisher and owns exclusive rights to his songs, and so works with AMRA or The Songwriters Guild of America, who cut a check directly to the songwriter instead of passing them to the publisher first.

3. They are signed to a publisher, but the songs are being released on albums by independent labels. In this case, the songwriter often works with AMRA since they have a focus on the independent music publishing market.

PERFORMING SONGWRITERS/ARTISTS
How do performing songwriters make money?

Performing songwriters and artists (if they write their own songs) make money just like non-performing songwriters, as described above, but they also make money through royalties made on the retail price of an album when it is sold online, in a store, etc.

What about all the stories of performing songwriters getting into bad deals?

The stories are generally true, but if they're smart, performing songwriters usually can hold on to the money they would be owed as songwriters (performing and mechanical royalties). But when it comes to retail sale royalties, all they will usually see is an "advance"—essentially a loan—which must then be paid off from record sales. You will not see a royalty check on retail sales until you're advance is paid off ("earned out"). If you are given a $600,000 advance, you will have to pay back the record company $600,000 out of your sales royalties before you see any more money.

Do performing songwriters and artists get to keep the advance?

Not really. If you have a manager who has gotten you a record deal, he will take his cut. You will probably be required in the contract to pay for the producer and studio time to make the album. Often the producer will take a percentage of subsequent royalties from album sales, which comes out of your pocket. Then there are also music video costs, promotion to radio stations, tour support, paying sidemen, etc. Just about anything you can think of is eventually paid for out of your advance or out of sales royalties. There are also deductions to royalties usually built in to record company contracts that make it harder to earn out an advance.

What should a performing songwriter wanting to sign with a major label do?

Their best option is to negotiate a fair contract, get as big of an advance as possible, and then manage that advance money the best they can. A good contract will keep the songwriting royalties described above completely separate from the flow of sales royalties, and will also cut down on the number of royalty deductions the record company builds into the contract. And because of the difficulty in earning out any size advance or auditing the record company, it makes sense to get as much cash up front as you can, then to manage that as best you can. You will need a good lawyer.

RECORD COMPANIES, PRODUCERS & MANAGERS, BOOKING AGENTS

How do music publishers make money?

A publisher works as a songwriter's agent, looks for profitable commercial uses for the songs he represents, and then takes a percentage of the profits. This is typically 50% of all earning from a particular song—often referred to as the *publisher's share*. A successful publisher stays in contact with several A&R reps, finding out what upcoming projects are in need of new material, and whether any songs he represents will be appropriate.

How do record companies make money?

Record companies primarily make their money from profits made selling CDs, cassettes, DVDs, etc. Record companies keep most of the profit after subtracting manufacturing costs, royalties to recording artists, distribution fees and the costs of promoting songs to radio (which for major labels can reach up to $300,000 per song). Record companies also usually have music publishing divisions that make money performing all the functions of publishers.

How do record producers make money?

Producers mostly make their money by charging a flat fee up front to helm a recording project, by sharing in the royalties from album sales, or both. A small independent producer might charge $10,000 (or sometimes less) up front to produce a small indie band, while a "name" producer such as Bob Rock, who regularly works with major label bands, might charge $300,000. Either of these might also take a share in sales royalties, referred to as "points"—as in "percentage points." A producer might say, "I'll produce you for $10,000 and 2 points." If an artist is getting a 15% royalty an album sales, then two of those percentage points will go to the producer instead. Producers also make money by co-writing with the artists to get publishing royalties, or they may ask for part of the publishing from songs written by outside songwriters.

How do managers make money?

Most managers make money by taking a percentage commission of their clients' income, usually 10-25%. If a touring band finishes a show and makes a $2,000 profit, a manager on 15% commission would get $300. If an artist gets a $40,000 advance from a mid-size label, the manager would get $6,000. Whether an artist's songwriting income is included in the manager's commission comes down to negotiation. *The commission should give the manager incentive to make things happen for your career, so avoid paying flat fees up front.*

What About Copyright?

How am I protected by the copyright laws?

Copyright protection applies to your songs the instant you put them down in fixed form—a recording, sheet music, lead sheet, etc. This protection lasts for your lifetime plus 70 years (or the lifetime of the last surviving writer, if you co-wrote the song with somebody else). When you prepare demos, place notification of copyright on all copies of your song—the lyric sheets, lead sheets and labels for cassettes, CDs, etc. The notice is simply the word "copyright" or the symbol © followed by the year the song was created (or published) and your name: © 2005 by John Q. Songwriter.

What parts of a song are protected by copyright?

Traditionally, only the melody line and the lyrics are eligible for copyright. Period. Chords and rhythm are virtually never protected. An incredibly original arrangement can sometimes qualify. Sound recordings can also be copyrighted, but this applies strictly to the actual sounds on the recording, not the song itself (this copyright is usually owned by record companies).

What songs are not protected?

Song titles or mere ideas for music and lyrics cannot be copyrighted. Very old songs in the "public domain" are not protected. You could quote a melody from a Bach piece, but you could not then stop someone else from quoting the same melody in their song.

When would I lose or have to share the copyright?

If you *collaborate* with other writers, they are assumed to have equal interests unless you state some other arrangement, in writing. If you write under a *work-for-hire* arrangement, the company or person who hired you to write the song then owns the copyright. Sometimes your spouse may automatically be granted an interest in your copyright as part of their *spousal rights*, which might then become important if you got divorced.

Should I register my copyright?

Registering your copyright with the Library of Congress gives the best possible protection. Registration establishes a public record of your copyright—even though a song is legally protected whether or not it is registered—and could prove useful in any future court cases involving the song. Registration also entitles you to a potentially greater settlement in a copyright infringement lawsuit.

How do I register my song?

To register your song, request government form PA from the Copyright Office. Call the 24-hour hotline at (202)707-9100 and leave your name and address on the messaging system. Once you receive the PA form, you must return it, along with a registration fee and a CD (or tape) and lead sheet of your song. Send these to the Register of Copyrights, Copyright Office, Library of Congress, Washington DC 20559. It may take several months to receive your certificate of registration from the Copyright Office, but your songs are protected from the date of creation (the date of registration will reflect the date you applied). For more information, call the Copyright Office's Public Information Office at (202)707-3000 or visit their Web site at www.copyright.gov.

Government Resources

For More Info

The Library of Congress's copyright website is your best source for current, complete information on the subject of copyright. Not only can you learn all you could possibly wish to know about intellectual property rights and U.S. copyright law (the section of the U.S. Code dealing with copyright is reprinted there in its entirety), but you can also download copyright forms directly from the site. The site also includes links to other copyright-related web pages, many of which will be of interest to songwriters, including ASCAP, BMI, SESAC, and the Harry Fox Agency. Check it out at **www.copyright.gov.**

How likely is it that someone will try to steal my song?

Copyright infringement is very rare. But, if you ever feel that one of your songs has been stolen—that someone has unlawfully infringed on your copyright—you must prove that you created the work and that the person you are suing had access to your song. Copyright registration is the best proof of a date of creation. You *must* have your copyright registered in order to file a lawsuit. Also, it's helpful if you keep your rough drafts and revisions of songs, either on paper or on tape.

Why did song sharks begin soliciting me after I registered my song?

This is one potential, unintended consequence of registering your song with the Library of Congress. The copyright indexes are a public record of your songwriting, and song sharks often search the copyright indexes and mail solicitations to songwriters who live out away from major music centers such as Nashville. They figure these songwriters don't know any better and are easy prey. *Do not allow this possibility to stop you from registering your songs!* Just be aware, educate yourself, and then throw the song sharks' mailings in the trash.

What if I mail a tape to myself to get a postmark date on a sealed envelope?

The "poor man's copyright" has not stood up in court, and is not an acceptable substitute for registering your song. If you feel it's important to shore up your copyright, register it with the Library of Congress.

Career Songwriting

What Should I Know?

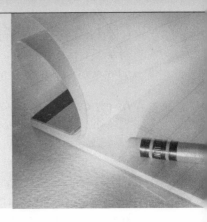

What career options are open to songwriters who do not perform?

The possibilities range from a beginning songwriter living away from a music center like Nashville who lands an occasional single-song publishing deal, to a staff songwriter signed to a major publishing company. And then there are songwriters like Desmond Child who operate independently, have developed a lot of connections, work with numerous artists, and have set up their own independent publishing operations.

What is "single-song" songwriting about?

In this case, a songwriter submits songs to many different companies. One or two songs gain interest from different publishers, and the songwriter signs separate contracts for each song with each publisher. The songwriter can then pitch other songs to other publishers. In Nashville, for instance, a single-song contract is usually the first taste of success for an aspiring songwriter on his way up the ladder. Success of this sort can induce a songwriter to move to a music center like Nashville (if they haven't already), and is a big boost for a struggling songwriter already living there. A series of single-song contracts often signals a songwriter's maturing skill and marketability.

What is a "staff songwriter"?

A staff songwriter usually works for a major publisher and receives a monthly stipend as an advance against the royalties he is likely to earn for the publisher. The music publisher has exclusive rights to everything the songwriter writes while signed to the company. The publisher also works actively on the writer's behalf to hook him or her up with co-writers and other opportunities. A staff songwriting position is highly treasured by many because it offers a steady income, and in Nashville is a sign the songwriter has "arrived."

What comes after the staff songwriting position?

Songwriters who go to the next level have a significant reputation for their ability to write hit songs. Famous artists seek them out, and they often write actively in several markets at once. They often write on assignment for film and television, and commonly keep their own publishing companies to maximize their income.

As my career grows what should I do about keeping track of expenses, etc.?
You should keep a ledger or notebook with records on all financial transactions related to your songwriting—royalty checks, demo costs, office supplies, postage, travel expenses, dues to organizations, class and workshop fees, plus any publications you purchase pertaining to songwriting. You may also want a separate checking account devoted to your songwriting activities. This will make record keeping easier and help to establish your identity as a business for tax purposes.

What should I know about taxes related to songwriting income?
Any royalties you receive will not reflect taxes or any other mandatory deductions. It is your responsibility to keep track of income and file the correct tax forms. For specific information, contact the IRS or talk to an accountant who serves music industry clients.

Music Biz Basics

What About Contracts?

CO-WRITING
What kind of agreements do I need with co-writers?

You may need to sign a legal agreement between you and a co-writer to establish percentages you will each receive of the writer's royalties. You will also have to iron out what you will do if another person, such as an artist, wants to change your song and receive credit as a cowriter. For example, in the event a major artist wants to cut your song for her album—but also wants to rewrite some lyrics and take a share of the publishing—you and your co-writer need to agree whether it is better to get a song on an album that might sell millions (and make a lot of money) or pass on it because you don't want to give up credit. The situation could be uncomfortable if you are not in sync on the issue.

When do I need a lawyer to look over agreements?

When it comes to doing business with a publisher, producer, or record company, you should always have the contract reviewed by a knowledgeable entertainment attorney. As long as the issues at stake are simple, the co-writers respect each other, and they discuss their business philosophies before writing a song together, they can probably write up an agreement without the aid of a lawyer.

SINGLE-SONG CONTRACTS
What is a single-song contract?

A music publisher offers a single-song contract when he wants to sign one or more of your songs, but doesn't want to hire you as a staff songwriter. You assign your rights to a particular song to the publisher for an agreed-upon number of years, so that he may represent the song and find uses profitable for both of you. This is a common contract and will probably be the first you encounter in your songwriting career.

What basic elements should every single-song contract contain?

Every contract should have the publisher's name, the writer's name, the song's title, the date, and the purpose of the agreement. The songwriter also declares the

When Does 50% Equal 100%?

NOTE: the publisher's and songwriter's share of the income are sometimes referred to as each being 100%—for 200% total! You might hear someone say, "I'll take 100% of the publisher's share." **Do not be needlessly confused!** If the numbers confuse you, ask for the terms to be clarified.

Tip

song is a original work and he is creator of the work. The contract *must* specify the royalties the songwriter will earn from various uses of the song, including performance, mechanical, print and synchronization royalties.

How should the royalties usually be divided in the contract?

The songwriter should receive no less than 50% of the income his song generates. That means the songwriter and publisher split the total royalties 50/50. The songwriter's half is called the "writer's share" and the publisher's half is called the "publisher's share." If there is more than one songwriter, the songwriters split the writer's share. Sometimes, successful songwriters will bargain for a percentage of the publisher's share, negotiating what is basically a co-publishing agreement. For a visual explanation of how royalties are collected and flow to the songwriter, see the chart called Music Publishing Royalties on page 29.

What should the contract say about a "reversion clause"?

Songwriters should always negotiate for a "reversion clause," which returns all rights back to the songwriter if some provision of the contract is not met. Most reversion clauses give a publisher a set amount of time (usually one or two years) to work the song and make money with it. If the publisher can't get the song recorded and released during the agreed-upon time period, the songwriter can then take his song to another publisher. The danger of *not* getting some sort of reversion clause is that you could wind up with a publisher sitting on your song for the entire life-plus-70-years term of the copyright—which may as well be forever.

Is a reversion clause difficult to get?

Some publishers agree to it, and figure if they can't get any action with the song in the first year or two, they're not likely to ever have much luck with it. Other publishers may be reluctant to agree to a reversion clause. They may invest a lot of time and money in demoing and pitching a song to artists and want to keep working at it for a longer period of time. Or, for example, a producer might put a song on hold for a while and then go into a lengthy recording project. A year can easily go by before the artist or producer decides which songs to release as singles.

Basic Song Contract Pointers

Tip

The following list, taken from a Songwriters Guild of America publication, enumerates the basic features of an acceptable songwriting contract:

1 **Work for Hire.** When you receive a contract covering just one composition, you should make sure the phrases "employment for hire" and "exclusive writer agreement" are *not* included. Also, there should be no options for future songs.

2 **Performing Rights Affiliation.** If you previously signed publishing contracts, you should be affiliated with either ASCAP, BMI, or SESAC. All performance royalties must be received directly by you from your performing rights organization and this should be written into your contract.

3 **Reversion Clause.** The contract should include a provision that if the publisher does not secure a release of a commercial sound recording within a specified time (one year, two years, etc.), the contract can be terminated by you.

4 **Changes in the Composition.** If the contract includes a provision that the publisher can change the title, lyrics or music, this should be amended so that only with your consent can such changes be made.

5 **Royalty Provisions.** You should receive fifty percent (50%) of all publisher's income on all licenses issued. If the publisher prints and sells his own sheet music, your royalty should be ten percent (10%) of the wholesale selling price. The royalty should not be stated in the contract as a flat rate ($.05, $.07, etc.).

6 **Negotiable Deductions.** Ideally, demos and all other expenses of publication should be paid 100% by the publisher. The only allowable fee is for the Harry Fox Agency collection fee, whereby the writer pays one half of the amount charged to the publisher for mechanical rights. The current mechanical royalty collected by the Harry Fox Agency is 9.1 cents per cut for songs under 5 minutes; and 1.75 cents per minute for songs over 5 minutes.

7 **Royalty Statements and Audit Provision.** Once the song is recorded, you are entitled to receive royalty statements at least once every six months. In addition, an audit provision with no time restriction should be included in every contract.

8 **Writer's Credit.** The publisher should make sure that you receive proper credit on all uses of the composition.

9 **Arbitration.** In order to avoid large legal fees in case of a dispute with your publisher, the contract should include an arbitration clause.

10 **Future Uses.** Any use not specifically covered by the contract should be retained by the writer to be negotiated as it comes up.

Music Biz Basics

This means you may have to agree to a longer time period, be flexible and trust the publisher has your best mutual interests in mind. Use your best judgment.

What other basic issues should be covered by a single-song contract?

The contract should also address these issues:

- will an advance be paid, and if so, how much will the advance be?
- when will royalties be paid (annually or semiannually)?
- who will pay for demos—the publisher, songwriter or both?
- how will lawsuits against copyright infringement be handled, including the cost of lawsuits?
- will the publisher have the right to sell its interest in the song to another publisher without the songwriter's consent?
- does the publisher have the right to make changes in a song, or approve changes by someone else, without the songwriter's consent?
- the songwriter should have the right to audit the publisher's books if he feels it is necessary and gives the publisher reasonable notice.

Where else can I go for advice on contracts?

The Songwriters Guild of America has drawn up a Popular Songwriter's Contract which it believes to be the best minimum songwriter contract available (see the Basic Song Contract Pointers sidebar on page 40). The Guild will send a copy of the contract at no charge to any interested songwriter upon request (see the Songwriters Guild of America listing in the Organizations section on page 321). SGA will also review—free of charge—any contract offered to its members, and will check it for fairness and completeness. Also see these two books published by Writer's Digest Books: *The Craft and Business of Songwriting, 3rd Edition*, by John Braheny and *The New Songwriter's Guide to Music Publishing, 3rd Edition*, by Randy Poe.

Music Biz Basics

The Poetry of the Song

Using Rhyme, Rhythm & Refrain

by Mary Harwell Sayler

Songwriting and poetry writing often sound discordant notes in the length, imagery, and terminology used to discuss techniques, and the variations that work well for one might not for the other. However, both song lyrics and poetry can hit a high note with each of the three R's: Rhyme, Rhythm, and Refrain.

WRITING A REFRAIN

Whether you write song lyrics or a traditional form of poetry that relies on repetition, try taking it from the flip side and start with a refrain. This might consist of a single sentence or a line or two, but regardless of the length, the refrain needs to be worth repeating. If you think about something that's important to you, chances are, other people will care about it too. The trick then is to hold that thought in a clear, conversational way so people can readily identify with what you sing or say.

Although a well-written refrain usually steers clear of clichés, you can put those old phrases to use before discarding them. Just list a few of your favorite expressions then keep playing with the words or thoughts until you find an unusual twist or view.

For example, I wanted to write a villanelle, which is a traditional form of poetry with a complex pattern repeat. I also wanted to tie the poem to the timely but timeless subject of the aftermath of war, so I started jotting down thoughts, such as, "We come along and tell them what to do, but who knows what is right for them or true?" I liked that thought and could see several possibilities for developing the idea. However, to keep in line with the form I'd chosen, I had to split the sentence in two, insert a variation, and weave each line back and forth until both came

MARY HARWELL SAYLER has authored over two dozen books of fiction and nonfiction and placed many poems in periodicals and anthologies. Since 1983, she's worked with other poets and writers, first through home study courses then her critique service and website, www.poetryofcourse.com.

together at the end. By then the thought had progressed enough to change "them" to "us," which gave the initial idea a little twist as well as a stronger connection between the "us" and "them" of this world.

To do something similar with song lyrics, just refresh an old thought or phrase to fit your lines to the cultural times. With songwriting you also have the advantage of musical timing to refresh a common theme or ordinary subject. For example, the flat statements, "You are so beautiful" and "I want to hold your hand," or the rather plainly put question, "Didn't we almost make it this time?" scored high with music-lovers because of the musical emphasis that accentuated each word and made familiar thoughts outstanding.

USING TRUE & SLANT RHYME

Besides musical emphasis, the naturally-occurring sound echoes of the spoken word can be used to emphasize your important thoughts. Since the most resounding echoes arise with the ring of true rhymes, those words will usually provide your strongest emphasis in writing song lyrics and poems. I say "usually" because all true rhymes do not have the same quality of freshness or strength of meaning. For example, notice the contrast between the true-ringing but cliché-singing pair of rhymes *of / above* and the stronger rhymes that typically occur with nouns *hand / sand* or active verbs, *give / live* or a combination of the two, *bird / heard*.

Generally, true rhymes are easy to recognize as you hear a single sound repeated in the last syllable of two or more words, each of which begins with a different letter of the alphabet, for example, *word / stirred*. As that example also demonstrates, spelling may vary, while the sound remains the same.

More Writing Tips

- Listen to the lyrics of contemporary songs you like, focusing on their use of the three R's.
- Study, too, song lyrics you don't like, analyzing what makes them less effective.
- Evaluate lyrics you've previously written to see if you have used the three R's well.
- Song lyrics occasionally hum with mystery, but unlike poems that rely on the eye, irony and subtle changes of meaning can be confusing to the ear.
- Let your lyrics be clear in sound and meaning.
- Make your choice of words, phrases, and refrain highly sing-able.
- Allow variation in your use of each of the three R's but have a good reason for any deviation from what the ear normally expects to hear.
- Read aloud or sing each revision to be sure nothing hinders the musicality.
- Revise your lyrics until you're satisfied with the results.
- As you consider the overall effectiveness of sound effects, let your ear be the final judge.
- If you haven't already done so, select a catchy title in keeping with the song's primary subject, mood, and theme.

Articles & Interviews

Compared to other languages, English offers relatively few choices for creating true rhymes. However, you can increase your sound options by using other types of echoes, such as those found in slant rhyme and alliteration. The words *summer/ simmer* provide an example of both since those words echo the consonants and almost rhyme, but don't.

Words beginning with the same letter of the alphabet create the sound effect known as alliteration, which, carried to extreme, can create humor, twist the tongue, and make a song almost impossible to sing. So as you write and revise your song lyrics, experiment with the effects you most want to hear. For instance, you might like the subtle sound of assonance, a form of alliteration that focuses the vocals on the vowels, such as those found in *blue / moon* and *alone / own.* Notice, too, how those long vowels act similarly to a held note, which means the musical timing can increase the emphasis even more.

How will you know such things? Experiment—experiment as you write but, even more so, as you revise. If you find that you still prefer the pure sound of true rhymes, attune your ear to notice which syllables seem most apt to rhyme. For instance, the sounds of such word-ending syllables as *and, ate, all, am* can often be heard in English, but if you listen for a word that rhymes with *orange,* disappointment and strange sounds will surely occur.

To help you find your rhyming options more readily, all sorts of rhyming dictionaries have become available online and in bookstores. If, however, you have neither book nor Internet connection, connect the sounds yourself by listing your key words. This can be a fun word game as you run through an alphabet of sounds, listening for potential rhymes that relate to the theme and content of your lyrics. More importantly, perhaps, playing with words, sounds, and meanings can open up unexpected options that you might not have noticed by glancing at a ready-made list instead of relying on your ear.

Once you have assured your mind and ear that you have adequate rhyming options, use those clear notes to establish a rhyme scheme. For example, traditional patterns of rhyme commonly include *abab* or *abba* or *xaxa,* which simply means that the "a" rhyme comes first, the "b" rhyme second, and "x" doesn't rhyme with anything.

As your ear will confirm, an "x" between a rhyming pair of words can soften the ring of true rhymes and make slant rhyme almost imperceptible. To test that artistic effect, sing or read aloud your lyrics. If you want to mix up the sound effects even more, try tossing an occasional rhyme inside a line instead of always plinking away at the end.

FINDING THE RHYTHM

True rhyme, slant rhyme, and alliteration help your listeners to hear the emphasis on each resounding word. These echoes also contribute to the rhythm of your song as the sounds increase or decrease. To hear this for yourself, read your lyrics aloud as you would a poem, listening especially for any off-beat sound or jarring effect that you did not intend. If you notice that a particular word or phrase causes a rough spot in the beat, find a more effective word choice as you revise. For instance, test each potential word replacement against your ear until you like the sound of a synonym that emphasizes other syllables.

Notice, too, the sense of each sound. In poetry, the popular two-syllable iamb ends on an accentuated syllable, making it upbeat, whereas the two-syllable trochee starts on a high note then drops the speaking voice down. Simply knowing this can help a poet to match words with the general tone or feelings, and songwriters can do this too. For instance, if the tempo is downbeat, your lyrics can correspond to that, increasing the effect of the mood. Conversely, an upbeat tune might call for lively lyrics.

That said, once you've mastered the technique of matching sound with sense, experiment. For instance, try using upbeat words in a downbeat song and vice verse, being aware, of course, that this could bring about either totally ridiculous or positively brilliant results. And that's another similarity between poetry writing and songwriting: Something unique and exciting often happens as you play around with words and try out new approaches.

Having a stable, established structure as the springboard for something new is one reason poets continue to write in traditional forms. You can do this, too, as you practice writing new lyrics to the tunes of old ballads, hymns, folk songs, or once-popular melodies now available for public use with, of course, proper acknowledgement but no payment or permission required. To find these songs on the Internet, begin your search with a relevant phrase, such as "music in the public domain" or "songs out of copyright."

As you hum a tune or listen to your favorite "oldies," write down whatever words the melody and refrain suggest to you. Let your thoughts flow without censoring yourself. Later, as you return to revise your work, build the lyrics toward a dramatic conclusion or insightful ending as you might in a poem, saving the best for last.

BEYOND THE R'S

For many people, poetry writing provides an opportunity to explore a visual image through figurative language, comparisons, or word plays, but for me, poems often start with music. Suddenly, a phrase catches my ear, and I write down that small beginning to see where the music might lead. This can happen in songwriting too, especially if you have been given a tune in need of lyrics.

Whatever writing method works for you, each song or poem needs to consider the content as well as the musicality. Depending on your unique blend of interests, this might be an interesting story told in a narrative ballad or lyrical love song. Or you might write a rave in a hard-rocking knock against hypocrisy, complacency, or the absurdity of violence and most fears. Regardless of your overriding emphasis, focus on a single but universal theme that will matter to almost everyone, for instance, life, death, love, war, relationships, or various aspects of change.

If you have not thought about a theme before now, don't worry. That's not uncommon. Poets and songwriters often finish a first draft before detecting the overriding theme that arises from the initial flow of creativity. Also, the song or poem itself can lead you into discovering a main premise, not only for one set of lyrics but major life themes as well.

If those thoughts or beliefs happen to relate to the very people you hope will hear your songs, so much the better. To be heard, cared about, and remembered, well-written song lyrics and poems will speak to and for other people. Then, with skillful use of each of the three R's, you just might have a poetic hit on your hands.

Get the Most Out of Songwriting Workshops

by Kerry Dexter

Perhaps you're just beginning to write songs. Maybe you've been at it for a while and band members tell you your songs are great, but you wonder how they'd sound to others. Maybe you've been writing in a certain style but you have ideas that don't seem to fit there. Could be you've got a sheaf of songs you know are great and you wonder how to get them recorded. Maybe you want to brush up on your playing skills to take your songwriting further. Could be you know you're a good writer but you've hit roadblocks in writing your songs or getting people to listen to them. Maybe you're wondering if your writing could be a career. Maybe you situation doesn't fit any of these scenarios. If you're considering taking a workshop, though—your first or your fifteenth—think about where you are with your songwriting, where you want to be, and how—and what kind—of songwriting workshop could help you get there.

KNOW YOURSELF AND YOUR GOALS

You'll want to think about how you learn best, and what sort of time and resources you have to invest. Your choices will become more clear as you research what's on offer—there are ideas about that to come. Right now, though:

- What's your favorite way of learning: having someone tell you, having someone show you, or hands on doing it yourself? That's going to vary with what you're learning, of course, but spend time thinking over what the best experiences have been for you so far. Then pair them up with the workshop descriptions you'll find as you research specific programs.
- When you are in a group or class, do like to sit back and take it all in, talk over

KERRY DEXTER is an independent writer, editor, and photgrapher in the U.S. and Europe. Her work has appeared in VH1.com, music magazine *Dirty Linen, Strings, Symphony, Wandering Educators*, and CMT, among others. She's contributed chapters to *Ireland and the Americas, The Dictionary of American History,* and *The Encyclopedia of Counterculture,* and writes about the arts at http://musicroad.blogspot.com.

things with your classmates, or sit up front and ask questions?

- How confident are you in sharing your music with others? Playing onstage, in class, other workshops, on your own or part of a group?
- How skilled are you at listening, both to musical ideas and in everyday conversation?

There are no right or wrong answers to these questions. They'll get you thinking about your learning styles, though, which will help you as you look at what workshops to take and again when you make your choice and go about learning from your instructor, your fellow musicians, and yourself.

"Choose a format that fits your learning goals," suggests Carrie Newcomer, a folk and Americana songwriter based in Indiana. "Some workshops are presented in a relaxed atmosphere, but still within a classroom method approach. Some workshops are presented more as up close concerts where the artist plays songs and answers song writing questions. Some workshops focus on critiquing previously written material and learning happens through listening and discussion. Some workshops focus on developing new tools for the craft and practical application through exercises and group writing experiences."

RESEARCH WHAT'S OUT THERE

If you already have a specific workshop in mind, it's still good to review your choice in light of what you've learned through thinking about the ideas above—that will help you make the most of your time at the workshop. If you're looking around, time, money, distance, length of course, subject matter, instructor style, and level of instruction, and how all this fits with your song writing goals are all things that will

Where to Look Online

Three sources for online songwriting workshops:
- www.berkleemusic.com
- www.nashvillesongwriters.com [NSAI]
- www.SongU.com

Artists' websites:
- Danny Arena—www.songu.com/pubwhoweare.asp
- Matt Heaton—www.mattandshannonheaton.com
- Shannon Heaton—www.mattandshannonheaton.com
- Corrina Hewat—www.corrinahewat.com
- Laurie Lewis—www.laurielewis.com
- Carrie Newcomer—www.carrienewcomer.com
- n Smith—www.johnsmithmusic.com
- Suggs—www.salt

influence your choice. You'll find hands-on, talk and interview, lecture, discussion, songwriter in the round, and just about every sort of workshop style in between. "Choose a workshop that focuses on the areas in which you hope to gain new experience," says Carrie Newcomer. California based bluegrass musician Laurie Lewis says "How do I know how to get the most out of a particular workshop unless I know how the workshop is being taught?"

Several places to look:

- **Local resources.** Is there a songwriter association in your town? It may offer courses or bring in guest speakers. Adult education programs and community centers are other places to start. Ask your librarian. Ask your musician friends and music teachers for leads. "It's not always the best move to jump to study with the most famous player, who may or may not have the slightest idea how to help other players. It can sometimes be worth taking a little time to gather word-of-mouth recommendations from other students," says Massachusetts based Shannon Heaton, who composes and plays Celtic music.

- **Nearby colleges, and universities.** Both academic departments (think music, English, education) and student organizations may have workshops or classes you'd like. Summer music schools sometimes take place on college campuses—such as The Swannanoa Gathering, held on the campus of Warren Wilson College in North Carolina; and Augusta, held on the campus of Davis Elkins College in West Virginia.

- **Music and arts festivals.** Workshops are often part of day time programs at these events. MerleFest in North Carolina, The Montana Irish Festival, and The Florida Folk Festival are just three of the many festivals that regularly offer workshops.

- **Your favorite artist's website.** Many artists teach in formal and informal situations. Check out the online presence of musicians you like, and see what's offered (see sidebar on previous page).

- **Online resources.** You've probably been using the Internet to help research all these possibilities, and while you are online, you might want to look into online song writing workshops. Berkleemusic and SongU are both well respected programs, and there is a range of others out there. The Nashville Songwriters Association (NSAI) offers online and live workshops to its members—and no, they are not all about writing country music. Read over the NSAI, Berklee and SongU sites (see sidebar on previous page) as benchmarks to use when evaluating other programs.

PREPARE

Knowing yourself and knowing your goals, you've made your choice. What's next? "Take care of the details ahead of time, so they don't distract you from the actual workshop," says Boston based guitarist and singer Matt Heaton. Some pre work you can do:

- Gather the practical details—time, date, place, how to get there, registration information—and have all that ready to take with you.
- If you're bringing your instrument recording device (ask if this is not addressed in the workshop materials), make sure all it is in working order. Check the batteries beforehand. Have it ready to go, so you don't have to ask the teacher to wait while you read the instruction manual.
- Bring a notebook, and more than one pen.
- Be on time.
- If it's a hands-on workshop, tune before you sit down.
- If you're taking a workshop with a specific artist, you may want to listen to his or her work.
- You may want to prepare a few questions. But do not feel you have to ask them.
- Review your goals, both short term and long term.
- Relax.

"I think most people like to come away from a hands-on workshop with a new song or two, says John Smith, a touring songwriter based in Wisconsin. "Of course, this means making a safe environment for fragile new starts."

FOCUS

Maybe your style is to jump right in, maybe you prefer to scope things out a bit first. Either way, pay attention to the vibe of the class. Be ready to play a song, if that's requested or seems appropriate. If you're to give a critique, be thoughtful and honest. Listen to the critiques given to and by others. Listen to all that goes on, record the class if allowed, and take notes. Be courteous and stay focused on the subject matter of the workshop in your comments and questions.

"Participate fully," advises Florida based singer and songwriter Del Suggs. "Lots of folks want to sit in the back of the class and only take notes. Get involved, volunteer to play your song when the teacher asks."

"Go with the flow," adds Matt Heaton. "Some workshops will not be what you expect them to be. Try to do whatever the teacher asks. If you don't understand something, ask a question. But don't ask questions that are designed to show how much you know. It is tempting, when pushed out of your comfort zone, to try to bolster that comfort zone ('well, I normally don't play this type of music, I play this other type'). A workshop isn't the place for that. When you're at a workshop, you are formally saying that you are there to learn. And you will, if you're open to it."

Scottish composer and singer Corrina Hewat agrees. It's a good idea to research the subject matter of the workshop a bit, she says, and then, "Go with an open mind and willingness to try anything. And go with confidence that you can achieve whatever is being asked of you, and what you are asking of yourself."

FOLLOW UP

Thank the workshop leader, briefly. Every other workshop participant probably has something to say to the leader too. Keep it brief and cheerful and save longer questions for another time or an e-mail, if offered.

Exchange contact information with other workshop participants if it's natural to do so. "While it's great to chat with the guest speakers and thank them for their time, it's just as important to get to know some of those attending the same workshop or class, whether online or in-person. You just might meet a future major label artist, the future collaborator on your first hit song, or a future Grammy-Award winning record producer who you'll be calling in a few years to listen to your songs," says songwriter and teacher Danny Arena, who is based in Nashville. "Sometimes my song writing group attendees establish an e-mail list and share new songs over the months following the workshop," adds John Smith.

Let what you've learned sink in, reflect on all that went on, and review your notes. Put what you've learned into practice in your music.

IF THINGS GO WRONG

Trust your instincts. Maybe a certain workshop, or this leader, isn't right for you, for any number of reasons. Give yourself permission to look for a better fit. Maybe you'll discover that working in a group isn't right for your goals just now.

If that's so, you might benefit from the sort of workshop where an artist plays and talks about his or her songs, rather than one where you play yours. You might also like taking a workshop that's about another area. Learning more about your instrument or looking into the history of a favorite style could inspire you. All of these options—including getting out of a situation that isn't working—are great ways to work on your song writing goals. "I would say that the most important thing to take away from any workshop situation is the fact that in order to write well, you must *begin* to write," says Laurie Lewis. "Sometimes this is the most difficult thing. Just starting the process."

"You can learn about the components, you can understand how the pieces fit together, you can grasp the nuances of melody and structure. But it's up to you to put all those parts together into a great song," says Del Suggs. "And you can do it— it's a matter of applying what you know and what you learn with what you feel."

"A workshop is a place to try out new ideas and skills. Some of these experiments will be more successful than others, but the point is to jump in the pool and paddle around until you get used to the water," says Carrie Newcomer. "Have fun!"

Take risks, trust yourself, and keep on learning.

Articles & Interviews

Scoring Songs

For TV, Film & Commercials

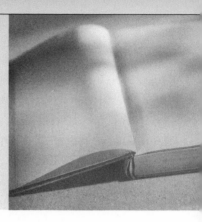

by David McPherson

Friday night. You are slumped back on the couch watching your favorite sitcom; the end credits roll, and there's one of your songs. Every songwriter's dream right? The thinking among musicians used to be you were "selling out" if one of your songs was used to sell product in a commercial on TV. Who can forget Neil Young's cheeky song, and accompanying video, "This Notes for You."

Today, though, the music business is tougher than ever for artists to crack and get their songs heard by the masses, so looking for alternative avenues to find new audiences such as TV, film and commercials is totally acceptable. So, how does one land songs in these media markets? Ask a bunch of seasoned songwriters and the advice is endless. Here follows tips from a handful of musicians who have had luck placing their songs in TV and films.

Royal Wood

Royal Wood is a Toronto-based songwriter. According to the bio on his website: "His approach to writing harkens back to traditions of song crafting that go straight to the heart of the relationship an artist creates with an audience. As great songwriting defies the whimsies of a trend, Royal's classic songs explore the architecture of emotions upon which our most cherished relationships are built. Named an iTunes Songwriter of the Year in 2008, Royal's music shares an emotional immediacy with the listener that creates a lingering feeling of intimacy with his recordings and live performances."

In 2008, Wood had his song "A Mirror Without" from his disc *A Good Enough Day*, air on the smash TV show *Grey's Anatomy*. His songs have also been featured on HBO programs and on CBC Television in Canada.

DAVID McPHERSON is a Toronto-based freelance writer with more than 17 years experience writing about music. A graduate of the University of Western Ontario, with a Masters in Journalism, David has published thousands of articles in daily newspapers, consumer magazines, and websites across North America, including *Bluegrass Unlimited, Paste, American Songwriter, Performing Songwriter* to name a few. His website is: www.davidmcpherson.ca.

The songsmith says he's never actively tried to pitch his songs. He advises to start by making contact with a licenser and approach them about trying to represent you for one record. Also, as an indie artist, a lot of indie films will contact you.

"It then goes from there," Wood says. "The more music you are making the more options people have to choose one of your songs. If you try to randomly pitch your songs to ABC television, for example, you are never going to get the right person. I have been at radio interviews or at some record label's office and I see these massive boxes in the corner filled with yellow, unopened manila envelopes.

Basic Song Contract Pointers

Tip

Songwriter Tamara Miller offers a two more tips to help you get your songs placed in TV and movies

1. **Be sure you have an amazing finished product** and aside from the actual recording, be sure to conduct as much research as you can about your genre of music and what shows/films are seeking your type of music. There are so many independent film makers out there who are looking for great music. Try the university and college campuses; you never know where that independent film maker will end up. The director might ask you to compose a piece for free, but think about all of the exposure you will receive and what other projects that will lead to...this is key. You also need to find the music supervisors who are responsible for finding that perfect song for film and television. Google is a wonderful thing. Research, research, research. Don't wait until your CD is complete, research ahead of time and work that into your plan.

2. **Know your rights.** You can make a great living from writing music for a film or television series. If your music gets picked up by the music supervisor based on your own self-promotion, you can obtain both the songwriter's half, referred to as the "writers share" and the publisher's half, referred to as the "publishers share." If your song is selected, you will most likely receive compensation from the company using your music. This is referred to as the license fee or fee for "renting your music" for their show. At least with a song placement in a television agreement, you should be paid both a license fee for your Master and a Synchronization fee (permission for the company to synch your music with picture); this depends on how your song will be used. Before any of this happens, you will most likely encounter a legal agreement/contract between the company and yourself; be sure to have this document reviewed by an entertainment lawyer. It will cost you, but it's worth every penny. The last thing you need to is to have to pay thousands of dollars in court trying to get out of the agreement. Research the company and make sure they are legit. Make sure you are a member of a performing rights organization.

"People are constantly taking that shot hoping someone is going to open up their package, but the sad reality is that there is so much music out there and so many people out there trying to make a living at it, that they need these filters to direct things to them … you are in a sea of artists/would be artists, to find a place to take a deep breath takes a long time." Once you get one song in though, Wood says it often snowballs from there.

"The more records I put out the more songs I had to pass around. Eventually I got a licenser who worked solely for me trying to place songs. He pitches songs, travelling back and forth to LA … that's his job. He gets tips of what types of songs producers are looking for and he pitches things to the director and producer that he thinks would fit."

Troy Campbell

"Take the words out," advises the Austin-based musician.

Campbell, originally from Ohio, was a past member of bands The Highwaymen and Loose Diamonds. Today, between performing solo and writing songs, he works as a music supervisor; he offers songwriters advice garnered from both sides of the table.

"I make a terrible supervisor because when a director says 'I would really like to use this song,' since I know what it costs, I immediately say 'You can't afford it.' and they get really broken hearted," he says.

Joking aside, Campbell's best advice to songwriters looking to land their creations in TV, film and commercials, is to strip out the vocals.

"I tell friends who are songwriters such as Gurf Morlix and Ray Wylie Hubbard, when making your records, make instrumental versions too since it increases your odds by 50 percent," Campbell says. "I would venture even more than 50 per cent sometimes based on what I've seen and the way I've been able to pick something for somebody. Give me copies without the vocals. A lot of the songwriters, especially singer-songwriters, have distinct voices. During the course of a movie, or on the end credits of *Grey's Anatomy*, that's beneficial because it's impactful. But if you are in the middle of the show, your voice is going to jar against the dialogue, so you have a lesser chance of getting your song in.

"My theory is your music is great, emotional and cool and they like you, but your voice is more of a distraction," he says. "So give me an instrumental version … just pull the vocals out when making your record."

Campbell says another option is to do what Gurf Morlix did for a recent movie project.

"He just put in other things and made a whole new record," he explains. "His song, which I co-wrote with him, 'Killing Time in Texas,' we recently put an instrumental version in a documentary called *Happiness Is*—a documentary about the pursuit of happiness in America…whatever that means. We put four tracks of

Gurf's in the film because it just worked. It opens him up to a bigger audience."

Another piece of advice Campbell offers is to put yourself in the music supervisor's shoes.

"As an independent, you are going to get my attention if you consider what I have to do," he explains. "A lot of times, I'm just under stress to come up with options and I really want to use my favorite people and independents, but a lot of time it's a hassle to get them to send me things."

Josh Finlayson

Co-founder, guitarist, and one of the chief songwriters for Canadian roots band The SkyDiggers, says, in a lot of cases, getting your songs on TV and film are the only ways you get exposure for your music today because commercial radio has become so limited in what they play. He also says landing songs in TV and films involves a bit of luck.

"Typically, the way this stuff happens is that there is someone—a director or a producer—someone who works in that arena, who discovers a CD or a song from a band and wants to use it in a movie or a TV show," he explains. "Early on for us, and it continues for our band, there are certain songs people have in their mind for certain scenes."

Finlayson says while there are avenues you can go and "flog your wares," it seems today, TV, film and commercials while once frowned upon, are now seen as a way to get your music out there.

An obvious example is Canadian artist Feist, whose song "1,2,3,4" promoted the launch of Apple's iPod Nano.

"Ten to fifteen years ago, the perception was seen as selling out a bit, but the reality now is although it is very easy to get your music out to the world through the Internet, how do you really make people conscious of it," says Finlayson. "I don't know what role that song played in helping Feist's career, but have to think it was significant."

Findlayson says the other side of the equation is traditionally music publishers played a big role in getting your music into films and onto TV shows, but today they are competing more and more with all kinds of independent people...boutique shops doing the same thing who have built up relationships with production companies and films.

Astrid Young

Astrid Young, Neil Young's half-sister, and a seasoned songwriter, is blunter in her advice, but it rings true; she says the best thing you can do is to "find out who all the music editors are and kiss their asses up and down."

"They're the ones who really call the shots, not the music supervisors or the execs," she says. "If they (the editors) slug something into an edit, it's likely to get in the film—that's the bottom line." Young also advises to get your music into music libraries.

"There is a whole world out there doing music for trailers and other commercials and it pays not bad," she says.

Like Campbell, she also believes cutting a second version of your song, minus the words, is good advice. "Make sure when you mix a song you've always got, in addition to your final mix, an instrumental mix. This goes a long way for versatility. [If one] of these guys ask for an instrumental mix, and if you don't have one, you might be out of luck."

Tamara Miller

The Toronto-based songwriter, who's CD *60 Seconds* was released in April 2008, says it all starts with the song.

"You need to have a belief and a passion that what you have created simply must be heard," she says. "It's something you want to share with the world and you stop at nothing to attain it."

Miller says she always wanted to compose music for film and television.

"I would often sit at the piano for hours and play 'abstract tinkles' on the ivories," she says. "The music took me away to places of possibility. I was told by random people I met while playing piano in a lobby of a hotel or a shopping mall that I should be writing for the screen. The more I heard it, the more I felt it while playing."

Eight months after Miller independently released her disc the title cut was selected for the hit television show, *Degrassi: The Next Generation*.

"I thought my heart was going to jump out of my chest," she recalls. "I just couldn't believe it. I had looked at a goal sheet I set the year before, and it consisted of recording a new CD, having my songs featured on radio, getting press, and having a song selected for TV. These items were all on the list! What I learned was that it was crucial to have a plan. I always had that positive vision, and always believed that anything is possible, even with all the competition out there. But I made sure it was going to happen by being organized and developing a plan. There are so many ways to make it in the music industry...it's just important to be creative both in your music and in the music business."

Baby Boomers & Songwriting

by Doris Bloodworth

It's only natural that the generation that came of age between Elvis Presley and Woodstock would make up a growing number of new songwriters. Born between 1946 and 1964, these men and women are finding new outlets for their passion and talents. And many are finding success.

Lots of baby boomers say that with childrearing and career-building behind them, they finally have the time and disposable income to pursue their long-dormant talents. Some say a health crisis, divorce or other life-changing event pushed them into songwriting as a way to cope.

Jack Speer, a 59-year-old Florida building project manager, says he had enjoyed writing songs for a band he founded during his teen years. But music took a backseat as he took on college, career and family responsibilities. It wasn't until the death of his parents several years ago that he turned again to songwriting as a catharsis. "Now I can't imagine a day when I'm not in my home studio working on a song," he says.

Like their younger counterparts, baby boomers are tapping the Internet for its wealth of "how-to" information on everything from writing lyrics to researching copyright laws to connecting with music publishers. These silver-haired songwriters have their own websites, MySpace and Facebook pages and stay in touch with the latest trends through music-industry message boards and e-newsletters—tools that have brought Nashville into homes across the country and around the world.

By day, these Beatle-generation composers are teachers, cops, engineers and grandparents. They rush home, eager to work on the latest melody or lyrics and spend hours at their computers and keyboards. Through networking groups, they

---

DORIS BLOODSWORTH is a Pulitzer-nominated writer, author and president of Crosswords Communications in Orlando, Fla. She is a former reporter for the *Wall Street Journal* and currently covers Florida federal courts for *Bloomberg News* in addition to freelance writing. Bloodsworth graduated from the University of Florida with highest honors and is a member of the Florida Writers Association.

find support, critiques, collaborators, mentors and friends.

Steve Desjardins, 61, was a Rhode Island police officer who grew up with no musical training. A chance meeting with songwriter Jimmie Crane, who wrote "If I Give My Heart to You" and "Hurt" among other hits, sparked Desjardins' interest in music. At age 35, when his friends were buying sports cars, Desjardins took his first piano lesson and started writing songs with Crane acting as mentor.

"He taught me about becoming the character in the song," Desjardins says. "He taught me to write lyrics that were clever and surprised people."

In 2003, Desjardins entered the Nashville Song Search Contest and earned an honorable mention. In 2006, his song "When He Comes Home to Her" was voted the top country song for Billboard's World Songwriting Contest. A mutual friend introduced him to legendary country singer and publisher Mel Tillis who listened to Desjardins' CD and signed a contract to publish four songs.

Although Desjardins is still waiting to have one of his songs recorded by a "Music Row" artist, several of his songs have been recorded by up-and-coming singers; and one of his songs was picked up for a movie with Jerry Springer.

Although some baby boomers gain satisfaction in just sharing their music on a local level, it is success stories such as Desjardin's that have others hoping their next song could be "the one."

What follow are tips—culled from dozens of interviews with baby boomer songwriters and industry professionals—that have proven helpful for aspiring newbies as well as veteran musicians.

HOW TO GET STARTED

It is important to find a support system as soon as possible. That might mean one-on-one coaching from a professional mentor or more often it's a group of fellow songwriters who encourage each other and offer feedback on songs. One of the most popular networks is the Nashville Songwriters Association International (NSAI), which sponsors peer critique groups around the world.

Although composing melodies and writing lyrics may be a solitary effort for many, experts encourage songwriters to join a support group, such as the NSAI, to become better educated about the music industry, to form connections to publishers and to get audience feedback. In smaller towns or rural areas, people can start their own group by posting a notice in the local paper, on community billboards, on songwriting forums or by contacting the music faculty at community colleges.

During the NSAI local meetings, the leader usually shares songwriting tips or the latest news from the music industry. Members then have an opportunity to get feedback on their latest songs. They bring a recording and copies of the lyrics for other members to review. After the song is played, fellow songwriters share their opinions on what they liked or thought could be improved. The emphasis is on being positive but frank.

Helpful Resources

For More Info

Organizations

- **Nashville Songwriters Association International (NSAI)**—A premiere site for songwriters for all genres and levels of experience. NSAI is the headquarters for local support groups around the world and features numerous educational and networking opportunities, including Tin Pan South, NSAI Spring Training, Songposium and weekly song camps in Nashville.

- **The American Society of Composers, Authors and Publishers (ASCAP)**—An association for U.S. songwriters, composers, lyricists and music publishers dedicated to protecting the rights of its members through licensing and distributing royalties.

- **Broadcast Music Inc. (BMI)**—BMI collects license fees from businesses that use music and then distributes the royalties to songwriters, composers and publishers.

Websites

- **Allmusicindustrycontacts.com**—One-stop website with explanations of who to contact in the music industry. The site includes the names of companies and executives for top label A&Rs, managers, producers and publishers.

- **Songwriterstipjar.com**—Tips and creative songwriting ideas from songwriters for songwriters. It includes an e-newsletters and discussion forums.

- **Paulreisler.com**—Reisler features several popular songwriting camps set in some of North America's most beautiful locations.

- **Nashvillesongwriters.com**—The website for one of the top educational and networking organizations for songwriters. Members can access webcasts that explain all aspects of the music industry.

- **Ascap.com**—The website for ASCAP, which includes a portal for songwriters that has numerous resources, such as "Playback Magazine" and advice on a variety of music-related topics.

- **Bmi.com**—User friendly explanations for songwriters about copyrighting and royalties.

- **Cdbaby.com**—Touts itself as the world's largest online distributor of independent music. Especially useful for songwriters who also are singers and want to market their music to download retailers, such as iTunes, Rhapsodiy and eMusic.

- **Broadjam.com**—Includes opportunities to blog and to expose music to indie music fans.

Articles & Interviews

Helpful Resources, cont.

For More Info

- **Indieheaven.com**—A resource for independent Christian musicians and songwriters with numerous services available to members. The online music store promises to pay members 100 percent for the gross sales of their music.

- **Sesac.com**—A performing rights organization that represents songwriters and publishers. It includes a section on "getting started."

- **Musesmuse.com**—A songwriting resource for all levels of experience. It includes news, a message board and a reference guide for frequently used terms in songwriting.

- **Songu.com**—An online connection to courses, coaching, people who will plug your songs to the music industry and collaborators.

- **Musicsubmit.com**—Get help getting your music submitted to online music directories, blogs, podcasts and radio stations.

- **Billboard.com**—Delivers the latest news on the music industry, including artists, songs and trends.

- **Bbhq.com**—Baby Boomers Headquarters includes a music page with a lyrics library.

- **Berkleemusic.com**—For those who want to polish their skills and earn a songwriting certificate online and connect to the renowned faculty at the college whose alumni include songwriting legends Melissa Etheridge, John Mayer, Donald Fagen and composer Quincy Jones. The site also has numerous blogs with insights about the latest software and cutting-edge songwriting opportunities, such as video games.

- **Songpluggers.net**—A host of services, including a link to highly rated song pluggers, who pitch songs to the recording studios and artists.

- **Taxi.com**—Touts itself as the world's leading independent artist and repertoire (A&R) company. The company helps songwriters connect to record companies, publishers and others shopping for music, such as filmmakers. The site includes practical tips for songwriters, such as how to avoid clichéd lyrics and the importance of contrast.

E-newsletters

- **ASCAP Daily Brief**—dailyref@ascap.com. Information about music, copyright and new technology affecting the music industry.

Books and Magazines

- *Songwriter's Market*
- *The Craft of Lyric Writing*, by Sheila Davis
- *Writing Better Lyrics*, by Pat Pattison

Members also have an opportunity to forward their songs to the NSAI group in Nashville for further objective feedback.

Whether songwriting is a hobby or a more serious pursuit, the songwriter will need to make an investment. A typical startup would include an instrument, such as a piano or guitar, a computer with sequencing software, a microphone, speakers and a headphone.

Sequencing software allows the songwriter to create, record, edit and mix vocals and instruments. Popular systems include Pro Tools, Cubase and Cakewalk, among others.

The Internet offers a wealth of free resources, such as rhymezone.com, which helps songwriters think of rhyming words and phrases. The NSAI and other trade industry sites, such as ASCAP.com, can help educate songwriters about copyrighting, licensing and other business issues so that they can protect and earn revenue for their efforts.

ALL ROADS LEAD TO NASHVILLE

Los Angeles, New York and a few other cities have major recording studios. But Nashville is still the center of the musical universe for most songwriters—not just for country music but for all genres.

Some songwriters who want to pursue the craft professionally move to Nashville. Tim Buppert, 50, spent 12 years on the road playing clubs from Florida to Pennsylvania before moving to Nashville to become a songwriter. Buppert has had several hits by some of the top recording artists, including a No. 1 single by Kevin Sharp, "She's Sure Taking It Well."

"I wish I'd moved here sooner," Buppert says. "It's a network-driven town and business. You have to be here so that if Kenny Chesney is going into the studio tomorrow and needs one more song, you'll be here to hear about it."

For many baby boomers, moving is not an option. After all, they have often invested decades in their day jobs and aren't close enough to retirement to pull up stakes. Music insiders say in that case, songwriters need to come to Nashville as often as possible. There are many opportunities, such as Tin Pan South, Songposium and NSAI's spring training. Songwriters have an opportunity to get professional critiques and to form relationships with Nashville's top publishers and song pluggers—people who pitch to the studios and artists throughout the year.

Desjardins, the retired cop turned songwriter, says he endeared himself to a number of music industry insiders, including a top executive at Warner Bros. Records, when he flew from Central Florida to Nashville every week for two months to take part in a songwriting camp.

"If you can't live there, then spend your money there," says Desjardins, who spends around $1,000 each time he gets professional demos of his songs made.

NSAI lists success stories on its Web site that show how trips to Nashville can pay off. Alice Lankford, 52, from Sapulpa, Okla., attended a symposium. A Banner Music executive heard Lankford's music at a critique session and ended up signing her to a contract.

NEW OPPORTUNITIES ARE EMERGING

Although it's true that CD sales are shrinking and the music industry is struggling, it's also just as true that new opportunities are evolving for songwriters—regardless of their age. Songwriters can open up their own virtual music shops online, pitch to indie labels, film studios, television and radio in addition to new outlets, such as video games and greeting cards.

Here is just a sample of baby boomer songwriters who have found success without leaving their hometowns:

- **Ed Kliman**, 55, of Austin, Texas, (TexasMusicForge.com), has won a couple of songwriting awards and had his music licensed for radio and television in the United States and Canada in addition to writing music for musical theater.
- **Leon Olguin**, 51, and **Sheryl Olguin**, 50, of Cocoa, Fla., (SoloCreativeMedia.com), have had songs published and recorded in the United States and the United Kingdom. Leon Olguin's "White as Snow," has been recorded more than 100 times and has earned a reputation as a classic praise song. His wife, Sheryl, has written themes for local radio and TV shows. "Having lived 50 years, I've experienced a lot that has added depth to what I write," Sheryl Olguin says. "This is the really helpful part of being a midlife boomer."
- **Terry Kitchen**, 50, of Boston, Mass., (TerryKitchen.com), has won numerous awards including first place in the USA Songwriting Competition. He has recorded about 100 songs and released them on his private label. Some of his songs have been used in documentary films. "Being a baby boomer is helpful in that much of my audience has the same cultural and musical landmarks that I have," Kitchen says.
- **Jeffrey Bosworth**, 47, of Altamonte Springs, Fla., (Bozmusic.com and ieminvest. com), runs a marketing company by day but spends his nights at the recording studio creating songs for his Island Estuary label. Bosworth's vision is to create a venue near the Walt Disney World and Universal Studios theme parks that would give more songwriters and artists a chance to share their music. "Being a bit older gives us a real demographic who love music and loved it through the '60s into the '90s when music was made more for art than money," Bosworth says.

WRITING FOR YOUNGER AUDIENCES

Jack Perricone, chair of the songwriting department at renowned Berklee College of Music in Boston, says baby boomers have to adapt in order to get their songs published for today's younger consumers.

"Melodic rhythms of today's music are more complex," Perricone says.

"Rhythms are faster and there are more words—both in pop and country, probably because of the influence of rap."

Perricone suggested baby boomers study the songs that are getting the most airplay on radio. Online courses are another way to prepare for a professional career in contemporary music. Berklee was the first college to offer a complete songwriting degree.

Debbie Cavalier, dean of the continuing education online school Berkleemusic. com, says the number of baby boomers enrolling in the school's online songwriting program has been rising.

"They say they are finally getting back to something they always wanted to do," she says.

Even veteran songwriters are struggling to compete in an industry in which new stars are teens, such as Taylor Swift and Miley Cyrus. Swift writes many of her own songs.

"As much as I hate to admit it, I don't have a clue what a 15-year-old girl thinks," says Buppert, who records demos for aspiring songwriters in addition to writing and performing his own songs.

NSAI boomer songwriter Robert Wagener of Belleville, Ill., says he thinks age neither helps nor hurts. "Age means nothing to the process," he says.

BOOM

Bruce Springsteen, "The Boss," turned 60 and graced the cover of AARP in its September-October 2009 edition. The multitalented actor and songwriter, Jeff Daniels, 54, pokes fun at baby boomers in the songs he's written for his one-man road show. Both have found no shortage of audiences.

At 75 million strong, U.S. baby boomers have too big an impact on the economy to be ignored—as songwriters or song buyers.

Passionate boomer songwriters, such as Desjardins, are not easily dissuaded. He says on one of his early trips a well known Nashville executive says, "Kiddo, what you're trying to do—the chances are a million to one," to which Desjardins says, "I believe I am that one in a million."

He encourages his peers to believe in themselves, believe in their songs and believe in their songwriting.

"Don't get discouraged," he says. "Enjoy the ride. Sometimes the journey is better than the destination."

The New Deal

A New Approach to Selling CDs
Based on Public Trust

by Grant Peeples

In the Fall of 2007 I began to develop a new idea about a way to sell CDs of the songs I was writing and recording. It all started as I licked an envelope into which I had just placed a check for $1,200, made out to someone in Hollywood, known to me only as: TellyMan.

Aside from the obviousness of the name, I had no idea who TellyMan was. I never once spoke with him on the phone. As I recall I didn't even have an e-mail address for him. But he had a blond, 1984 Fender Telecaster listed on eBay that fit the criteria of the instrument I had been hunting. And the price was right. After a few question-and-answer transmissions through the enchanting eBay portal of dream and profit, I pulled the trigger. I told TellyMan I wanted the guitar and that the proverbial check was in the mail.

Bam. Welcome to commerce in the 21st Century. It was a pleasure doing business with you. Whoever you are.

Less than two weeks after my check set out on its 2,000 mile journey to TellyMan in California, my new guitar was plugged in to a Fender twin amplifier and I was assaulting the countryside where I live with cranked up twang and liquid reverb.

It would be a little while before I got back to that new idea I had about how to sell those records of mine. The first thing I had to deal with was the deputy sheriff who was coming up the drive. Somebody had called the law on my songs.

The selling of recorded music has changed radically over the last 10 years. The development of MP3s, digital downloading, and the sharing and distribution of music files has done to the corner record store what Henry Ford did to the horse and buggy. There has developed, too, a corresponding ethical disconnect between an artist's proprietary right to his creation and what the public feels it owes him for it.

GRANT PEEPLES is a touring Americana singer/songwriter out of Tallahassee, Florida. His bio, songs, videos and performance schedule can be found at www.grantpeeples.com.

This became patently clear to me at a gig last winter in South Florida. After my show I was in the lobby of the club selling CDs at a small table I had set up. I was chatting with two couples who were on their way out when one of men said to me: "Hey, I don't have your first CD. I should get that now."

He was reaching for his wallet and I was I was reaching for a CD to hand to him when the female half of the other couple gleefully weighed in. "Oh, you don't need to do that, Les. I already have that one. I'll just burn a copy for you." Though the blood drained from my own face, all four of them were all smiles. It must have seemed like a plausible and sensible idea. It never occurred to any of them that there might be anything improper or unfair or embarrassing—not to mention illegal or unethical—to what the woman had proposed. To them, I guess, this was no different than if she had offered to loan him a copy of a book so that he didn't have to purchase one. And of course one might wonder: what *is* he difference?

Though there is no shortage of arguments for either side of that question, the only really pertinent issue for the independent musician is: can I make a record of my songs and get compensated for my creations and efforts to the extent that I will be able to carry on with my artistic life and...make yet another record at some date in the future?

Making a record—not just any record, but a really good record, with production values equal to what the industry's best studios were issuing 20 years ago—is easier and far less expensive than any of us ever imagined back before the personal computer worked its way into the heart and soul of recording studios. But *selling* a record has never been more challenging than it is today.

(You might have noticed I often us the term "record," when referring to music on a CD. I like to argue that in spite of all the changes in technology, a musical recording is still a "record" of music, a document, and that the CD is merely the conveyor of a creation, like paper or film or canvas or...vinyl.)

Not only have the conventional channels of distribution gone the way of the 8-track tape, virtually anyone who has ever played three chords on a guitar now has a recording of their work. And like any artist worth the eviction notice tacked to his door, they want to share their vision and creations with others. So there's more music out there than there ever has been, but only a fraction remains of the distribution points where it could once be featured and retailed. In other words: there's a sonic log jam in the frothy wake of the Digital Age.

So...what's a Bob Dylan wannabe to do?

Which leads us back (almost) to me licking that envelope I was sending off to TellyMan.

On my first record my sales approach was....what? Well, to do what everybody else seemed to be doing. I joined CD Baby (www.cdbaby.com), that hugely popular web distribution company for independent artists. I did the same with the behemoth and unwieldy Amazon. I also linked up with PayPal, which enabled me to sell directly from my own website.

I did okay with CD Baby, (they are, in fact, a good company, very user friendly and helpful, and I still distribute through them today) but it cost $30 to join and list the record, and they award themselves four dollars from every CD sold from their site. Additionally, I had to pay the shipping to them in Oregon, where the CDs were stocked. Amazon takes a whopping 50 percent from each sale, which I found, frankly, larcenous, but again—everybody else seemed to be doing it. PayPal took a much smaller cut, (essentially, they are just money collectors, not involved in fulfillment, as are CD Baby and Amazon) but the process was cumbersome. And in all three cases (unless you were PayPal member with a credit balance), people had to whip out their credit card and type a lot of personal information into little boxes on a computer screen. For my taste, this has always been a loathsome impediment and deterrent when it comes to being excited about buying something new. Moreover, having the ubiquitous PayPal icon there on my web page just seemed tacky. Still, artistic indignation notwithstanding, the biggest issue was that I just wasn't happy with the sales I was getting from my marketing strategy.

It was at this juncture that my dealings with TellyMan cracked open a door for me. And I began to wonder about a new approach to my second record. It began with the redoubtable question: WHAT IF?

What if I just sent out a blast to my e-mail list, (at that time, about a thousand people) and told them I had a new record, and that I had come up with a real easy way for them to get their hands on it. That all they had to do was *tell* me they wanted it, and to give me their mailing address, and that I would mail it to them. And that I would include an envelope, addressed to me, into which they could put their payment to me. In other words, they were to pay for the CD *after* they got it.

And what if I put a banner on my web page that very much the same thing? Inviting anyone out there is cyber space to request a CD, and leave it up to them and their conscience to pay for it?

What would happen? Would this painless way of requesting and receiving the new record spur sales? And—this was the real kicker—what percentage of people would actually send the payment?

It seemed to me that the somewhat impulsive buyer (with whom, I admit, I am duly sympathetic) would be much more likely to buy the CD than if he had to go through all the rigmarole of pulling out his credit card and laboring through the miasma of an Internet order, which statistics, surely, prove no customer *ever* gets through the first time without having to go back and fix some mistake they made in the process. I figured that if 25 percent of the people did *not* pay me, I would still be way ahead of the game even if the strategy didn't increase the number of purchases, which I could not imagine it not doing. But more than anything, I just liked the idea, the feel, its premise of trusting people out there in the cyber heartland, (most of whom I didn't even know). It felt right making it incumbent upon them to decide whether or not they would live up to the tenets of my original proposition, which I promptly and very unoriginally named: The New Deal.

I bounced it off a few fellow musicians. The consensus was that my idea was interesting but risky. But I think all were curious just how it might pan out, and most seemed to think I didn't have that much to lose. They, too, had been struggling with record sales. They knew.

In any event, when my new CD, "It's Later Than You Think," was delivered by the duplicator in April of 2008, I posted a New Deal banner on my web page, and sent out this blast to my e-mail list:

> **Hey folks, my new record, "It's Later Than You Think," is out. And I think it might be...good. It might even be real good. If you would like a copy, all you have to do is just hit reply and send me your mailing address. I'll send you the new CD, and I'll also include a self-addressed envelope. After you get the CD, stick the money in that envelope and mail it to me. Quick, easy and painless.**

Within 48 hours I had sold a hundred and fifty CDs at $15 each. (The price included postage.) Fifteen percent of my mailing list had placed an order. I quickly made a run for envelopes and stamps. The living room was soon awash with mailroom clutter.

Sensing I might now be on to something, a week after sending out the blast, I re-sent it, this time with a link to a video I had recently made of one of the songs that was on the record. More than 50 more orders came back.

And then the checks starting arriving at the big rural mail box at the end of my drive. In the parlance of today's Youth: "Swee-eet."

Between May of 2008 and May of 2009 I send out another 20 or so blasts to my e-mail list, which I now worked steadily to broaden and increase in number. No matter what the blast was about—gigs, reviews, radio play, etc.—I always included the New Deal in it, and always got at least a few sales. I made a personal decision that it wasn't overtly unethical to "pirate" an occasional list of e-mail addresses from someone who had sent out a blast of their own without blind copying their recipients. (I always blind copy my own.) But I absolved myself by never forgetting to put a red note at the top of every mailing saying that if the recipient wanted off the list, all they had to do was hit return and say "remove."

During that year I also opened and began to build a Facebook page, reconnecting with old friends and finding new ones whose musical taste and world view jibed with my own. And in the spring of 2009, when my next record, "PawnShop," was ready to be shipped (yes, thanks to the sales through the New Deal I was able to return to the studio), I had 2,700 names on my e-mail list, and 500 Facebook friends. I sent two blasts in 10 days, redesigned my web page with even more emphasis on the New Deal, and sent a note to all my Facebook friends letting them know how they, too, could get the record. The printed copy on the CD packaging also talks about the New Deal and gives the e-mail address to write to should someone want another copy or if they would like to have a copy sent to somebody else. (In this case I send the CD to one address, and the envelope to another.) The first month that "PawnShop" was out I sold more than 400 copies on my own, without paying a nickel's commission to anybody.

Of course the 64-dollar question in all of this is: Did the public live up to their end of the deal? Did they follow through with their commitment and send in their money? To date I have sold more than 1,100 CDs through the New Deal as it is presented through e-mail blasts, my web page and Facebook. And my collection rate is over 95 percent.

Maybe it's just me, but I find that a very revealing number when it comes to how an artist can think about selling his wares these days.

I made a decision early on that if somebody didn't pay, I was not going to chase them down or otherwise play collection agency with them. People often write and ask me for my address, saying they have misplaced the envelope I sent with the CD for remittance. On several occasions I have had people come up to me at gigs and hand me money, saying that they had lost the envelope or had just never gotten around to sending me a check. I find that continuing to send e-mail blasts that mention the New Deal reminds people who might have forgotten that they have not yet paid for the CD they received. Checks seem to just wander in.

At the root of all this, of course, is a fact about us humans that I think we often forget about in our daily interactions with each other—and that is that trust is an empowering thing. To trust someone is to establish a relationship with them, ipso facto. For musicians this is crucial knowledge, because our business is all about establishing relationships, whether it's from the stage, through a pair of speakers, or in the public forum of cyber space. A musical performance itself, a least a good one, balances on the trust the performer has of his audience to hear him out, let him open up his heart to them and have his say. Likewise, it is trust that brings the audience to the performer, trust that he will be honest and forthright and worthy of their time and attention. That's what puts the checks in the mailbox.

Gene Shay

'You've Got to Work at It.'

by Ruth Heil

Y ou're sure your song has the potential to be a hit. You've reworked it, recorded it, and even packaged it—but how do you get a DJ to play it? To find out, I spoke with Gene Shay, a professional broadcaster in the song-playing business for almost 50 years.

On the Philadelphia folk scene, Shay is a legend. Philadelphians heard Bob Dylan for the first time when Shay introduced him. After arranging Dylan's regional debut, Shay even gave him a lift from the train station the day before the 300-seat Rittenhouse Square show. Shay cofounded the Philadelphia Folk Festival in 1962, and he returns every year to emcee at this still-running, general interest folk festival. His love of music—starting with musical comedy, show tunes and other Americana standards, continuing through a stint playing jazz and pop on Armed Forces Radio and prevailing for decades through his work in the folk arena—draws in the audience. They trust him to play well-written music.

Shay hosts shows on WXPN in Philadelphia and online at FolkAlley.com. He and he alone decides which songs fill the airwaves during his enduring Sunday evening folk show on WXPN. Shay may draw a paycheck from the station, but he ultimately answers to his listeners: the people who buy music.

His responses to my questions about the business are filled with harsh realities, but a motivated songwriter in any genre or with any measure of experience or talent will benefit from the answers. Key among them: "You've got to work at it."

My first question: What can it mean for a songwriter's career to know Gene Shay? In his typical lighthearted, yet honest, fashion he responds, "We'll they're not going to make a million dollars from it." A positive encounter with someone willing

---

RUTH HEIL is a 35-year musician and freelance writer. She strives to bring solutions to creative-minded and environmentally conscious individuals so that they may find success in business.

to give you a break is not a guarantee of success. When talented Joni Mitchell met Shay, she was an unknown. He may have helped her, but it was Mitchell who crafted her music, made connections, put herself out there and worked hard. You cannot lean on any one person and expect him or her to make it happen for you.

You can, however, build on the association. Shay's friend, singer/songwriter Susan Werner, describes it this way: "From the first time I met Gene and played for him in 1990, I could sense what many songwriters know: that Gene listens as an individual, of course, but also as a member of the larger community. He listens with an ear to whether the song speaks for just the writer, or whether the song speaks to and for many others. So knowing Gene, and playing for Gene, makes you want to write the best songs you possibly can. He's actually pulling for you, and pulling for the song, which is a wonderful feeling. I'm pretty sure I speak for many when I say that Gene has inspired several generations of songwriters to write great, big, broad, kind songs, and that we're all the richer for it."

Today Shay's two shows are both commercial free and listener supported, and licensing does not restrict what he can play. He finds content from numerous places, but the songwriters themselves (or their representatives) submit the bulk of fresh discoveries. Of the 15 to 20 CDs that come to him each week, one might have a hit, and it's his job to dig through the pile and find it for his listeners.

"People who do shows like myself, we're not paid huge amounts of money and we don't do it on a full-time basis where we have a staff to sit around and pre-listen for us and say hey, of the 500 that came in this past month, here are four of the best. We have to do it. We have to listen, and quite often we don't have the time." He must start by ruling out the ones he doesn't like.

CATCH THEIR ATTENTION

"My main criticism with most contemporary songs is that the melodies are not very strong. They don't have anything memorable or the words are clichés," says Shay. He disregards lyricists who take the easy way out. "They're not using words in an imaginative, creative way. Too many use common phrases like ' 'cause I love you so much my heart is in my throat.' Where have we heard that before?"

The music must be captivating from the very beginning. Shay likes a song that is "a little off the wall, but just enough to make you sit up and take notice and say, 'Hey this guy is pretty clever.' The idea, of course, is not to draw the attention to the writer as being clever; the idea is get a song that sticks in your brain."

To do that you need to write things in a way that relates to your audience. Current events and comical situations often work. Tom Paxton once wrote "Thank You, Republic Airlines" in 1985 about the airline breaking his guitar. Many traveling musicians found it very funny so they bought the album.

People will often hand a CD to Shay and say, "Tell me what you think about it." He cringes at these requests. "I don't want to have to be put in that position. If it sucks, I'm not going to tell you that, and I don't want to lie to you."

THE SELECTION PROCESS

"It's rare for me to have to sit down and listen to an album all the way through." Sadly for aspiring musicians, he will not listen to half of the CDs he receives. He starts with a spot check of the song titles. A weak list contains "songs that are all sort of lovey dovey like 'I miss you so much,' 'When are you coming home Harry?', 'Why did you leave me?' "

If there is an unusual title, "I'll go in for the cuts that sound interesting. I usually go for the first two cuts just because that's where artists usually put their best two songs. But not always." Shay prefers track five ("The Babysitter's Here") on Dar Williams' 1995 album, *The Honesty Room* because it was funny and he thought it was a great novelty song.

Most often, though, he listens to the first cut and maybe 30 seconds of the second. By the third, "if nothing grabs me, I just put it in the reject pile. I won't throw it away; I'll hold it for six months. Sometimes one that was rejected became popular, and I'll realize that I have that album." Right now, there are about 800 to 1,000 CDs on that rejection shelf, and Shay's genuine voice turns solemn as he says, "It's a cruel business. I think of these guys and gals—they spent a lot of money, putting this album together and taking the picture for the cover, and beautiful artwork and all that."

People like Shay hold an encyclopedia of music within their heads. He will know if, as you claim, your song is unique. He acts as both a gatekeeper, guarding his listener from the ordinary, and a door opener, exposing songs that make people laugh, cry, contemplate, hum, or sway to the rhythm.

PUT YOURSELF OUT THERE

In addition to titles, Shay scours the cover for something to indicate the artist invested him or herself into the success of the project.

He looks to see if it was produced by someone he has heard of; if it was recorded in a familiar studio; if the songwriter collaborated with another musician whose name he recognizes; or if there is a local connection somehow. He looks for hard work.

While we are talking, Shay notices that the CD in front of him is by Kristin Andreassen who was the John Lennon Song Contest Grand Prize '07 winner for the song "Crayola Doesn't Make a Color for Your Eyes." Contest-winning and the like is evidence that the artist is serious and has something special.

Networking is another great way for a performer to make connections. Through the years, Shay has participated in events staged by the Northeast Regional Folk Alliance (www.nerfa.org), Broadcast Music Inc (www.bmi.com) as well as many, many festivals; in fact he is preparing to leave for the Woody Guthrie Festival in Oklahoma as we speak. "If the artist can afford it, it's a good idea to get to those things, to sing in front of DJs and in front of record producers and other singers. After a while, somebody becomes a friend of yours and they lead you to other gigs, not only booking and clubs in their area but they also can help you with your songwriting."

WORD GETS AROUND

In order to stay at the top of his game, Shay listens to as much as he can. Besides submitted demos, he's always listening to satellite radio and other folk shows because they provide insight into audience interest.

And he's not the only DJ staying in touch. Shay explains how a group of about 150 to 250 disc jockeys from licensed broadcast folk radio stations all around the country e-mail their playlists to Richard Gillman of KBCS in Bellevue, Washington, who has created an automated counting program. Each month, Richard creates an airplay tally, and then lists the top 70 albums and the top three songs from those albums on www.folkradio.org. "Most of those shows are folk shows on college stations or public radio stations. Most are done by volunteers. The DJs all seem to like the same artists.

"It's a great gauge for me to see if I'm picking the right cuts." If he sees a top listing that he is not playing, he can retrieve the CD from his rejection shelf and give it a second chance. "Sometimes three years later I discover a song on an album that is every bit as good as the one I am playing, or even better, and how it passed me buy I don't know, but I find that out by listening, for instance, to satellite radio."

So an artist who is discovered in Philadelphia today may burst onto the scene in Minneapolis tomorrow because of this communication. Catch the attention of *your* local radio personality who is playing the tunes in your genre, and the buzz will start from there.

Shay also notes, "It behooves a singer/songwriter to go onto these playlists from time to time and see if their own album is on there and see where it's going."

FIND YOUR OWN CONNECTION

Shay is still launching careers and spinning tunes on air and online. He has watched the business grow and change. He remembers a day when more performers bought songs, and more journeyman songwriters connected with buyers through publishing companies. People like recording artist Kathy Mattea still buy songs from writers, but he notes that Neil Diamond and James Taylor pioneered the now-common practice of performing their own songs, narrowing the opportunities for the non-performing songwriter.

Meanwhile, Shay has watched diversity increase and technology costs decrease, leveling the playing field and opening the competitive doors. He is watching as the middleman is being cut out, and he sees artists now selling their own album directly at a price that exceeds the cost of duplication.

Can a songwriter truly make money in the music industry today? "If they have a hit on their hands. If not, if they have good quality songs," says Shay.

Leonard Cohen once said in an interview that he wrote and reworked almost 85 verses to a song for which he needed six. Work hard to create a strong melody, be clever with your words and build the right connections. Then, the audience will buy your recordings, cheer at your concerts, and camp out at festivals to see you perform. Then you will know they like your song.

Gretchen Peters

*Respect Your Voice, Encourage
Your Instincts*

by Kerry Dexter

I think if you're going to write something really lasting, you have to look at the big things," Gretchen Peters says. She's done that in ways that have moved Faith Hill, Bonnie Raitt, Bryan Adams, Patty Loveless, Martina McBride, and George Strait, among others, to record her songs, And she fills up listening rooms in Europe, and the U.S. on her own, too, offering songs that often look at the hard choices and changes of life. Whether those song are dark or light, happy or sad, Peters anchors the big subjects in small and vivid detail. The taste of bitter coffee, children's faces peering around a door frame, a snowfall through a window are three telling ones she's used to mark the end of a long relationship, consider divorce, and look at the pain that is present in life's changes. "It's always more powerful to talk a around the thing than to describe it directly," Peters says.

Recently the Nashville-based songwriter came across an old notebook, one that she began keeping when she was about 10, and continued to write in until she was 17. "I wrote out lyrics in it, lyrics to all the songs I liked, and eventually the songs that I played in my first performances," she says, "and although I didn't know it at the time, it became sort of my school of songwriting. Writing out lyrics forces you to think about what the song is about. It forces you to look at the song structure, and the weight in each line, in each word." She put those songs to use playing in bands, duos, and trios where she was living in Colorado, covering a mix of songs that leaned toward music from Bonnie Raitt, Emmylou Harris, and Rodney Crowell and included the occasional Dire Straits cover as well.

One night, Peters went to see Dolly Parton play in Denver. "When I saw Dolly,

KERRY DEXTER is an independent writer, editor, and photgrapher in the U.S. and Europe. Her work has appeared in VH1. com, music magazine *Dirty Linen, Strings, Symphony, Wandering Educators,* and CMT, among others. She's contributed chapters to *Ireland and the Americas, The Dictionary of American History,* and *The Encyclopedia of Counterculture,* and writes about the arts at http://musicroad.blogspot.com.

it sank in that the songs she wrote could only have been written by her. I was so inspired by that that after that show, I sat down and wrote what I still consider a pretty good song. I mean it's young, it's naive, but there's something in there," she says. What was in there, as it turned out, was the seed of a talent that would lead her to write songs that would top the country charts. Peters moved to Nashville a few years later without much in the way of prospects, which, she recalls, "was scary, it was crazy—it was one of the craziest things I've ever done in my life."

She also found parts of it baffling. People asked her whether she was a singer or a writer. She was both, but more doors opened in writing. Peters found her own voice and style, telling stories of characters facing chance and change in songs such as "Chill of an Early Fall," recorded by George Strait; "High Lonesome, recorded by Longview; "Water Into Wine," recorded by Patty Loveless; "On a Bus to Saint Cloud," recorded by Trisha Yearwood; and "Independence Day," recorded by Martina McBride.

FINDING HER PLACE

Though Peters has a clear and engaging soprano and the relaxed yet compelling stage presence of a storyteller, after her move to Nashville she found country audiences didn't quite know what to do with her a performer. In the U.K., she found warm reception on stage, but in the U.S., the path was not as clear. "With my first album, my record company felt that they had to break me as a country artist," Peters says, "and when that didn't happen, nobody—and I should have done it myself, I'm not laying the blame on anybody—nobody said to me hey, maybe that's not who you are. Maybe you need to go another route."

Eventually, she did, finding a place for herself on the folk circuit. "Tom Russell, who encouraged me a lot, introduced me to his booking agent. She said, 'You'll have to reintroduce yourself to this market, 'cause these people aren't going to know who you are. But if you're willing to do that, sure, there's a place for you here.' I said, 'Yes, send me anywhere; I just want to play,'" Peters recalls. "I guess I wasn't cut out to be a writer who sits at home and only writes songs for other people to sing. I'm thrilled and delighted that other people have recorded my songs and I hope they record more of them, but I have to get out and play too."

TELLING HER STORIES

It's a varied bag of songs Peters brings to her audiences. "I remember early on I had to struggle to make sure I had enough songs of my own to fill an evening," she says. At a recent concert broadcast over the Internet, though, fans around the world sent in enough requests to fill a week of shows.

The material she works with now comprises character songs, such as her mainstream country hits "Independence Day," "Let That Pony Run," and "Love and Texaco," a few well chosen covers including Tom Russell's "Guadalupe" and Kim Richey and Will Kimbrough's "Careful How You Go," and songs drawn from

Articles & Interviews

material in her own life, such as "Northern Lights" and "Ghost."

"I'm really a story song writer," she says, "I write a lot of fictional characters in stories. I found myself, about five or six years ago, shifting more toward stuff from my own life, There was a desire to do that, and there was fear around it.

"My first thought was, I'm not interesting enough, these characters are a lot more interesting than I am—Circus Girl, she's a lot more colorful, and Independence Day, those characters are a lot more dramatic, and I don't really have anything like that, why would anybody care?

"That was the first wave of fear about it, but of course the deeper fear, the more real fear, is revealing yourself. That's a tough one," she continues. "I went ahead and did it anyway, because the writer in me is stronger than the fear in me, and also because I was feeling really depleted and didn't have any ideas for characters or stories, and I thought, I have to write, and this my material, this is what I have, my life. A lot of the material for my album *Halcyon* came out of that. And what I found was, revealing yourself is scary—and the real example for me would be *Burnt Toast & Offerings* because that's all completely—me," she says.

Among the material Peters had to draw on for that album was the end of her long marriage, changes in her life and work, and taking a chance on new love, all of which turn up in the songs. "It is scary, but what you find is that these things that are so specifically you are so incredibly universal. You find that out by playing the songs for people, talking with people who have the music, and you see how it resonates, and you see, this is my story, but it' s their story too.

"Loneliness, alienation, the end of a relationship, all that stuff—it's all completely universal stuff. We all feel that way, and seeing that helped me get over the hump of feeling that I could write this sort of confessional stuff and do it well," Peters says. Part of the reason these songs connect so strongly with listeners is Peters' approach to writing them.

"I have a real dislike of navel gazing song writing. I don't ever want to be guilty of that," she says. "I'm very aware all the time that, if I'm going to write this song about me, I still have to apply all the skills that I have acquired as a writer to make sure it is a good song. Of course writing about your own stuff and putting it out in front of everyone is terrifying! I think if you're going to write something that is true, then you may uncover some stuff that you don't want to look at, don't want to reveal to other people—but the gift in revealing it is this wonderful sense of community. I guarantee you if you do it, and you do it well, it will resonate. That *Burnt Toast* album has brought me so much in terms of an audience that got it, and, I think, appreciated having it expressed for them, in a sense." It's not that she wasn't putting herself into the character songs as well, Peters says. "Oh, I was, to such an extent that I wasn't even really aware of it. Two years later I'd be singing a line and go Oh my God, that's about me! and not even realize it until way, way after the fact. I think I had just reached a point where I was ready not to clothe those ideas in someone else's life and trappings, so to speak. And there are a lot of great characters—I'd love to do some more character songs. But I hope there'd be more of me in them," she says.

Peters finds writing songs one of the most creative and amazing—and hardest—experiences she has. Reflecting what she's learned, she says, "I think a lot of young writers look at veterans and think they've got it down. They just go in and they just write and they know a secret we don't know. In a very real sense it never gets any easier—actually it in some ways gets harder, because your target gets higher and higher and farther away, the more you write, the more you listen and the more you realize it's an awesome thing to attempt. That can seem discouraging but actually it's encouraging, because you can relax and go, OK, it's not going to get any easier, so let's put that off the table.

Making time and space to hear your own voice is another thing Peters finds vital, and wrestles with. "All of us who are singer songwriters are doing at least three jobs, and there's a lot of left brain stuff going on with touring and promotion and all of that, and it's hard to turn that off. I think it's the transition that's hard for me—when I'm doing the left brain stuff I find that very satisfying, and then to get to the writing side I have to space out and go through the agony of nothing working for a couple of days, and then when I get into the creative space and ideas are flowing, I don't want to come out of that—coming out of that is like walking into a room where the lights are too bright and the noise is too loud, you know?" she says.

Respecting your voice is what it is all about in the end, and in the beginning, Peters thinks. "I think one of the mistakes young, hungry writers make is not identifying and listening to and encouraging their own instincts, their own gut. I know I was that way in the beginning, I was so anxious for feedback, so anxious to get my songs to work in the marketplace, to have anything happening, that it was a struggle to balance that with my own voice.

"It's easy to have your voice twisted and worn down by external cues, by too much co-writing, by paying attention to the marketplace and to what people tell you," Peters says. "I'm not saying don't listen to advice, but you really have to develop this inner sense of what you're trying to say, and have you said it well? Is it any good? If—and this is a really big if—you really are a writer, I'm a big believer that there's an internal mechanism, a gut, a truth bone—call it what you want—and your job as a writer is listening to it when it tells you this song or this line or this melody needs to be this way, this is way this goes. If it needs to be changed, you know what needs to be changed. That's internal, that comes from within. And if what you're writing about is true, and authentic, and it moves you—if it has emotional truth—then people will stand up and take notice."

Cathie Ryan

Weaving a Tapestry of Song

by Kerry Dexter

Carrick a Rede is a place in County Antrim, Northern Ireland, where there is a rope bridge high over the sea. It's also the name of a song by Irish American songwriter Cathie Ryan (www.cathieryan.com). When Ryan was at "Carrick a Rede" not long ago, a stranger walking behind her was singing the song. The woman had no idea who Ryan was," and I didn't say a word," Ryan says. "But I thought, that's lovely. This place has a song now."

Place and landscape often provide first sparks of song ideas for Ryan, and a landscape image will also sometimes be the catalyst that draws together ideas she's been mulling about emotion, history, and character. Those landscapes and characters might equally be from Ireland or America. Ryan was born in Detroit to parents who had emigrated from Ireland, and she spent childhood summers visiting her grandparents back in Kerry and Tipperary. Growing up, she took in sounds including very traditional Irish music, American country from the likes of Loretta Lynn, Merle Haggard, and Emmylou Harris, mainstream Irish music such as that of the Clancy Brothers, Appalachian ballads, and a bit of Motown as well. All of those would form the background to her own music. "I've always been an Irish American singer," she says.

As an adult, Ryan has spent time living in both Ireland and America. As a touring musician she's also spent many days on the road, which is where the lyric for "Carrick a Rede" came to her. "I was in a plane, and we were delayed and sat on the runway for a long time," she recalls, "I was going to meet up with guitarist John Doyle to work on songs for [her third album] *Somewhere Along the Road*, and I knew there was something missing. There was a song I wanted on the album, medium tempo happy kind of song that wasn't a throwaway. I sat on the plane and

KERRY DEXTER is an independent writer, editor, and photgrapher in the U.S. and Europe. Her work has appeared in VH1.com, music magazine *Dirty Linen, Strings, Symphony, Wandering Educators*, and CMT, among others. She's contributed chapters to *Ireland and the Americas, The Dictionary of American History*, and *The Encyclopedia of Counterculture*, and writes about the arts at http://musicroad.blogspot.com.

the lyrics came to me, clean. I handed it to John and he said, 'I don't think I can do anything with this, Cathie, the meter is strange.' I left it with him anyway, and when I got back home and turned on my answering machine, it was John, playing the melody for 'Carrick a Rede.' For me that was a bit of magic."

It's a joyous and lively tale, with a melody to match, of a couple heading off over the bridge to "Carrick a Rede" for a bit of lovemaking. Happy love songs are rare in Irish tradition, a fact that Ryan has fun with when introducing the song in concert. It is, however, more than just an upbeat song to fill a slot. "It lives on several levels, I think," Ryan says. "On a very basic level it's about how do you get across to Carrick a Rede? You hold on tight, you let go, and that's the only way, when you're afraid of something, because the impulse, for me anyway, is to hold on for dear life. But the only way through is to let go." That's as true whether you're negotiating a rope bridge 80 feet above the sea or the dynamics of a relationship, Ryan says. "On the second level it's about that—giving your heart is a very similar process, holding on and letting go, how much do you give, how much do you hold back? Then a lot of people just see it as a great song about a couple going off to have a romp on 'Carrick a Rede,' and I think you can take it that way as well," she says, laughing.

She wasn't thinking of those layers when she was writing it, Ryan points out, "but I used to teach English, and when I'd be explicating a story students would raise their hands and say. 'Oh, c'mon, the writer wasn't thinking all that when they were writing it!' and I'd say, 'On some level it was being thought.' I do believe that's the case with songs, as well as with any writing. You bring so much power to the words, to the intention and the meaning."

THE SONGWRITING PROCESS

Ryan usually starts with the words and finds the melody in them, but for a song called "What's Closest to the Heart" on her fourth album, *The Farthest Wave*, it was a different experience, "and it's one of the hardest things I've ever done," she says. "I said to John Doyle, 'There's this old Irish expression that I love: What's closest to the heart comes out." And I've got this little snippet of a lyric and sort of said the snippet to him, 'what's closest next or near it, listen you'll hear it,' and I said, 'I have some ideas about what I'd like it to be about but I haven't fleshed it out.' He just started groovin' on the sound of the consonants, the meter of the words."

They were at producer and fiddle player John McCusker's house working on other songs for the record, "and John McCusker came in with the idea for the fiddle break, and said, 'Oh, I really want to do this, we've got to really rock it out, and then guitarist Kris Drever came over, and John said. 'Listen to this, no words yet but really likin' the melody.' And the two them sat down together with their guitars and came up with this really intense, just mesmerizing groove, which I just fell in love with, and I said, 'Let's record it now!—I'll just sing la la la la' And that's what we did.

I went home with the track, and then I thought, 'What have I gotten myself into?' I listened back to it and thought, 'I'm never gonna be able to find words for this melody.'" Eventually Ryan took herself to the town library for a bit of quiet and a change of scenery, and there she was able to get the words to work. The result is a swirling, shape shifting groove of melody with lyrics that raise more questions than they answer, in both English and Irish—an enigmatic song that, while it fits well with Ryan's other work, is rather different from most of it. "I love doing that song live now, it's just exciting to do that song live," she says.

At Ryan's live shows, as well as on her recordings, she weaves a tapestry of song from Irish tradition, the American folk song bag, and contemporary writers such as Karine Polwart and John Spillane along with her own music. Each of her albums has a central idea around which she chooses the songs "although I hate to say concept, because that doesn't seem organic enough; it seems a bit technical. But maybe that's what it is."

GOING SOLO, BUILDING BRIDGES

Her first solo album, called simply *Cathie Ryan*, "is an assertion," she says. Ryan was a founding member of the internationally respected band Cherish the Ladies, and for nearly eight years, lead singer with them. "The Back Door," a song about undocumented Irish immigrants which was the first song of her own Ryan sang out publicly, became the title track of the band's first album. She looks back on her time with Cherish as a good musical experience, and people still identify her with the band, "but it seems like another lifetime to me now," she says.

"A lot of the songs on the *Cathie Ryan* album were songs I brought to Cherish the Ladies and that they didn't like, that they didn't want to do. So it was a way of declaring some independence." Her second album, *The Music of What Happens*, is named from a well known phrase in Irish legend. Reflection on that mythology was her central idea there. "It's Finn McCool being asked, what's the most beautiful music in the world? The music of what happens," she says. The music she chose to answer that question included a traditional lament sung in Irish, a song about immigration, emigration and identity by Gerry O'Beirne, a love song from Scotland, and Ryan's own songs "I'm Going Back" and "At the Foot of Knocknarae."

Somewhere Along the Road, her third recording, "was really about who I was in the world being Irish American," Ryan says. That's an identity which offers Ryan a deep well of ideas, and it's also an identity which comes with a deep well of stereotypes. Ryan's work has more in common with the adventurous approaches of country Grammy winner Kathy Mattea and top international star Mary Black than it does with hearty pub drinking songs and highly embellished traditional song styling often thought of when Irish music is mentioned.

"When I was with Cherish, I got so much flak for doing contemporary songs, from people who only wanted to hear really traditional material," she recalls. As a solo artist, she has headlined most major Celtic festivals and also played not so Celtic clubs and concert halls including the Cactus Cafe in Austin, The Ark in Ann Arbor, Lincoln Center in New York City, and the Kennedy Center in Washington, DC. "It took a lot of really hard work and having a substantial body of work to get there," she says. "The promoters didn't know what to do with me—I was this artist with one foot in each world, standing in the threshold."

Standing in a different sort of threshold was part of idea centering her fourth album, *The Farthest Wave*. "There had been some huge, huge changes in my life—it was the end of my life as I knew it, and it was about trying to come to terms with being somebody different. There's also this idea in mythology, if you're banished from the island you're sent out beyond the waves, with only your coracle and no oars, and have to make your way to land again," she says. Ryan chose John Spillane's "The Wild Flowers," about flourishing outside the garden, and Karine Polwart's "Follow the Heron," about the coming of spring after the cold of winter, to be on the record. One of her own songs for the album is called *Be Like the Sea*. "That was an important part of the process of that record for me, talking about casting things off and beginning again. I was reading a lot of poetry by Rumi at the time, and that's an influence too—there's a line in the song about give up the small ground that comes from taking in his work.

As she often does in her music, Ryan found in the natural world around her a poetic way to connect her ideas. "I love the sea, the life in it, and the idea that it constantly renews itself—and we make that so hard!" Ryan says. "I was meditating while I was working on the record, and that comes into it too, there's a line that says down below these waves, in the deepest depth, there are echoes sounding, true as your breath, and I'd think of my breath, like waves coming up to the shore."

People don't come up to Ryan after her shows to talk about meditation or geography, though. "When you write a song, if it's a good one, it means something different to each person who hears it," Ryan says. "They take it in and make it their own."

With "Be Like the Sea," "Carrick a Rede," "What's Closest to the Heart," and the other songs she writes and sings, Cathie Ryan continues to walk the territory of being an artist who sees things in two worlds, who makes music that creates bridges between Ireland and America, myth and reality, past and present, natural landscapes and landscapes of the heart. She's working on ideas for songs which may become her next album. "I'm looking forward to seeing where they take me," Ryan says.

Articles & Interviews

Steve Seskin

Teaching Others to Be Better Songwriters

by Laura Louise Renegar

Steve Seskin has written seven number one hits. His work has been recorded by Tim McGraw, John Michael Montgomery, Ricochet, and Kenny Chesney, just to name a few. Seskin's "Grown Men Don't Cry" was nominated for a Grammy. He writes, performs, records, and is a songwriting teacher for organizations such as the West Coast Songwriters Association and the Nashville Songwriters Association International. But lately, he has been co-writing with a younger crowd.

For the last four years, Steve has been an artist in residence in many different schools helping teach kids to write songs. Most of the lyrics he writes with students focus on self-esteem, diversity, and strong character traits.

Seskin packs his own music with the same heart he encourages children to use. His award-winning song "Don't Laugh at Me" was recorded by Peter, Paul, and Mary, and became the catalyst for Operation Respect/Don't Laugh at Me. This program has been used in schools to discourage bullying and encourage kids to be compassionate.

In addition to working with kids, Seskin has been writing books for them. *Don't Laugh at Me* and *A Chance to Shine* are two picture books based on songs co-written by Steve Seskin and Allen Shamblin.

How long have you been writing songs, and how did you get started?
I've been writing songs for 35 years. I started singing as a kid and was always attracted to material that lyrically spoke to me. I decided it was something I could do and wrote my first song at age 22. It wasn't very good.

LAURA LOUISE RENEGAR is a children's book writer and freelancer. She lives in Clemmons, North Carolina, and cheats all bar chords. Visit her website, www.laurarenegar.blogspot.com.

Who are some of your musical influences?

Paul Simon; James Taylor; The Beatles; Joni Mitchell; Jackson Browne; Crosby, Stills & Nash; Steely Dan; Michael McDonald; Peter, Paul, and Mary; Pete Seeger; Bob Dylan.

As a singer/songwriter, are you ever disappointed by another artist's interpretation of your song?

Sometimes. I'm always flattered that someone chooses to record one of my songs, but I'm not always happy with the results.

How much time do you usually spend rewriting a song? How do you know when it's done?

It varies, but I'll spend as long as it takes to get it right. It's done when your gut says every word and every note feel like they're the best they can be. Songwriting is never a math problem. There's more than one right answer.

Do you write from your own experiences or from your imagination?

Both. I think writing about your own life is a great place to start but not a great place to stop. There's always something interesting going on in someone's world. I try to keep my eyes and ears open all the time to gather in what the universe is offering.

How do you use emotional truth to write a fictional song?

Sometimes I try to imagine what it would feel like to be a particular character, or I call up the emotions I felt a long time ago when something similar happened to me. I also believe in the catalyst theory that allows me to transfer the emotional energy of a story to another set of facts. For instance, "Grown Men Don't Cry" was sparked by a passage in a book where the father tells his 17-year-old son not to cry because he is a grown man. One stereotype in our society is that men shouldn't be as emotional as women. They are often taught to "suck it up" and "be a man." I think that's unhealthy and offensive. I transferred that energy to a song giving men permission to cry if and when they feel like it. The particulars of the story in the book were not part of the story in the song.

What are the advantages and disadvantages of co-writing?

When it's a good union, the old adage of "two heads are better than one" can certainly apply. There are people I love writing with because we produce a hybrid creation where both writers feel like the song is better due to our combined efforts. Co-writing also offers exposure to different types of music. The disadvantages can occur when personalities don't mesh and both people feel unable to assert themselves. Part of co-writing is making the other writer feel comfortable so they can do their best work. Sometimes co-writers disagree on what should stay in the song and when to dig a little deeper. If that happens on a regular basis it's probably a sign that it's not a good creative pairing. I always try to give my co-writer the benefit of the doubt. If they feel like something isn't right in a song, I'm willing to take another look at it, even if I don't agree. We're both there to serve the song, not our egos.

How should a new songwriter approach someone about co-writing?

I would start with an honest appraisal of your own talents. What are your strengths as a writer? What are your weaknesses? When it comes to lyric writing are you better at starting ideas or finishing them? Are you better at big picture, chorus ideas or descriptive details more often found in verses? Musically some people are better at grooves, others at hearing melodies when someone else supplies the groove/chord background. Look for someone who complements your talents as a writer. I'd also want to hear some of the potential co-writer's work, and vice versa, so there's an initial feeling that it would work on a level of being different enough but not too large a gap between styles. A good place to approach possible co-writers is at writers' nights where both people get a chance to hear each other. Many songwriting organizations host these kinds of gatherings.

You live in California but also spend a lot of time in Nashville. What are some of the differences you've noticed between the music business in Nashville and L.A.?

This is changing all the time, but for many years the difference has been that Nashville was a place where writers co-wrote on a regular basis, and their only goal was to write a great song. Throughout the '90s there was not much target writing (trying to write a song for a specific artist), or inside writing where you had a better chance of getting the song recorded if you wrote it with the artist. In Los Angeles there is not as much of an active search for songs. More often the artist or band is self-contained completely, or the songs are supplied by the producer's camp or co-written with the artist. Target writing and inside writing are happening a lot more in Nashville now than in years past. To me it takes the heart, soul, and creativity out of the process. Create your art from a pure place and when you're done, figure out who might want to buy it.

How do you decide who to approach when pitching a song?

It's kind of like casting a movie. Usually my publisher and I will make a list of who might be interested in a song, based on what they've done in the past and what we've heard they're looking for now. If I've had success with an artist, I might be able to get a song directly to him or her. If I haven't, I might have to pitch it to someone who will have to play it for several other people before the artist would ever get to hear it.

What words of wisdom do you have for a new songwriter putting together a demo?

If they are the artist, they have a lot more latitude in terms of how they produce the recording and what they can do in terms of sound or even the content of the songs themselves. When you're trying to get songs recorded by other artists, you have to be aware of what the marketplace is doing at any given time and keep things somewhat in the confines of the flavor of the month. Artists break new ground in popular music much more often than writers.

How did you meet Peter Yarrow and become a part of Operation Respect/ Don't Laugh at Me?

I was teaching a songwriting class at the Kerrville Folk Festival in Texas. One of the lessons was about point of view. I always use "Don't Laugh at Me" as an example of a song that uses first person in an unusual way. At the end of the class a young woman came up and said she really liked that song, and that her dad needed to hear it. It turned out she was Bethany Yarrow, Peter's daughter. The next night she brought him to see my show. He loved the song. Peter, Paul, and Mary started singing it, and a year later he decided it would make a great centerpiece for an arts-based character education curriculum. Allen Shamblin and I donated the song for usage in the program, and Operation Respect was born. I became personally involved when Peter asked me if I'd develop an assembly program for schools to impart messages of kindness and respect using music as the delivery system. It's the most rewarding work I've ever done. Nine years later, the program has now been implemented in over 25,000 schools in 35 states and seven foreign countries. Peter also enlisted me to do assembly programs in schools and has been instrumental in facilitating all my work with children.

How did "Don't Laugh at Me" become a book?

My friend Robert Stricker is a literary agent. After the school program began, he thought an illustrated book would be a good companion piece to the song. He pitched it to Ten Speed Press. They enlisted illustrator Glin Dibley, and the book was born. It's now been printed in five additional languages including Spanish, Taiwanese, Croatian, Hebrew, and Arabic.

Why did you decide to start teaching children to write songs?

My songwriting with kids came as a result of my assembly program. I combined my passion for writing songs and teaching songwriting with my dedication to furthering character education and arts education in the schools. I spend about 60 days a year teaching kids how to write songs. In the process we write one together which lyrically is almost always geared to some aspect of good character. I hope to help kids realize that they can be creative and use their talents to share with the world how they feel about any issue.

How do the students decide on a song topic?

I poll the class for titles and ideas, and I bring in a few as well. We vote to come up with one that the majority likes. I give them some parameters to keep the effort from being too silly and to hopefully make the song about something that will benefit the whole school.

What happens to the songs you co-write with students after you leave?

I put recordings up on my website, www.steveseskin.com, so that students all over the world can be inspired. Twelve of the songs have been turned into my latest children's book, *Sing My Song*. A school in Oregon sent a song we wrote together called "Yes We Can" to President Obama.

How is teaching songwriting to kids different from teaching adults?

It's not very different. I do have to take into consideration the level I'm working with in terms of vocabulary and comprehension. Kids have amazing imaginations. They are often more forthcoming and unafraid to express themselves than adults.

In a competitive market, why do you choose to teach others how to be better songwriters?

I feel like it's part of my legacy to pass on the knowledge I've gathered over 30 plus years of writing songs. I think it's fabulous that people write songs. I believe that the greatest gift in life is sharing your gift with others. I'm not worried about the competitive aspect of it. I celebrate anyone who can get somewhere in this crazy music business. I love when one of my students has success and relish in the thought that I might have had a little something to do with it.

Richard Flohil

Marketing Advice from a Seasoned Promoter

by David McPherson

Richard Flohil recently turned 75. The grey, shoulder-length wispy hair epitomizes the experience of this Toronto music publicist, promoter and passionate champion of roots music.

Walk through his house in midtown Toronto and immediately you know you are in the midst of a music lover; his shelves—from the bathroom to the living room—are lined with more than 11,000 vinyl and CD records, along with hundreds of music books. His electronic Rolodex is 3,500 names and counting.

Catch up with him and you may find him nursing a mild hangover and charming a young songwriter—telling her how to get started in the music biz; then you watch him kill (or reply to) 100 e-mails. Next, he figures out the guest list for that evening's show at Hugh's Room before, as he says, "wrestling" an Ian Tyson biography to the ground.

Flohil emigrated to Canada in 1957; he started out working in journalism for various trade publications before moving into PR in the late 60s. In 1970, Richard Flohil & Associates was born and 39 years later this boutique PR agency that handles publicity for musicians, record companies, concert tours and club gigs is still going strong.

He has promoted concerts for the likes of Muddy Waters, BB King, and k.d. lang over the years. He has worked with the Downchild Blues band for 37 years, Stony Plain Records for 27 years and Loreena McKennitt for 20 years. The Renaissance man has also contributed liner notes to more than 100 albums and written hundreds of bios for musicians.

DAVID McPHERSON is a Toronto-based freelance writer with more than 17 years experience writing about music. A graduate of the University of Western Ontario, with a Masters in Journalism, David has published thousands of articles in daily newspapers, consumer magazines, and websites across North America, including *Bluegrass Unlimited, Paste, American Songwriter, Performing Songwriter* to name a few. His website is: www.davidmcpherson.ca.

Here follows some marketing advice for songwriters from this veteran publicist.

GENERAL RULES OF PROMOTING ONESELF

These apply regardless of what media you use. You use media to spread the word faster than word-of-mouth can spread it. Word-of-mouth is still the most reliable, effective method of making people believe in what you do, your music, and you as a person, but it is impractical to reach a mass audience.

The bio

A certain degree of hyperbole and hype is permitted. Downright lying is not. It's surprising the number of people…they don't really lie, but they exaggerate past the point of no return. If you are writing a bio there are various elements you have to consider. Who are you, what do you do…make these things as objective as possible. You can use them on your MySpace, Facebook, and Sonic Bids pages, but be objective.

Do not say, "I'm Joe Blow, I'm the best singer-songwriter to come out of North America in the last 20 years and I've been compared to Bob Dylan, etc." There is no believability. People turn off instantly. It is perfectly permissible though to carefully use other people's quotes. For example, if *The New York Times* says, "We regard Fred Smith as one of the best folk singers in Ontario." That's OK since it's not you [saying it].

Objective bio material is step No.1. If you've got a penchant for writing objectively about yourself, fair enough, you can write it, otherwise get someone to do it. You also need a hook. I helped a client write her bio recently. She has a tattoo on her wrist in Sanskrit or something and I asked "What does that read?" And she said, 'Tell the truth.' There's your angle.

Learning Never Stops

Flohil Talks with Randy Newman

"Some people never stop learning," says Richard Flohil.

That point was driven home during an on-stage interview Flohil did with Randy Newman. Here's how he recounts the end of his conversation with the singer-songwriter:

Flohil: You are a recording artist, you've done stuff for movies; is there anything like an average day in your house?"

Newman: "Yea, I watch the baby, middle of the day I may go for my piano lesson…"

Flohill: "Wait a minute…"

Newman: "Yeah, I'm studying classical piano."

Flohill: You play a Beethoven sonata?

Newman: Sure.

Good photographs

Do not let your brother-in-law's sister take your picture. There are specific needs for pictures. Good photos are important. I sound like a broken record on this one, especially with photographers I work with who continue to ignore it, but the media needs, likes and gives bigger space to horizontal images, rather than vertical images. A vertical image can very easily be made into a single column shot.

The book

Your music isn't enough. I hate to say that, but to be successful, and you can define success any way you like, making a living is a good way in this climate. Forget about Gold records and multi-million dollar this and that as it probably won't happen. If it does, nice, but don't bang your head against the wall trying to get there.

Apart from the music, you have to be focused and ambitious. You have to go for it. The fact is that most people will screw up parts of their life in search of this golden rainbow. You may screw up your relationships, your family…whatever. It behoves you to go for it, especially if you are young…let the relationships and the other things go by the wall if you want to be successful. If you want a domestic life, terrific, that's your decision, but it's hard to do both. If you are very young, that's a hook.

When I first started working with Serena Ryder, she was 17 and that was the hook. Yes, she had an amazing voice, but her youth was the hook. Being old is also a hook. I have an e-mail quote from Teddy Thompson, son of Richard Thompson, the line is, "You can be hip until you are 30 and then after that there is a period of limbo and then after 60 you can be a legend."

The music itself is not so much a hook, although that's what grabs new listeners. When I was working with k.d. lang, I did the very first dates in Toronto at a blues bar and she was doing her neo-country thing at the time, so that was an interesting experiment. Take music out of its normal context and put it somewhere else. You have to be careful because if it's too over the top, or too artificial or too manufactured, media people in particular spot it, unless it is so bizarre they have to cover it. Think in country music: Garth Brooks, black hat, never seen without it; Dolly Parton's wigs and her enhanced figure, never seen without it. Because it is so over the top it's incredibly likeable. Longevity is a hook for some people: think Gordon Lightfoot.

Join together

I think this is self-evident, but any successful artist, no matter what stage in their career, needs a team around them. When Serena Ryder was 16 she had a friend who did her press and hyped her to the local media and sent out cassettes to people like me saying, "What do you think?" My response was it's astonishing, amazing, can I help? Part of that help was I introduced her to Hawksley Workman who produced her first real record. Hawksley introduced her to her manager who is still on the scene. Building a team is important. I think this works universally throughout North America and Europe.

When you are looking for a manager or agent and you are still a very baby artist, you are going to be lucky to find one because those parts of the music industry by tradition, by custom and by practice, are based on a percentage of your earnings. If you are not earning anything, why would you expect a manager or agent to invest time and money working with you when the income is non-existent or very small. Find a friend to get involved in an evangelical way…it's called looking for a believer. You may find an experienced manager or agent who susses you out and thinks you have an unusual talent and signs you; it does happen, but not very often. The first person on your team would be a family member or a friend. Sooner or later that has to give way to someone with more connections.

As a publicist who has been at the business for a long time, we don't want a percentage, we want a fee. It may be that your first professional team member in your search for a believer is somebody like myself who have music industry contacts, we didn't lie too many times, so we have credibility attached to what we say. And, on our part, as a sidebar, we are very careful about who we take on… don't want to take on a turkey as their reputation rests on you and you on them.

Get out & play

A newcomer has to hone the art of the act. Any acoustic artist should look for work in the folk festivals, regardless of the dubious image of the "f" word because you can be exposed to huge audiences who didn't expect to see you; if you are good you will surprise them. If you are going to be doing a showcase, don't expect media to come unless there is a hook. Where you hold it is a hook. The act has to be together and you have to pack it with friends, relatives, uncles, whoever, so it gives the appearance to the handful of media you might entice out, they go "Oh my god!" Have to have the songs down, new strings on your guitar if need be and pace your set.

THESE RULES WERE MADE TO BE BROKEN

The other thing about the music industry is that it's covered and covered with layers and layers of rules, the biggest of which is that there are no rules. Anything that is a standard practice or normal can be broken, can be different or changed. Learn the rules, but once you know them, it's like writing songs, once you have them down, you can break them and make better songs maybe or different songs. One person I know learned to play piano so she could write songs on piano instead of guitar because they would come out different than ones she created on guitar.

Joe Ashley

He Writes the Songs
(& the Commercials Between Them)

by Noell Wolfgram Evans

For more than 40 years Joe Ashley has made a living writing songs. Almost from the start, his career has been split—he's had hits on the country chart, won numerous awards, and written for talented artists including John Denver. On the other side, his jingles have interrupted our television programs, his corporate anthems have taught employees the merits of their chosen company, and his melodies have injected life into business theatre events across the country.

Ashley, a self-professed "non-risk taker," has cautiously created a career balanced between the dreams of commercial songwriting and the practicalities (and stability) of industrial work. He has managed to find success in both with an innate ability to conceptualize an idea or a feeling and translate that into a song that tells a *story*, be it the story of a love lost or one extolling the virtues of a heating company. This balance also helps him to maintain a grounded sensibility about what it is he gets to do each and every day.

"I have something to say and I say it. And that's what it's all about really."

In many ways, Ashley's story plays like one of the country music songs that he loves. Born in West Virginia, his father (a somewhat amateur musician) got fourth-grader Joe a guitar and sent him off for music lessons. Ashley showed no lasting interest though, particularly in practicing, and he was shortly relieved of his burden.

THE CHOICE IS MADE

Ashley returned to playing music in college where he took up the bongos and the congas—but there were perhaps more personal than artistic reasons guiding that. "The Moment" would finally come for him in 1965 as he was driving from Lima,

---

NOELL WOLFGRAM EVANS, a playwright and two-time winner of the Thurber Treat Award for humor writing, has had productions in New York City, Chicago, Cleveland, Louisville, and Palm Springs. He is the Theatre Editor for Umbrella Publishing and an advisor for Group Creativity Improv Projects. The thing he enjoys most, though, is laughing with his family.

Ohio to Charleston, South Carolina for his brother's wedding. His brother's friend—and that friend's guitar—were along for the ride. During the trip the guitar never saw the inside of its case. Music floated out the windows and down the highway (Ashley particularly remembers multiple renditions of "Don't Think Twice" by Peter, Paul, and Mary) and it was somewhere on the pavement of I-75 that he had The Moment. As soon as he returned he *had* to get a guitar. This was more than just some vacation interest like a souvenir sand dollar; this was "an intense understanding that my life was changing," he says. When he returned to Lima he bought a guitar and a "How to Play" book and worked on completing those fourth grade lessons.

"I had a very technical musical style at first. It took years of playing, listening, and writing before I was really able to understand the variances and differences in writing a song."

Part of that understanding came from a girl he was seeing. A fellow musician, she helped him understand how to infuse his work with emotion and move beyond his textbook. While the relationship didn't last, the influence remains.

He was also influenced, as all good writers are, by the events of the day. It was the charged atmosphere on college campuses that led him to his first song writing "credit." He wrote a darkly humorous song about students burning draft cards which ended up being printed in the local paper. It may not have been a top of the charts recording, but when you're starting off, there is a certain thrill in a published song, no matter where it appears.

While there are many people whose work he admires, there is not one particular writer held up as an ideal. It's a conscious decision he's made to keep his writing "clean." "There are a lot of great songwriters. But I've found, for me, that if I study them too hard, I end up writing too close to them and everything becomes just an imitation."

INTO THE ADVERTISING GAME

Following college, Ashley moved into a copywriter position at an advertising agency and it was there that he finally started to get paid for writing songs (jingles, industrial melodies, corporate anthems, etc). He went on to write hundreds of jingles including pieces for Delaware Punch, Franklin University, The Columbus Zoo, Atlas Butler, and Germain Ford. While there is a satisfying feeling hearing your songs on the radio, advertising can be a taxing job. "It came be a time-intensive process, with so many people and opinions. That's why it's important to invest the time in developing your skills as a writer."

Along with strengthening his skills, he's also had to work hard to polish his pitch tactics. "One thing I've learned in writing for industrial clients that has helped me with *everything* I write is that you only get once chance. The client will only sit there captive to your idea for a short moment so you have one chance to do it as well as you can."

During this time he never gave up on his dream of writing commercial music. In fact as he wrote more and more for corporate clients, his songwriting skills improved and his confidence jumped. So much so that in the late '70s he made a dedicated push to see some of his work taken on by recording artists. It was a good choice and his efforts culminated in 1979 when he had several songs published with a few even finding their way into the onto the country charts. He ended the year receiving an ASCAP Country Music Award for "It's Too Soon to Say Goodbye" which was recorded by Terri Hollowell. While he was one of *many* receiving an award that year, it was a huge confidence boost. "Standing there on stage with people like Don Schlitz (writer of "The Gambler" and co-writer of "Forever and Ever, Amen"), whose work is just amazing, made me think, 'I might be good at this.'"

At this point one would think Ashley could officially be called a songwriter but it's a distinction he plays down with dark glee. "If someone asked me my thoughts on songwriting as a career I'd say it was an enormous waste of time. You'd be better off standing around looking for money on the ground." But he continues, "You shouldn't write songs in an attempt to make money, you should write them because it's the only way you can express yourself."

Ashley continued to write songs both corporate and commercial and often found that the two genres overlapped. For example, he was commissioned to write a song for John Denver to sing at the United Nations Environmental Awards. Later he was selected by NASCAR to write the lyrics for a set of original songs honoring Winston Cup Winners. In both cases the songs had to fit their venues, performers, and messages while providing an emotional pop—in other words these were commercial songs gone corporate.

A CHANGING MARKET

2003 saw the birth of Ashley Words, his move to break free from the ever consolidating agency world and take greater control of his career. Since the late 1970's Ashley has called Columbus, Ohio home and so it only made sense for him to base his studio there. In typical Ashley fashion, even though he's spent half of his life in Columbus, started a family, and carved out a successful writing career there, he wonders if Columbus is the right place to be: "I always say that you eat in the restaurant you're in. There are no complaints but you always wonder how things would be if you were living where people are doing and interested in the same things you are."

Recently Ashley's musical output for industrial clients has diminished. It's a mixture of choice and circumstance. As writer's we constantly praise the Internet and its ability to open opportunities in the marketplace to us. What we too often forget though is that this means there is greater competition for work as well. And that's where the problem lies—in the competition.

Articles & Interviews

"Guys who spend all day playing piano at the Holiday Inn are suddenly songwriters, creating commercials, and jingles, and all sorts of things. They'll knock out this thing for a thousand dollars and the client is happy because it's cheap but most clients are inexperienced and don't fully understand their true needs. And these people come in and throw this thing together without any thought to the message or the advertising that should be driving the work."

So, how can you expect to compete in a marketplace that not only encourages underbidding but rewards it? According to Ashley it's two simple words: "Relationships and Contacts." By building a solid roster of clients in his area he makes it easier for someone to pick up the phone instead of immediately jumping online when they need a song.

These relationships also make it easier for him to be less reliant on the feast or famine Internet job search. Following this model, his greatest sales and marketing tool is himself and the face-to-face connection he can make.

NEW SONGS

Ashley recently played out for the first time in his life and is planning on recording a CD of his songs. "It's time," he says with his characteristic fatalistic attitude. "I'm not sure if these will go anywhere but I feel like I need to get them out there. I usually write for someone else. I generally hear a women's voice, but I figured…" As his voice trails off I know exactly what he means to say: "Sometime's it's easier to just do it on your own."

THE PROCESS

After 40 years in the business Ashley still suffers from the same uncertainty as when he was plucking guitar strings in his dorm room. "It's the creative dilemma isn't it? We never know exactly how we've done something and so we spend half our time working to try to replicate it and the other half worrying we won't be able to."

Because his career has encompassed so many types of songs, Ashley has had to be flexible in his writing style—sometimes he'll come up with the lyrics first, sometimes the music, and sometime's he's given the music and told to go. Where he goes depends on the mood of the day. He doesn't have a rigid writing area or process which seems to allow a more spontaneous creativity to emerge with inspiration from his surroundings, be they the local Panera, his kitchen table, or the banks of the Scioto River.

Patience is also a huge part of the process, as it can take time for an idea to really play its self out. When he was writing "Son of a Coal Miner," he had, he felt, a great open and a great close but no way to make the two meet. No matter what he tried, he was stuck with two decent halves of a song. He eventually shelved the project and moved on. Over a year later he was working on a completely separate song, for an industrial client, when suddenly a line came to him. He pulled "Son of a Coal Miner" back out and found that it was the piece he had been searching for.

WHY WE DO IT

"I had just written the book and lyrics for a Wright Brothers stage show and I was in the conference room, pitching it to the client and I was reading it to everyone at the table and all of a sudden, for the first time, I realized that I didn't care if they liked it or not. Of course I wanted them to like it, I was proud of it, and I wanted the work—but that's the thing, whether they liked it or not, nothing could take away the fact that I wrote this stupid song. It took me a long time to get to that point but it's a wonderful place to be." (The client ended up going with Ashley's pitch and this mini-musical celebration of the Wright Brothers flight at Kitty Hawk became a finalist at the New York Festival Awards.)

Music Publishers

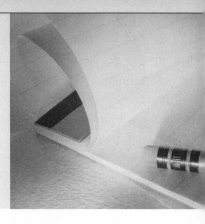

Music publishers find songs and then get them recorded. In return for a share of the money made from your songs, they work as an agent for you by plugging your songs to recording artists, taking care of paperwork and accounting, setting you up with co-writers (recording artists or other songwriters), and so on.

HOW DO MUSIC PUBLISHERS MAKE MONEY FROM SONGS?

Music publishers make money by getting songs recorded onto albums, Film and TV soundtracks, commercials, etc. and other areas. While this is their primary function, music publishers also handle administrative tasks such as copyrighting songs; collecting royalties for the songwriter; negotiating and issuing synchronization licenses for use of music in films, television programs and commercials; arranging and administering foreign rights; auditing record companies and other music users; suing infringers; and producing new demos of new songs. In a small, independent publishing company, one or two people may handle all these jobs. Larger publishing companies are more likely to be divided into the following departments: creative (or professional), copyright, licensing, legal affairs, business affairs, royalty, accounting and foreign.

HOW DO MUSIC PUBLISHERS FIND SONGS?

The *creative department* is responsible for finding talented writers and signing them to the company. Once a writer is signed, it is up to the creative department to develop and nurture the writer so he will write songs that create income for the company. Staff members often put writers together to form collaborative teams. And, perhaps most important, the creative department is responsible for securing commercial recordings of songs and pitching them for use in film and other media. The head of the creative department—usually called the "professional manager"— is charged with locating talented writers for the company.

HOW DO MUSIC PUBLISHERS GET SONGS RECORDED?

Once a writer is signed, the professional manager arranges for a demo to be made of the writer's songs. Even though a writer may already have recorded his own demo, the publisher will often re-demo the songs using established studio musicians in an effort to produce the highest-quality demo possible.

Once a demo is produced, the professional manager begins shopping the song to various outlets. He may try to get the song recorded by a top artist on his or her next album or get the song used in an upcoming film. The professional manager uses all the contacts and leads he has to get the writer's songs recorded by as many artists as possible. Therefore, he must be able to deal efficiently and effectively with people in other segments of the music industry, including A&R personnel, recording artists, producers, distributors, managers and lawyers. Through these contacts, he can find out what artists are looking for new material, and who may be interested in recording one of the writer's songs.

HOW IS A PUBLISHING COMPANY ORGANIZED?

After a writer's songs are recorded, the other departments at the publishing company come into play.

- The *licensing and copyright departments* are responsible for issuing any licenses for use of the writer's songs in film or TV and for filing various forms with the copyright office.
- The *legal affairs department and business affairs department* works with the professional department in negotiating contracts with its writers.
- The *royalty and accounting departments* are responsible for making sure that users of music are paying correct royalties to the publisher and ensuring the writer is receiving the proper royalty rate as specified in the contract and that statements are mailed to the writer promptly.
- Finally, the *foreign department*'s role is to oversee any publishing activities outside of the United States, to notify sub-publishers of the proper writer and ownership information of songs in the catalogue and update all activity and new releases, and to make sure a writer is being paid for any uses of his material in foreign countries.

LOCATING A MUSIC PUBLISHER

How do you go about finding a music publisher that will work well for you? First, you must find a publisher suited to the type of music you write. If a particular publisher works mostly with alternative music and you're a country songwriter, the contacts he has within the industry will hardly be beneficial to you.

Each listing in this section details, in order of importance, the type of music that publisher is most interested in; the music types appear in **boldface** to make them easier to locate. It's also very important to submit only to companies interested in your level of experience (see A Sample Listing Decoded on page 12). You will also want to refer to the Category Indexes on page 370, which list companies by the type of music they work with. Publishers placing music in film or TV will be proceded by a ▨ (see the Film & TV Index on page 417 for a complete list of these companies).

Do your research!

It's important to study the market and do research to identify which companies to submit to.

- Many record producers have publishing companies or have joint ventures with major publishers who fund the signing of songwriters and who provide administration services. Since producers have an influence over what is recorded in a session, targeting the producer/publisher can be a useful avenue.
- Since most publishers don't open unsolicited material, try to meet the publishing representative in person (at conferences, speaking engagements, etc.) or try to have an intermediary intercede on your behalf (for example, an entertainment attorney; a manager, an agent, etc.).
- As to demos, submit no more than 3 songs.
- As to publishing deals, co-publishing deals (where a writer owns part of the publishing share through his or her own company) are relatively common if the writer has a well-established track record.
- Are you targeting a specific artist to sing your songs? If so, find out if that artist even considers outside material. Get a copy of the artist's latest album, and see who wrote most of the songs. If they were all written by the artist, he's probably not interested in hearing material from outside writers. If the songs were written by a variety of different writers, however, he may be open to hearing new songs.
- Check the album liner notes, which will list the names of the publishers of each writer. These publishers obviously have had luck pitching songs to the artist, and they may be able to get your songs to that artist as well.
- If the artist you're interested in has a recent hit on the *Billboard* charts, the publisher of that song will be listed in the "Hot 100 A-Z" index. Carefully choosing which publishers will work best for the material you write may take time, but it will only increase your chances of getting your songs heard. "Shotgunning" your demo packages (sending out many packages without regard for music preference or submission policy) is a waste of time and money and will hurt, rather than help, your songwriting career.

Once you've found some companies that may be interested in your work, learn what songs have been successfully handled by those publishers. Most publishers are happy to provide you with this information in order to attract high-quality material. As you're researching music publishers, keep in mind how you get along with them personally. If you can't work with a publisher on a personal level, chances are your material won't be represented as you would like it to be. A publisher can become your most valuable connection to all other segments of the music industry, so it's important to find someone you can trust and feel comfortable with.

Icons

For more instructional information on the listings in this book, including explanations of symbols (**N** ✔ ▽ 🗔 🍁 🌐 ○ ◑ ◔ ∅), read the article *How To Use Songwriter's Market* on page 7.

For More Info

Independent or major company?

Also consider the size of the publishing company. The publishing affiliates of the major music conglomerates are huge, handling catalogs of thousands of songs by hundreds of songwriters. Unless you are an established songwriter, your songs probably won't receive enough attention from such large companies. Smaller, independent publishers offer several advantages. First, independent music publishers are located all over the country, making it easier for you to work face-to-face rather than by mail or phone. Smaller companies usually aren't affiliated with a particular record company and are therefore able to pitch your songs to many different labels and acts. Independent music publishers are usually interested in a smaller range of music, allowing you to target your submissions more accurately. The most obvious advantage to working with a smaller publisher is the personal attention they can bring to you and your songs. With a smaller roster of artists to work with, the independent music publisher is able to concentrate more time and effort on each particular project.

SUBMITTING MATERIAL TO PUBLISHERS

When submitting material to a publisher, always keep in mind that a professional, courteous manner goes a long way in making a good impression. When you submit a demo through the mail, make sure your package is neat and meets the particular needs of the publisher. Review each publisher's submission policy carefully, and follow it to the letter. Disregarding this information will only make you look like an amateur in the eyes of the company you're submitting to.

Listings of companies in Canada are preceded by a 🍁, and international markets are designated with a 🌐. You will find an alphabetical list of these companies at the back of the book, along with an index of publishers by state in the Geographic Index (see page 418).

PUBLISHING CONTRACTS

Once you've located a publisher you like and he's interested in shopping your work, it's time to consider the publishing contract—an agreement in which a songwriter grants certain rights to a publisher for one or more songs. The contract specifies any advances offered to the writer, the rights that will be transferred to the publisher, the royalties a songwriter is to receive and the length of time the contract is valid.

- When a contract is signed, a publisher will ask for a 50-50 split with the writer.

This is standard industry practice; the publisher is taking that 50% to cover the overhead costs of running his business and for the work he's doing to get your songs recorded.

- It is always a good idea to have a publishing contract (or any music business contract) reviewed by a competent entertainment lawyer.
- There is no "standard" publishing contract, and each company offers different provisions for their writers.

Make sure you ask questions about anything you don't understand, especially if you're new in the business. Songwriter organizations such as the Songwriters Guild of America (SGA) provide contract review services, and can help you learn about music business language and what constitutes a fair music publishing contract. Be sure to read What About Contracts? on page 38 for more information on contracts. See the Organizations section, beginning on page 302 of this book, for more information on the SGA and other songwriting groups.

When signing a contract, it's important to be aware of the music industry's unethical practitioners. The "song shark," as he's called, makes his living by asking a songwriter to pay to have a song published. The shark will ask for money to demo a song and promote it to radio stations; he may also ask for more than the standard 50% publisher's share or ask you to give up all rights to a song in order to have it published. Although none of these practices is illegal, it's certainly not ethical, and no successful publisher uses these methods. *Songwriter's Market* works to list only honest companies interested in hearing new material. (For more on "song sharks," see How Do I Avoid the Rip-Offs? on page 21.)

ADDITIONAL PUBLISHERS

There are **more publishers** located in other sections of the book! On page 144 use the list of Additional Publishers to find listings within other sections who are also music publishers.

◪ ABEAR PUBLISHING (BMI)/SONGTOWN PUBLISHING (ASCAP)

323 N. Walnut St., Murfreesboro TN 37130. (615)890-1878. Fax: (615)890-3771. E-mail: info@songtownpublishing.com. Website: www.songtownpub.com. **Contact:** Ron Hebert, publisher. Estab. 2000. Pays standard royalty.

How to Contact Submit demo by mail. Unsolicited submissions are OK. Prefers CD of 5 songs with lyric sheets. "Finished demos only, please." Does not return material. Responds in 2 weeks if interested.

Music Mostly **country**, **country/pop**, **pop**, **dance**, and **Christian**.

⬆ ◪ ACKEAN MUSIC PUBLISHING/PROMOTION/CRITIQUE (SOCAN)

5454 198th St., Suite 208, Langley BC V3A 1G2 Canada. (604)532-9203. E-mail: pamelaroyal47@shaw.ca. Website: www.ackeanmusic.net. **Contact:** Pamela Royal, professional manager (country). Professional Managers: Kim McLeod (traditional country); Cristine Royal (instrumental country). Music publisher and Promotion/Critique. Estab. 2005. Publishes 6 songs/year. Publishes 3 new songwriters/year. Staff size: 2. Pays standard royalty of 50%.

Affiliates Crowe Entertainment. "Crowe Entertainment is our co-publisher in Nashville"

How to Contact *Write first and obtain permission to submit a demo.*Prefers CD with 3 songs with lyric sheets and cover letter. Include SASE or SAE and IRC for outside Canada. "Please include SASE, cover letter, and clean typed lyric sheets." Responds in 2 months.

Film & TV Places 2 songs/year in film. Music Supervisor: Joe Lenders (Minnot Lenters Music, Florida). Recently selected "Someone Like You" and "Heart on the Line" (singles by Angie Bull), recorded by Marie Willson, in *Terror Inside* (film).

Music Mostly **country**, **traditional country**, and **instrumental country**; also **instrumental music for film**. Published "Someone Like You" and "The Cheater's Out of Town" (single by Angie Bull) from *Rock Hard Lovin'* (album), recorded by Marie Willson (traditional country), released independently in 2006; "Where My Truck Stops" (single) from *Where My Truck Stops* (album), written and recorded by Wolfe Milestone(country), released in 1999.

Tips "Professional demos only, best one to three songs, great voice. Keep the hook exciting. First impression is important. Serious writers only, please. We also pitch songs to TV/film/movie companies, so music should be broadcast quality. Interested also in instrumental music for film productions. Please have songs registered and copyrighted. Ackean Music is a new company and will work hard for the songwriters and artists we publish and promote. We also offer a critique service. See our website under critique for song submissions. 3 songs maximum. Ackean Music will not review songs before critiquing."

▦ ◻ ALL ROCK MUSIC

P.O. Box 1200, 3260 AE Oud Beijerland The Netherlands. (31) 186-604266. Fax: (32) 0186-

604366. E-mail: info@collectorrecords.nl. Website: www.collectorrecords.nl. **Contact:** Cees Klop, president. Music publisher, record company (Collector Records) and record producer. Estab. 1967. Publishes 40 songs/year; publishes several new songwriters/year. Staff size: 3. Pays standard royalty.

- Also see the listings for Collector Records in the Record Companies and Record Producers sections of this book.

Affiliates All Rock Music (United Kingdom).

How to Contact Submit demo package by mail. Unsolicited submissions are OK. Prefers cassette. SAE and IRC. Responds in 2 months.

Music Mostly '50s rock, rockabilly and country rock; also piano boogie woogie. Published *Rock Crazy Baby* (album), written and recorded by Art Adams (1950s rockabilly), released 2004; *Marvin Jackson* (album), by Marvin Jackson (1950s rockers), released 2005; *Western Australian Snake Pit R&R* (album), recorded by various (1950s rockers), released 2005, all on Collector Records.

Tips "Send only the kind of material we issue/produce as listed."

ALPHA MUSIC INC.

Dept. SM, One International Blvd Ste. 212, Mahwah NJ 07495. (201)335-0005. Fax: (201)335-0004. E-mail: alpha@trfmusic.com. Website: www.trfmusic.com. **Contact:** Michael Nurko. Music publisher. Estab. 1931. Pays standard royalty.

Affiliates Dorian Music Publishers, Inc. (ASCAP) and TRF Music Inc.

- Also see listing for TRF Production Music Libraries in the Advertising, Audiovisual & Commercial Music Firms section of this book.

How to Contact "We accept submissions of new compositions. Submissions are not returnable."

Music All categories, mainly instrumental and acoustic suitable for use as production music, including theme and background music for television and film. "Have published over 50,000 titles since 1931."

ANTELOPE PUBLISHING INC. (BMI)

P.O. Box 55, Rowayton CT 06853. **Contact:** Tony LaVorgna, owner/president. Music publisher. Estab. 1982. Publishes 5-10 new songs/year; publishes 3-5 new songwriters/year. Pays standard royalty.

How to Contact Submit demo by mail. Unsolicited submissions are OK. Prefers cassette with lead sheet. Does not return material. Responds in 1 month "only if interested."

Music Only bebop and 1940s swing. Does not want anything electronic. Published "Somewhere Near" (single by Tony LaVorgna) from *Just For My Friends* (album), recorded by Jeri Brown (easy listening); "Cookie Monster" and "The Lady From Mars" (singles by Tony LaVorgna) from *Just For My Friends* (album), recorded by Tony LaVorgna (jazz/easy listening), released 2007 on Antelope.

Tips "Put your best song first with a short intro."

☐ BARKIN' FOE THE MASTER'S BONE

405 Broadway St., Suite 900, Cincinnati OH 45202-3329. (513)546-2537 (cell). E-mail: autoredcurtis@aol.com. Website: www.1stbook.com. Company Owner (rock, R&B): Kevin Curtis. Professional Managers: Shonda Barr (country, jazz, pop, rap, gospel, soul, soft rock). Music publisher. Estab. 1989. Publishes 4 songs/year; publishes 1 new songwriter/year. Staff size: 4. Pays standard royalty.

Affiliates Beat Box Music (ASCAP) and Feltstar (BMI).

How to Contact Submit demo by mail. Unsolicited submissions are OK. Prefers CD (or VHS videocassette) with 3 songs. Include SASE. Responds in 2 weeks.

Music Mostly **top 40** and **pop**; also **soul**, **gospel**, **rap** and **jazz**. Does not want classical. Published "Lover, Lover" (single by J Tea/Jay B./Skylar) from The Time Has Come (album), recorded by J-Trey (rap), released 2003 on East Side Records; "Been A Long Time" (single by J Tea/Jay B./Skylar), from The Time Has Come (album), recorded by J-Trey (rap), released 2003 on East Side Records; "No Worries" (single by Mejestic/7-Starr/D-Smooy/Hardhead), from Home Grown (album), recorded by Low Down Boyz (rap), released 2002 on Untamed Records.

⊕ BEARSONGS (PRS)

Box 944, Birmingham B16 8UT United Kingdom. 44-121-454-7020. E-mail: jim@bigbearmusic.com. Website: www.bigbearmusic.com. Managing Director: Jim Simpson. Professional Manager: Russell Fletcher. Music publisher and record company (Big Bear Records). Member PRS, MCPS. Publishes 25 songs/year; publishes 15-20 new songwriters/year. Pays standard royalty.

- Also see the listings for Big Bear Records in the Record Companies section and Big Bear in the Record Producers section of this book.

How to Contact Submit demo by mail. Unsolicited submissions are OK. Prefers CD. Does not return material. Responds in 3 months.

Music Mostly **blues**, **swing** and **jazz**. Published Blowing With Bruce and Cool Heights (by Alan Barnes), recorded by Bruce Adams/Alan Barnes Quintet; and Blues For My Baby (by Charles Brown), recorded by King Pleasure & The Biscuit Boys, all on Big Bear Records.

Tips "Have a real interest in jazz, blues, swing."

☐ BRANDON HILLS MUSIC, LLC (BMI)/HEATH BROWN MUSIC (ASCAP)/STEVEN LYNN MUSIC (SESAC)

N. 3425 Searle County Line Rd., Brandon WI 53919. (920)398-3279 or (cell) (920)570-1076. E-mail: marta@dotnet.com. **Contact:** Marsha Brown, president. Music publishers. Estab. 2005. Publishes 4 new songwriters/year. Staff size: 2. Pays standard royalty of 50%.

How to Contact Submit demo package by mail. Unsolicited submissions are OK. Prefers CD with 1-4 songs and cover letter. Does not return submissions. Responds only if interested.

Music Mostly **country (traditional, modern, country rock)**, **contemporary Christian**, **blues**; also **children's** and **bluegrass** and **rap**. Published "Let It Rain," recorded by Steff Nevers, written by Larry Migliore and Kevin Gallarello (Universal Records, Norway); "Do You Like My Body," recorded by Ginger-Ly, written by Nisa McCall (SEI Corp and Big Daddy G Music, CA); "Did I Ever Thank You Lord," recorded by Jacob Garcia, written by Eletta Sias (TRW Records); "Honky Tonk In Heaven," recorded by Buddy Lewis, written by Mike Heath and Bob Alexander (Ozark Records).

Tips "We prefer studio-produced CDs. The lyrics and the CD must match. Cover letter, lyrics, and CD should have a professional look. Demos should have vocals up front and every word should be distinguishable. Please make sure your lyrics match your song. Submit only your best. The better the demo, the better of chance of getting your music published and recorded."

☐ CALIFORNIA COUNTRY MUSIC (BMI)

112 Widmar Pl., Clayton CA 94517. (925)833-4680. **Contact:** Edgar J. Brincat, owner. Music publisher and record company (Roll On Records). Estab. 1985. Staff size: 1. Pays standard royalty.

Affiliates Sweet Inspirations Music (ASCAP).

• Also see the listing for Roll On Records in the Record Companies section of this book.

How to Contact Submit demo by mail. Unsolicited submissions are OK. "Do not call or write. Any calls will be returned collect to caller." Send CD with 3 songs and lyric sheet. Include SASE. Responds in 6 weeks.

Music Mostly **MOR**, **contemporary country** and **pop**. Does not want rap, metal or rock. Published *For Realities Sake* (album by F.L. Pittman/R. Barretta) and *Maddy* (album by F.L. Pittman/M. Weeks), both recorded by Ron Banks & L.J. Reynolds on Life & Bellmark Records; and *Quarter Past Love* (album by Irwin Rubinsky/Janet Fisher), recorded by Darcy Dawson on NNP Records.

▨ ☑ CHRISTMAS & HOLIDAY MUSIC

26642 Via Noveno, Mission Viejo CA 92691. (949)859-1615. E-mail: justinwilde@christmassongs.com. Website: www.christmassongs.com. **Contact:** Justin Wilde, president. Music publisher. Estab. 1980. Publishes 8-12 songs/year; publishes 8-12 new songwriters/year. Staff size: 1. "All submissions must be complete songs (i.e., music and lyrics)." Pays standard royalty.

Affiliates Songcastle Music (ASCAP).

How to Contact Submit demo CD by mail. Unsolicited submissions are OK. *Do not call. Do not send unsolicited mp3s or links to Web sites.* See website for submission guidelines. "First Class Mail only. Registered or certified mail not accepted." Prefers CD with no more than 3 songs with lyric sheets. Do not send lead sheets or promotional material, bios, etc." Include SASE but does not return material out of the US. Responds only if interested.

Film & TV Places 10-15 songs in TV/year. Published Barbara Streisand's "It Must Have Been the Mistletoe."

Music Strictly **Christmas**, **Halloween**, **Hanukkah**, **Mother's Day**, **Thanksgiving**, **Father's Day** and **New Year's Eve music** in every style imaginable: easy listening, rock, pop, blues, jazz, country, reggae, rap, children's secular or religious. *Please do not send anything that isn't a holiday song.* Published "It Must Have Been the Mistletoe" (single by Justin Wilde/Doug Konecky) from *Christmas Memories* (album), recorded by Barbra Streisand (pop Christmas), by Columbia; "What Made the Baby Cry?" (single by Toby Keith) and "Mr. Santa Claus" (single by James Golseth) from *Casper's Haunted Christmas* soundtrack (album), recorded by Scotty Blevins (Christmas) on Koch International.

Tips "We only sign one out of every 200 submissions. Please be selective. If a stranger can hum your melody back to you after hearing it twice, it has 'standard' potential. Couple that with a lyric filled with unique, inventive imagery, that stands on its own, even without music. Combine the two elements, and workshop the finished result thoroughly to identify weak points. Submit to us only when the song is polished to perfection. Submit positive lyrics only. Avoid negative themes like 'Blue Christmas'."

☑ CHRYSALIS MUSIC GROUP (ASCAP, BMI)

8500 Melrose Ave., Suite 207, Los Angeles CA 90069. (310)652-0066. Fax: (310)652-5428. E-mail: enquiries@chrysalis.com. Website: www.chrysalis.com. **Contact:** Mark Friedman, vice president of A&R. Music publisher. Estab. 1968.

How to Contact *Chrysalis Music does not accept any submissions.*

Music Published "Sum 41" (single), written and recorded by OutKast; "Light Ladder" (single), written and recorded by David Gray. Administer, David Lee Roth, Andrea Boccelli, Velvet Revolver, and Johnta Austin.

☑ COME ALIVE COMMUNICATIONS, INC. (ASCAP)

348 Valley Rd., Suite A, P.O. Box 436, West Grove PA 19390-0436. (610)869-3660. Fax: (610)869-3660. E-mail: info@comealivemusic.com. Website: www.comealivemusic.com. Professional Managers: Joseph L. Hooker (pop, rock, jazz); Bridget G. Hylak (spiritual, country, classical). Music publisher, record producer and record company. Estab. 1985. Publishes 4 singles/year. Staff: 7. Pays standard royalty of 50%.

• Come Alive Communications received a IHS Ministries Award in 1996, John Lennon Songwriting Contest winter, 2003.

How to Contact *Call first to obtain permission to submit a demo.* For song publishing submissions, prefers CD with 3 songs, lyric sheet, and cover letter. Does not return submissions. Responds only if interested.

Music Mostly **pop**, **easy listening**, **contemporary Christian**, and **patriotic**; also **country**

and **spiritual**. Does not want obscene, suggestive, violent, or morally offensive lyrics. Produced "In Search of America" (single) from *Long Road to Freedom* (album), written and recorded by J. Hooker (patriotic), released 2003 on ComeAliveMusic.com; "Our Priests/ Nuestros Sacerdotes," named CMN's official theme song for the Vatican Designated Year of the Priest (2009-10). See www.ourpriests.com.

◙ COPPERFIELD MUSIC GROUP/PENNY ANNIE MUSIC (BMI)/TOP BRASS MUSIC (ASCAP)/BIDDY BABY MUSIC (SESAC)

1400 South St., Nashville TN 37212. (615)726-3100. E-mail: ken@copperfieldmusic.com. Website: www.copperfieldmusic.com **Contact**: Ken Biddy, president/CEO.

How to Contact Contact first and obtain permission to submit a demo by e-mail only. Does not return submissions or accept phone calls. Responds only if interested.

Music Mostly **country**; also **modern bluegrass**. Does not want rap or heavy/metal/rock. Recently published "Daddy Won't Sell the Farm" from *Tattoos and Scars* (album), recorded by Montgomery Gentry (country).

▢ CORELLI MUSIC GROUP (BMI/ASCAP)

P.O. Box 2314, Tacoma WA 98401-2314. (253)273-6205. E-mail: JerryCorelli@yahoo.com. Website: www.CorelliMusicGroup.com. **Contact:** Jerry Corelli, owner. Music publisher, record company (Omega III Records), record producer (Jerry Corelli/Angels Dance Recording Studio) and booking agency (Tone Deaf Booking). Estab. 1996. Publishes 12 songs/year; publishes 6 new songwriters/year. Staff size: 3. Pays standard royalty.

Affiliates My Angel's Songs (ASCAP); Corelli's Music Box (BMI).

How to Contact Submit demo by mail. Unsolicited submissions are OK. "No phone calls, e-mails, or letters asking to submit." CD only with 3 songs, lyric sheet and cover letter. "*We DO NOT accept mp3s vie e-mail.* We want love songs with a message and overtly Christian songs. Make sure all material is copyrighted. *You MUST include SASE or we DO NOT respond!*" Responds in 2 months

Music Mostly **contemporary Christian**, **Christian soft rock** and **Christmas**; also **love songs**, **ballads** and **new country**. Does not want songs without lyrics or lyrics without music. Published "I Can't Believe I'm Yours (by Jerry Corelli), "Grandfather Moon" (by Kevin Mannarino & Jerry Corelli), and "What'd I Even Came Here For" (by Rich Green), all from *Grandfather Moon* (album), released 2008 on Omega III Records.

Tips "Success is obtained when opportunity meets preparation! If a SASE is not sent with demo, we don't even listen to the demo. Be willing to do a rewrite. Don't send material expecting us to place it with a Top Ten artist. Be practical. Do your songs say what's always been said, except differently? Don't take rejection personally. Always send a #10 self-adhesive envelope for your SASE."

THE CORNELIUS COMPANIES/GATEWAY ENTERTAINMENT, INC. (BMI, ASCAP, SESAC)

Dept. SM, 1710 Grand Ave., Nashville TN 37212. (615)321-5333. E-mail: corneliuscomps@bellsouth.net. Website: www.gatewayentertainment.com. **Contact:** Ron Cornelius, owner/president. Music publisher and record producer (Ron Cornelius). Estab. 1986. Publishes 60-80 songs/year; publishes 2-3 new songwriters/year. Occasionally hires staff writers. Pays standard royalty.

Affiliates RobinSparrow Music (BMI), Strummin' Bird Music (ASCAP) and Bridgeway Music (SESAC).

How to Contact *Contact by e-mail or call for permission to submit material.* Submit demo package by mail. Unsolicited submissions are OK. "Send demo on CD format only with 2-3 songs." Include SASE. Responds in 2 months.

Music Mostly **country** and **pop**; also **positive country**, **gospel** and **alternative**. Published songs by Confederate Railroad, Faith Hill, David Allen Coe, Alabama and over 50 radio singles in the positive Christian/country format.

Tips "Looking for material suitable for film."

CRINGE MUSIC (PRS, MCPS)

The Cedars, Elvington Lane, Folkestone Kent CT18 7AD United Kingdom. (01)(303)893-472. Fax: (01)(303)893-833. E-mail: info@cringemusic.co.uk. Website: www.cringemusic.co.uk. **Contact:** Christopher Ashman. Music publisher and record company (Red Admiral Records). Estab. 1979. Staff size: 2.

How to Contact Submit demo package by mail. Unsolicited submissions are OK. CD only with unlimited number of songs and lyric sheet, lead sheet. Submission materials are not returned. Responds if interested.

Music All styles.

THE CROSSWIND CORPORATION

PO Box 120816, Nashville TN 37212. (615)467-3860. Fax: (615)467-3859. E-mail: tdchoate@aol.com. **Contact:** Terry Choate.

CUPIT MUSIC GROUP (ASCAP, BMI)

P.O. Box 121904, Nashville TN 37212. (615)731-0100. Fax: (615)731-3005. E-mail: dan@cupitmusic.com. Website: www.cupitmusic.com. **Contact:** Publishing Division. Music publisher, record producer, record company, entertainment division and recording studio. Estab. 1986. Staff size: 12. Pays standard royalty.

Affiliates Cupit Memaries (ASCAP) and Cupit Music (BMI).

• Also see the listing for Jerry Cupit Productions in the Record Producers section. Cupit Music's "Jukebox Junkie" won BMI Millionair Award.

How to Contact *Please visit cupitmusic.com for our submission policy.* Prefers CD with lyric sheet. "We will return a response card." Include SASE. Usually responds in 2 months.

Music Mostly **country**, **bluegrass**, **blues**, **pop**, **gospel** and **instrumental**. Does not want rap, hard rock or metal. Published "He'll Never Be A Lawyer Cause He Can't Pass the Bar" (single), recorded by Mustang Creek (country), released 2007 on Cupit Records; "Your Love Reaches Me" (single), recorded by Kevin Sharp (country), released 2007 on Cupit Records; "I Bought the Shoes (That Just Walked Out On Me)" (single) from *Dierks Bentley* (album), recorded by Dierks Bentley (country), released 2005 on Cupit Records; and "I Know What You Got Up Your Sleeve" (single) from *Maverick* (album), recorded by Hank Williams, Jr. (country), released 2001 on Curb Records.

◙ JOF DAVE MUSIC

1055 Kimball Ave., Kansas City KS 66104. (913)593-3180. **Contact:** David Johnson, CEO. Music publisher, record company (Cymbal Records). Estab. 1984. Publishes 30 songs/year; publishes 12 new songwriters/year. Pays standard royalty.

How to Contact *Contact first and obtain permission to submit.* Prefers CD. Include SASE. Responds in 1 month.

Music Mostly **gospel** and **R&B**. Published "The Woman I Love" (single) from *Sugar Bowl (*album), written and recorded by King Alex, released 2001 on Cymbal Records; and "Booty Clap" (single by Johnny Jones) from *Gotta Move On* (album), recorded by Jacuzé, released 2005 on Cymbal Records.

DEFINE SOMETHING IN NOTHING MUSIC (ASCAP)

11213 W. Baden St., Avondale AZ 85323. (360)421-9225. E-mail: definesinm@gmail.com. **Contact**: Jaime Reynolds, president. Estab. 2008. Music Publisher. Staff Size: 5. Pays 75% of gross revenue.

How to Contact Prefers MP3s sent to e-mail only. "Please do not contact for permission, just send your music." Does not return submissions. Responds in 2 weeks.

Music Interested in all styles. "We welcome everything all over the world."

Tips "Please e-mail 4 of your strongest mp3s, best quality. No phone calls or mail, no CDs or cassettes."

◙ DELEV MUSIC COMPANY (ASCAP, BMI)

7231 Mansfield Ave., Philadelphia PA 19138-1620. (215)276-8861. Fax: (215)276-4509. E-mail: delevmusic@msn.com. President/CEO: William L. Lucas. A&R: Darryl Lucas. Music publisher. Publishes 6-10 songs/year; publishes 6-10 new songwriters/year. Pays standard royalty.

Affiliates Sign of the Ram Music (ASCAP) and Delev Music (BMI).

How to Contact *Does not accept unsolicited material. Write or call first to obtain permission to submit.* Prefers CD format only—no cassettes—with 1-4 songs and lyric sheet. "We will not accept certified mail or SASE." Does not return material. Responds in 1-2 months.

Music Mostly **R&B ballads** and **dance-oriented**; also **pop ballads**, **Christian/gospel**, **crossover** and **country/western**. We do not accept rap song material. Published "Angel Love" (single by Barbara Heston/Geraldine Fernandez) from *The Silky Sounds of Debbie G* (album), recorded by Debbie G (light R&B/easy listening), released 2000 on Blizzard Records; *Variety* (album), produced by Barbara Heston, released on Luvya Records; and "Ever Again" by Bernie Williams, released 2003 on SunDazed Records.

Tips "Persevere regardless if it is sent to our company or any other company. Most of all, no matter what happens, believe in yourself."

THE EDWARD DE MILES MUSIC COMPANY (BMI)

10573 W. Pico Blvd., #352, Los Angeles CA 90064-2348. (310)948-9652. Fax: (310)474-7705. E-mail: info@edmsahara.com. Website: www.edmsahara.com. **Contact:** Professional Manager. Music publisher, record company (Sahara Records), record producer, management, bookings and promotions. Estab. 1984. Publishes 50-75 songs/year; publishes 5 new songwriters/year. Hires staff songwriters. Pays standard royalty.

• Also see the listings for Edward De Miles in the Record Producers and Managers & Booking Agents sections, and Sahara Records And Filmworks Entertainment in the Record Companies section of this book.

How to Contact *Write first and obtain permission to submit.* Prefers CD with 1-3 songs and lyric sheet. Does not return material. Reponds in 1 month.

Music Mostly **top 40 pop/rock**, **R&B/dance** and **country**; also **musical scores for TV, radio, films** and **jingles**. Published "Dance Wit Me" and "Moments" (singles), written and recorded by Steve Lynn; "Games" (single), written and recorded by D'von Edwards (jazz), all on Sahara Records. Other artists include Multiple Choice.

Tips "Copyright all materials before submitting. Equipment and showmanship a must."

DEMI MONDE RECORDS & PUBLISHING LTD.

Foel Studio, Llanfair, Caereinion Wales POWYS United Kingdom. E-mail: demi-monde@ dial.pipex.com. Website: www.demi.monde.co.uk/demimonde. **Contact:** Dave Anderson, managing director. Music publisher, record company (Demi Monde Records & Publishing Ltd.), record producer (Dave Anderson). Member MCPS. Estab. 1983. Publishes 50-70 songs/year; publishes 10-15 new songwriters/year. Pays standard royalty.

How to Contact Submit demo tape by mail. Unsolicited submissions are OK. Prefers cassette or VHS videocassette with 3-4 songs. Does not return material. Responds in 6 weeks.

Music Mostly **rock**, **R&B** and **pop**. Published "I Feel So Lazy" (by D. Allen), recorded by Gong (rock); "Phalarn Dawn" (by E. Wynne), recorded by Ozric Tentacles (rock); and "Pioneer" (by D. Anderson), recorded by Amon Dual (rock), all on Demi Monde Records.

☑ DISNEY MUSIC PUBLISHING (ASCAP, BMI)

500 S. Buena Vista St., Burbank CA 91521-6182. (818)567-5069. Website: http://home. disney.go.com/music/. **Contact:** Ashley Saunig, DMP creative department.

Affiliates Seven Peaks Music and Seven Summits Music.

• Part of the Buena Vista Music Group.

How to Contact *"We cannot accept any unsolicited material."*

☐ DREAM SEEKERS PUBLISHING

21 Coachlight Dr., Danville IL 61832-8240. (615)822-1160. President: Sally Sidman. Music publisher. Estab. 1993. Publishes 25-50 songs/year; publishes 15-20 new songwriters/ year. Pays standard royalty.

Affiliates Dream Builders Publishing (ASCAP).

How to Contact Submit demo by mail. Unsolicited submissions are OK. "Please do not call to request permission—just submit your material. There are no code words. We listen to everything." Prefers CD with 2 songs and lyric sheet. "If one of your songs is selected for publishing, we prefer to have it available on CD for dubbing off copies to pitch to artist." Include SASE. Responds in 6 weeks.

Music Mostly **country**. "All types of **country** material, but mostly in need of up -tempo songs, preferably with positive lyrics." Does not want rap, jazz, classical, children's, hard rock, instrumental or blues. Published "Hang On Tight" (single by Germain Brunet) from *Fantasy* (album), recorded by Cheryl K. Warner (country), released 2007 on CKW Records; "Burn Your Memory Down" (single by Jeff Moxcey/Catharine Haver) from *Who Am I to You* (album), recorded by Jennifer LeMoss (country), released 2007 on Vision Way Records; and "80 Mile from Memphis" (single by Mark Collie) from *Rose Covered Garden* (album), recorded by Mark Collie (country), released 2006 on Sixteen Ton.

Tips "Be willing to work hard to learn the craft of songwriting. Be persistent. Nobody is born a hit songwriter. It often takes years to achieve that status."

☒ DUNSDON MUSIC PUBLISHING

P.O. Box 635, Montvale NJ 07645. Estab. 2006. (212)400-7662. Fax: (201)426-2366. E-mail: info@dunsdonmusic.com. Website: www.dunsdonmusic.com. **Contact:** Ian Dunsdon. Estab. 2006. Published 3 songs in the last year; published 2 new songwriters in the last year. Staff size: 2. Hires staff writers. Pays standard royalty of 50%.

Affiliates Newave Music Publishing (BMI).

How to Contact Contact first and obtain permission to submit a demo. Include CD or e-mail a download link, lyric sheet, and cover letter. Does not return submissions. Responds only if interested.

Film & TV Placed 3 songs in film/year. Recently published "Pennyless," "Already Know by Now," and "Coming Down" by Mark Mullane, recorded by The Misery Loves, in

Jumping Up and Down (film) (Pragma Records).

Music Mostly **rock/pop, hip hop**, and **dance**; also **country** and **alternative**.

EARITATING MUSIC PUBLISHING (BMI)

P.O. Box 1101, Gresham OR 97030. Music publisher. Estab. 1979. Pays individual per song contract, usually greater than 50% to writer.

How to Contact Submit demo package by mail. Unsolicited submissions are OK. Prefers CD with lyric sheet. "Submissions should be copyrighted by the author. We will deal for rights if interested." Does not return material. Responds only if interested.

Music Mostly **rock**, **country** and **folk**. Does not want rap.

Tips "Melody is most important, lyrics second. Style and performance take a back seat to these. A good song will stand with just one voice and one instrument. Also, don't use staples on your mailers."

EARTHSCREAM MUSIC PUBLISHING CO. (BMI)

8377 Westview Dr., Houston TX 77055. (713)464-GOLD. E-mail: jeffwells@ soundartsrecording.com. Website: www.soundartsrecording.com. **Contact:** Jeff Wells; Peter Verkerk. Music publisher, record company and record producer. Estab. 1975. Publishes 12 songs/year; publishes 4 new songwriters/year. Pays standard royalty.

- Also see the listings for Surface Records in the Record Companies section and Sound Arts Recording Studio in the Record Producers section of this book.

Affiliates Reach For The Sky Music Publishing (ASCAP).

How to Contact Submit demo by mail. Unsolicited submissions are OK. Prefers CD or videocassette with 2-5 songs and lyric sheet. Does not return material. Responds in 6 weeks.

Music Mostly **new rock**, **country**, **blues** and **top 40/pop**. Published "Baby Never Cries" (single by Carlos DeLeon), recorded by Jinkies on Surface Records (pop); "Telephone Road" (single), written and recorded by Mark May(blues) on Icehouse Records; "Do You Remember" (single by Barbara Pennington), recorded by Perfect Strangers on Earth Records (rock), and "Sheryl Crow" (single), recorded by Dr. Jeff and the Painkillers (pop); "Going Backwards" (single), written and recorded by Tony Vega (Gulf swamp blues), released on Red Onion Records.

EAST MADISON MUSIC PUBLISHING (ASCAP)

9 Music Square South, #143, Nashville TN 37203. (615)838-4171. E-mail: eastmadisonmusic@ charter.net. Website: www.emmrecordsnashville.com. **Contact:** Dean Holmen, publisher. Music publisher, record company (East Madison Music Records), and record producer (Dean Holmen). Estab. 2003 Published 6 songs/year; publishes 3 new songwriters/year. Staff size: 2. Pays standard royalty.

- East Madison Music Publishing received a First Place Award in 2005 for "If Teardrops

Played the Juke Box" and First Place in 2006 for "I Should Get 30 Years" from Songwriters of Wisconsin.

Affiliates Ricki Lynn Publishing (BMI).

How to Contact Submit demo by mail. Unsolicited submissions are OK. Prefers CD with 1-3 songs with lyric sheet and cover letter. Does not return submissions. Responds only if interested.

Music Mostly **traditional country** and **gospel**; does not want rock or hip-hop. Published "Weekend Willie Nelson," "I Gave My Heart Away," and "Don't Ever Leave Me" (singles by Tim Schweeberger) from *Heartaches & Honky Tonks*, recorded by Dean Holmen (traditional country), released 2006 on EMM Records.

Tips "Please follow submission guidelines. If you follow our guidelines, your song will be reviewed. If not, it will be disregarded. Don't overlook the independent artist. Most songs cut today are cut by them."

☑ ELECTRIC MULE PUBLISHING COMPANY (BMI)/NEON MULE MUSIC (ASCAP)

1500 Clifton Ln., Nashville TN 37215. E-mail: emuleme@aol.com. **Contact:** Jeff Moseley, President.

☑ EMF PRODUCTIONS (ASCAP)

1000 E. Prien Lake Rd., Suite D, Lake Charles LA 70601. E-mail: emfprod@aol.com. Website: www.emfproductions.com. President: Ed Fruge. Music publisher and record producer. Estab. 1984. Pays standard royalty.

How to Contact Submit demo package by mail. Unsolicited submissions are OK. Prefers CD or DVDs with 3 of your best songs and lyric sheets. Does not return material. Responds in 6 weeks.

Music Mostly **R&B**, **pop** and **rock**; also **country** and **gospel**.

☑ EMI CHRISTIAN MUSIC PUBLISHING (ASCAP, BMI, SESAC)

P.O. Box 5085, Brentwood TN 37024. (615)371-6800. Website: www.EMICMGPublishing. com. Music publisher. Publishes more than 100 songs/year. Hires staff songwriters. Pays standard royalty.

Affiliates Birdwing Music (ASCAP), Sparrow Song (BMI), His Eye Music (SESAC), Ariose Music (ASCAP), Straightway Music (ASCAP), Shepherd's Fold Music (BMI), Songs of Promise (SESAC), Dawn Treader Music (SESAC), Meadowgreen Music Company (ASCAP), River Oaks Music Company (BMI), Stonebrook Music Company (SESAC), Bud John Songs, Inc. (ASCAP), Bud John Music, Inc. (BMI), Bud John Tunes, Inc. (SESAC), WorshipTogether Songs, ThankYou Music, Thirst Moon River.

How to Contact *"We do not accept unsolicited submissions."*

Music Published Chris Tomlin, Toby Mac, David Crowder, Jeremy Camp, Stephen Curtis Chapman, Delirious, Tim Hughes, Matt Redman, Demon Hunter, Underoath, Switchfoot,

Third Day, Casting Crowns, and many others.

Tips "Do what you do with passion and excellence and success will follow; just be open to new and potentially more satisfying definitions of what 'success' means."

✪ EMI MUSIC PUBLISHING

1290 Avenue of the Americas, 42nd Floor, New York NY 10104. (212)492-1200. Website: www.emimusicpub.com. Music publisher.

How to Contact *EMI does not accept unsolicited material.*

Music Published "All Night Long" (by F. Evans/R. Lawrence/S. Combs), recorded by Faith Evans featuring Puff Daddy on Bad Boy; "You" (by C. Roland/J. Powell), recorded by Jesse Powell on Silas; and "I Was" (by C. Black/P. Vassar), recorded by Neal McCoy on Atlantic.

Tips "Don't bury your songs. Less is more—we will ask for more if we need it. Put your strongest song first."

☑ EMSTONE MUSIC PUBLISHING (BMI)

Box 398, Hallandale FL 33008. (305)936-0412. E-mail: michael@emstonemusicpublishing. com. **Contact:** Michael Gary, creative director. President: Mitchell Stone. Vice President: Madeline Stone. Music publisher. Estab. 1997. Pays standard royalty.

How to Contact Submit demo CD by mail with any number of songs. Unsolicited submissions are OK. Does not return material. Responds only if interested. Also check our sister company at SongwritersBestSong.com.

Music All types. Published *Greetings from Texas* (2009) (album), by Greetings From Texas; "Gonna Recall My Heart" (written by Dan Jury) from *No Tears* (album), recorded by Cole Seaver and Tammie Darlene, released on CountryStock Records; and "I Love What I've Got" (single by Heather and Paul Turner) from *The Best of Talented Kids* (compilation album) recorded by Gypsy; "My Christmas Card to You" (words and music by Madeline and Mitchell Stone); and "Your Turn to Shine" (words and music by Mitchell Stone).

Tips "Keep the materials inside your demo package as simple as possible. Just include a brief cover letter (with your contact information) and lyric sheets. Avoid written explanations of the songs; if your music is great, it'll speak for itself. We only offer publishing contracts to writers whose songs exhibit a spark of genius. Anything less can't compete in the music industry."

▧ FATT CHANTZ MUSIC (BMI)

2535 Winthrope Way, Lawrenceville GA 30044. (770)982-7055. Fax: (770)982-1882. E-mail: hitcd@bellsouth.net. Website: www.jeromepromotions.com. Contact: Bill Jerome, president and CEO. Music Publisher. Estab. 2009. Staff size: 3. Pays standard royalty of 50%.

How to Contact Contact first and obtain permission to submit a demo. Include CD or mp3 and cover letter. Does not return submissions. Responds in 1 week.

Music Top 40, alt country. Also **alternative**, crossover **R&B** and **hip-hop**. Does not want rap, gospel, country. Published "She's My Girl," written by Lefkowith/Rogers, recorded by Hifi on Red/Generic (2009).

☐ FIFTH AVENUE MEDIA, LTD. (ASCAP)

1208 W. Broadway, Hewlett NY 11557. (212)691-5630. Fax: (212)645-5038. E-mail: thefirm@thefirm.com. Website: www.thefirm.com. Professional Managers: Bruce E. Colfin(rootsy bluesy rock/reggae, Jam Bands/alternative rock/heavy metal); Jeffrey E. Jacobson (hip-hop/R&B/dance). Music publisher and record company (Fifth Avenue Media, Ltd.). Estab. 1995. Publishes 2 songs/year. Staff size: 4. Pays standard royalty.

Music Published "Analog" (single by Paul Byrne) from Paul Byrne & the Bleeders (album), recorded by Paul Byrne (pop rock), released 2001 on Independent.

⊞ ⊠ ☐ FIRST TIME MUSIC (PUBLISHING) U.K.

Sovereign House, 12 Trewartha Road, Praa Sands, Penzance, Cornwall TR20 9ST United Kingdom. (01736)762826. Fax: (01736)763328. E-mail: panamus@aol.com. Website: www.panamamusic.co.uk. **Contact:** Roderick G. Jones, CEO. Music publisher, record company (Digimix Records Ltd www.digimaxrecords.com, Rainy Day Records, Mohock Records, Pure Gold Records). Estab. 1986. Publishes 500-750 songs/year; 20-50 new songwriters/year. Staff size: 6. Hires staff writers. Pays standard royalty; "50-60% to established and up-and-coming writers with the right attitude."

Affiliates Scamp Music Publishing, Panama Music Library, Musik Image Library, Caribbean Music Library, PSI Music Library, ADN Creation Music Library, Promo Sonor International, Eventide Music, Melody First Music Library, Piano Bar Music Library, Corelia Music Library, Panama Music Ltd, Panama Music Productions, Digimix Worldwide Digital Distribution Services.

How to Contact Submit demo package by mail. Unsolicited submissions are OK. Submit on CD only, "of professional quality" with unlimited number of songs/instrumentals and lyric or lead sheets. Responds in 1 month. SAE and IRC required for reply.

Film & TV Places 200 songs in film and TV/year. "Copyrights and phonographic rights of Panama Music Limited and its associated catalogue idents have been used and subsist in many productions broadcasts and adverts produced by major and independent production companies, television, film/video companies, radio broadcasters (not just in the UK, but in various countries world-wide) and by commercial record companies for general release and sale. In the UK & Republic of Ireland they include the BBC networks of national/regional television and radio, ITV network programs and promotions (Channel 4, Border TV, Granada TV, Tyne Tees TV, Scottish TV, Yorkshire TV, HTV, Central TV, Channel TV, LWT, Meridian TV, Grampian TV, GMTV, Ulster TV, Westcountry TV, Channel TV, Carlton

TV, Anglia TV, TV3, RTE (Ireland), Planet TV, Rapido TV, VT4 TV, BBC Worldwide, etc.), independent radio stations, satellite Sky Television (BskyB), Discovery Channel, Learning Channel, National Geographic, Living Channel, Sony, Trouble TV, UK Style Channel, Hon Cyf, CSI, etc., and cable companies, GWR Creative, Premier, Spectrum FM, Local Radio Partnership, Fox, Manx, Swansea Sound, Mercury, 2CRFM, Broadland, BBC Radio Collection, etc. Some credits include copyrights in programs, films/videos, broadcasts, trailers and promotions such as *Desmond's*, *One Foot in the Grave*, *EastEnders*, *Hale* and *Pace*, *Holidays from Hell*, *A Touch of Frost*, *999 International*, and *Get Away*."

Music All styles. Published "I Get Stoned" (hardcore dance), recorded by AudioJunkie & Stylus, released by EMI records (2009) on *Hardcore Nation 2009*; "Long Way to Go" (country/MOR) on *Under Blue Skies*, recorded by Charlie Landsborough, released on Rosette Recordss (2008); "Mr Wilson" (folk) from *Only the Willows are Weeping*, released on Digimix Records (2009); "Collusion Illusion" (progressive rock/goth), recorded by Bram Stoker on *Rock Paranoia*, released by Digimix Records and many more.

Tips "Have a professional approach—present well produced demos. First impressions are important and may be the only chance you get. Writers are advised to join the Guild of International Songwriters and Composers in the United Kingdom (www.songwriters-guild.co.uk and www.myspace.com/guildofsongwriters)."

⊡ ◻ FRESH ENTERTAINMENT

1315 Simpson Rd., Atlanta GA 30314. E-mail: whunter1122@yahoo.com. **Contact:** Willie W. Hunter, managing director. Music publisher and record company. Publishes 5 songs/year. Staff size: 4. Hires staff songwriters. Pays standard royalty.

Affiliates !Hserf Music (ASCAP), Blair Vizzion Music (BMI), Santron Music (BMI), G.I. Joe Muzick Publishing (BMI), and Bing-O Productions.

How to Contact Submit demo package by mail. Unsolicited submissions are OK. Prefers cassette or videocassette with 3 songs and lyric sheet. "Send photo if available." Include SASE. Responds in 6 weeks.

Film & TV Places 1 song in TV/year. Published the theme song for BET's *Comic Vue* (by Charles E. Jones), recorded by Cirocco.

Music Mostly **rap**, **R&B** and **pop/dance**. Published *Ancestral Spirits* (album), written and recorded by Robert Miles (jazz), released 2004 on Sheets of Sound/Fresh Entertainment; *My Life My Hustle* (album), written and recorded by Jamal Smith (rap/hip-hop), released 2004 on Vision Vibe/Fresh Entertainment; "Go Sit Down" (single), by Maceo, released 2005 on Quick Flip/Fresh Entertainment; Bob Miles' *Nubian Woman* 2009; Lissen (R&B/hip hop); "As the World Turns" by Kaz & Kardi (Bing-O Productions).

◻ GLAD MUSIC CO.

14340 Torrey Chase, Suite 380, Houston TX 77014. (281)397-7300. Fax: (281)397-6206. E-mail: hwesdaily@gladmusicco.com. Website: www.gladmusicco.com. **Contact:** Wes

Daily, A&R Director (country). Music publisher, record company and record producer. Estab. 1958. Publishes 5 songs/year; publishes 2 new songwriters/year. Staff size: 4. Pays standard royalty.

Affiliates Bud-Don (ASCAP) and Rayde (SESAC).

How to Contact *Write first and obtain permission to submit.* CDs only with 2 songs maximum, lyric sheet and cover letter. Does not return material. Responds in 6 weeks. SASE or e-mail address for reply.

Music Mostly **country**. Does not want weak songs. Published **Love Bug** (album by C. Wayne/W. Kemp), recorded by George Strait, released 1995 on MCA; *Walk Through This World With Me* (album), recorded by George Jones; and *Race Is On* (album by D. Rollins), recorded by George Jones, both released 1999 on Asylum.

⊘ G MAJOR PUBLISHING

P.O. Box 3331, Fort Smith AR 72913-3331. E-mail: Alex@gmajor.org. Website: www. GMajorPublishing.com. Professional Managers: Alex Hoover. Music publisher. Estab. 1992. Publishes 10 songs/year; publishes 2 new songwriters/year. Staff size: 2. Pays standard royalty.

How to Contact *No unsolicited submissions.* Submit inquiry by mail with SASE. Prefers CD or mp3. Submit up to 3 songs with lyrics. Include SASE. Responds in 4-6 weeks.

Music Mostly **country** and **contemporary Christian**. Published *Set The Captives Free* (album by Chad Little/Jeff Pitzer/Ben Storie), recorded by Sweeter Rain (contemporary Christian), for Cornerstone Television; "Hopes and Dreams" (single by Jerry Glidewell), recorded by Carrie Underwood (country), released on Star Rise; and "Be Still" (single by Chad Little/Dave Romero/Bryan Morse/Jerry Glidewell), recorded CO3 (contemporary Christian), released on Flagship Records.

Tips "We are looking for 'smash hits' to pitch to the Country and Christian markets."

☐ L.J. GOOD PUBLISHING (ASCAP)

P.O. Box 1696, Omak WA 98841.(509)422-1400. Fax: (509)267-8611. E-mail: lonnie@ ljgood.com. Website: www.wingsforchrist.com. **Contact:** Lonnie Good, president. Music publisher. Estab. 2006. Publishes 5 songs/year. Publishes 1 new songwriters/year. Staff size: 1. Pays standard royalty of 50%.

Affiliates L.J. Good Publishing (ASCAP).

How to Contact Prefers CD or mp3 with 3 songs and lyric sheet, cover letter. Does not return submissions.

Music Mostly **country**, **blues**, **soft rock**, **contemporary Christian/Praise and Worship**.

☐ R L HAMMEL ASSOCIATES, INC.

"Consultants to the Music, Recording & Entertainment Industries," P.O. Box 531,

Alexandria IN 46001-0531. E-mail: info@rlhammel.com. Website: www.rlhammel.com. **Contact:** A&R Department. President: Randal L. Hammel. Music publisher, record producer and consultant. Estab. 1974. Staff size: 3-5. Pays standard royalty.

Affiliates LADNAR Music (ASCAP) and LEMMAH Music (BMI).

How to Contact Submit demo package and brief bio by mail. Unsolicited submissions are OK. Prefers CD, DAT or VHS/8mm videocassette with a maximum of 3 songs and typed lyric sheets. "Please notate three (3) best songs—no time to listen to a full project." Does not return material. Responds ASAP. "No fixed timeline."

Music Mostly **pop**, **R&B** and **Christian**; also **MOR**, **light rock**, **pop country** and **feature film title cuts**. Produced/arranged *The Wedding Collection Series* for WORD Records. Published *Lessons For Life* (album by Kelly Hubbell/Jim Boedicker) and *I Just Want Jesus* (album by Mark Condon), both recorded by Kelly Connor, released on iMPACT Records.

⊞ ☐ HAPPY MELODY

VZW, Paul Gilsonstraat 31, St-Andries 8200 Belgium. 00 32 50-316380. Fax: 00 32 50-315235. E-mail: happymelody@skynet.be. **Contact:** Eddy Van Mouffaert, general manager. Music publisher, record company (Jump Records) and record producer (Jump Productions). Member SABAM S.V., Brussels. Publishes 100 songs/year; publishes 8 new songwriters/year. Staff size: 2. Pays standard royalty via SABAM S.V.

How to Contact Submit demo CD or tape by mail. Unsolicited submissions are OK. Prefers CD. Does not return material. Responds in 2 weeks.

Music Mostly **easy listening**, **disco** and **light pop**; also **instrumentals**. Published "Football Mania" (single by R. Mondes/J. Towers/D. Winters), recorded by Le Grand Julot (accordion), released 2005 on Scorpion; *Don't Give Up Your Dream* (album), written and recorded by Chris Clark (pop), released 2004 on 5 Stars; and *Instrumental Delight* (album), written and recorded by various artists (pop), released 2005 on Belstar.

Tips "Music wanted with easy, catchy melodies (very commercial songs)."

⊞ ▣ ◉ HEUPFERD MUSIKVERLAG GMBH

Ringwaldstr. 18, Dreieich 63303. Germany. E-mail: heupferd@t-online.de. Website: http://www.heupferd-musik.de. **Contact:** Christian Winkelmann, general manager. Music publisher and record company (Viva La Difference). GEMA. Publishes 30 songs/year. Staff size: 3. Pays "royalties after GEMA distribution plan."

Affiliates Song Buücherei (book series). "Vive La Difference!" (label).

How to Contact *Does not accept unsolicited submissions.*

Film & TV Places 1 song in film/year. Published "El Grito Y El Silencio" (by Thomas Hickstein), recorded by Tierra in *Frauen sind was Wunderbares* .

Music Mostly **folk**, **jazz** and **fusion**; also **New Age**, **rock** and **ethnic music**. Published "Mi Mundo" (single by Denise M'Baye/Matthias Furstenberg) from *Havana—Vamos A Ver* (album), recorded by Havana (Latin), released 2003 on Vive La Difference. Printed *Andy Irvine: Aiming For the Heart—Irish Song Affairs*, released in 2007.

☐ HOME TOWN HERO'S PUBLISHING (BMI)

112 West Houston, Leonard TX 75452. E-mail: hometownheroes1@verizon.net. Website: www.myspace.com/hometownherospublishing1. **Contact:** Tammy Wood, owner. Music publisher. Estab. 2003. Staff size: 2. Pays standard royalty.

How to Contact Submit demo by mail. Unsolicited submissions are OK. Prefers CD with 3-6 songs, lyric sheet, and cover letter. Does not return submissions. Responds only if interested.

Music Mostly **country (all styles)**, **pop**, **Southern rock**; also **ballads**, **gospel**, and **blues**. Does not want heavy metal and rap.

Tips "Most of all, believe in yourself. The best songs come from the heart. Don't get discouraged, be tough, keep writing, and always think positive. Songwriters, no calls please. I will contact you if interested. Send me your best."

IAMA (INTERNATIONAL ACOUSTIC MUSIC AWARDS)

2881 E. Oakland Park Blvd., Fort Lauderdale FL 33306. (954)537-3127. E-mail: info@inacoustic.com. Website: www.inacoustic.com.

☒ IDOL PUBLISHING

P.O. Box 720043, Dallas TX 75372. Estab. 1992. (214)321-8890. E-mail: info@idolrecords.com. Website: www.IdolRecords.com. **Contact:** Erv Karwelis, president. Record publisher. Estab. 1992. Releases 30 singles, 80 LPs, 20 EPs and 10-15 CDs/year. Pays negotiable royalty to artists on contract; negotiable rate to publisher per song on record.

How to Contact See Web site at www.IdolRecords.com for submission policy. No phone calls or e-mail follow-ups.

Music Mostly **rock**, **pop**, and **alternative**; also some **hip-hop**. Released *The Boys Names Sue-The Hits Vol. Sue!* (album), The O's - *We are the Os* (album), Little Black Dress — *Snow in June (album)*, *The Man,* recorded by Sponge (alternative); *Movements* (album), recorded by Black Tie Dynasty (alternative); In Between Days (album), recorded by Glen Reynolds (rock), all released 2006/2006 on Idol Records. Other artists include Flickerstick, DARYL, Centro-matic, The Deathray Davies, GBH, PPT, The Crash that Took Me, Shibboleth, Trey Johnson.

⊕ ▣ ⊘ INTOXYGENE SARL

283 Fbg St. Antoine, Paris 75011 France. 011(33)1 43485151. Fax: 011(33)1 43485753. Website: www.intoxygene.com or www.intoxygene.net. E-mail: infos@intoxygene.com. **Contact:** Patrick Jammes, managing director. Music publisher and record company. Estab. 1990. Staff size: 1. Publishes 30 songs/year. Pays 50% royalty.

How to Contact *Does not accept unsolicited submissions.*

Film & TV Places 3/5 songs in film and in TV/year.

Music Mostly **new industrial** and **metal**, **lounge**, **electronic**, and **ambient**. Publisher for Peepingtom (trip-hop), Djaimin (house), Missa Furiosa by Thierry Zaboitzeff (progressive), The Young Gods (alternative), Alex Carter, Love Motel, Steve Tallis, and lo'n, amongst others.

⊕ ◻ ISLAND CULTURE MUSIC PUBLISHERS (BMI)

7005 Bordeaux, St. John 00830-9510. U.S. Virgin Islands. E-mail: L_monsanto@hotmail.com. Website: www.IslandKingRecords.com. **Contact:** Liston Monsanto, Jr., president. Music publisher and record company (Island King Records). Estab. 1996. Publishes 10 songs/year; publishes 3 new songwriters/year. Hires staff songwriters. Staff size: 3. Pays standard royalty.

How to Contact Submit demo package by mail. Unsolicited submissions are OK. Prefers CD with 8 songs and lyric sheet. Send bio and 8 × 10 glossy. Does not return material. Responds in 1 month.

Music Mostly **reggae**, **calypso**, and **zouk**; also **house**. Published *De Paris a Bohicon* (album), recorded by Rasbawa (reggae), released 2006 on Island King Records; "Jah Give Me Life" (single by Chubby) from *Best of Island King* (album), recorded by Chubby (reggae), released 2003 on Island King Records; "When People Mix Up" (single by Lady Lex/L. Monsanto/Chubby) and "I Am Real" (single by L. Monsanto) from *Best of Island King* (album), recorded by Lady Lex (reggae), released 2003 on Island King Records.

◻ IVORY PEN ENTERTAINMENT (ASCAP)

P.O. Box 1097, Laurel MD 20725. Fax: (240)786-6744. E-mail: ivorypen@comcast.net. Professional Managers: Steven Lewis (R&B, pop/rock, inspirational); Sonya Lewis (AC, dance) Wandaliz Colon (Latin, Ethic). Music publisher. Estab. 2003. Publishes 10 songs/year. Staff size: 4. Pays standard royalty.

How to Contact Submit demo package by mail. Unsolicited submissions are OK. Prefers CD with 3-5 songs and cover letter. Does not return material. Responds in 4 months. "Don't forget contact info with e-mail address for faster response! Always be professional when you submit your work to any company. Quality counts."

Music Mostly **R&B**, **dance**, **pop/rock**, **Latin**, **adult contemporary**, and **inspirational**. Published Ryan Vetter (single), writer recorded by Alan Johnson (/pop/rock), released on Ivory Pen Entertainment; and "Mirror" (single), by Angel Demone, on Vox Angel Inc./Ivory Pen Entertainment.

Tips "Learn your craft. Always deliver high quality demos. 'Remember, if you don't invest in yourself, don't expect others to invest in you. Ivory Pen Entertainment is a music publishing company that caters to the new songwriter, producer, and aspiring artist. We also place music tracks (no vocals) with artists for release."

◪ JANA JAE MUSIC

P.O. Box 35726, Tulsa OK 74153. (918)786-8896. Fax: (918)786-8897. E-mail: janajae@

janajae.com. Website: www.janajae.com. **Contact:** Kathleen Pixley, secretary. Music publisher, record company (Lark Record Productions, Inc.) and record producer (Lark Talent and Advertising). Estab. 1980. Publishes 5-10 songs/year; publishes 1-2 new songwriters/year. Staff size: 8. Pays standard royalty.

How to Contact Submit demo by mail. Unsolicited submissions are OK. Prefers CD or DVD with 3-4 songs and typed lyric and lead sheet if possible. Does not return material. Responds only if accepted for use.

Music Mostly **country**, **bluegrass**, **jazz** and **instrumentals** (**classical** or **country**). Published *Mayonnaise* (album by Steve Upfold), recorded by Jana Jae; and *Let the Bible Be Your Roadmap* (album by Irene Elliot), recorded by Jana Jae, both on Lark Records.

⊕ ☐ JA/NEIN MUSIKVERLAG GMBH (GEMA)

Oberstr. 14 A, D - 20144, Hamburg Germany. Fax: (49)(40)448 850. E-mail: janeinmv@aol.com. General Manager: Mary Dostal. Music publisher, record company and record producer. Member of GEMA. Publishes 50 songs/year; publishes 5 new songwriters/year. Staff size: 3. Pays 50-66% royalty.

Affiliates Pinorrekk Mv., Star-Club Mv. (GEMA).

How to Contact Submit audio (visual) carrier by mail. Unsolicited submissions are OK. "We do not download unsolicited material, but visit known websites." Prefers CD or DVD. Enclose e-mail address. Responds in maximum 2 months.

Music Mostly **jazz**, **world** (**klezmer**), **pop**, **rap** and **rock**.

Tips "We do not return submitted material. Send your best A-Side works only, please. Indicate all rights owners, like possible co-composer/lyricist, publisher, sample owner. Write what you expect from collaboration. If artist, enclose photo. Enclose lyrics. Be extraordinary! Be fantastic!"

☐ JERJOY MUSIC (BMI)

P.O. Box 1264, 6020 W. Pottstown Rd., Peoria IL 61654-1264. (309)673-5755. Fax: (309)673-7636. E-mail: uarltd@A5.com. Website: www.unitedcyber.com and www.myspace.com/jerryhanlon. **Contact:** Jerry Hanlon, professional manager. Music publisher and record company (UAR Records). Estab. 1978. Publishes 6 songs/year; publishes 6 new songwriters/year. Staff size: 3. Pays standard royalty.

• Also see the listing for Kaysarah Music in this section and UAR Records in the Record Companies section of this book.

Affiliates Kaysarah Music (ASCAP); Abilite Music (BMI).

How to Contact *Write first and obtain permission to submit. "WE DO NOT RESPOND TO TELEPHONE CALLS.* Unsolicited submissions are OK, but be sure to send SASE and/or postage or mailing materials if you want a reply and/or a return of all your material. *WE DO NOT OFFER CRITIQUES OF YOUR WORK UNLESS SPECIFICALLY ASKED.* Simple demos—vocal plus guitar or keyboard—are acceptable. We DO NOT require a major demo production to interpret the value of a song." Prefers CD with 4-8 songs and lyric sheet. Responds in 2 weeks.

Music Mostly **American country, Irish Country** and **religious**. Published "Philomena From Ireland," "I Wanted You for Mine," and "Lisa, Dance with Me" written by The Heggarty Twins of Northern Ireland (recorded by The Heggarty Twins and Jerry Hanlon, country), and "things My Daddy Used to Do" written by Mark Walton (recorded by Jerry Hanlon, country); "That Little Irish Church" written and recorded by Jerry Hanlon, country gospel Irish). "I'd Better Stand Up" written by Gene Gillen and Will Herring (recorded by The Heggarty Twins and Jerry Hanlon, country); "Rainbow" written by Dwight Howell (recorded by The Heggarty Twins and Jerry Hanlon, Irish country). "All Your Little Secrets" and "The Girl from Central High" written by Ron Czikall (recorded by Tracy Wells, country); all released on UAR Records.

Tips "Don't submit any song that you don't honestly feel is well constructed and strong in commercial value. Be critical of your writing efforts. Be sure you use each and every one of your lyrics to its best advantage. 'Think Big!' Make your songs tell a story and don't be repetitious in using the same or similar ideas or words in each of your verses. Would your musical creation stand up against the major hits that are making the charts today? Think of great hooks you can work into your song ideas."

KAUPPS & ROBERT PUBLISHING CO. (BMI)

P.O. Box 5474, Stockton CA 95205. (209)948-8186. Fax: (209)942-2163. Website: www. makingmusic4u.com. **Contact:** Melissa Glenn, A&R coordinator (all styles). Production Manager (country, pop, rock): Rick Webb. Professional Manager (country, pop, rock): Bruce Bolin. President: Nancy L. Merrihew. Music publisher, record company (Kaupp Records), manager and booking agent (Merri-Webb Productions and Most Wanted Bookings). Estab. 1990. Publishes 15-20 songs/year; publishes 5 new songwriters/year. Pays standard royalty.

How to Contact *Write first and obtain permission to submit.* Prefers cassette or VHS videocassette (if available) with 3 songs maximum and lyric sheet. "If artist, send PR package." Include SASE. Responds in 6 months.

Music Mostly **country, R&B** and **A/C rock**; also **pop, rock** and **gospel**. Published "Rushin' In" (singles by N. Merrihew/B. Bolin), recorded by Valerie; "Goin Postal" (singles by N. Merrihew/B. Bolin), recorded by Bruce Bolin (country/rock/pop); and "I Gotta Know" (single by N. Merrihew/B. Bolin), recorded by Cheryl (country/rock/pop), all released on Kaupp Records.

Tips "Know what you want, set a goal, focus in on your goals, be open to constructive criticism, polish tunes and keep polishing."

KAYSARAH MUSIC (ASCAP, BMI)

P.O. Box 1264, 6020 W. Pottstown Rd., Peoria IL 61654-1264. (309)673-5755. Fax: (309)673-7636. E-mail: uarltd@A5.com. Website: www.unitedcyber.com and www.myspace.com/

jerryhanlon. **Contact:** Jerry Hanlon, owner/producer. Music Publisher, record company (UAR Records), and record producer. Estab. 2000. Publishes 2 new songwriters/year. Staff size: 3. Pays standard royalty.

- Also see the listing for Jerjoy Music in this section and UAR Records in the Record Companies section of this book.

Affiliates Jerjoy Music (BMI); Abilite Music (BMI).

How to Contact *Write first and obtain permission to submit. "WE DO NOT RESPOND TO TELEPHONE CALLS.* Unsolicited submissions are OK, but be sure to send SASE and/or postage or mailing materials if you want a reply and/or a return of all your material. *WE DO NOT OFFER CRITIQUES OF YOUR WORK UNLESS SPECIFICALLY ASKED."* Prefers CD with 4 songs and lyric sheet and cover letter. Include SASE. Responds in 2 weeks.

Music Mostly **traditional country** and **country gospel**; also **Irish country**, **Irish ballads** and **Irish folk/traditional**.

Tips "Be honest and self-critical of your work. Make every word in a song count. Attempt to create work that is not over 2:50 minutes in length. Compare your work to the songs that seem to be what you hear on radio. A good A&R person or professional recording artist with a creative mind can determine the potential value of a song simply by hearing a melody line (guitar or keyboard) and the lyrics. DON'T convince yourself that your work is outstanding if you feel that it will not be able to compete with the tough competition of today 's market."

☑ LARI-JON PUBLISHING

P.O. Box 216, Rising City NE 68658. (402)542-2336. **Contact:** Larry Good, owner. Music publisher, record company (Lari-Jon Records), management firm (Lari-Jon Promotions) and record producer (Lari-Jon Productions). Estab. 1967. Publishes 20 songs/year; publishes 2-3 new songwriters/year. Staff size: 1. Pays standard royalty.

How to Contact Submit demo by mail. Unsolicited submissions are OK. Prefers CD with 5 songs and lyric sheet. "Be professional." Include SASE. Responds in 2 months.

Music Mostly **country**, **Southern gospel** and **'50s rock**. Does not want rock, hip-hop, pop or heavy metal. Published "Bluegrass Blues" and "Carolina Morning" (singles by Larry Good) from *Carolina Morning* (album), recorded by Blue Persuasion (country), released 2002 by Bullseye; "Those Rolling Hills of Glenwood" (single by Tom Campbell) from *Single* (album), recorded by Tom Campbell (country), released 2001 by Jeffs-Room-Productions.

🔁 🖼 ☐ LILLY MUSIC PUBLISHING

61 Euphrasia Dr., Toronto ON M6B 3V8 Canada. (416)782-5768. Fax: (416)782-7170. E-mail: panfilo@sympatico.ca. **Contact:** Panfilo Di Matteo, president. Music publisher and record company (P. & N. Records). Estab. 1992. Publishes 20 songs/year; publishes 8 new songwriters/year. Staff size: 3. Pays standard royalty.

Affiliates San Martino Music Publishing and Paglieta Music Publishing (CMRRA).

How to Contact Submit demo by mail. Unsolicited submissions are OK. Prefers CD (or videocassette if available) with 3 songs and lyric and lead sheets. "We will contact you only if we are interested in the material." Responds in 1 month.

Film & TV Places 12 songs in film/year.

Music Mostly **dance**, **ballads** and **rock**; also **country**. Published "I'd Give It All" (single by Glenna J. Sparkes), recorded by Suzanne Michelle (country crossover), released 2005 on Lilly Records.

☐ LITA MUSIC (ASCAP)

2831 Dogwood Place, Nashville TN 37204. (615)269-8682. Fax: (615)269-8929. Website: www.songsfortheplanet.com. **Contact:** Justin Peters, president. Music publisher. Estab. 1980.

Affiliates Justin Peters Music, Platinum Planet Music and Tourmaline (BMI).

How to Contact Submit demo package by mail. Unsolicited submissions are OK. Prefers CD with 5 songs and lyric sheet. Does not return material. "Place code '2010' on each envelope submission."

Music Mostly **country**, **classic rock**, **Southern rock, inspirational AC Pop, Southern gospel/Christian,** and **worship songs**. Published "The Bottom Line" recorded by Charley Pride on Music City Records (written by Art Craig, Drew Bourke, and Justin Peters); "No Less Than Faithful" (single by Don Pardoe/Joel Lyndsey), recorded by Ann Downing on Daywind Records, Jim Bullard on Genesis Records and Melody Beizer (#1 song) on Covenant Records; "No Other Like You" (single by Mark Comden/Paula Carpenter), recorded by Twila Paris and Tony Melendez (#5 song) on Starsong Records; "Making A New Start" and "Invincible Faith" (singles by Gayle Cox), recorded by Kingdom Heirs on Sonlite Records; "I Don't Want To Go Back" (single by Gayle Cox), recorded by Greater Vision on Benson Records; and "HE HAD MERCY ON ME" (by Constance and Justin Peters) recorded by Shining Grace.

☐ M & T WALDOCH PUBLISHING, INC. (BMI)

4803 S. Seventh St., Milwaukee WI 53221. (414)482-2194. VP, Creative Management (rockabilly, pop, country): Timothy J. Waldoch. Professional Manager (country, top 40): Mark T. Waldoch. Music publisher. Estab. 1990. Publishes 2-3 songs/year; publishes 2-3 new songwriters/year. Staff size: 2. Pays standard royalty.

How to Contact Submit demo package by mail. Unsolicited submissions are OK. Prefers CD with 3-6 songs and lyric or lead sheet. "We will also accept a studio produced demo tape." Include SASE. Responds in 3 months.

Music Mostly **country/pop**, **rock**, **top 40 pop**; also **melodic metal**, **dance**, **R&B**. Does not want rap. Published "It's Only Me" and "Let Peace Rule the World" (by Kenny LePrix), recorded by Brigade on SBD Records (rock).

Tips "Study the classic pop songs from the 1950s through the present time. There is a reason why good songs stand the test of time. Today's hits will be tomorrow's classics. Send your best well-crafted, polished song material."

☑ MAKERS MARK GOLD PUBLISHING (ASCAP)

534 W. Queen Lane, Philadelphia PA 19144. E-mail: MakersMark@verizon.net. **Contact:** Paul Hopkins, producer/publisher. Music publisher and record producer. Estab. 1991. Pays standard royalty.

How to Contact Submit demo CD or tape by mail. Unsolicited submissions are OK. Prefers 2-4 songs. Does not return material. Responds in 6 weeks if interested.

Music "Our publishing and productions has changed to total **Christian/Inspirational. gospel/christian** only. All genres **contemporary, traditional, pop, dance, hip-hop gospel**." Historically mostly **R&B**, **hip-hop**, **gospel**, **pop** and **house**. Published "Silent Love," "Why You Want My Love" and "Something for Nothing," (singles), written and recorded by Elaine Monk, released on Black Sands Records/Metropolitan Records; "Get Funky" (single), written and recorded by Larry Larr, released on Columbia Records; and "He Made A Way" (single by Kenyatta Arrington), "We Give All Praises Unto God" (single by Jacqueline D. Pate), "I Believe He Will" (single by Pastor Alyn E. Waller), and "Psalms 146" (single by Rodney Roberson), all songs recorded by The Enon Tabernacle Mass Choir from *Pastor Alyn E. Waller Presents: The Enon Tabernacle Mass Choir*, released on ECDC Records (www.enontab.org). Also produces and publishes music for Bunim/ Murray productions network television, MTV's *Real World*, *Road Rules*, *Rebel Billionaire*, *Simple Life*, and movie soundtracks worldwide. Also produced deep soul remixes for Brian McKnight, Musiq Souchild, Jagged Edge, John Legend, and Elaine Monk.

🔄 ☑ MANY LIVES MUSIC PUBLISHERS (SOCAN)

RR #1, Kensington PE COB 1MO Canada. (902)836-4571 (studio). E-mail: paul.milner@ summerside.ca. **Contact:** Paul C. Milner, publisher. Music publisher. Estab. 1997. "Owners of Shell Lane Studio www.shelllanestudio.com complete in-house production facility. Many Lives Music Publishers was also involved in the production and recording of all projects listed below." Pays standard royalty.

How to Contact Submit demo by mail, myspace, or SonicBids. Unsolicited submissions are OK. Prefers CD and lyric sheet (lead sheet if available). Does not return material. Responds in 3 months if interested.

Music All styles. *Six Pack EP* and *Colour*(album), written and recorded by Chucky Danger (Pop/Rock), released 2005 on Landwash Entertainment. Chucky Danger's *Colour* album was named Winner Best Pop Recording at the East Coast Music Awards 2006, "Sweet Symphony" was nominated for Single of the Year, and Chucky Danger was nominated for Best New Group. Released *Temptation* (album by various writers), arrangement by Paul Milner, Patrizia, Dan Cutrona (rock/opera), released 2003 on United One Records; *The*

Edge Of Emotion (album by various writers), arrangement by Paul Milner, Patrizia, Dan Cutrona (rock/opera), released 2006 on Nuff entertainment /United One Records. The Single "Temptation" won a SOCAN #1 award. *Saddle River Stringband* (album) written and recorded by The Saddle River Stringband (Bluegrass) released on Panda Digital/ Save As Music 2007. Winners of best Bluegrass recording East Coast Music Awards 2007. *Pat Deighan and the Orb Weavers* (album) "In A Fever In A Dream" (Alternative Rock) written by Pat Deighan, released on Sandbar Music April 2008.

MATERIAL WORTH PUBLISHING (ASCAP)

PO Box 162, Walden NY 12586. (845) 283-0795. E-mail: franksardella@ materialworthpublishing.com. Website: www.materialworthpublishing.com. **Contact:** Frank Sardella, owner. Music publisher. Estab. 2003. Staff size: 3. Pays standard royalty of 50%.

How to Contact *Visit Web site for how to obtain permission to submit. Must have permission before sending. Do not call first.* Prefers CD, lyric sheet, and cover letter. Does not return submissions. Responds in 4-6 weeks.

Music Mostly **female pop** or **pop/country crossover**, **singer-songwriter, male pop alternative rock**.

◪ MCCLURE & TROWBRIDGE PUBLISHING, LTD (ASCAP, BMI)

P.O. Box 148548, Nashville TN 37214. (615) 902-0509. Website: www.TrowbridgePlanetEarth. com. Contact: Miig Miniger, director of marketing. Music publisher, and record label (JIP Records) and production company (George McClure, producer). Estab. 1983. Publishes 35 songs/year. Publishes 5 new songwriters/year. Staff size: 8. Pays standard royalty of 50%.

How to Contact Do not e-mail. *Follow directions ONLINE ONLY—obtain Control Number to submit a demo via US Mail.* Requires CD with 1-5 songs, lyric sheet, and cover letter. Does not return submissions. Responds in 3 weeks if interested.

Music Pop, **country**, **gospel**, **Latin** and **swing**. Publisher of Band of Writers (BOW) series. Published "Playboy Swing", released 2008 on JIP Records; "You're One In A Million" (single), recorded by Layni Kooper (R&B/pop), released 2007 on JIP Records; "My Way or Hit the Highway" (single), written and recorded by Jacqui Watson (Americana), released 2005 on Artist Choice CD; and "I'm A Wild One" (single), recorded by Veronica Leigh, released 2006 on Artist Choice CD.

◻ JIM MCCOY MUSIC (BMI)

25 Troubadour Lane, Berkeley Springs WV 25411. (304)258-9381. E-mail: mccoytroubadour@aol.com. Website: www.troubadourlounge.com. **Contact:** Bertha and Jim McCoy, owners. Music publisher, record company (Winchester Records) and record producer (Jim McCoy Productions). Estab. 1973. Publishes 20 songs/year; publishes 3-5

new songwriters/year. Pays standard royalty.

Affiliates New Edition Music (BMI).

How to Contact Submit demo by mail with lyric sheet. Unsolicited submissions are OK. Prefers cassette or CD with 6 songs. Include SASE. Responds in 1 month.

Music Mostly **country**, **country/rock** and **rock**; also **bluegrass** and **gospel**. Published *Jim McCoy and Friends Remember Ernest Tubb*; "She's the Best" recorded by Matt Hahn on Troubadour Records (written by Jim McCoy); "Shadows on My Mind" recorded by Sandy Utley (written by Jim McCoy), "Rock and Roll Hillbilly Redneck Girl" recorded by Elani Arthur (written by Jim McCoy), released in 2007.

☑ MIDI TRACK PUBLISHING (BMI)

P.O. Box 1545, Smithtown NY 11787. (718)767-8995. E-mail: info@allrsmusic.com. Website: www.allrsmusic.com. **Contact:** Renee Silvestri-Bushey, president. F.John Silvestri, founder; Leslie Migliorelli, director of operations. Music publisher, record company (MIDI Track Records), music consultant, artist management, record producer. Voting member of NARAS/National Academy of Recording Arts and Sciences (The Grammy Awards), voting member of the Country Music Association (CMA Awards); SGMA/Southern Gospel Music Association, SGA/Songwriters Guild of America (Diamond Member). Estab. 1994. Staff size: 6. Publishes 3 songs/year; publishes 2 new songwriters/year. Pays standard royalty.

Affiliates ALLRS Music Publishing Co. (ASCAP).

How to Contact "Write or e-mail first to obtain permission to submit. We do not accept unsolicited submissions." Prefers CD with 3 songs, lyric sheet and cover letter. Does not return material. Responds in 6 months only if interested.

Film & TV Places 1 song in film/year. Published "Why Can't You Hear My Prayer" (single by F. John Silvestri/Leslie Silvestri), recorded by Iliana Medina in a documentary by Silvermine Films.

Music Mostly **country**, **gospel**, **top 40**, **R&B**, **MOR** and **pop**. Does not want showtunes, jazz, classical or rap. Published "Why Can't You Hear My Prayer" (single by F. John Silvestri/Leslie Silvestri), recorded by eight-time Grammy nominee Huey Dunbar of the group DLG (Dark Latin Groove), released on MIDI Track Records (including other multiple releases); "Chasing Rainbows" (single by F. John Silvestri/Leslie Silvestri/Darin Kelly), recorded by Tommy Cash (country), released on MMT Records (including other multiple releases); "Because of You" (single by F. John Silvestri/Leslie Silvestri), recorded by Iliana Medina, released 2002 on MIDI Track Records (including other multiple releases also recorded by three-time Grammy nominee Terri Williams, of Always, Patsy Cline, Grand Ole Opry member Ernie Ashworth), released on KMA Records; also recorded by Grand Ole Opry member Ernie Ashworth, released 2004 on KMA Records; "My Coney Island" (single by F. John Silvestri/Leslie Silvestri), recorded by eight-time Grammy nominee Huey Dunbar, released 2005-2009 on MIDI Track Records.

Tips "Attend workshops, seminars, and visit our blog on our Web site for advise, tips, and info on the music industry."

⚡ ☑ MONTINA MUSIC (SOCAN)

P.O. Box 32, Snowdon Station, Montreal QC H3X 3T3 Canada. **Contact:** David P. Leonard, professional manager. Music publisher and record company (Monticana Records). Estab. 1963. Pays negotiable royalty.

Affiliates Saber-T Music (SOCAN).

How to Contact Unsolicited submissions are OK. Prefers CD. SAE and IRC. Responds in 3 months.

Music Mostly **top 40**; also **bluegrass**, **blues**, **country**, **dance-oriented**, **easy listening**, **folk**, **gospel**, **jazz**, **MOR**, **progressive**, **R&B**, **rock** and **soul**. Does not want heavy metal, hard rock, jazz, classical or New Age.

Tips "Maintain awareness of styles and trends of your peers who have succeeded professionally. Understand the markets to which you are pitching your material. Persevere at marketing your talents. Develop a network of industry contacts, first locally, then regionally, nationally and internationally."

⬜ MOON JUNE MUSIC

4233 SW Marigold, Portland OR 97219. (507)777-4621. Fax: (503)277-4622. **Contact:** Bob Stoutenburg, president. Music publisher. Estab. 1971. Staff size: 1. Pays standard royalty.

How to Contact Submit demo by mail. Unsolicited submissions are OK. Prefers cassette or CD with 2-10 songs.

Music Country.

☑ MUST HAVE MUSIC (ASCAP, BMI)

P.O. Box 361326, Los Angeles CA 90036-1326. (323)932-9524. E-mail: info@musthavemusic. com. Website: www.musthavemusic.com. **Contact:** Kenneth R. Klar, managing director. Music publisher and music library. Estab. 1990. Pays standard royalty.

Affiliates Must Have More Music (ASCAP); Must Have Music (BMI).

How to Contact Submit demo by mail with your personal e-mail address included for directors response. Unsolicited submissions are OK. Prefers CD with lyric sheet and cover letter. Does not return submissions. Responds in 2 months.

Film & TV Music supervisor: Ken Klar, managing director.

Music Mostly **pop/ R& B**, **pop/country** and **rock**; also **AAA**, **adult contemporary**, and **contemporary Christian/gospel**. Does not want instrumental music. "We only work with completed songs with lyric and vocal." Published "Come to the Table" (single by Ken Klar/Steve Massey) from *Worship Leader Magazine's Song Discovery, Vol. 26* (album), recorded by various artists, released 2002 on Worship Leader; "Fool" (single by Ken Klar) from *If You Want My Love* (album), recorded by Jennifer Young (pop/R&B), released 2002 on Independent; and "Blame It On My Heart" (single by Ken Klar/Steve Kir wan) from *Blame It On My Heart* (album), recorded by Steve Kirwan (adult contemporary), released 2001 on Independent.

Tips "Write what you know and what you believe. Then re-write it!"

⊞ ☐ NERVOUS PUBLISHING

5 Sussex Crescent, Northolt, Middlesex UB5 4DL United Kingdom. +44(020) 8423 7373. Fax: +44(020) 8423 7773. E-mail: info@nervous.co.uk. Website: www.nervous.co.uk. **Contact:** Roy Williams, owner. Music publisher, record company (Nervous Records) and record producer. MCPS, PRS and Phonographic Performance Ltd. Estab. 1979. Publishes 100 songs/year; publishes 25 new songwriters/year. Pays standard royalty; royalties paid directly to US songwriters.

- Nervous Publishing's record label, Nervous Records, is listed in the Record Companies section.

How to Contact Submit demo by mail. Unsolicited submissions are OK. Prefers CD with 3-10 songs and lyric sheet. "Include letter giving your age and mentioning any previously published material." SAE and IRC. Responds in 3 weeks.

Music Mostly **psychobilly, rockabilly** and **rock** (impossibly fast music—e.g.: Stray Cats but twice as fast); also **blues, country, R&B** and **rock** ('50s style). Published *Trouble* (album), recorded by Dido Bonneville (rockabilly); *Rockabilly Comp* (album), recorded by various artists; and *Nervous Singles Collection* (album), recorded by various artists, all on Nervous Records.

Tips "Submit *no* rap, soul, funk—we want *rockabilly*."

☑ NEWBRAUGH BROTHERS MUSIC (ASCAP, BMI)

228 Morgan Lane, Berkeley Springs WV 25411-3475. (304)261-0228. E-mail: Nbtoys@verizon.net. **Contact:** John S. Newbraugh, owner. Music publisher, record company (NBT Records, BMI/ASCAP). Estab. 1967. Publishes 124 songs/year. Publishes 14 new songwriters/year. Staff size: 1. Pays standard royalty.

Affiliates NBT Music (ASCAP) and Newbraugh Brothers Music (BMI).

How to Contact Submit demo by mail. Unsolicited submissions are OK. Prefers cassette or CD with any amount of songs, a lyric sheet and a cover letter. Include SASE. Responds in 6 weeks. "Please don't call for permission to submit. Your materials are welcomed."

Music Mostly **rockabilly, hillbilly, folk** and **bluegrass**; also **rock, country**, and **gospel**. "We will accept all genres of music except songs with vulgar language." Published Released *Ride the Train Series Vol. 24; Layin' It On the Line* by Night Drive (2008); *Country Like It Ought to Be* by Bobby "Swampgrass" Anderson (2008) and *The Gospel Songbird* Vol. 2 by Wanda Sue Watkins (2008).

Tips "Find out if a publisher/record company has any special interest. NBT, for instance, is always hunting 'original' train songs. Our 'registered' trademark is a train and from time to time we release a compilation album of all train songs. We welcome all genres of music for this project."

◪ A NEW RAP JAM PUBLISHING (BMI)

P.O. Box 683, Lima OH 45802. E-mail: just_chilling_2002@yahoo.com. Professional Managers: William Roach (rap, clean); James Milligan (country, 70s music, pop). **Contact:** A&R Dept. Music publisher and record company (New Experience/Faze 4 Records, Pump It Up Records, and Rough Edge Records). Estab. 1989. Publishes 40 songs/year; publishes 2-3 new songwriters/year. Hires staff songwriters. Staff size: 6. Pays standard royalty.

Affiliates Party House Publishing (BMI), Creative Star Management, and Rough Edge Records. Distribution through NER/SONY/BMG/SMD.

How to Contact *Write first to arrange personal interview or submit demo CD by mail.* Unsolicited submissions are OK. Prefers CD with 3-5 songs and lyric or lead sheet. Include SASE. Responds in 6-8 weeks. "Visit www.NewExperienceRecords.com for more information."

Music Mostly **R&B**, **pop**, **blues** and **rock/rap** (clean); also **contemporary**, **gospel**, **country** and **soul**. Published "Lets Go Dancing" (single by Dion Mikel), recorded and released 2006 on Faze 4 Records/New Experience Records; "The Broken Hearted" (single) from The Final Chapter (album), recorded by T.M.C. the milligan connection (R&B/gospel), released 2003/2007 on New Experience/Pump It Up Records. Other artists include singer-songwriter James, Jr. on Faze 4 Records/Rough Edge Records/Sonic Wave/SONY/BMG.

Tips "We are seeking hit artists 70s, 80s, and 90s who would like to be signed, as well as new talent and female solo artists. Send any available information supporting the group or act. We are a label that does not promote violence, drugs or anything that we feel is a bad example for our youth. Establish music industry contacts, write and keep writing and most of all believe in yourself. Use a good recording studio but be very professional. Just take your time and produce the best music possible. Sometimes you only get one chance. Make sure you place your best song on your demo first. This will increase your chances greatly. If you're the owner of your own small label and have a finished product, please send it. And if there is interest we will contact you. Also be on the lookout for new artists on Rough Edge Records. now reviewing material. Please be aware of the new sampling laws and laws for digital downloading. It is against the law. People are being jailed and fined for this act. Do your homework. Read the new digital downloading contracts carefully or seek legal help if need be. Good luck and thanks for considering our company for your musical needs."

◪ ⊘ OLD SLOWPOKE MUSIC (BMI)

P.O. Box 52626, Tulsa OK 74152-0626. (918)742-8087. E-mail: ryoung@cherrystreetrecords. com. Website: www.cherrystreetrecords.com. **Contact:** Steve Hickerson, professional manager. President: Rodney Young. Music publisher and record producer. Estab. 1977. Publishes 10- 20 songs/year; publishes 2 new songwriters/year. Staff size: 2. Pays standard royalty.

How to Contact CDs only, no cassettes.

Film & TV 1 song in film/year. Recently published "Samantha," written and recorded by

George W. Carroll in Samantha. Placed two songs for Tim Drummond in movies "Hound Dog Man" in *Loving Lu Lu* and "Fur Slippers" in a CBS movie *Shake, Rattle & Roll*.

Music Mostly **rock**, **country** and **R&B**; also **jazz**. Published *Promise Land* (album), written and recorded by Richard Neville on Cherry Street Records (rock).

Tips "Write great songs. We sign only artists who play an instrument, sing and write songs."

☑ ORCHID PUBLISHING

Bouquet-Orchid Enterprises, P.O. Box 1335, Norcross GA 30091. Phone/fax: (770)339-9088. **Contact:** Bill Bohannon, president. Music publisher, record company, record producer (Bouquet-Orchid Enterprises) and artist management. Member: CMA, AFM. Publishes 10-12 songs/year; publishes 3 new songwriters/year. Pays standard royalty.

How to Contact Submit demo by mail. Unsolicited submissions are OK. Prefers cassette or CD with 3-5 songs and lyric sheet. "Send biographical information if possible—even a photo helps." Include SASE. Responds in 1 month.

Music Mostly **religious** ("Amy Grant, etc., contemporary gospel"); **country** ("Garth Brooks, Trisha Yearwood-type material"); and **top 100/pop** ("Bryan Adams, Whitney Houston-type material"). Published "Blue As Your Eyes" (single), written and recorded by Adam Day; "Spare My Feelings" (single by Clayton Russ), recorded by Terri Palmer; and "Trying to Get By" (single by Tom Sparks), recorded by Bandoleers, all on Bouquet Records.

⊕ ☑ PEGASUS MUSIC

1 Derwent Street, Oamaru 9400, Otago, New Zealand. E-mail: peg.music@xtra.co.nz. Website: www.pegasusmusic.biz. Professional Managers: Errol Peters (country, rock); Ginny Peters (gospel, pop). Music publisher and record company. Estab. 1981. Publishes 20-30 songs/year; publishes 5 new songwriters/year. Pays standard royalty.

How to Contact Submit demo package by mail. Unsolicited submissions are OK. Prefers CD with 3-5 songs and lyric sheet. SAE and IRC. Responds in 1 month.

Music Mostly **country**; also **bluegrass**, **easy listening** and **top 40/pop**. Published "Beyond the Reason," written and recorded by Ginny Peters (Pegasus Records); "I Only See You," written by Ginny Peters, recorded by Dennis Marsh (Rajon Records, New Zealand); "The Mystery of God," written and recorded by Ginny Peters (NCM Records, England).

Tips "Get to the meat of the subject without too many words. Less is better."

☑ PERLA MUSIC (ASCAP)

134 Parker Ave., Easton PA 18042-1361. (212)957-9509. E-mail: PM@PMRecords.Org. Website: www.PMRecords.org. **Contact:** Gene Perla (jazz). Music publisher, record company (PMRecords.org), record producer (Perla.org), studio production (TheSystemMSP.com) and Internet Design (CCINYC.com). Estab. 1971. Publishes 5 songs/year. Staff size: 5. Pays 75%/25% royalty.

How to Contact *E-mail first and obtain permission to submit.*
Music Mostly **jazz** and **rock**.

☐ JUSTIN PETERS MUSIC (BMI)

P.O. Box 40251, Nashville TN 37204. (615)269-8682. Fax: (615)269-8929. Website: www. songsfortheplanet.com. **Contact:** Justin Peters, president. Music publisher. Estab. 1981.
Affiliates Platinum Planet Music(BMI), Tourmaline (BMI) and LITA Music (ASCAP).
How to Contact Submit demo package by mail. Unsolicited submissions are OK. Prefers CD with 5 songs and lyric sheet. Does not return material. "Place code '2010' on each envelope submission."
Music Mostly **pop**, **reggae**, **country** and **comedy**. Published "Saved By Love" (single), recorded by Amy Grant on A&M Records; "Nothing Can Separate Us", recorded by Al Denson; "A Gift That She Don't Want" (single), recorded by Bill Engvall on Warner Brother Records; "The Bottom Line," recorded by Charley Pride on Music City Records, cowritten by Justin Peters; "Heaven's Got to Help Me Shake These Blues" (single), written by Vickie Shaub and Justin Peters, recorded by B.J. Thomas; "Virginia Dreams" and "Closer to You" (Jimmy Fortune/Justin Peters), recorded by Jimmy Fortune.

☑ PIANO PRESS (ASCAP)

P.O. Box 85, Del Mar CA 92014-0085. (619)884-1401. Fax: (858)755-1104. E-mail: pianopress@pianopress.com. Website: www.pianopress.com. **Contact:** Elizabeth C. Axford, M.A., owner. Music publisher and distributor. Publishes songbooks & CD's for music students and teachers. Estab. 1998. Licenses 32-100 songs/year; publishes 1-24 new songwriters/year. Staff size: 5. Pays standard print music and/or mechanical royalty; songwriter retains rights to songs.
How to Contact *E-mail first to obtain permission to submit.* Prefers CD with 1-3 songs, lyric and lead sheet, cover letter and sheet music/piano arrangements. "Looking for children's songs for young piano students and arrangements of public domain folk songs of any nationality." Currently accepting submissions for various projects. Include SASE. Responds in 2-3 months.
Music Mostly **children's songs**, **folk songs** and **holiday songs**; also **teaching pieces**, **piano arrangements**, **lead sheets with melody, chords and lyrics** and **songbooks**. Published *My Halloween Fun Songbook* and CD and *My Christmas Fun Songbook* series, *The Holiday Fun* series, *The Pieces for Piano* series, *The Piano Composers* series, and *The Kidtunes* series.
Tips "Songs should be simple, melodic and memorable. Lyrics should be for a juvenile audience and well-crafted."

☐ PLATINUM PLANET MUSIC, INC. (BMI)

2831 Dogwood Place, Nashville TN 37204. (615)269-8682. Fax: (615)269-8929. Website:

www.songsfortheplanet.com. **Contact:** Justin Peters, president. Music publisher. Estab. 1997.

Affiliates Justin Peters Music (BMI), Tourmaline (BMI) and LITA Music (ASCAP).

How to Contact Submit demo package by mail. Unsolicited submissions are OK. Prefers CD with 5 songs and lyric sheet. Does not return material. "Place code '2010' on each envelope submission."

Music Mostly **R&B**, **reggae, sports themes**, **dance** and **country**; also represents many **Christian** artists/writers. Published "Happy Face" (single by Dez Dickerson/Jordan Dickerson), recorded by Squirt on Absolute Records; "Buena Vida" (Daron Glenn and Justin Peters), recorded by Daron Glenn on PPMI; "Love's Not A Game" (single), written by Art Craig and J. Peters and recorded by Kashief Lindo on Heavybeat Records; "Place Called Heaven" written by Armond Morales and Kevin Wicker and released by the Imperials, "Love Won't Let Me Leave" (Art Craig and Justin Peters), recorded by Jason Rogers on Independent; and "Loud" (single), written and recorded by These Five Down on Absolute Records.

☑ POLLYBYRD PUBLICATIONS LIMITED (ASCAP, BMI, SESAC)

P.O. Box 261488, Encino CA 91426. (818)506-8533. Fax: (818)506-8534. E-mail: pplzmi@aol.com. Website: www.pplzmi.com. Branch office: 468 N. Camden Drive Suite 200, Beverly Hills CA 90210. **Contact:** Dakota Hawk, vice president. Professional Managers: Cisco Blue (country, pop, rock); Tedford Steele (hip-hop, R&B). Music publisher, record company (PPL Entertainment) and Management firm (Sa'mall Management). Estab. 1979. Publishes 100 songs/year; publishes 25-40 new songwriters/year. Hires staff writers. Pays standard royalty.

Affiliates Kellijai Music (ASCAP), Pollyann Music (ASCAP), Ja'Nikki Songs (BMI), Velma Songs International (BMI), Lonnvanness Songs (SESAC), PPL Music (ASCAP), Zettitalia Music, Butternut Music (BMI), Zett Two Music (ASCAP), Plus Publishing and Zett One Songs (BMI).

How to Contact *Write first and obtain permission to submit.* No phone calls. Prefers CD, cassette, or videocassette with 4 songs and lyric and lead sheet. Include SASE. Responds in 2 months.

Music Published "Return of the Players" (album) by Juz-Cuz 2004 on PPL; "Believe" (single by J. Jarrett/S. Cuseo) from *Time* (album), recorded by Lejenz (pop), released 2001 on PRL/Credence; *Rainbow Gypsy Child* (album), written and recorded by Riki Hendrix (rock), released 2001 on PRL/Sony; and "What's Up With That" (single by Brandon James/Patrick Bouvier) from *Outcast* (album), recorded by Condottieré; (hip-hop), released 2001 on Bouvier.

Tips "Make those decisions—are you really a songwriter? Are you prepared to starve for your craft? Do you believe in delayed gratification? Are you commercial or do you write only for yourself? Can you take rejection? Do you want to be the best? If so, contact us—if not, keep your day job."

⊘ PORTAGE MUSIC (BMI)

16634 Gannon Ave. W., Rosemount MN 55068. (952)432-5737. E-mail: olrivers@ earthlink.net. President: Larry LaPole. Music publisher. Publishes 0-5 songs/year. Pays standard royalty.

How to Contact *Call or e-mail first for permission to submit.*

Music Mostly **country** and **country rock**. Published "Lost Angel," "Think It Over" and "Congratulations to Me" (by L. Lapole), all recorded by Trashmen on Sundazed.

Tips "Keep songs short, simple and upbeat with positive theme."

⊡ PRESCRIPTION COMPANY (BMI)

Box 222249, Great Neck NY 11021. (415)553-8540. E-mail: therxco@yahoo.com. President: David F. Gasman. Vice President of Sales: Bruce Brennan. Vice President of Finance: Robert Murphy. Music publisher and record producer. Staff size: 7. Pays standard royalty.

- Also see the listing for The Prescription Co. in the Record Producers section of this book.

How to Contact *Write or call first and obtain permission to submit.* Prefers cassette with any number of songs and lyric sheet. "Send all submissions with SASE (or no returns)." Responds in 1 month.

Music Mostly **bluegrass**, **blues**, **children's** and **country**, **dance-oriented**; also **easy listening**, **folk**, **jazz**, **MOR**, **progressive**, **R&B**, **rock**, **soul** and **top 40/pop**. Published "The World's Most Dangerous Man," "Here Comes Trouble" and "Automated People" (singles by D.F. Gasman) from *Special EP No. 1* (album), all recorded by Medicine Mike (rock), released 2003 on Prescription.

Tips "Songs should be good and written to last. Forget fads—we want songs that'll sound as good in ten years as they do today. Organization, communication and exploration of form are as essential as message (and sincerity matters, too)."

⊡ ⊡ QUARK, INC.

P.O. Box 452, Newtown, CT 06470. (917)687-9988. E-mail: quarkent@aol.com. **Contact:** Curtis Urbina, manager. Music publisher, record company (Quark Records) and record producer (Curtis Urbina). Estab. 1984. Publishes 12 songs/year; 2 new songwriters/year. Staff size: 4. Pays standard royalty.

Affiliates Quarkette Music (BMI), Freedurb Music (ASCAP), and Quark Records.

How to Contact Prefers CD only with 2 songs. No cassettes. Include SASE. Responds in 2 months.

Film & TV Places 10 songs in film/year. Music Supervisor: Curtis Urbina.

Music Pop. Does not want anything short of a hit.

⊡ ⊘ RAINBOW MUSIC CORP.

45 E. 66 St., New York NY 10021. (212)988-4619. Fax: (212)861-9079. E-mail: fscam45@ aol.com. **Contact:** Fred Stuart, vice president. Music publisher. Estab. 1990. Publishes 25 songs/year. Staff size: 2. Pays standard royalty.

Affiliates Tri-Circle (ASCAP).

How to Contact *Only accepts material referred by a reputable industry source.* Prefers CD with 2 songs and lyric sheet. Include SASE. Responds in 1 week.

Film & TV Published "You Wouldn't Lie To An Angel, Would Ya?" (single by Diane Lampert/Paul Overstreet) from Lady of the Evening (album), recorded by Ben te Boe (country), released 2003 on Mega International Records; "Gonna Give Lovin' A Try" (single by Cannonball Adderley/Diane Lampert/Nat Adderley) from The Axelrod Chronicles (album), recorded by Randy Crawford (jazz), released 2003 on Fantasy Records; "Breaking Bread" (single by Diane Lampert/Paul Overstreet) from Unearthed (album), recorded by Johnny Cash (country), released 2003 on Lost Highway Records; "Gonna Give Lovin' A Try" (single by Cannonball Adderley/Diane Lampert/Nat Adderley) from Day Dreamin' (album), recorded by Laverne Butler (jazz), released 2002 on Chesky Records; "Nothin' Shakin' (But the Leaves on the Trees)" (single by Diane Lampert;John Gluck, Jr./Eddie Fontaine/Cirino Colcrai) recorded by the Beatles, from *Live at the BBC* (album).

Music Mostly **pop**, **R&B** and **country**; also **jazz**. Published "Break It To Me Gently" (single by Diane Lampert/Joe Seneca) from *TIME/LIFE* compilations *Queens of Country* (2004), *Classic Country* (2003), and *Glory Days of Rock 'N Roll* (2002), recorded by Brenda Lee.

⊠ RAZOR & TIE ENTERTAINMENT

214 Sullivan St., Suite 4A, New York NY 10012. (212)473-9173. E-mail: info@ razorandtiemusicpublishing.com. Website: www.razorandtiemusicpublishing.com Music publisher.

How to Contact *Does not accept unsolicited material.*

Music Songwriters represented include Natalie Grant, Phillip LaRue, Matisyahu, Drive-By Truckers, Dave Barnes, Melinda Watts, and many more.

▢ RED SUNDOWN MUSIC (BMI)

1920 Errel Dowlen Rd., Pleasant View TN 37146. (615)746-0844. E-mail: rsdr@bellsouth. net. **Contact:** Ruby Perry.

How to Contact *Does not accept unsolicited submissions.* Submit CD and cover letter. Does not return submissions.

Music Country, **rock**, and **pop**. Does not want rap or hip-hop. Published "Take A Heart" (single by Kyle Pierce) from *Take Me With You* (album), recorded by Tammy Lee (country) released in 1998 on Red Sundown Records.

☑ ROCKFORD MUSIC CO. (ASCAP, BMI)

150 West End Ave., Suite 6-D, New York NY 10023. **Contact:** Danny Darrow, manager. Music publisher, record company (Mighty Records), record and video tape producer (Danny Darrow). Publishes 1-3 songs/year; publishes 1-3 new songwriters/year. Staff size: 3. Pays standard royalty.

Affiliates Corporate Music Publishing Company (ASCAP), Stateside Music Company (BMI), and Rockford Music Co. (BMI).

How to Contact Submit demo by mail. Unsolicited submissions are OK. "No phone calls and do not write for permission to submit." 3 songs and lyric sheet. Does not return material. Responds in 2 weeks.

Music Mostly **MOR** and **top 40/pop**; also **adult pop**, **country**, **adult rock**, **dance-oriented**, **easy listening**, **folk** and **jazz**. Does not want rap. Published "Look to the Wind" (single by Peggy Stewart/Danny Darrow) from *Falling in Love* (album), recorded by Danny Darrow (movie theme); "Doomsday" (single by Robert Lee Lowery/Danny Darrow) from *Doomsday* (album), recorded by Danny Darrow (euro jazz), all released 2004 on Mighty Records; and "Telephones" (single Robert Lee Lowery/Danny Darrow) from *Telephones* (album), and "Love to Dance" (single by Robert Lee Lowery/Danny Darrow) from *Love to Dance* (album), both recorded by Danny Darrow (trance dance), released 2006 on Mighty Records.

Tips "Listen to Top 40 and write current lyrics and music."

☐ SANDALPHON MUSIC PUBLISHING (BMI)

P.O. Box 29110, Portland OR 97296. (503)957-3929. E-mail: jackrabbit01@comcast.net. **Contact:** Ruth Otey, president. Music publisher, record company (Sandalphon Records), and management agency (Sandalphon Management). Estab. 2005. Staff size: 2. Pays standard royalty of 50%.

How to Contact Submit demo by mail. Unsolicited submissions are OK. Prefers cassette or CD with 1-5 songs, lyric sheet, and cover letter. Include SASE or SAE and IRC for outside United States. Responds in 6-8 weeks.

Music Mostly **rock**, **country**, and **alternative**; also **pop**, **blues**, and **gospel**.

☐ SILICON MUSIC PUBLISHING CO.

222 Tulane St., Garland TX 75043-2239. President: Gene Summers. Vice President: Deanna L. Summers. Public Relations: Steve Summers. Music publisher and record company (Front Row Records). Estab. 1965. Publishes 10-20 songs/year; publishes 2-3 new songwriters/year. Pays standard royalty.

- Also see the listing for Front Row Records in the Record Companies section of this book.

How to Contact Submit demo package by mail. Unsolicited submissions are OK. Prefers cassette with 1-2 songs. Does not return material. Responds ASAP.

Music Publishers

Music Mostly **rockabilly** and **'50s material**; also **old-time blues/country** and **MOR**. Published "Rockaboogie Shake" (single by James McClung) from *Rebels and More* (album), recorded by Lennerockers (rockabilly), released 2002 on Lenne (Germany); "Be-Bop City" (single by Dan Edwards), "So" (single by Dea Summers/Gene Summers), and "Little Lu Ann" (single by James McClung) from *Do Right Daddy* (album), recorded by Gene Summers (rockabilly/'50s rock and roll), released 2004 on Enviken (Sweden).

Tips "We are very interested in '50s rock and rockabilly original masters for release through overseas affiliates. If you are the owner of any '50s masters, contact us first! We have releases in Holland, Switzerland, United Kingdom, Belgium, France, Sweden, Norway and Australia. We have the market if you have the tapes! Our staff writers include James McClung, Gary Mears (original Casuals), Robert Clark, Dea Summers, Shawn Summers, Joe Hardin Brown, Bill Becker and Dan Edwards."

⊠ ⊘ SILVER BLUE MUSIC/OCEANS BLUE MUSIC (ASCAP, BMI)

3940 Laurel Canyon Blvd., Suite 441, Studio City CA 91604. (818)980-9588. E-mail: jdiamond20@aol.com. **Contact:** Joel Diamond, president. Music publisher and record producer (Joel Diamond Entertainment). Estab. 1971. Publishes 50 songs/year. Pays standard royalty.

How to Contact *Does not accept unsolicited material.* "No tapes returned."

Film & TV Places 4 songs in film and 6 songs in TV/year.

Music Mostly **pop** and **R&B**; also **rap** and **classical**. Produced and managed The 5 Browns-3 #1 CDs on Sony. Published "After the Lovin" (by Bernstein/Adams), recorded by Engelbert Humperdinck; "This Moment in Time" (by Alan Bernstein/Ritchie Adams), recorded by Engelbert Humperdinck. Other artists include David Hasselhoff, Kaci (Curb Records), Ike Turner, Andrew Dice Clay, Gloria Gaynor, Tony Orlando, Katie Cassidy, and Vaneza.

⊕ ⊘ SINUS MUSIK PRODUKTION, ULLI WEIGEL

Geitnerweg 30a, D-12209, Berlin Germany. +49-30-7159050. Fax: +49-30-71590522. E-mail: ulli.weigel@arcor.de. Website: www.ulli-weigel.de. **Contact:** Ulli Weigel, owner. Music publisher, record producer and screenwriter. Wrote German lyrics for more than 500 records. Member: GEMA, GVL. Estab. 1976. Publishes 20 songs/year; publishes 6 new songwriters/year. Staff size: 3. Pays standard royalty.

Affiliates Sinus Musikverlag H.U. Weigel GmbH.

How to Contact Submit demo package by mail. Prefers CD or cassette with up to 10 songs and lyric sheets. If you want to send mp3 attachments, you should contact me before. Attachments from unknown senders will not be opened. Responds in 2 months by email. "If material should be returned, please send 2 International Reply Coupons (IRC) for cassettes and 3 for a CD. No stamps."

Music Mostly **rock**, **pop** and **New Age**; also **background music for movies and audio**

books. Published "Simple Story" (single), recorded by MAANAM on RCA (Polish rock); *Die Musik Maschine* (album by Klaus Lage), recorded by CWN Productions on Hansa Records (pop/German), "Villa Woodstock" (film music/comedy) Gebrueder Blattschuss, Juergen Von Der Lippe, Hans Werner Olm (2005).

Tips "Take more time working on the melody than on the instrumentation. I am also looking for master-quality recordings for non-exclusive release on my label (and to use them as soundtracks for multimedia projects, TV and movie scripts I am working on)."

☒ ☒ ☒ S.M.C.L. PRODUCTIONS, INC.

P.O. Box 84, Boucherville QC J4B 5E6 Canada. (450)641-2266. **Contact:** Christian Lefort, president. Music publisher and record company. SOCAN. Estab. 1968. Publishes 25 songs/year. Pays standard royalty.

Affiliates A.Q.E.M. Ltee, Bag Music, C.F. Music, Big Bazaar Music, Sunrise Music, Stage One Music, L.M.S. Music, ITT Music, Machine Music, Dynamite Music, Cimafilm, Coincidence Music, Music and Music, Cinemusic Inc., Cinafilm, Editions La Fete Inc., Groupe Concept Musique, Editions Dorimen, C.C.H. Music (PRO/SDE) and Lavagot Music.

How to Contact *Write first and obtain permission to submit.* Prefers CD with 4-12 songs and lead sheet. SAE and IRC. Responds in 3 months.

Film & TV Places songs in film and TV. Recently published songs in French-Canadian TV series and films, including *Young Ivanhoe*, *Twist of Terror*, *More Tales of the City*, *Art of War*, *Lance & Comte (Nouvelle Generation)*, *Turtle Island* (TV series), *Being Dorothy*, *The Hidden Fortress*, *Lance et Compte:La Revanche* (TV series), and *A Vos Marques, Party* (film).

Music Mostly **dance**, **easy listening** and **MOR**; also **top 40/pop** and **TV and movie soundtracks**. Published *Always and Forever* (album by Maurice Jarre/Nathalie Carien), recorded by N. Carsen on BMG Records (ballad); *Au Nom De La Passion* (album), written and recorded by Alex Stanke on Select Records.

☒ SME PUBLISHING GROUP (ASCAP, BMI)

P.O. Box 1150, Tuttle OK 73089. (405)381-3754. Fax: (405)381-3754. E-mail: smemusic@ juno.com. Website: www.smepublishinggroup.com. Professional Managers: Cliff Shelder (southern gospel); Sharon Kinard (country gospel). Music publisher. Estab. 1994. Publishes 6 songs/year; publishes 2 new songwriters/year. Staff size: 2. Pays standard royalty.

Affiliates Touch of Heaven Music (ASCAP) and SME Music (BMI).

How to Contact Submit demo package by mail. Unsolicited submissions are OK. Prefers CD with 3 songs and lyric sheet. Make sure tapes and CDs are labeled and include song title, writer's name, e-mail address, and phone number. Do not send SASE. Does not return or critique material. Responds only if interested.

Music Mostly **Southern gospel**, **country gospel** and **Christian country**. Does not want Christian rap, rock and roll, and hard-core country. Released "Come See A Man" (single by Mike Spanhanks) from *God Writes Our Story* (album), recorded by The Jody Brown Indian Family (southern gospel) on Crossroads Records; "Look Who's in the Ship" (Single by Mike Spanhanks) from *How I Picture Me* (album), recorded by the Skyline Boys (Southern Gospel) on Journey Records; "What Kinda Car" (single by Quint Randle and Jeff Hinton) from *Heaven's Not that Far* (album) recorded by Joshua Creek (Christian country) on Covenant Records.

Tips "Always submit good quality demos. Never give up."

⊘ SONY/ATV MUSIC PUBLISHING (ASCAP, BMI, SESAC)

8 Music Square W., Nashville TN 37203. (615)726-8300. Fax: (615)242-3441. E-mail: info@sonyatv.com. Website: www.sonyatv.com. **Santa Monica**: 10635 Santa Monica Blvd., Suite 300, Los Angeles CA 90025. (310)441-1300. **New York**: 550 Madison Ave., 5th Floor, New York NY 10022. (212)833-7730.

How to Contact *Sony/ATV Music does not accept unsolicited submissions.*

⊕ ▧ ◌ SUCCES

Pijnderslaan 84, Dendermonde 9200 Belgium. (052)218 987. Fax: (052) 225 260. E-mail: deschuyteneer@hotmail.com. **Contact:** Deschuyteneer Hendrik, director. Music publisher, record company and record producer. Estab. 1978. Publishes 400 songs/year. Hires staff songwriters. Staff size: 4. Pays standard royalty.

How to Contact Submit demo by mail. Unsolicited submissions are OK. Prefers cassette or VHS videocassette with 3 songs. SAE and IRC. Responds in 2 months.

Film & TV Places songs in TV. Recently released "Werkloos" (by Deschuyteneer), recorded by Jacques Vermeire in Jacques Vermeire Show.

Music Mostly **pop**, **dance** and **variety**; also **instrumental** and **rock**. Published "Hoe Moet Dat Nou" (single by Henry Spider), recorded by Monja (ballad), released 2001 on MN; "Liefde" (single by H. Spider), recorded by Rudy Silvester (rock), released 2001 on Scorpion; and "Bel Me Gauw" (single by H. Spider), recorded by Guy Dumon (ballad), released 2001 on BM Records.

▧ ◌ THISTLE HILL (BMI)

P.O. Box 707, Hermitage TN 37076. (615)889-7105. E-mail: billyherzig@hotmail.com. **Contact:** Arden Miller.

How to Contact Submit demo by mail. Unsolicited submissions OK. Prefers CD with 3-10 songs. *No* lyric sheets. Responds only if interested.

Music Country, **pop**, and **rock**; also **songs for film/TV**. Published "Angry Heart " (single) from *See What You Wanna See* (album), recorded by Radney Foster (Americana); and "I Wanna be Free" (single) from *I Wanna be Free* (album), recorded by Jordon MyCoskie

(Americana), released 2003 on Ah! Records; "Que Vamos Hacer" (single) from *Rachel Rodriguez* (album), recorded by Rachel Rodriguez.

○ TIKI ENTERPRISES, INC. (ASCAP, BMI)

195 S. 26th St., San Jose CA 95116. (408)286-9840. E-mail: onealproduction@juno.com. Website: www.onealprod.com. **Contact:** Gradie O'Neal, president. Professional Manager: Jeannine O'Neil. Music publisher, record company (Rowena Records) and record producer (Jeannine O'Neal and Gradie O'Neal). Estab. 1967. Publishes 40 songs/year; publishes 12 new songwriters/year. Staff size: 3. Pays standard royalty.

Affiliates Tooter Scooter Music (BMI), Janell Music (BMI) and O'Neal & Friend (ASCAP).

How to Contact Submit demo by mail. Unsolicited submissions are OK. Prefers CD with 3 songs and lyric or lead sheets. Include SASE. Responds in 2 weeks.

Music Mostly **country**, **Mexican**, **rock/pop**, **gospel**, **R&B** and **New Age**. Does not want atonal music. Published "You're Looking Good To Me" (single) from *A Rock 'N' Roll Love Story* (album), written and recorded by Warren R. Spalding (rock 'n' roll), released 2003-2004; "I Am Healed" (single) from *Faith On The Front Lines* (album), written and recorded by Jeannine O'Neal (praise music), released 2003-2004; and "It Amazes Me" (single by David Davis/Jeannine O'Neal) from *The Forgiven Project* (album), recorded by David Davis and Amber Littlefield, released 2003, all on Rowena Records.

Tips "For up-to-date published titles, review our Web site. Keep writing and sending songs in. Never give up—the next hit may be just around the bend."

☑ TOURMALINE MUSIC, INC. (BMI)

2831 Dogwood Place, Nashville TN 37204. (615)269-8682. Fax: (615)269-8929. Website: www.songsfortheplanet.com. **Contact:** Justin Peters, president. Music publisher. Estab. 1980.

Affiliates Justin Peters Music (BMI), LITA Music (ASCAP) and Platinum Planet Music (BMI).

How to Contact Submit demo package by mail. Unsolicited submissions are OK. Prefers CD with 5 songs and lyric sheet. Does not return material. "Place code '2010' on each envelope submissions."

Music Mostly **rock and roll**, **classy alternative**, **adult contemporary**, **classic rock**, **country**, **Spanish gospel**, and some **Christmas music**. Published "Making War In The Heavenlies," written by George Searcy, recorded by Ron Kenoly (Integrity); "The Hurt is Worth The Chance," by Justin Peters/Billy Simon, recorded by Gary Chapman on RCA/BMG Records, and "The Bottom Line," by Art Craig, Drew Bourke, and Justin Peters, recorded by Charley Pride (Music City Records).

◪ ◿ TOWER MUSIC GROUP (ASCAP, BMI)

30 Music Square W., Suite 103, Nashville TN 37203. (615)401-7111. Fax: (615)401-7119. E-mail: castlerecords@castlerecords.com. Website: www.castlerecords.com. **Contact:** Dave Sullivan, A&R Director. Professional Managers: Ed Russell; Eddie Bishop. Music publisher, record company (Castle Records) and record producer. Estab. 1969. Publishes 50 songs/year; publishes 10 new songwriters/year. Staff size: 15. Pays standard royalty.

Affiliates Cat's Alley Music (ASCAP) and Alley Roads Music (BMI).

How to Contact See submission policy on Web site. Prefers CD with 3 songs and lyric sheet. Does not return material. "You may follow up via e-mail." Responds in 3 months only if interested.

Film & TV Places 2 songs in film and 26 songs in TV/year. Published "Run Little Girl" (by J.R. Jones/Eddie Ray), recorded by J.R. Jones in Roadside Prey.

Music Mostly **country** and **R&B**; also **blues**, **pop** and **gospel**. Published "If You Broke My Heart" (single by Condrone) from *If You Broke My Heart* (album), recorded by Kimberly Simon (country); "I Wonder Who's Holding My Angel Tonight" (single) from Up Above (album), recorded by Carl Butler (country); and "Psychedelic Fantasy" (single by Paul Sullivan/Priege) from *The Hip Hoods* (album), recorded by The Hip Hoods (power/ metal/y2k), all released 2001 on Castle Records. "Visit our Web site for an up-to-date listing of published songs."

Tips "Please follow our Submission Policy at our website www.CastleRecords.com."

⊕ ◪ ◿ TRANSAMERIKA MUSIKVERLAG KG

Wilhelmstrasse 10, Bad Schwartau 23611 Germany. (00) (49) 4512 1530. E-mail: transamerika@online.de. Website: www.TRANSAMERIKAmusik.de. General Manager: Pia Kaminsky. **Hamburg:** Knauerstr 1, 20249 Hamburg, Germany. Phone: 0049-40-46 06 3394. E-mail: transamerika@t-online.de. License Manager: Kirsten Jung. Member: GEMA, KODA, NCB. Music publisher and administrator. Estab. 1978. Staff size: 3. Pays 50% royalty if releasing a record; 85% if only administrating.

Affiliates Administrative agreements with: German Fried Music, Rock and Roll Stew Music (UK), Origin Network PLC Australia Pty. Ltd. (Sydney), MCS Music America, Inc. (USA), Native Tongue Music Pty. (New Zealand), Pacific Electric Music Publishing (USA), Evolution Music Partners (USA).

How to Contact "We accept only released materials—no demos!" Submit CD or MP3. Does not return material. Responds only if interested.

Film & TV administration.

Music Mostly **pop**; also **rock**, **country**, **reggae,** and especially **film music**.

Tips "We are specializing in administering (filing, registering, licensing and finding unclaimed royalties, and dealing with counter-claims) publishers worldwide."

⬚ TRANSITION MUSIC CORPORATION (ASCAP, BMI, SESAC)

P.O. Box 2586, Toluca Lake CA 91610. (323)860-7074. Fax: (323)860-7986. E-mail: onestopmus@aol.com. Website: www.transitionmusic.com. Creative Director: Todd Johnson. Chief Administrator: Mike Dobson. Music publisher. Estab. 1998. Publishes 250 songs/year; publishes 50 new songwriters/year. Variable royalty based on song placement and writer.

Affiliates Pushy Publishing (ASCAP), Creative Entertainment Music (BMI) and One Stop Shop Music (SESAC).

How to Contact Address submissions to: New Submissions Dept. Unsolicited submissions are accepted. Prefers CD with no more than 3 songs per. **Responses will not be given due to the high volume of submissions daily. Please do not call/email to inquire about us receiving your submission. TMC will only contact who they intend on signing**.

Film & TV "TMC provides music for all forms of visual media. Mainly television. "Music-all styles.

Tips "Supply master quality material with great songs."

⬚ UNIVERSAL MUSIC PUBLISHING (ASCAP, BMI, SESAC)

2220 Colorado Av., Santa Monica CA 90404. (310)235-4700. **New York**: 1755 Broadway, 3rd Floor, New York NY 10019. (212)841-8000. **Tennessee:** 1904 Adelicia St., Nashville TN 37212. (615)340-5400. Website: www.umusicpub.com or www.synchexpress.com.

- In 1999, MCA Music Publishing and PolyGram Music Publishing merged into Universal Music Publishing.

How to Contact *Does not accept unsolicited submissions.*

⬚ UNKNOWN SOURCE MUSIC (ASCAP)

120-4d Carver Loop, Bronx NY 10475. E-mail: unknownsourcemusic@hotmail.com. **Contact:** James Johnson, A&R. Music publisher, record company (Smokin Ya Productions) and record producer. Estab. 1993. Publishes 5-10 songs/year; publishes 5-10 new songwriters/year. Hires staff songwriters. Staff size: 10. Pays standard royalty.

Affiliates Sundance Records (ASCAP), Critique Records, WMI Records, and Cornell Entertainment.

How to Contact *Send e-mail first then mail.* Unsolicited submissions are OK. Prefers mp3s. Responds within 6 weeks.

Music Mostly **rap/hip-hop**, **R&B**, and **alternative**. Published "LAH" recorded by Force Dog; "Changed My World" recorded by Crysto.

Tips "Keep working with us, be patient, be willing to work hard. Send your very best work."

⬚ VAAM MUSIC GROUP (BMI)

P.O. Box 29550, Hollywood CA 90029-0550. E-mail: pmarti3636@aol.com. Website:

www.VaamMusic.com. **Contact:** Pete Martin, president. Music publisher and record producer (Pete Martin/Vaam Productions). Estab. 1967. Publishes 9-24 new songs/year. Pays standard royalty.

- Also see the listings for Blue Gem Records in the Record Companies section of this book and Pete Martin/Vaam Music Productions in the record Producers section of this book.

Affiliates Pete Martin Music (ASCAP).

How to Contact Send CD or cassette with 2 songs and lyric sheet. Include SASE. Responds in 1 month. "Small packages only."

Music Mostly **top 40/pop**, **country**, and **R&B**. "Submitted material must have potential of reaching top 5 on charts."

Tips "Study the top 10 charts in the style you write. Stay current and up-to-date with today's market."

☑ VINE CREEK MUSIC (ASCAP)

P.O. Box 171143, Nashville TN 37217. (615)366-1326. Fax: (615)367-1073. E-mail: vinecreek1@aol.com. Website: www.myspace.com/vinecreekmusic. **Contact:** Darlene Austin, Brenda Madden. Administration: Jayne Negri. Creative Director: Brenda Madden.

How to Contact *Vine Creek Music does not accept unsolicited submissions.* "Only send material of good competitive quality. We do not return tapes/CDs unless SASE is enclosed."

☐ WALKERBOUT MUSIC GROUP (ASCAP, BMI, SESAC)

(formerly The Goodland Music Group, Inc.), P.O. Box 24454, Nashville TN 37202. (615)269-7071. Fax: (615)269-0131. E-mail: info@walkerboutmusic.com. Website: www.walkerboutmusic.com. **Contact:** Matt Watkins, publishing coordinator. Estab. 1988. Publishes 50 songs/year; 5-10 new songwriters/year. Pays standard royalty.

Affiliates Goodland Publishing Company (ASCAP), Marc Isle Music (BMI), Gulf Bay Publishing (SESAC), Con Brio Music (BMI), Wiljex Publishing (ASCAP), Concorde Publishing (SESAC).

How to Contact "Please see Web site for submission information."

Music Mostly **country/Christian** and **adult contemporary**.

☑ ☑ WARNER/CHAPPELL MUSIC, INC.

10585 Santa Monica Blvd., Third Floor, Los Angeles CA 90025. (310)441-8600. Fax: (310)470-3232. **New York:** 1290 Avenue of the Americas, 23rd floor, New York NY 10104. (212)707-2600. Fax: (212)405-5428. **Nashville:** 20 Music Square E., Nashville TN 37203. (615)733-1880. Fax: (615)733-1885. Website: www.warnerchappell.com. Music publisher.

How to Contact *Warner/Chappell does not accept unsolicited material.*

☑ WEAVER OF WORDS MUSIC (BMI)

(administered by Bug Music), P.O. Box 803, Tazewell VA 24651. (276)988-6267. E-mail: cooksong@verizon.net. Website: www.weaverofwordsmusic.com. **Contact:** H.R. Cook, president. Music publisher and record company (Fireball Records). Estab. 1978. Publishes 12 songs/year. Pays standard royalty.

Affiliates Weaver of Melodies Music (ASCAP).

How to Contact Submit demo by mail. Unsolicited submissions are OK. Prefers CD with 3 songs and lyric or lead sheets. "We prefer CD submissions but will accept mp3s- limit 2." Include SASE. Responds in 3 weeks.

Music Mostly **country**, **pop**, **bluegrass**, **R&B**, **film and television** and **rock**. Published "Zero To Love" (single by H. Cook/Brian James Deskins/Rick Tiger) from *It's Just The Night* (album), recorded by Del McCoury Band (bluegrass), released 2003 on McCoury Music; "Muddy Water" (Alan Johnston) from *The Midnight Call* (album), recorded by Don Rigsby (bluegrass), released 2003 on Sugar Hill; "Ol Brown Suitcase" (H.R. Cook) from *Lonesome Highway* (album), recorded by Josh Williams (bluegrass), released 2004 on Pinecastle; and "Mansions of Kings" from *Cherry Holmes II* (album), recorded by IBMA 2005 Entertainer of the Year Cherry Holmes (bluegrass), released 2007 on Skaggs Family Records.

⊕ ◻ BERTHOLD WENGERT (MUSIKVERLAG)

Hauptstrasse 36, Pfinztal-Söllingen, D-76327 Germany. **Contact:** Berthold Wengert. Music publisher. Pays standard GEMA royalty.

How to Contact Prefers cassette and complete score for piano. SAE and IRC. Responds in 1 month. "No cassette returns!"

Music Mostly **light music** and **pop**.

☑ YOUR BEST SONGS PUBLISHING (ASCAP)

1402 Auburn Way N, Suite 396, Auburn WA 98002. (877)672-2520. **Contact:** John Markovich, general manager. Music publisher. Estab. 1988. Publishes 1-5 songs/year; publishes 1-3 new songwriters/year. Query for royalty terms.

How to Contact *Write first and obtain permission to submit.* Prefers CD with 1-3 songs and lyric sheet. "Submit your 1-3 best songs per type of music. Use separate CDs per music type and indicate music type on each CD." Include SASE. Responds in 3 months.

Music Mostly **country**, **rock/blues**, and **pop/rock**; also **progressive**, **A/C**, some **heavy metal** and **New Age**. Published "Sea of Dreams," written and recorded by J.C. Mark on Cybervoc Productions, Inc. (New Age).

Tips "We just require good lyrics, good melodies and good rhythm in a song. We absolutely do not want music without a decent melodic structure. We do not want lyrics with foul language or lyrics that do not inspire some form of imaginative thought."

ADDITIONAL MUSIC PUBLISHERS

The following companies are also music publishers, but their listings are found in other sections of the book. Read the listings for submission information.

Record Companies

Record companies release and distribute records, cassettes and CDs—the tangible products of the music industry. They sign artists to recording contracts, decide what songs those artists will record, and determine which songs to release. They are also responsible for providing recording facilities, securing producers and musicians, and overseeing the manufacture, distribution and promotion of new releases.

MAJOR LABELS & INDEPENDENT LABELS

Major labels and independent labels—what's the difference between the two?

The majors

As of this writing, there are four major record labels, commonly referred to as the "Big 4":

- **The EMI Group** (Capitol Music Group, Angel Music Group, Astralwerks, Chrysalis Records, etc.)
- **Sony BMG** (Columbia Records, Epic Records, RCA Records, Arista Records, J Records, Provident Label Group, etc.)
- **Universal Music Group** (Universal Records, Interscope/Geffen/A&M, Island/Def Jam, Dreamworks Records, MCA Nashville Records, Verve Music Group, etc.)
- **Warner Music Group** (Atlantic Records, Bad Boy, Asylum Records, Warner Bros. Records, Maverick Records, Sub Pop, etc.)

Each of the "Big 4" is a large publicly-traded corporation beholden to shareholders and quarterly profit expectations. This means the major labels have greater financial resources and promotional muscle than a smaller "indie" label, but it's also harder to get signed to a major. A big major label may also expect more contractual control over an artist or band's sound and image.

As shown in the above list, they also each act as umbrella organizations for numerous other well-known labels—former major labels in their own right, well-respected former independent/boutique labels, as well as subsidiary "vanity" labels fronted by successful major label recording artists. Each major label also has its own related worldwide product distribution system, and many independent labels will contract with the majors for distribution into stores.

If a label is distributed by one of these major companies, you can be assured any release coming out on that label has a large distribution network behind it. It will most likely be sent to most major retail stores in the United States.

The independents

Independent labels go through smaller distribution companies to distribute their product. They usually don't have the ability to deliver records in massive quantities as the major distributors do. However, that doesn't mean independent labels aren't able to have hit records just like their major counterparts. A record label's distributors are found in the listings after the **Distributed by** heading.

Which do I submit to?

Many of the companies listed in this section are independent labels. They are usually the most receptive to receiving material from new artists. Major labels spend more money than most other segments of the music industry; the music publisher, for instance, pays only for items such as salaries and the costs of making demos. Record companies, at great financial risk, pay for many more services, including production, manufacturing and promotion. Therefore, they must be very selective when signing new talent. Also, the continuing fear of copyright infringement suits has closed avenues to getting new material heard by the majors. Most don't listen to unsolicited submissions, period. Only songs recommended by attorneys, managers and producers who record company employees trust and respect are being heard by A&R people at major labels (companies with a referral policy have a ⊘ preceding their listing). But that doesn't mean all major labels are closed to new artists. With a combination of a strong local following, success on an independent label (or strong sales of an independently produced and released album) and the right connections, you could conceivably get an attentive audience at a major label.

But the competition is fierce at the majors, so you shouldn't overlook independent labels. Since they're located all over the country, indie labels are easier to contact and can be important in building a local base of support for your music (consult the Geographic Index at the back of the book to find out which companies are located near you). Independent labels usually concentrate on a specific type of music, which will help you target those companies your submissions should be sent to. And since the staff at an indie label is smaller, there are fewer channels to go through to get your music heard by the decision makers in the company.

HOW RECORD COMPANIES WORK

Independent record labels can run on a small staff, with only a handful of people running

The Case for Independents

Tip

If you're interested in getting a major label deal, it makes sense to look to independent record labels to get your start. Independent labels are seen by many as a stepping stone to a major recording contract. Very few artists are signed to a major label at the start of their careers; usually, they've had a few independent releases that helped build their reputation in the industry. Major labels watch independent labels closely to locate up-and-coming bands and new trends. In the current economic atmosphere at major labels—with extremely high overhead costs for developing new bands and the fact that only 10% of acts on major labels actually make any profit—they're not willing to risk everything on an unknown act. Most major labels won't even consider signing a new act that hasn't had some indie success.

But independents aren't just farming grounds for future major label acts; many bands have long term relationships with indies, and prefer it that way. While they may not be able to provide the extensive distribution and promotion that a major label can (though there are exceptions), indie labels can help an artist become a regional success, and may even help the performer to see a profit as well. With the lower overhead and smaller production costs an independent label operates on, it's much easier to "succeed" on an indie label than on a major.

the day-to-day business. Major record labels are more likely to be divided into the following departments: A&R, sales, marketing, promotion, product management, artist development, production, finance, business/legal and international.

- The *A&R department* is staffed with A&R representatives who search out new talent. They go out and see new bands, listen to demo tapes, and decide which artists to sign. They also look for new material for already signed acts, match producers with artists and oversee recording projects. Once an artist is signed by an A&R rep and a record is recorded, the rest of the departments at the company come into play.

- The *sales department* is responsible for getting a record into stores. They make sure record stores and other outlets receive enough copies of a record to meet consumer demand.

- The *marketing department* is in charge of publicity, advertising in magazines and other media, promotional videos, album cover artwork, in-store displays, and any other means of getting the name and image of an artist to the public.

- The *promotion department*'s main objective is to get songs from a new album played on the radio. They work with radio programmers to make sure a product gets airplay.

- The *product management department* is the ringmaster of the sales, marketing and promotion departments, assuring that they're all going in the same direction when promoting a new release.
- The *artist development department* is responsible for taking care of things while an artist is on tour, such as setting up promotional opportunities in cities where an act is performing.
- The *production department* handles the actual manufacturing and pressing of the record and makes sure it gets shipped to distributors in a timely manner.
- People in the *finance department* compute and distribute royalties, as well as keep track of expenses and income at the company.
- The *business/legal department* takes care of contracts, not only between the record company and artists but with foreign distributors, record clubs, etc.
- And finally, the *international department* is responsible for working with international companies for the release of records in other countries.

LOCATING A RECORD LABEL

With the abundance of record labels out there, how do you go about finding one that's right for the music you create? First, it helps to know exactly what kind of music a record label releases. Become familiar with the records a company has released, and see if they fit in with what you're doing. Each listing in this section details the type of music a particular record company is interested in releasing. You will want to refer to the Category Index on page 370 to help you find those companies most receptive to the type of music you write. You should only approach companies open to your level of experience (see A Sample Listing Decoded on page 12). Visiting a company's website can also provide valuable information about a company's philosophy, the artists on the label and the music they work with.

Networking

Recommendations by key music industry people are an important part of making contacts with record companies. Songwriters must remember that talent alone does not guarantee success in the music business. You must be recognized through contacts, and the only way to make contacts is through networking. Networking is the process of building an interconnecting web of acquaintances within the music business. The more industry people you meet, the larger your contact base becomes, and the better are your chances of meeting someone with the clout to get your demo into the hands of the right people. If you want to get your music heard by key A&R representatives, networking is imperative.

Networking opportunities can be found anywhere industry people gather. A good place to meet key industry people is at regional and national music conferences and workshops. There are many held all over the country for all types of music (see the Workshops and Conferences section for more information). You should try to attend at least one or two of these events each year; it's a great way to increase the number and quality of your music industry contacts.

Icons

For More Info

For more instructional information on the listings in this book, including explanations of symbols ( ), read the article *How To Use Songwriter's Market* on page 7.

Creating a buzz

Another good way to attract A&R people is to make a name for yourself as an artist. By starting your career on a local level and building it from there, you can start to cultivate a following and prove to labels that you can be a success. A&R people figure if an act can be successful locally, there's a good chance they could be successful nationally. Start getting booked at local clubs, and start a mailing list of fans and local media. Once you gain some success on a local level, branch out. All this attention you're slowly gathering, this "buzz" you're generating, will not only get to your fans but to influential people in the music industry as well.

SUBMITTING TO RECORD COMPANIES

When submitting to a record company, major or independent, a professional attitude is imperative. Be specific about what you are submitting and what your goals are. If you are strictly a songwriter and the label carries a band you believe would properly present your song, state that in your cover letter. If you are an artist looking for a contract, showcase your strong points as a performer. Whatever your goals are, follow submission guidelines closely, be as neat as possible and include a top-notch demo. If you need more information concerning a company's requirements, write or call for more details. (For more information on submitting your material, see the article Where Should I Send My Songs? on page 10 and Demo Recordings: What Should I Know? on page 14.)

RECORD COMPANY CONTRACTS

Once you've found a record company that is interested in your work, the next step is signing a contract. Independent label contracts are usually not as long and complicated as major label ones, but they are still binding, legal contracts. Make sure the terms are in the best interest of both you and the label. Avoid anything in your contract that you feel is too restrictive. It's important to have your contract reviewed by a competent entertainment lawyer. A basic recording contract can run from 40-100 pages, and you need a lawyer to help you understand it. A lawyer will also be essential in helping you negotiate a deal that is in your best interest.

Recording contracts cover many areas, and just a few of the things you will be asked to consider will be: What royalty rate is the record label willing to pay you? What kind of advance are they offering? How many records will the company commit to? Will they offer tour support? Will they provide a budget for video? What sort of a recording budget are they offering? Are they asking you to give up any publishing rights? Are they offering you a publishing advance? These are only a few of the complex issues raised by a recording contract, so it's vital to have an entertainment lawyer at your side as you negotiate.

ADDITIONAL RECORD COMPANIES

There are **more record companies** located in other sections of the book! On page 194 use the list of Additional Record Companies to find listings within other sections who are also record companies.

N ⊕ 4AD

Beggar's Group, 17-19 Alma Road, London UK SW18 1AA. 020 8870 9912. E-mail: 4AD@4AD.com. Website: www.4ad.com.

How to Contact Submit demo (CD or vinyl only) by mail, attention A&R, 4AD. "Sadly, there just aren't enough hours in the day to respond to everything that comes in. We'll only get in touch if we really like something."

Music Mostly rock, indie/alternative. Current artists include Blonde Redhead, Bon Iver, Camera Obscura, The Breeders, The National, TV On The Radio, and more.

⊏ 28 RECORDS

P.O. Box 88456, Los Angeles CA 90009-8456. E-mail: rec28@aol.com. Website: www.28records.com. **Contact:** Eric Diaz, president/CEO/A&R. Record company. Estab. 1994. Staff size: 1. Releases 2 LPs and 4 CDs/year. Pays 12% royalty to artists on contract; statutory rate to publisher per song on record.

Distributed By Rock Bottom-USA.

How to Contact Online submissions only. Unsolicited online submissions are OK. Send us your myspace links or Sonicbids EPK. Responds in 6 weeks.

Music Mostly **hard rock/modern rock**, **metal** and **alternative**; also **punk** and **death metal**. Released *Julian Day* (album), recorded by Helltown's Infamous Vandal (modern/hard rock); *Fractured Fairy Tales* (album), written and recorded by Eric Knight (modern/hard rock); and *Mantra* (album), recorded by Derek Cintron (modern rock), all on 28 Records.

Tips "Be patient and ready for the long haul. We strongly believe in nurturing you, the artist/songwriter. If you're willing to do what it takes, and have what it takes, we will do whatever it takes to get you to the next level. We are looking for artists to develop. We are a very small label but we are giving the attention that is a must for a new band as well as developed and established acts. Give us a call."

☑ ALTERNATIVE TENTACLES

Attn: New Materials, P.O. Box 419092, San Francisco CA 94141. (510) 596-8981. Fax: (510) 596-8982. E-mail: jello@alternativetentacles.com. Website: www.alternativetentacles.com. **Contact:** Jello Biafra. Estab. 1979. Staff size: 4. Releases 15-20 albums/year.

Distributed By Lumberjack/Mordam Records.

How to Contact Unsolicited submissions OK. Prefers CD or cassette. Does not return material. Responds only if interested. *"We accept demos by postal mail ONLY! We do not accept mp3s sent to us.* We will not go out and listen to your mp3s on Web sites. If you are interested in having ATR hear your music, you need to send us a CD, tape or vinyl. We cannot return your demos either, so please don't send us your originals or ask us to send them back. Sometimes Jello replies to people submitting demos; sometimes he doesn't. There is no way for us to check on your 'status', so please don't ask us."

Music Mostly **punk rock**, **spoken word**, **Brazilian hardcore**, **bent pop**, **faux-country**, and **assorted rock & roll**. Released *It's Not the Eat, It's the Humidity* (album), recorded by the Eat (punk); *Fuck World Trade* (album), recorded by Leftover Crack (punk); *Live from the Armed Madhouse* (album), recorded by Greg Palast (spoken word); *Dash Rip Rock* (album), recorded by Hee Haw Hell (southern country punk); *Homem Inimigo Do Homem* (album), recorded by Ratos De Parao (Brazilian hardcore). Other artists include Jello Biafra, The (International) Noise Conspiracy, Subhumans, Butthole Surfers, Dead Kennedys, DOA, Pansy Division, and Melvins.

☑ ANGEL RECORDS

150 Fifth Ave., 6th Floor, New York NY 10011. (212)786-8600. Website: www.angelrecords. com. Record company. Labels include EMI Classics, Manhattan Records, and Virgin Classics.

- Angel Records is a subsidiary of the EMI Group, one of the "Big 4" major labels. EMI is a British-based company.

Distributed By EMI Music Distribution.

How to Contact Angel/EMI Records does not accept unsolicited submissions.

Music Artists include Sarah Brightman, Sir Paul McCartney, and Bernadette Peters.

☑ ARIANA RECORDS

1312 S. Avenida Polar, Tucson AZ 85710. Website: www.arianarecords.net. **Contact:** James M. Gasper, president. Vice President (pop, rock): Tom Dukes. Partners: Tom Privett (funk, experimental, rock); Scott Smith (pop, rock, AOR). Labels include Smart Monkey Records, The MoleHole Studio, Chumway Studios. Record company, music publisher (Myko Music/BMI) and record producer. Estab. 1980. Releases 5 CDs a year and 1 compilation/year. Pays negotiable rates.

Distributed By LoneBoy Records London, The Yellow Record Company in Germany, and Groovetune Music distributors in Alberta, Canada.

How to Contact "Send finished masters only. No demos! Unsolicited material okay."

Music Mostly **rock**, **funk**, **jazz**, **anything weird**, **strange**, or **lo-fi** (must be mastered to CD). Released "Rustling Silk (electronic) by BuddyLoveBand; "PornMuzik 2" (ambient); "T.G.I.F4" (electronica); "UnderCover Band"; "2010" (pop rock and funk); "Catch the Ghost" (hard rock).

Tips "Keep on trying."

☑ ASTRALWERKS

ATTN: A&R Dept. 101 Avenue of the Americas, 10th Floor, New York NY 10013. E-mail: A&R@astralwerks.net. Website: www.astralwerks.com/demo.html. **Contact:** A&R. Record company. Estab. 1979. Releases 10-12 12" singles and 100 CDs/year. Pays varying royalty to artists on contract; statutory rate to publisher per song.

- Astralwerks is a subsidiary of the EMI Group, one of the "Big 4" major labels. EMI is a British-based company.

How to Contact Send submissions to: "A&R Dept." to address above. No unsolicited phone calls please. Prefers CD. "Please include any pertinent information, including your group name, track titles, names of members, bio background, successes, and any contact info. Do not send e-mail attachments."

Music Mostly **alternative/indie/electronic**. Artists include VHS or BETA, Badly Drawn boy, The Beta Band, Chemical Brothers, Turin Breaks, and Fatboy Slim.

Tips "We are open to artists of unique quality and enjoy developing artists from the ground up. We listen to all types of 'alternative' music regardless of genre. It's about the aesthetic and artistic quality first. We send out rejection letters so do not call to find out what's happening with your demo."

☐ ATLAN-DEC/GROOVELINE RECORDS

2529 Green Forest Court, Snellville GA 30078-4183. (770)985-1686. Fax: (877)751-5169. E-mail: atlandec@prodigy.net. Website: www.ATLAN-DEC.com. President/Senior A&R Rep: James Hatcher. A&R Rep: Wiletta J. Hatcher. Record company, music publisher and record producer. Estab. 1994. Staff size: 2. Releases 3-4 singles, 3-4 LPs and 3-4 CDs/ year. Pays 10-25% royalty to artists on contract; statutory rate to publisher per song on record.

Distributed By C.E.D. Entertainment Dist.

How to Contact Submit demo package by mail. Unsolicited submissions are OK. Prefers CD with lyric sheet. Does not return material. Responds in 3 months.

Music Mostly **R&B/urban**, **hip-hop/rap**, and **contemporary jazz**; also **soft rock**, **gospel**, **dance**, and **new country**. Released "Temptation" by Shawree, released 2004 on Atlan-Dec/Grooveline Records; *Enemy of the State* (album), recorded by Lowlife (rap/hip-hop); *I'm The Definition* (album), recorded by L.S. (rap/hip-hop), released 2007; "AHHW" (single), recorded by LeTebony Simmons (R&B), released 2007. Other artists include Furious D (rap/hip-hop), Mark Cocker (new country), and Looka, "From the Top" (rap/ hip-hop) recorded in 2008.

⚡ ⊘ ATLANTIC RECORDS

1290 Avenue of the Americas, New York NY 10104. (212)707-2000. Fax: (212)581-6414. Website: www.atlanticrecords.com. **New York:** 1290 Avenue of the Americas, New York, NY 10104. **Los Angeles:** 3400 W. Olive Ave., 3rd Floor, Burbank CA 91505. (818)238-6800 Fax: (310)205-7411. **Nashville:** 20 Music Square East, Nashville TN 37203. (615)272-7990. Labels include Big Beat Records, LAVA, Nonesuch Records, Atlantic Classics, and Rhino Records. Record company. Pays negotiable royalty to artists on contract; negotiable rate to publisher per song on record.

- Atlantic Records is a subsidiary of Warner Music Group, one of the "Big 4" major labels.

Distributed By WEA.

How to Contact *Does not accept unsolicited material.* "No phone calls please."

Music Artists include Missy Elliott, Simple Plan, Lupe Fiasco, Phil Collins, Gnarls Barkley, and Metallica.

☑ AWAL.COM

P.O. Box 879, Ojai CA 93024. (805)640-7399. Fax: (805)646-6077. E-mail: mike@awal. com. Website: www.awal.com. **Contact:** A&R Department. President: Denzyl Feigelson. Record company. Estab. 1996. Staff size: 3.

Distributed By Primarily distributes via digital downloads but physical distribution available.

How to Contact Submit demo by mail. Unsolicited submissions are OK. Prefers CD with 5 songs, lyric sheet, cover letter and press clippings. Does not return materials.

Music Mostly **pop**, **world**, and **jazz**; also **techno**, **teen**, and **children's**. Released *Go Cat Go* (album by various), recorded by Carl Perkins on ArtistOne.com; *Bliss* (album), written and recorded by Donna Delory (pop); and *Shake A Little* (album), written and recorded by Michael Ruff, both on Awal Records.

☑ AWARE RECORDS

624 Davis St., 2nd Floor, Evanston IL 60201. (874)424-2000. E-mail: info@awaremusic. com. Website: www.awaremusic.com. A&R: Steve Smith. President: Gregg Latterman. Record company. Estab. 1993. Staff size: 7. Releases 5 LPs, 1 EP and 3 CDs/year. Pays negotiable royalty to artists on contract; statutory rate to publisher per song on record.

Distributed By Sony/Columbia.

How to Contact *Does not accept unsolicited submissions.*

Music Mostly **rock/pop**. Artists include John Mayer, Five for Fighting, Newton Faulkner, Angel Taylor, and Guster.

⊞ BIG BEAR RECORDS

P.O. Box 944, Birmingham B16 8UT United Kingdom. 44-121-454-7020. Fax: 44-121-454-9996. E-mail: jim@bigbearmusic.com. Website: www.bigbearmusic.com. A&R Director: Jim Simpson. Labels include Truckers Delight and Grandstand Records. Record company, record producer and music publisher (Bearsongs). Releases 6 LPs/year. Pays 8-10% royalty to artists on contract; 81/4% to publishers for each record sold. Royalties paid directly to songwriters and artists or through US publishing or recording affiliate.

• Big Bear's publishing affiliate, Bearsongs, is listed in the Music Publishers section, and Big Bear is listed in the Record Producers section of this book.

How to Contact Submit demo by mail. Unsolicited submissions are OK. Prefers CD. Does not return material. Responds in 3 weeks.

Music Blues and **jazz**. Released *I've Finished with the Blues* and *Blues for Pleasure* (by

Skirving/Nicholls), both recorded by King Pleasure and the Biscuit Boys (jazz); and *Side-Steppin'* (by Barnes), recorded by Alan Barnes/Bruce Adams Quintet (jazz), all on Big Bear Records. Other artists include Lady Sings the Blues, Drummin' Man, Kenny Baker's Dozen, Tipitina, and Dr. Teeth Big Band.

☑ BLACKHEART RECORDS

636 Broadway, New York NY 10012. (212)353-9600. Fax: (212)353-8300. E-mail: blackheart@blackheart.com. Website: www.blackheart.com. **Contact:** Zander Wolff, a&r. Record label. Estab. 1982.

How to Contact Unsolicited submissions are OK. Prefers CD with 1-3 songs and lyric sheets. Include SASE. Responds only if interested.

Music Mostly **rock**. Artists include Joan Jett & the Blackhearts, The Dollyrots, The Vacancies, Girl In A Coma, and The Eyeliners.

☐ BLUE GEM RECORDS

P.O. Box 29550, Hollywood CA 90029. (323)664-7765. E-mail: pmarti3636@aol.com. Website: www.bluegemrecords.com. **Contact:** Pete Martin. Record company, music publisher (Vaam Music Group) and record producer (Pete Martin/Vaam Productions). Estab. 1981. Pays 6-15% royalty to artists on contract; statutory rate to publisher per song on record.

- Also see the listings for Vaam Music Group in the Music Publishers section of this book and Pete Martin/Vaam Music Productions in the Record Producers section of this book.

How to Contact Submit demo by mail. Unsolicited submissions are OK. Prefers CD or cassette with 2 songs. Include SASE. Responds in 3 weeks.

Music Mostly **country** and **R&B**; also **pop/top 40** and **rock**.

☑ BOUQUET RECORDS

Bouquet-Orchid Enterprises, P.O. Box 1335, Norcross GA 30091. Phone/fax: (770)339-9088. **Contact:** Bill Bohannon, president. Record company, music publisher (Orchid Publishing/BMI), record producer (Bouquet-Orchid Enterprises) and management firm (Bouquet-Orchid Enterprises). Releases 3-4 singles and 2 LPs/year. Pays 5-8% royalty to artists on contract; pays statutory rate to publishers for each record sold.

How to Contact Submit demo by mail. Unsolicited submissions are OK. Prefers cassette or CD with 3-5 songs and lyric sheet. Include SASE. Responds in 1 month.

Music Mostly **religious** (contemporary or country-gospel, Amy Grant, etc.), **country** ("the type suitable for Kenny Chesney, George Strait, Carrie Underwood, Patty Loveless, etc.") and **top 100** ("the type suitable for Billy Joel, Whitney Houston, R.E.M., etc."); also **rock**, and **MOR**. Released *Blue As Your Eyes* (by Bill Bohannon), recorded by Adam Day (country); *Take Care of My World* (by Bob Freeman), recorded by Bandoleers (top

40); and *Making Plans* (by John Harris), recorded by Susan Spencer (country), all on Bouquet Records.

Tips "Submit 3-5 songs on a cassette tape or CD with lyric sheets. Include a short biography and perhaps a photo. Enclose SASE."

◖ CANTILENA RECORDS

740 Fox Dale Ln. Knoxville, TN. 37934. E-mail: llzz@aol.com. Website: www. cantilenarecords.com. A&R: Laurel Zucker, owner. A&R: B. Houseman. Record company. Estab. 1993. Releases 3 CDs/year. Pays Harry Fox standard royalty to artists on contract; statutory rate to publishers per song on record.

How to Contact *Write first and obtain permission to submit or to arrange personal interview.* Prefers CD. Does not return material.

Music Classical, jazz. Released "Caliente!" (single by Christopher Caliendo) from *Caliente! World Music for Flute & Guitar* (album), recorded by Laurel Zucker and Christopher Caliendo! (world crossover); *Suites No. 1 & 2 For Flute & Jazz Piano Trio* (album by Claude Bolling), recorded by Laurel Zucker, Joe Gilman, David Rokeach, Jeff Neighbor (jazz); and *HOPE! Music for Flute, Soprano, Guitar* (album by Daniel Akiva, Astor Piazzolla, Haim Permont, Villa-Lobos) (classical/world), recorded by Laurel Zucker, Ronit Widmann-Levy, Daniel Akiva, all released in 2004 by Cantilena Records. Other artists include Tim Gorman, Prairie Prince, Dave Margen, Israel Philharmonic, Erkel Chamber Orchestra, Samuel Magill, Renee Siebert, Robin Sutherland, and Gerald Ranch.d

◩ CAPITOL RECORDS

1750 N. Vine St., Hollywood CA 90028-5274. (323)462-6252. Fax: (323)469-4542. Website: www.hollywoodandvine.com. Nashville: 3322 West End Ave., 11th Floor, Nashville TN 37203. (615)269-2000. Labels include Blue Note Records, Grand Royal Records, Pangaea Records, The Right Stuff Records and Capitol Nashville Records. Record company.

• Capitol Records is a subsidiary of the EMI Group, one of the "Big 4" major labels.

Distributed By EMD.

How to Contact *Capitol Records does not accept unsolicited submissions.*

Music Artists include Coldplay, The Decemberists, Beastie Boys, Liz Phair, Interpol, Lily Allen, and Auf der Maur.

▢ CHATTAHOOCHEE RECORDS

2544 Roscomare Rd., Los Angeles CA 90077. (818)788-6863. Fax: (310)471-2089. E-mail: cyardum@prodigy.net. **Contact:** Robyn Meyers, Music Director/A&R. Music Director: Chris Yardum. Record company and music publisher (Etnoc/Conte). Member NARAS. Releases 4 singles/year. Pays negotiable royalty to artists on contract.

How to Contact : Submit demo by e-mail. Will respond only if interested.

Music Mostly **rock**. Released *Don't Touch It Let It Drip* (album), recorded by Cream House (hard rock), released 2000 on Chattahoochee Records. Artists include DNA, Noctrnl, and Vator.

CHERRY STREET RECORDS

P.O. Box 52626, Tulsa OK 74152. (918)742-8087. Fax: (918)975-9736. E-mail: info@ cherrystreetmusic.com. Website: www.cherrystreetrecords.com. President: Rodney Young. Vice President: Steve Hickerson. Record company and music publisher. Estab. 1990. Staff size: 2. Releases 2 CD/year. Pays 50% royalty to artists on contract; statutory rate to publisher per song on record.

Distributed By Internet.

How to Contact *Write first and obtain permission to submit.* Prefers cassette or videocassette with 4 songs and lyric sheet. Include SASE. Responds in 4 months.

Music Rock, **country**, and **R&B**; also **jazz**. Released *Promised Land* (album), written and recorded by Richard Neville on Cherry Street (rock). Other artists include George W. Carroll and Chris Blevins.

Tips "We sign only artists who play an instrument, sing, and write songs. Send only your best 4 songs."

COLLECTOR RECORDS

P.O. Box 1200, 3260 AE oud beyerland Holland. (31)186 604266. Fax: (31)186 604366. E-mail: cees@collectorrec.com. Website: www.collectorrecords.nl. **Contact:** Cees Klop, president. Manager: John Moore. Labels include All Rock, Downsouth, Unknown, Pro Forma and White Label Records. Record company, music publisher (All Rock Music Publishing) and record producer (Cees Klop). Estab. 1967. Staff size: 4. Release 25 LPs/ year. Pays 10% royalty to artist on contract.

How to Contact Submit demo package by mail. Unsolicited submissions are OK. Prefers cassette. SAE and IRC. Responds in 2 months.

Music Mostly **'50s rock**, **rockabilly**, **hillbilly boogie** and **country/rock**; also **piano boogie woogie**. Released *Rock Crazy Baby* (album), by Art Adams (1950s rockabilly), released 2005; *Marvin Jackson* (album), by Marvin Jackson (1950s rockers), released 2005; *Western Australian Snake Pit R&R* (album), recorded by various (1950s rockers), released 2005, all on Collector Records. Other artists include Henk Pepping, Rob Hoeke, Eric-Jan Overbeek, and more. "See our Web site."

COLUMBIA RECORDS

555 Madison Ave., 10th Floor, New York NY 10022. (212)833-4000. Fax: (212)833-4389. E-mail: sonymusiconline@sonymusic.com. Website: www.columbiarecords.com. **Santa Monica:** 2100 Colorado Ave., Santa Monica CA 90404. (310)449-2100. Fax: (310)449-2743. **Nashville:** 34 Music Square E., Nashville TN 37203. (615)742-4321. Fax: (615)244-2549. Labels include So So Def Records and Ruffhouse Records. Record company.

• Columbia Records is a subsidiary of Sony BMG, one of the "Big 4" major labels.

Distributed By Sony.

How to Contact *Columbia Records does not accept unsolicited submissions.*

Music Artists include Aerosmith, Marc Anthony, Beyonce, Bob Dylan, and Patti Smith.

✪ COSMOTONE RECORDS

2951 Marina Bay Dr., Ste. 130, League City TX 77573-2733. E-mail: marianland@ earthlink.net. Website: www.cosmotonerecords.com. Record company, music publisher (Cosmotone Music, ASCAP) and record producer (Rafael Brom). Estab. 1984.

Distributed By marianland.com.

How to Contact "Sorry, we do not accept material at this time." Does not return materials.

Music Mostly **Christian pop/rock**. Released *Dance for Padre Pio*, *Peace of Heart*, *Music for Peace of Mind*, *The Sounds of Heaven*, *The Christmas Songs*, *Angelophany*, *The True Measure of Love*, *All My Love to You Jesus* (albums), and *Rafael Brom Unplugged* (live concert DVD), *Life is Good, Enjoy it While You Can* (album), "Change," by Rafael Brom.

▢ CREATIVE IMPROVISED MUSIC PROJECTS (CIMP) RECORDS

CIMP LTD, Cadence Building, Redwood NY 13679. (315)287-2852. Fax: (315)287-2860. E-mail: cimp@cadencebuilding.com Website: www.cimprecords.com. **Contact:** Bob Rusch, producer. Labels include Cadence Jazz Records. Record company and record producer (Robert D. Rusch). Estab. 1980. Releases 25-30 CDs/year. Pays negotiable royalty to artists on contract; pays statutory rate to publisher per song on record.Distributed by North Country Distributors.

• CIMP specializes in jazz and creative improvised music.

How to Contact Submit demo by mail. Unsolicited submissions are OK. Prefers cassette or CD. "We are not looking for songwriters but recording artists." Include SASE. Responds in 1 week.

Music Mostly **jazz** and **creative improvised music**. Released *The Redwood Session* (album), recorded by Evan Parker, Barry Guy, Paul Lytton, and Joe McPhee; *Sarah's Theme* (album), recorded by the Ernie Krivda Trio, Bob Fraser, and Jeff Halsey; and *Human Flowers* (album), recorded by the Bobby Zankel Trio, Marily Crispell, and Newman Baker, all released on CIMP (improvised jazz). Other artists include Arthur Blythe, Joe McPhee, David Prentice, Anthony Braxton, Roswell Rudd, Paul Smoker, Khan Jamal, Odean Pope, etc.

Tips "CIMP Records are produced to provide music to reward repeated and in-depth listenings. They are recorded live to two-track which captures the full dynamic range one would experience in a live concert. There is no compression, homogenization, eq-ing, post-recording splicing, mixing, or electronic fiddling with the performance. Digital recording allows for a vanishingly low noise floor and tremendous dynamic range. This

Record Companies

compression of the dynamic range is what limits the 'air' and life of many recordings. Our recordings capture the dynamic intended by the musicians. In this regard these recordings are demanding. Treat the recording as your private concert. Give it your undivided attention and it will reward you. CIMP Records are not intended to be background music. This method is demanding not only on the listener but on the performer as well. Musicians must be able to play together in real time. They must understand the dynamics of their instrument and how it relates to the others around them. There is no fix-it-in-the-mix safety; either it works or it doesn't. What you hear is exactly what was played. Our main concern is music not marketing."

☑ CURB RECORDS

48 Music Square E., Nashville TN 37203. (615)321-5080. Fax: (615)327-1964. Website: www.curb.com. **Contact:** John Ozler, A&R coordinator. Record company.

How to Contact Curb Records does not accept unsolicited submissions; accepts previously published material only. *Do not submit without permission.*

Music Released *Everywhere* (album), recorded by Tim McGraw; *Sittin' On Top of the World* (album), recorded by LeAnn Rimes; and *I'm Alright* (album), recorded by Jo Dee Messina, all on Curb Records. Other artists include Mary Black, Merle Haggard, Kal Ketchum, David Kersh, Lyle Lovett, Tim McGraw, Wynonna, and Sawyer Brown.

ℕ DEEP ELM RECORDS

210 N. Church St. #2502, Charlotte NC 28202-2385. E-mail: INFO@deepelm.com. Website: www.deepelm.com.

How to Contact Accepts unsolicited submissions. DO NOT e-mail sound files. "We are most interested in receiving completed full-length albums (at least 10 songs) that are available for immediate worldwide release. Send a CD or CDR with the BAND NAME, PHONE and E-MAIL directly written on the face of the CD. If the CD has artwork on it, write the information on a label, white sticker or piece of making tape and affix it to the face of the CD. Send your CD in a jewel case or with a piece of cardboard to protect it from breaking. Forget the fancy folders, bios, reviews and photos...we don't need it. It's only the music that matters. Send your CD by Regular Mail ONLY (absolutely no Express Mail, Fedex, DHL, UPS) to: Deep Elm Records - Music Submission, 210 N. Church Street #2502, Charlotte, NC 28202-2385 USA. If we are interested in your music, WE will be in contact with you. PLEASE do not call, e-mail or contact us. Assume we received your package if it has not been returned to you in the mail, as we cannot track unsolicited packages. Sorry, packages cannot be returned and we do not comment on music that we pass on. More details here: www.deepelm.com/submit."

Music Public Radio, Moving Mountains, Nathan Xander, 500 Miles to Memphis, This Drama, Goonies Never Say Die, Latterman, Desoto Jones, Track A Tiger, The Emo Diaries, The Appleseed Cast.

☐ DEEP SOUTH ENTERTAINMENT

P.O. Box 17737, Raleigh NC 27619-7737. (919)844-1515. Fax: (919)847-5922. E-mail: info@ deepsouthentertainment.com. Website: www.deepsouthentertainment.com. Manager: Amy Cox. Record company and management company. Estab. 1996. Staff size: 10. Pays negotiable royalty to artists on contract; statutory rate to publisher per song on record.

Distributed By Redeye Distribution, Valley, Select-O-Hits, City Hall, AEC/Bassin, Northeast One Stop, Pollstar, and Koch International.

How to Contact Submit demo by mail. Unsolicited submissions are OK. Prefers cassette or CD with 3 songs, cover letter, and press clippings. Does not return material. Responds only if interested.

Music Mostly **pop**, **modern rock**, and **alternative**; also **swing**, **rockabilly**, and **heavy rock**. Does not want rap or R&B. Artists include Bruce Hornsby, Little Feat, Mike Daly, SR-71, Stretch Princess, Darden Smith, and Vienna Teng.

▦ ◪ DEMI MONDE RECORDS AND PUBLISHING, LTD.

Foel Studio, Llanfair Caereinion, Powys, Wales, United Kingdom. (01938)810758. E-mail: demi.monde@dial.pipex.com. Website: www.demimonde.co.uk/demimonde. Managing Director: Dave Anderson. Record company, music publisher (Demi Monde Records & Publishing, Ltd.) and record producer (Dave Anderson). Estab. 1983. Releases 5 12" singles, 10 LPs and 6 CDs/year. Pays 10% royalty to artists on contract; statutory rate to publisher per song on record.

Distributed By Pinnacle, Magnum and Shellshock.

How to Contact Submit demo tape by mail. Unsolicited submissions are OK. Prefers cassette with 3-4 songs. Does not return material. Responds in 6 weeks.

Music Mostly **rock**, **R&B** and **pop**. Released *Hawkwind*, *Amon Duul II & Gong* and *Groundhogs* (by T.S. McPhee), all on Demi Monde Records.

☐ DENTAL RECORDS

P.O. Box 20058, New York NY 10017. E-mail: info@dentalrecords.com. Website: www. dentalrecords.com. **Contact:** Rick Sanford, owner. Record company. Estab. 1981. Staff size: 2. Releases 1-2 CDs/year. Pays negotiable royalty to artists on contract; statutory rate to publisher per song on record.

Distributed By Dutch East India Trading.

How to Contact *Not currently accepting unsolicited submissions.* Prefers CD with any number of songs, lyric sheet, and cover letter. "Check our website to see if your material is appropriate." Include SASE. Responds only if interested.

Music Pop-derived structures, **jazz-derived harmonies**, and **neo-classic-wannabee-pretenses**. Does not want urban, heavy metal, or hard core. Released *Perspectivism* (album), written and recorded by Rick Sanford (instrumental), released 2003 on Dental Records. Other artists include Les Izmor.

☑ DRUMBEAT INDIAN ARTS, INC.

4143 N. 16th St., Suite 1, Phoenix AZ 85016. (602)266-4823. Website: www. DrumbeatIndianArts.com **Contact:** Bob Nuss, president. Record company and distributor of American Indian recordings. Estab. 1984. Staff size: 8. Releases 100 CDs/year. Royalty varies with project.

- Note that Drumbeat Indian Arts is a very specialized label, and only wants to receive submissions by Native American artists.

How to Contact *Call first and obtain permission to submit.* Include SASE. Responds in 2 months.

Music Music by American Indians—any style (must be enrolled tribal members). Does not want New Age "Indian style" material. Released Pearl Moon (album), written and recorded by Xavier (native Amerindian). Other artists include Black Lodge Singers, R. Carlos Nakai, Lite Foot, and Joanne Shenandoah.

Tips "We deal only with American Indian performers. We do not accept material from others. Please include tribal affiliation."

☒ EARACHE RECORDS

43 W. 38th St., New York NY 10018. (212)840-9090. Fax: (212)840-4033. E-mail: usaproduction@earache.com. Website: www.earache.com. Estab. 1993 (US).

Music Rock, industrial, heavy metal techno, death metal, grindcore. Artists include Municipal Waste, Dillinger Escape Plan, Bring Me the Horizon, Deicide, Oceano, and more.

☑ ELEKTRA RECORDS

75 Rockefeller Plaza, 17th Floor, New York NY 10019. Website: www.elektra.com. Labels include Elektra Records, Eastwest Records, and Asylum Records. Record company.

- Elektra Records is a subsidiary of Warner Music Group, one of the "Big 4" major labels.

Distributed By WEA.

How to Contact *Elektra does not accept unsolicited submissions.*

Music Mostly alternative/modern rock. Artists include Cee Lo, Justice, Little Boots, and *True Blood.*

☑ EPIC RECORDS

550 Madison Ave., 21st Floor, New York NY 10022. (212)833-8870. Fax: (212)833-4054. Website: www.epicrecords.com. Senior Vice Presidents A&R: Ben Goldman, Rose Noone. **Santa Monica:** 2100 Colorado Ave., Santa Monica CA 90404. (310)449-2100 Fax: (310)449-2848. A&R: Pete Giberga, Mike Flynn. Labels include Epic Soundtrax, LV Records, Immortal Records, and Word Records. Record company.

- Epic Records is a subsidiary of Sony BMG, one of the "Big 4" major labels.

Distributed By Sony Music Distribution.

How to Contact *Write or call first and obtain permission to submit* (New York office only). Does not return material. Responds only if interested. *Santa Monica and Nashville offices do not accept unsolicited submissions.*

Music Artists include Celine Dion, Macy Gray, Modest Mouse, Fuel, Jennifer Lopez, B2K, Incubus, Ben Folds.

Tips "Do an internship if you don't have experience or work as someone's assistant. Learn the business and work hard while you figure out what your talents are and where you fit in. Once you figure out which area of the record company you're suited for, focus on that, work hard at it and it shall be yours."

ⓃEYEBALL RECORDS

751 Kearny Ave., Kearny NJ 07032. E-mail: info@eyeballrecords.com. Website: www. eyeballrecords.com. **Contact:** A&R.

How to Contact "Familiarize yourself with the bands we work with." Submit demo by mail. "You don't have to call or e-mail us to follow up."

Music New London Fire, Pompeii, The Blackout Pact, United Nations, Wolftron, and more.

ⓃFATT CHANTZ RECORDS

2535 Winthrope Way, Lawrenceville GA 30044. (770)982-7055. Fax: (770)982-1882. E-mail: hitcd@bellsouth.net. Website: www.jeromepromotions.com. **Contact:** Bill Jerome, president and CEO. Estab: 2009. Record company. Staff size: 3. Royalties are negotiable.

How to Contact Contact first and obtain permission to submit a demo. Include CD with 5 songs and cover letter. Does not return submissions. Responds in 1 week.

Music Mostly interested in **top 40**, **adult contemporary, hot AC**; also **R&B, alternative,** and **hip-hop crossover**. Does not want rap, country, gospel, hard rock.

FAT WRECK CHORDS

P.O. Box 193690, San Francisco CA 94119. E-mail: mailbag@fatwreck.com. Website: www.fatwreck.com. Contact: Mike.

How to Contact Accepts demos by mail at: Asian Man Records, ATTN: Mike, P.O. Box 35585, Monte Soreno, CA 95030. Responds via e-mail or through the post "in time."

Music Punk, rock, alternative. Artists include NOFX, Rise Against, The Lawrence Arms, Anti-Flag, Me First and the Gimme Gimmes, Propagandhi, Dillinger Four, Against Me, and more.

ⓃFEARLESS RECORDS

13772 Goldenwest St. #545, Westminster CA 92683. E-mail: bridget@fearlessrecords.

com. Website: www.fearlessrecords.com.

How to Contact Send all demos to mailing address. "Do not e-mail us about demos or with links to mp3s."

Music Alternative, indie, rock. Artists include The Maine, At the Drive-In, Every Avenue, Plain White T's, Sugarcult, Portugal The Man, Blessthefall, A Static Lullaby, and more.

✷ FIREANT

2009 Ashland Ave., Charlotte NC 28205. E-mail: lewh@fireantmusic.com. Website: www.fireantmusic.com. **Contact:** Lew Herman, owner. Record company, music publisher (Fireant Music) and record producer (Lew Herman). Estab. 1990. Releases several CDs/year. Pays negotiable royalty to artists on contract; statutory royalty to publisher per song on record.

Distributed By eMusic.com.

How to Contact Submit demo by mail. Unsolicited submissions are OK. Prefers cassette, DAT, or videocassette. Does not return material.

Music Mostly **progressive**, **traditional**, and **musical hybrids**. "Anything except New Age and MOR." Released *Loving the Alien: Athens Georgia Salutes David Bowie* (album), recorded by various artists (rock/alternative/electronic), released 2000 on Fireant; and *Good Enough* (album), recorded by Zen Frisbee. Other artists include Mr. Peters' Belizean Boom and Chime Band.

☐ FRESH ENTERTAINMENT

1315 Simpson Rd. NW, Suite 5, Atlanta GA 30314. E-mail: whunter1122@yahoo.com. **Contact:** Willie W. Hunter, managing director. Record company and music publisher (Hserf Music/ASCAP, Blair Vizzion Music/BMI). Releases 5 singles and 2 LPs/year. Pays 7-10% royalty to artists on contract; statutory rate to publisher per song on record.

Distributed By Ichiban International and Intersound Records.

How to Contact Submit demo package by mail. Unsolicited submissions are OK. Prefers cassette or VHS videocassette with at least 3 songs and lyric sheet. Include SASE. Responds in 2 months.

Music Mostly **R&B**, **rock** and **pop**; also **jazz**, **gospel** and **rap**. Released in 2008: *Nubian Woman* by Bob Miles (Jazz); Lissen (R&B/hip hop); *You Know I'm From the A* by Joe "Da Bingo" Bing (rap); "As the World Turns" by Kaz & Cardi (rap).

☐ FRONT ROW RECORDS

Ridgewood Park Estates, 222 Tulane St., Garland TX 75043. **Contact:** Gene or Dea Summers. Public Relations/Artist and Fan Club Coordinator: Steve Summers. A&R: Shawn Summers. Labels include Juan Records. Record company and music publisher (Silicon Music/BMI). Estab. 1968. Releases 5-6 singles and 2-3 LPs/year. Pays negotiable royalty to artists on contract; standard royalty to songwriters on contract.

Distributed by Crystal Clear Records.

- Also see the listing for Silicon Music Publishing Co. in the Music Publishers section of this book.

How to Contact Submit demo by mail. Unsolicited submissions are OK. Prefers cassette or VHS videocassette with 1-3 songs. "We request a photo and bio with material submission." Does not return material. Responds ASAP.

Music Mostly '50s **rock/rockabilly**; also **country**, **bluegrass**, **old-time blues**, and **R&B**. Released "Domino" (single), recorded by Gene Summers on Pollytone Records (rockabilly); "Goodbye Priscilla" and "Cool Baby" (singles), both recorded by Gene Summers on Collectables Records.

Tips "If you own masters of 1950s rock and rockabilly, contact us first! We will work with you on a percentage basis for overseas release. We have active releases in Holland, Switzerland, Belgium, Australia, England, France, Sweden, Norway, and the US at the present. We need original masters. You must be able to prove ownership of tapes before we can accept a deal. We're looking for little-known, obscure recordings. We have the market if you have the tapes! We are also interested in country and rockabilly artists who have not recorded for awhile but still have the voice and appeal to sell overseas."

FUELED BY RAMEN

P.O. box 1803, Tampa FL 33601. Website: www.fueledbyramen.com. Contact: Johnny Minardi.

How to Contact Send demos by mail to address above.

Music Alternative, Rock, Indie. Artists include The Academy Is..., Cobra Starship, Cute Is What We Aim For, Gym Class Heroes, The Hush Sound, Panic At the Disco, Paramore, A Rocket to the Moon, This Providence, and more.

MARTY GARRETT ENTERTAINMENT

320 West Utica Place, Broken Arrow OK 74011. (888)HE4-GAVE. E-mail: musicbusiness@telepath.com. Website: www.breakintothemusicbiz.com and www.martygarrettentertainment.com. Marty R. Garrett, president. Labels include MGE Records Lonesome Wind Records. Record company, record producer, music publisher, and entertainment consultant. Estab. 1988. Releases 1-2 EPs and 1 CD/year. Pays negotiable royalty to artists on contract; statutory rate to publisher per song on record.

How to Contact *Call or check Internet site first and obtain permission to submit.* Prefers CD with 4-5 songs and lyric or lead sheet with chord progressions listed. Does not return material. No press packs or bios, unless specifically requested. Responds in 4-6 weeks.

Music Mostly **honky tonk**, **progressive/traditional country**, or **scripture-based**

gospel. Released *Drinking the New Wine* (album) by Marty Garrett on MGE Records. Released singles include "He Brought Me Back Again", "My Father Made The Jailhouse Rock", "Drinking the New Wine", "Get Myself Off My Mind", "What Would God Say Then"; all singles released on MGE Records.

Tips "We help artists secure funding to record and release major label quality CD products to the public for sale through 1-800 television and radio advertising and on the Internet. Although we do submit finished products to major record companies for review, our main focus is to establish and surround the artist with their own long-term production, promotion and distribution organization. Professional studio demos are not required, but make sure vocals are distinct, up-front and up-to-date. I personally listen and respond to each submission received, so check Web site to see if we are reviewing for an upcoming project."

☐ GENERIC RECORDS, INC.

433 Limestone Rd., Ridgefield CT 06877. (203)438-9811. Fax: (203)431-3204. E-mail: hifiadd@aol.com. President: Gary Lefkowith. A&R: Bill Jerome. Labels include Outback, GLYN and Teec. Record company, music publisher (Sotto Music/BMI) and record producer. Estab. 1976. Staff size: 5. Releases 6 singles and 2 CDs/year. Pays 15% royalty to artists on contract; statutory rate to publisher per song on record.

Distributed By RED/Sony Music.

How to Contact Submit demo package by mail. Unsolicited submissions are OK but it is best to call or e-mail first. Prefers CD with 2-3 songs. Include SASE. Responds in 2-4 weeks.

Music Mostly **alternative rock**, **rock**, and **pop**; also **country** and **rap**. Released "She's My Girl," and "Oh" by HiFi; "I'll Be the One" and "Kansas City Woman" by JNB; "I's So Hard" and "Going Nowhere Fast" by Loose Change, featuring David Ruskay. Produced 4 singles for the legendary Chubby Checker: "Limbo Rock Remix," "Knock Down the Walls," "The Original Master of the Dance Hall Beat," and "The Fly."

Tips "Love what you're doing. The music comes first."

☐ GOTHAM RECORDS

Attn: A&R, P.O. Box 7185, Santa Monica CA 90406. E-mail: ar@gothamrecords.com. Website: www.gothamrecords.com. Record company. Estab. 1994. Staff size: 3. Releases 8 LPs and 8 CDs/year. Pays negotiable royalty to artists on contract; statutory rate to publisher per song on record. "We now have a new division (Gotham Music Placement) that places songs with motion picture, TV, advertising, and video game companies."

Distributed By KOCH Distribution and Sony RED.

How to Contact Submit demo by mail "in a padded mailer or similar package." Unsolicited submissions are OK. Prefers cassette or CD and bios, pictures, and touring information. Does not return material. Responds in 6 weeks.

Music Mostly **rock**, **pop**, **alternative**, and **AAA**. New artists include SLANT, Red Horizon, The Day After..., The Vicious Martinis.

Tips "Send all submissions in regular packaging. Spend your money on production and basics, not on fancy packaging and gift wrap."

�🅽 HOLOGRAPHIC RECORDING COMPANY

700 West Pete Rose Way PMB 18, Cincinnati OH 45203. (513)442-4405. Fax: (513)834-9390. E-mail: info@holographicrecords.com. Website: holographicrecords.com. **Contact**: James Sfarnas, president. Label. Estab. 1983. Releases recordings from artists and groups from anywhere; current roster includes 7 acts.

How to Contact Call first and obtain permission to submit.

Music Jazz, progressive. Current acts include Acumen (progressive jam rock), John Novello (fusion), Alex Skolnick Trio (progressive jazz), Jeff Berlin (jazz), Poogie Bell Band (urban jazz), Dave LaRue (fusion), Mads Eriksen (fusion).

☐ HOTTRAX RECORDS

1957 Kilburn Dr., Atlanta GA 30324. (770)662-6661. E-mail: hotwax@hottrax.com. Website: www.hottrax.com. **Contact:** George Burdell, vice president, A&R. Labels include Dance-A-Thon and Hardkor. Record company and music publisher (Starfox Publishing). Staff size: 6. Releases 8 singles and 3-4 CDs/year. Pays 5-15% royalty to artists on contract.

- Also see the listing for Alexander Janoulis Productions/Big Al Jano Productions in the Record Producers section of this book.

Distributed By Get Hip Inc., DWM Music and Super D.

How to Contact *Write first and obtain permission to submit.* Prefers CD with 3 songs and lyric sheet. Does not return material. Responds in 6 months. "When submissions get extremely heavy, we do not have the time to respond/return material we pass on. We do notify those sending the most promising work we review, however. Current economic conditions may also affect song acceptance and response."

Music Mostly **blues/blues rock**, some **top 40/pop, rock**, and **country**; also **hardcore punk** and **jazz-fusion**. Released *Power Pop Deluxe* (album), by Secret Lover featuring Delanna Protas, *Some of My Best Friends Have the Blues* (album), by Big Al Jano, *Hot to Trot* (album), written and recorded by Starfoxx (rock); *Lady That Digs The Blues* (album), recorded by Big Al Jano's Blues Mafia Show (blues rock); and *Vol. III, Psychedelic Era. 1967-1969* (album), released 2002 on Hottrax. Other artists include Big Al Jano, Sammy Blue, and Sheffield & Webb. Scheduled for 2010: *So Much Love* (album) by Michael Rozakis & Yorgos, *Yuck! What Kind of Music Is This?* (album) by Schmaltz, *Psychedelic Covers*, by Little Phil and the Night Shadows.

☑ IDOL RECORDS

P.O. Box 720043, Dallas TX 75372. (214)321-8890. E-mail: info@idolrecords.com. Website: www.IdolRecords.com. **Contact:** Erv Karwelis, president. Record company. Estab. 1992. Releases 30 singles, 80 LPs, 20 EPs and 10-15 CDs/year. Pays negotiable royalty to artists on contract; negotiable rate to publisher per song on record.

Distributed By Super D (SDID).

How to Contact See Web site at www.IdolRecords.com for submission policy. No phone calls or e-mail follow-ups.

Music Mostly **rock**, **pop**, and **alternative**; also some **hip-hop**. Released *The Boys Names Sue-The Hits Vol. Sue!* (album), The O's - *We are the Os* (album), Little Black Dress — *Snow in June (album), The Man,* recorded by Sponge (alternative); *Movements* (album), recorded by Black Tie Dynasty (alternative); In Between Days (album), recorded by Glen Reynolds (rock), all released 2006/2006 on Idol Records. Other artists include Flickerstick, DARYL, Centro-matic, The Deathray Davies, GBH, PPT, The Crash that Took Me, Shibboleth, Trey Johnson.

☐ IMAGINARY RECORDS

P.O. Box 66, Whites Creek TN 37189-0066. E-mail: jazz@imaginaryrecords.com. Website: www.imaginaryrecords.com. **Contact:** Lloyd Townsend, proprietor. Labels include Imaginary Records, Imaginary Jazz Records. Record company. Estab. 1981. Staff size: 1. Releases 1-3 CDs/year. Pays negotiable royalty to artists on contract; statutory rate to publisher per song on record.

Distributed By North Country, Gats Production LTD, Tokyo, Japan, and Imaginary Distribution.

How to Contact *Write first to obtain permission to submit.* "We do not act as a publisher placing songs with artists." Prefers CD with 3-5 songs (or full-length album), cover letter, and press clippings. Include SASE. Responds in 4 months if interested.

Music Mostly **mainstream jazz**, **swing jazz**, and **classical**. Does not want country, rap, hip-hop or metal. Released *Fifth House* (album), recorded by New York Trio Project (mainstream jazz), released 2001; *Get Out of Town* by Stevens, Siegel, and Ferguson (Mainstream Jazz), released 2006.

Tips "Be patient, I'm slow. I'm primarily considering mainstream jazz or classical—other genre submissions are much less likely to get a response."

☑ ☑ INTERSCOPE/GEFFEN/A&M RECORDS

2220 Colorado Ave., Santa Monica CA 90404. (310)865-1000. Fax: (310)865-7908. Website: www.interscoperecords.com. Labels include Death Row Records, Nothing Records, Rock Land, Almo Sounds, Aftermath Records, and Trauma Records. Record company.

- Interscope/Geffen/A&M is a subsidiary of Universal Music Group, one of the "Big 4" major labels.

How to Contact *Does not accept unsolicited submissions.*

Music Released *Worlds Apart*, recorded by... And You Will Know Us By The Trail Of Dead; and *Guero*, recorded by Beck. Other artists include U2, M.I.A, Keane, and Marilyn Manson.

ISLAND/DEF JAM MUSIC GROUP

825 Eighth Ave., 29th Floor, New York NY 10019. (212)333-8000. Fax: (212)603-7654. Website: www.islanddefjam.com. Los Angeles: 8920 Sunset Blvd, 2nd Floor, Los Angeles CA 90069. (310)276-4500. Fax: (310)242-7023. Executive A&R: Paul Pontius. Labels include Mouth Almighty Records, Worldly/Triloka Records, Blackheart Records, Private Records, Slipdisc Records, Thirsty Ear, Blue Gorilla, Dubbly, Little Dog Records, Rounder, and Capricorn Records. Record company.

- Island/Def Jam is a subsidiary of Universal Music Group, one of the "Big 4" major labels.

How to Contact *Island/Def Jam Music Group does not accept unsolicited submissions. Do not send material unless requested.*

Music Artists include Bon Jovi, Fall Out Boy, Kanye West, Rihanna, The Killers, Jay-Z, and Ludacris.

J RECORDS

745 Fifth Ave., 6th Floor, New York NY 10151. (646)840-5600. Website: www.jrecords. com.

How to Contact *J Records does not accept unsolicited submissions.*

Music Artists include Faithless, Alicia Keys, and Annie Lennox.

KAUPP RECORDS

P.O. Box 5474, Stockton CA 95205. (209)948-8186. **Contact:** Melissa Glenn. Record company, music publisher (Kaupps and Robert Publishing Co./BMI), management firm (Merri-Webb Productions) and record producer (Merri-Webb Productions). Estab. 1990. Releases 1 single and 4 LPs/year. Pays standard royalty to artists on contract; statutory rate to publisher per song on record.

Distributed By Merri-Webb Productions and Cal-Centron Distributing Co.

How to Contact *Write first and obtain permission to submit or to arrange personal interview.* Prefers cassette or VHS videocassette with 3 songs. Include SASE. Responds in 3 months.

Music Mostly **country**, **R&B**, and **A/C rock**; also **pop**, **rock**, and **gospel**. Mostly **country**, **R&B** and **A/C rock**; also **pop**, **rock** and **gospel**. Published "Rushin' In" (singles by N. Merrihew/B. Bolin), recorded by Valerie; "Goin Postal" (singles by N. Merrihew/B. Bolin), recorded by Bruce Bolin (country/rock/pop); and "I Gotta Know" (single by N. Merrihew/B. Bolin), recorded by Cheryl (country/rock/pop), all released on Kaupp Records.

☑ KILL ROCK STARS

E-mail: krs@killrockstars.com. Website: www.killrockstars.com. **Contact:** Record company. Estab. 1991. Releases 4 singles, 10 LPs, 4-6 EPs and 35 CDs/year. Pays 50% of net profit to artists on contract; negotiated rate to publisher per song on record.

Distributed By Redeye Distribution.

How to Contact *Does not accept or listen to demos sent by mail.* Will listen to links online only if in a touring band coming through Portland. "If you are not touring through Portland, don't send us anything." Prefers link to Web page or EPK. Does not return material.

Music Mostly **punk rock**, **neo-folk** or **anti-folk** and **spoken word**. Artists include Deerhoof, Xiu Xiu, Mary Timony, The Gossip, Erase Errata, and Two Ton Boa.

Tips "We will only work with touring acts, so let us know if you are playing Olympia, Seattle or Portland. Particularly interested in young artists with indie-rock background."

☑ KINGSTON RECORDS

15 Exeter Rd., Kingston NH 03848. (603)642-8493. E-mail: kingstonrecords@comcast. net. Website: www.kingstonrecords.com. **Contact:** Harry Mann, coordinator. Record company, record producer and music publisher (Strawberry Soda Publishing/ASCAP). Estab. 1988. Releases 10 singles, 12 CDs/year. Pays 3-5% royalty to artists on contract; statutory rate to publisher per song.

How to Contact *E-mail first and obtain permission to submit.* Prefers CD, cassette, DAT, 15 ips reel-to-reel or videocassette with 3 songs and lyric sheet. Does not return material. Responds in 2 months.

Music Mostly **rock**, **country**, and **pop**; "no heavy metal." Released *Two Lane Highway*, *Count the Stars*, and *Leaving Tracks* written and recorded by CMA winner Doug Mitchell, released 1999-2008, all on Kingston Records.

Tips "Working only with N.E. and local talent."

☑ LARI-JON RECORDS

P.O. Box 216, Rising City NE 68658. (402)542-2336. **Contact:** Larry Good, owner. Record company, management firm (Lari-Jon Promotions), music publisher (Lari-Jon Publishing/ BMI) and record producer (Lari-Jon Productions). Estab. 1967. Staff size: 1. Releases 15 singles and 5 LPs/year. Pays varying royalty to artists on contract.

How to Contact Submit demo by mail. Unsolicited submissions are OK. Prefers CD with 5 songs and lyric sheet. Include SASE. Responds in 2 months.

Music Mostly **country**, **Southern gospel** and **'50s rock**. Released "Glory Bound Train" (single), written and recorded by Tom Campbell; *The Best of Larry Good* (album), written and recorded by Larry Good (country); and *Her Favorite Songs* (album), written and recorded by Johnny Nace (country), all on Lari-Jon Records. Other artists include Kent Thompson and Brenda Allen.

☑ LARK RECORD PRODUCTIONS, INC.

P.O. Box 35726, Tulsa OK 74153. (918)786-8896. Fax: (918)786-8897. E-mail: janajae@ janajae.com. Website: www.janajae.com. **Contact:** Kathleen Pixley, vice president. Record company, music publisher (Jana Jae Music/BMI), management firm (Jana Jae Enterprises) and record producer (Lark Talent and Advertising). Estab. 1980. Staff size: 8. Pays negotiable royalty to artists on contract; statutory rate to publisher per song on record.

How to Contact Submit demo by mail. Unsolicited submissions are OK. Prefers CD or DVD with 3 songs and lead sheets. Does not return material. Responds only if interested.

Music Mostly **country**, **bluegrass**, and **classical**; also **instrumentals**. Released "Fiddlestix" (single by Jana Jae); "Mayonnaise" (single by Steve Upfold); and "Flyin' South" (single by Cindy Walker), all recorded by Jana Jae on Lark Records (country). Other artists include Sydni, Hotwire, and Matt Greif.

☒ LIVING MUSIC

P.O. Box 72, Litchfield CT 06759. (860)567-4276. E-mail: info@livingmusic.com. Website: www.livingmusic.com. Record company. Estab. 1980.

Music Classical, jazz, folk, progressive, world, New Age.

☑ LUCIFER RECORDS, INC.

P.O. Box 263, Brigantine NJ 08203-0263. (609)266-2623. Fax: (609)266-4870. **Contact:** Ron Luciano, president. Labels include TVA Records. Record company, music publisher (Ciano Publishing and Legz Music), record producer (Pete Fragale and Tony Vallo), management firm and booking agency (Ron Luciano Music Co. and TVA Productions). "Lucifer Records has offices in South Jersey; Palm Beach, Florida."

How to Contact *Call or write to arrange personal interview.* Prefers cassette with 4-8 songs. Include SASE. Responds in 3 weeks.

Music Mostly **dance**, **easy listening**, **MOR**, **rock**, **soul**, and **top 40/pop**. Released "I Who Have Nothing," (single), by Spit-N-Image (rock); "Lucky" (single), by Legz (rock); and "Love's a Crazy Game" (single), by Voyage (disco/ballad). Other artists include Bobby Fisher, Jerry Denton, FM, Zeke's Choice, Al Caz, Joe Vee, and Dana Nicole.

☒ ☑ MATADOR RECORDS

Beggar's Group, 304 Hudson St., New York NY 10013. (212)995-5882. Fax: (212)995-5883. E-mail: webmaster@matadorrecords.com. Website: www.matadorrecords.com. UK address: 17-19 Alma Road, London, SW18 1AA United Kingdom.

How to Contact "We are sorry to say that we *no longer accept unsolicited demo submissions.*"

Music Alternative rock. Artists include Lou Reed, Pavement, Belle and Sebastian, Cat Power, Jay Reatard, Sonic Youth, Yo La Tengo, Mogwai, The New Pornographers, and more.

Record Companies

☑ ⊘ MCA NASHVILLE

(formerly MCA Records), 1904 Adelicia St., Nashville TN 37212. (615)244-8944. Fax: (615)880-7447. Website: www.mca-nashville.com. Record company and music publisher (MCA Music).

- MCA Nashville is a subsidiary of Universal Music Group, one of the "Big 4" major labels.

How to Contact MCA Nashville cannot accept unsolicited submissions.

Music Artists include Tracy Byrd, George Strait, Vince Gill, The Mavericks, and Trisha Yearwood.

⊘ METAL BLADE RECORDS

2828 Cochran St., PMB 302, Simi Valley CA 93065. (805)522-9111. Fax: (805)522-9380. E-mail: metalblade@metalblade.com. Website: www.metalblade.com. **Contact:** A&R. Record company. Estab. 1982. Releases 20 LPs, 2 EPs and 20 CDs/year. Pays negotiable royalty to artists on contract.

How to Contact Submit demo by mail. Unsolicited submissions are OK. Prefers CD with 3 songs. Does not return material. Responds in 3 months.

Music Mostly **heavy metal** and **industrial**; also **hardcore**, **gothic** and **noise**. Released "Gallery of Suicide," recorded by Cannibal Corpse; "Voo Doo," recorded by King Diamond; and "A Pleasant Shade of Gray," recorded by Fates Warning, all on Metal Blade Records. Other artists include As I Lay Dying, The Red Chord, The Black Dahlia Murder, and Unearth.

Tips "Metal Blade is known throughout the underground for quality metal-oriented acts."

⊘ MIGHTY RECORDS

150 West End, Suite 6-D, New York NY 10023. Manager: Danny Darrow. Labels include Mighty Sounds & Filmworks. Record company, music publisher (Rockford Music Co./BMI, Stateside Music Co./BMI and Corporate Music Publishing Co./ASCAP) and record producer (Danny Darrow). Estab. 1958. Releases 1-2 singles, 1-2 12" singles and 1-2 LPs/year. Pays standard royalty to artists on contract; statutory rate to publisher per song on record.

Distributed By Amazon.com and CDBaby.com.

How to Contact Submit demo package by mail. Unsolicited submissions are OK. "No phone calls." Prefers cassette or CD with 2 songs and lyric sheet. Does not return material. Responds in 1 month only if interested.

Music Mostly **pop**, **country** and **dance**; also **jazz**. Released "Look to the Wind" (single by Peggy Stewart/Danny Darrow) from *Falling in Love* (album), recorded by Danny Darrow (movie theme); "Doomsday" (single by Robert Lee Lowery/Danny Darrow) from *Doomsday* (album), recorded by Danny Darrow (euro jazz), all released 2004 on Mighty

Records; "Telephones" (single Robert Lee Lowery/Danny Darrow) from *Telephones* (album), and "Love to Dance" (single by Robert Lee Lowery/Danny Darrow) from *Love to Dance* (album), both recorded by Danny Darrow (trance dance), released 2006 on Mighty Records.

☐ MODAL MUSIC, INC.™

P.O. Box 6473, Evanston IL 60204-6473. (847)864-1022. E-mail: info@modalmusic.com. Website: www.modalmusic.com. President: Terran Doehrer. Assistant: J. Distler. Record company and agent. Estab. 1988. Staff size: 2. Releases 1-2 LPs/year. Pays negotiable royalty to artists on contract; negotiable rate to publisher per song on record.

How to Contact Submit demo package by mail. Unsolicited submissions are OK. Prefers CD with bio, PR, brochures, any info about artist and music. Does not return material. Responds in 4 months.

Music Mostly **ethnic** and **world**. Released "St. James Vet Clinic" (single by T. Doehrer/Z. Doehrer) from *Wolfpak Den Recordings* (album), recorded by Wolfpak, released 2005; "Dance The Night Away" (single by T. Doehrer) from *Dance The Night Away* (album), recorded by Balkan Rhythm Band™; "Sid Beckerman's Rumanian" (single by D. Jacobs) from *Meet Your Neighbor's Folk Music*™ (album), recorded by Jutta & The Hi-Dukes™; and *Hold Whatcha Got* (album), recorded by Razzemetazz™, all on Modal Music Records. Other artists include Ensemble M'chaiya™, Nordland Band™ and Terran's Greek Band™.

Tips "Please note our focus is primarily traditional and traditionally-based ethnic which is a very limited, non-mainstream market niche. You waste your time and money by sending us any other type of music. If you are unsure of your music fitting our focus, please call us before sending anything. Put your name and contact info on every item you send!"

◘ ◙ MONTICANA RECORDS

P.O. Box 32, Snowdon Station, Montreal QC H3X 3T3 Canada. **Contact:** David P. Leonard, general manager. Record company, record producer (Monticana Productions) and music publisher (Montina Music/SOCAN). Estab. 1963. Staff size: 1. Pays negotiable royalty to artists on contract.

How to Contact Submit demo package by mail. Unsolicited submissions are OK. Prefers CD. Include SASE.

Music Mostly **top 40**, **blues**, **country**, **dance-oriented**, **easy listening**, **folk** and **gospel**; also **jazz**, **MOR**, **progressive**, **R&B**, **rock** and **soul**.

Tips "Be excited and passionate about what you do. Be professional."

☐ NBT RECORDS

228 Morgan Lane, Berkeley Springs WV 25411-3475. (304)261-0228. E-mail: nbtoys@ verizon.net. **Contact:** John S. Newbraugh, owner. Record company, music publisher

(Newbraugh Brothers Music/BMI, NBT Music/ASCAP). Estab. 1967. Staff size: 1. Releases 4 singles and 52 CDs/year. Pays negotiable royalty to artists on contract; statutory royalty to publishers per song on record.

Distributed By "Distribution depends on the genre of the release. Our biggest distributor is perhaps the artists themselves, for the most part, depending on the genre of the release. We do have product in some stores and on the Internet as well."

How to Contact Submit demo package by mail. Unsolicited submissions are OK. Prefers CD or cassette with any amount of songs, lyric sheet and cover letter. Include SASE. Responds in 4-6 weeks. "Please don't call for permission to submit. Your materials are welcomed."

Music Mostly **rockabilly**, **hillbilly**, **folk** and **bluegrass**; also **rock**, **country** and **gospel**. Does not want any music with vulgar lyrics. "We will accept all genres of music except songs that contain vulgar language." Released *"Ride the Train Series Vol. 24; Layin' It On the Line* by Night Drive (2008); *Rockin' The Oldies* by Dale Brooks (2009) and *The Gospel Songbird* Vol. 2 by Wanda Sue Watkins (2008).

Tips "We are best known for our rockabilly releases. Reviews of our records can be found on both the American and European rockabilly websites. Our 'registered' trademark is a train. From time to time, we put out a CD with various artists featuring original songs that use trains as part of their theme. We use all genres of music for our train releases. We have received train songs from various parts of the world. All submissions on this topic are welcomed."

NERVOUS RECORDS

5 Sussex Crescent, Northolt, Middlesex UB5 4DL England. 44(20)8423 7373. E-mail: nervous@compuserve.com. Website: www.nervous.co.uk. **Contact:** R. Williams, managing director. Record company (Rage Records), record producer and music publisher (Nervous Publishing and Zorch Music). Member: MCPS, PRS, PPL, ASCAP, NCB. Releases 10 CDs/year. Pays 8-12% royalty to artists on contract; statutory rate to publisher per song on records. Royalties paid directly to US songwriters and artists or through US publishing or recording affiliate.

- Nervous Records' publishing company, Nervous Publishing, is listed in the Music Publishers section.

How to Contact Submit demo tape by mail. Unsolicited submissions are OK. Prefers cassette with 4-15 songs and lyric sheet. SAE and IRC. Responds in 3 weeks.

Music Mostly **psychobilly** and **rockabilly**. "No heavy rock, AOR, stadium rock, disco, soul, pop—only wild rockabilly and psychobilly." Released "Extra Chrome", written and recorded by Johnny Black; "It's Still Rock 'N' Roll to Me", written and recorded by The Time. Other artists include Restless Wild and Taggy Tones.

☐ NORTH STAR MUSIC

338 Compass Circle A1, North Kingstown RI 02852. (401)886-8888 or (800)346-2706. Fax: (401)886-8880. E-mail: info@northstarmusic.com. Website: www.northstarmusic. com. **Contact:** Richard Waterman, president. Record company. Estab. 1985. Staff size: 15. Releases 12-16 LPs/year. Pays 9% royalty to artists on contract; 3/4 statutory rate to publisher per song on record.

Distributed By Goldenrod and in-house distribution.

How to Contact Submit demo CD by mail. Unsolicited submissions are OK. Prefers finished CD. Does not return material. Responds in 2 months.

Music Mostly **instrumental**, **traditional** and **contemporary jazz**, **New Age**, **traditional world (Cuban, Brasilian, singer/songwriter, Hawaiian and Flamenco)** and **classical**. Released *Sacred* (album), written and recorded by David Tolk (inspirational), released 2003; *An Evening In Tuscany* (album), written and recorded by Bruce Foulke/Howard Kleinfeld (contemporary instrumental), released 2004; *Always & Forever* (album), written and recorded by David Osborne (piano), released 2003, all on North Star Music. Other artists include Judith Lynn Stillman, David Osborne, Emilio Kauderer, Gerry Beaudoin, Cheryl Wheeler and Nathaniel Rosen.

◐ OGLIO RECORDS

P.O. Box 404, Redondo Beach CA 90277. (310)791-8600. Fax: (310)791-8670. E-mail: getinfo4@oglio.com. Website: www.oglio.com. Record company. Estab. 1992. Releases 20 LPs and 20 CDs/year. Pays negotiable royalty to artist on contract; statutory rate to publisher per song on record.

How to Contact No unsolicited demos.

Music Mostly **alternative rock** and **comedy**. Released *Shine* (album), recorded by Cyndi Lauper (pop); *Live At The Roxy* (album), recorded by Brian Wilson (rock); *Team Leader* (album), recorded by George Lopez (comedy).

◪ OUTSTANDING RECORDS

P.O. Box 2111, Huntington Beach CA 92647. (714)377-7447 E-mail: beecher@ outstandingmusic.com Website: www.outstandingmusic.com. **Contact:** Earl Beecher, owner. Labels include Outstanding, Morrhythm (mainstream/commercial), School Band (educational/charity), Church Choir (religious charity), and Empowerment (educational CDs and DVDs). Record company, music publisher (Earl Beecher Publishing/BMI and Beecher Music Publishing/ASCAP) and record producer (Earl Beecher). Estab. 1968. Staff size: 1. Releases 100 CDs/year. Pays $2/CD royalty to artists on contract; statutory rate to publisher per song on record.

Distributed By All full CDs listed on the Web site can be ordered directly through the Web site. Most of them are now available via download through iTunes, Napster, Rhapsody, Amazon/mp3, Emusic, or Yahoo. Whenever wholesale distributors contact me for specific orders, I am happy to work with them, especially distributors overseas.

How to Contact Submit demo by mail. Unsolicited submissions are OK. Prefers CD (full albums), lyric sheet, photo and cover letter. Include SASE. Responds in 3 weeks.

Music Mostly **jazz**, **rock** and **country**; also **everything else especially Latin**. Does not want music with negative, anti-social or immoral messages. "View our website for a listing of all current releases."

Tips "We prefer to receive full CDs, rather than just three numbers. A lot of submitters suggest we release their song in the form of singles, but we just can't bother with singles at the present time. Especially looking for performers who want to release their material on my labels. Some songwriters are pairing up with performers and putting out CDs with a 'Writer Presents the Performer' concept. No dirty language. Do not encourage listeners to use drugs, alcohol or engage in immoral behavior. I'm especially looking for upbeat, happy, danceable music."

⬚ ◯ P. & N. RECORDS

61 Euphrasia Dr., Toronto ON M6B 3V8 Canada. (416)782-5768. Fax: (416)782-7170. E-mail: panfilo@sympatico.ca. **Contact:** Panfilo Di Matteo, president, A&R. Record company, record producer and music publisher (Lilly Music Publishing). Estab. 1993. Staff size: 2. Releases 10 singles, 20 12" singles, 15 LPs, 20 EPs and 15 CDs/year. Pays 25-35% royalty to artists on contract; statutory rate to publisher per song on record.

How to Contact Submit demo by mail. Unsolicited submissions are OK. Prefers CD or videocassette with 3 songs and lyric or lead sheet. Does not return material. Responds in 1 month only if interested.

Music Mostly **dance**, **ballads** and **rock**. Released *Only This Way* (album), written and recorded by Angelica Castro; *The End of Us* (album), written and recorded by Putz, both on P. & N. Records (dance); and "Lovers" (single by Marc Singer), recorded by Silvana (dance), released 2001 on P. and N. Records.

⬚ ◪ THE PANAMA MUSIC GROUP OF COMPANIES

(formerly Audio-Visual Media Productions), Sovereign House, 12 Trewartha Rd., Praa Sands, Penzance, Cornwall TR20 9ST England. +44 (0)1736 762826. Fax: +44 (0)1736 763328. E-mail: panamus@aol.com. Website: www.songwriters-guild.co.uk and www. panamamusic.co.uk. **Contact:** Roderick G. Jones, CEO, A&R. Labels include Pure Gold Records, Panama Music Library, Rainy Day Records, Panama Records, Mohock Records, Digimix Records (www.digimixrecords.com and www.myspace.com/digimixrecords). Registered members of Phonographic Performance Ltd. (PPL). Record company, music publisher, production and development company (Panama Music Library, Melody First Music Library, Eventide Music Library, Musik Image Music Library, Promo Sonor International Music Library, Caribbean Music Library, ADN Creation Music Library, Piano Bar Music Library, Corelia Music Library, PSI Music Library, Scamp Music,

First Time Music Publishing U.K.), registered members of the Mechanical Copyright Protection Society (MCPS) and the Performing Right Society (PRS) (London, England UK), management firm and record producer (First Time Management & Production Co.). Estab. 1986. Staff size: 6. Pays variable royalty to artists on contract; statutory rate to publisher per song on record subject to deal.

Distributed By Media U.K. Distributors and Digimix Worldwide Digital Distribution.

How to Contact Submit demo package by mail. Unsolicited submissions are OK. CD only with unlimited number of songs/instrumentals and lyric or lead sheets where necessary. "We do not return material so there is no need to send return postage. We will, due to volume of material received only respond to you if we have any interest. Please note: no MP3 submissions, attachments, downloads, or referrals to Web sites in the first instance via e-mail. Do not send anything by recorded delivery or courier as it will not be signed for. If we are interested, we will follow up for further requests and offers as necessary."

Music All styles. Published by Scamp Music: "Chill Out" written by Richard Hinsley (single), recorded and released by Panama Productions / Panama Music Library (Film & TV library music) used in Ray Mears' "Wild Food" programme/documentary for BBC television networks and published by Scamp Music (mcps/prs) (www.panamamusic. co.uk and www.myspace.com/scampmusicpublishing); "I Get Stoned" (hardcore dance) recorded by AudioJunkie & Stylus, released by EMI Records on *Hardcore Nation 2009*; "Don't Want This Night to End" (dance/club) from *Clubland 14*, recorded by Club Generation & MC Whizzkid, released on Universal Records (2009); "Lord of the Ringside" (Brit Rock/indie) from *Cosmic Cabaret*, recorded by Toots Earl & Clown, released on Digimix Records, and more.

N PAPER + PLASTICK

Website: http://paperandplastick.com. **Contact:** through form on website. Paper + Plastick handles both visual artwork and music.

Music Andrew Dost, Coffee Project, Foundation, Gatorface, Blacklist Royals, Landmines, We are the Union, and more.

PARLIAMENT RECORDS

357 S. Fairfax Avenue #430, Los Angeles CA 90036. (323)653-0693. E-mail: parlirec@ aol.com. Website: www.parliamentrecords.com. **Contact:** Ben Weisman, owner. Record company, record producer (Weisman Production Group) and music publisher (Audio Music Publishers, Queen Esther Music Publishing). Estab. 1965. Produces 30 singles/ year. Fee derived from sales royalty when song or artist is recorded.

How to Contact Submit demo package by mail. Unsolicited submissions are OK. Prefers CD with 3-10 songs and lyric sheet. Include SASE. "Mention Songwriter's Market. Please make return envelope the same size as the envelopes you send material in, otherwise we cannot send everything back." Responds in 6 weeks.

Music Mostly **R&B**, **soul**, **dance**, and **top 40/pop**; also **gospel** and **blues**. Artists include Rapture 7 (gospel), Wisdom (male gospel singers), Chosen Recovery Ministry (female gospel group), Jewel With Love (gospel), Apostle J. Dancy (gospel), Mirac (rap), L'nee (R&B/pop/hip-hop).

Tips "Parliament Records will also listen to 'tracks' only. If you send tracks, please include a letter stating what equipment you record on—ADAT, Protools or Roland VS recorders."

☑ QUARK RECORDS

P.O. Box 452, Newtown CT 06470. (917)687-9988. E-mail: quarkent@aol.com. **Contact:** Curtis Urbina. Record company and music publisher (Quarkette Music/BMI and Freedurb Music/ASCAP). Estab. 1984. Releases 3 singles and 3 LPs/year. Pays negotiable royalty to artists on contract; 3/4 statutory rate to publisher per song on record.

How to Contact Prefers CD with 2 songs (max). Include SASE. "Must be an absolute 'hit' song!" Responds in 6 weeks.

Music POP and Dance music only.

☑ RAVE RECORDS, INC.

Attn: Production Dept., 13400 W. Seven Mile Rd., Detroit MI 48235. E-mail: info@raverecords.com. Website: www.raverecords.com. **Contact:** Carolyn and Derrick, production managers. Record company and music publisher (Magic Brain Music/ASCAP). Estab. 1992. Staff size: 2. Releases 2-4 singles and 2 CDs/year. Pays various royalty to artists on contract; statutory rate to publisher per song on record.

Distributed By Action Music Sales.

How to Contact *"We do not accept unsolicited submissions."* Submit demo package by mail. Prefers CD with 3 songs, lyric sheet. "Include any bios, fact sheets, and press you may have. We will contact you if we need any further information." Does not return materials.

Music Mostly **alternative rock** and **dance**. Artists include Cyber Cryst, Dorothy, Nicole, and Bukimi 3.

☑ ☑ RCA RECORDS

1540 Broadway, 36th Floor, New York NY 10036. (212)930-4936. Fax: (212)930-4447. E-mail: info@rcarecords.com. Website: www.rcarecords.com. A&R: Donna Pearce. Beverly Hills: 8750 Wilshire Blvd., Beverly Hills CA 90211. (310)358-4105 Fax: (310)358-4127. Senior Vice President of A&R: Jeff Blue. Nashville: 1400 18th Ave. S., Nashville TN 37212. A&R Director: Jim Catino. Labels include Loud Records, Deconstruction Records and Judgment/RCA Records. Record company.

• RCA Records is a subsidiary of Sony BMG, one of the "Big 4" major labels.

Distributed By BMG.

How to Contact *RCA Records does not accept unsolicited submissions.*
Music Artists include The Strokes, Dave Matthews Band, Anti-Flag, Christina Aguilera, and Foo Fighters.

RED ADMIRAL RECORDS LLP

The Cedars, Elvington Lane, Folkestone Kent CT18 7AD United Kingdom. Estab. 1979. (01)(303)893-472. Fax: (01)(303)893-833. E-mail: info@redadmiralrecords.com. Website: www.redadmiralrecords.com. **Contact:** Chris Ashman. Registered members of MCPS, PRS, and PPL. Record company and music publisher (Cringe Music (MCPS/PRS)). Estab. 1979.
How to Contact Submit demo package by mail. Unsolicited submissions are OK. Submit CD only with unlimited number of songs. Submission materials are not returned. Responds if interested.
Music All styles. Artists include Crispian St. Peters, Rik Waller, Wim Hautekiet, Mirkwood, David Hay, The Silent Kingdom, Peter Dinsley, Carmen Wiltshire Hardly Mozart, The Sharpee's.

REDEMPTION RECORDS

P.O. Box 10238, Beverly Hills CA 90213. E-mail: info@redemption.net. Website: www. redemption.net. A&R Czar: Ryan D. Kuper (indie rock, power pop, rock, etc.). Record company. Estab. 1990. Staff size: varies. Releases 2-3 (various)/year. "We typically engage in profit splits with signed artists."
Distributed By GoDigital (digital); misc. (physical).
How to Contact Submit via e-mail with link to digital tracks. Include accomplishments and goals. Responds only if interested.
Music Mostly **indie rock** and **power pop**. Artists include Race For Titles, Vicious Vicious, Motion City Soundtrack, and The Working Title.
Tips "We only sign acts that will tour in support of their releases. Make sure your line-up is secure."

RED SKY RECORDS

P.O. Box 27, Stroud, Glos. GL6 0YQ United Kingdom. 01453-836877. Fax: 01453-836877. Website: www.redskyrecords.co.uk. **Contact:** Johnny Coppin, producer. Record company and record producer (Johnny Coppin). Estab. 1985. Staff size: 1. Releases 1 album/year. Pays 8-10% to artists on contract; statutory rate to publisher per song on record.
Distributed By Proper Music Distribution.
How to Contact *Write first and obtain permission to submit.* Does not return material. Responds in 6 months.
Music Mostly **singer-songwriters, folk** and **roots music**. Released *Keep the Flame* (album) and *The Winding Stair* (album), written and recorded by Johnny Coppin (singer/

songwriter); *Breaking the Silence* (album), written and recorded by Mike Silver and Johnny Coppin. Other artists include Paul Burgess.

☑ REPRISE RECORDS

3300 Warner Blvd., 4th Floor, Burbank CA 91505. (818)846-9090. Fax: (818)840-2389. Website: www.repriserecords.com. Labels include Duck and Sire. Record company.
- Reprise Records is a subsidiary of Warner Music Group, one of the "Big 4" major labels.

Distributed By WEA.

How to Contact *Reprise Records does not accept unsolicited submissions.*

Music Artists include Eric Clapton, My Chemical Romance, The Used, Muse, The Distillers, Talking Heads, The Who, Tom Petty, Green Day, Jane's Addiction, and Neil Young.

☒ RISE RECORDS

917 SW Oak St., Suite 422, Portland OR 97205. E-mail: Matthew@RiseRecords.com. Website: www.riserecords.com.

How to Contact E-mail a link to music, either on Purevolume or MySpace. "Please save your money and don't mail a presskit."

Music Rock, metal, alternative. Artists include Dance Gavin Dance; Drop Dead, Gorgeous; Emarose; Oceana; The Devil Wears Prada; Tides of Man, and more.

☒ ROADRUNNER RECORDS

902 Broadway, 8th Floor, New York NY 10010. (212)274-7500. Fax: (212)505-7469. E-mail: roadrunner@roadrunnerrecords.com. Website: www.roadrunnerrecords.com.

How to Contact "We are not currently accepting demos at this time."

Music Rock, metal, alternative. Artists include Amanda Palmer, Killswitch Engage, The Wombats, Opeth, Nickelback, Biffy Clyro, Lynyrd Skynyrd, Megadeth, Slipknot, and more.

☑ ROBBINS ENTERTAINMENT LLC

35 Worth St., 4th Floor, New York NY 10013. (212)675-4321. Fax: (212)675-4441. E-mail: info@robbinsent.com. Website: www.robbinsent.com. **Contact:** Matt D'Arduini, Manager/ A&R. Record company and music publisher (Rocks, No Salt). Estab. 1996. Staff size: 10. Releases 25 singles and 12-14 CDs/year. Pays negotiable royalty to artists on contract; statutory rate to publisher per song on record.

Distributed By Sony/BMG.

How to Contact Accepts unsolicited radio edit demos as long as it's dance music. Prefers CD with 2 songs or less. "Make sure everything is labeled with the song title information and your contact information. This is important in case the CD and the jewel case get separated. Do not call us and ask if you can send your package. The answer is yes."

Music Commercial **dance** only. Released top 10 pop smashes, "Heaven" (single), recorded by DJ Sammy; "Everytime We Touch" (single), recorded by Cascada; "Listen To Your Heart" (single), recored by DHT; as well as Hot 100 records from Rockell, Lasgo, Reina and K5. Other artists include Ian Van Dahl, September, Andain, Judy Torres, Jenna Drey, Marly, Dee Dee, Milky, Kreo and many others.

Tips "Do not send your package 'Supreme-Overnight-Before-You-Wake-Up' delivery. Save yourself some money. Do not send material if you are going to state in your letter that, 'If I had more (fill in the blank) it would sound better.' We are interested in hearing your best and only your best. Do not call us and ask if you can send your package. The answer is yes. We are looking for dance music with crossover potential."

☐ ROLL ON RECORDS

112 Widmar Pl., Clayton CA 94517. (925)833-4680. E-mail: rollonrecords@aol.com. **Contact:** Edgar J. Brincat, owner. Record company and music publisher (California Country Music). Estab. 1985. Pays 10% royalty to artists on contract; statutory rate to publisher per song on record. Member of Harry Fox Agency.

Distributed By Tower.

How to Contact Submit demo package by mail. Unsolicited submissions are OK. "Do not call or write for permission to submit, if you do you will be rejected." Prefers CD or cassette with 3 songs and lyric sheet. Include SASE and phone number. Responds in 6 weeks.

Music Mostly **contemporary/country** and **modern gospel**. Released "Broken Record" (single by Horace Linsley/Dianne Baumgartner), recorded by Edee Gordon on Roll On Records; Maddy and For Realities Sake (albums both by F.L. Pittman/Madonna Weeks), recorded by Ron Banks/L.J. Reynolds on Life Records/Bellmark Records.

Tips "Be patient and prepare to be in it for the long haul. A successful songwriter does not happen overnight. It's rare to write a song today and have a hit tomorrow. If you give us your song and want it back, then don't give it to us to begin with."

☐ ROTTEN RECORDS

Attn: A&R Dept., P.O. Box 56, Upland CA 91785. (909)920-4567. E-mail: rotten@ rottenrecords.com. Website: www.rottenrecords.com. President: Ron Peterson. Promotions/Radio/Video: Andi Jones. Record company. Estab. 1988. Releases 3 LPs, 3 EPs and 3 CDs/year.

Distributed By RIOT (Australia), Sonic Rendezvous (NL), RED (US) and PHD (Canada).

How to Contact Submit demo package by mail. Unsolicited submissions are OK. Prefers CD or MySpace link. Does not return material.

Music Mostly **rock**, **alternative** and **commercial**; also **punk** and **heavy metal**. Released *Paegan Terrorism* (album), written and recorded by Acid Bath; *Kiss the Clown* (album by K. Donivon), recorded by Kiss the Clown; and *Full Speed Ahead* (album by Cassidy/ Brecht), recorded by D.R.T., all on Rotten Records.

Tips "Be patient."

☒ ⊛ ROUGH TRADE RECORDS

Beggar's Group, 66 Golborne Road, London W10 5PS.020 8960 9888. Fax: 020 8968 6715. Website: www.roughtraderecords.com.

How to Contact Demos should be marked for attention of Paul Jones.

Music Alternative. Artists include Super Furry Animals, Jarvis Cocker, The Hold Steady, Emiliana Torrini, British Sea Power, The Libertines, My Morning Jacket, Jenny Lewis, The Strokes, The Mystery Jets, the Decemberists, and more.

☐ ROWENA RECORDS

195 S. 26th St., San Jose CA 95116. (408)286-9840. E-mail: gradie@sbcglobal.net. Website: www.onealprod.com. Owner/A&R (country, Mexican, gospel): Gradie O'Neal. A&R (all styles): Jeannine O'Neal. Record company and music publisher (Tiki Enterprises). Estab. 1967. Staff size: 3. Releases 8-12 LPs and 8-12 CDs/year. Pays negotiable royalty to artists on contract; pays statutory rate to publisher per song on record.

- Also see the listing for Tiki Enterprises Inc. in the Music Publishers section of this book.

How to Contact Submit demo by mail. Unsolicited submissions are OK. Prefers CD with 2 songs and lyric sheet. Include SASE. Responds in 2 weeks.

Music Mostly **gospel**, **country** and **pop**; also **Mexican** and **R&B**. Released "It Amazes Me" (single by David Davis/Jeannine O'Neal) from *Forgiven* (album), recorded by Amber Littlefield/David Davis (Christian), released 2003-2004; "I'm Healed" (single by Jeannine O'Neal) from *Faith On the Front Lines* (album), recorded by Jeannine O'Neal, released 2004; and "You're Looking Good to Me" (single by Warren R. Spalding) from *A Rock 'N' Roll Love Story* (album), recorded by Warren R. Spalding, released 2003-2004, all on Rowena Records.

Tips "For up-to-date releases, view our website."

☒ RUSTIC RECORDS

6337 Murray Lane, Brentwood TN 37027. (615)371-0646. Fax: (615)370-0353. E-mail: rusticrecordsinc@aol.com. Website: www.rusticrecordsinc.com. President: Jack Schneider. Executive VP & Operations Manager: Nell Schneider. VP Publishing and Catalog Manager: Amanda Mark. VP Marketing and Promotions: Ross Schneider. Videography, Photography, and Graphic Design: Wayne Hall. Image consultant: Jo Ann Rossi. Independent traditional country music label and music publisher (Iron Skillet Music/ASCAP, Covered Bridge/ BMI, Old Towne Square/ SESAC). Estab. 1979. Staff size: 6. Releases 2-3/year. Pays negotiable royalty to artists on contracts; statutory royalty to publisher per song on record.

Distributed By CDBaby.com and available on iTunes, MSN Music, Rhapsody, and more.

How to Contact Submit professional demo package by mail. Unsolicited submissions are OK. CD only; no mp3s or e-mails. Include no more than 4 songs with corresponding lyric sheets and cover letter. Include appropriately-sized SASE. Responds in 4 weeks.

Music Good combination of traditional and modern **country**. 2008-09 releases: *Ready to Ride* - debut album from Nikki Britt, featuring "C-O-W-B-O-Y," "Do I Look Like Him," "Star in My Car," and "You Happened"; *Hank Stuff* from DeAnna Cox - featuring "I'm a Long Gone Mama," and "I'm so Lonesome I Could Cry."

Tips "Professional demo preferred."

☐ RUSTRON/WHIMSONG MUSIC PRODUCTIONS

1156 Park Lane, West Palm Beach FL 33417-5957. (561)686-1354. E-mail: rmp_wmp@ bellsouth.net. **Contact:** Sheelah Adams, office administrator. Executive Director: Rusty Gordon (folk fusions, blues, women's music, adult contemporary, electric-acoustic, New Age instrumentals, children's, cabaret, pop ballads). Director A&R: Ron Caruso (all styles). Associate Director of A&R: Kevin Reeves (pop, country, blues, R&B, jazz, folk). Labels include Rustron Records and Whimsong Records. "Rustron administers 20 independent labels for publishing and marketing." Record company, record producer, management firm and music publisher (Whimsong Music Publishing/ASCAP and Rustron Music Publishing/BMI). Estab. 1970. Releases 5-10 CDs/year. Pays variable royalty to artists on contract. "Artists with history of product sales get higher percent than those with no sales track record." Pays statutory rate to publisher.

How to Contact *Songwriters may write or call first to discuss your submission.* You may send a snail-mail request for current submission guidelines. Include a SASE or International Response Coupon (IRC) for all correspondence, including sending submissions. No Exceptions. E-mail gets the quickest response. Song submissions should include a cover letter that explains why you are submitting and what type of review you want. You may want a combined publishing and record company review. If your songs are already published, let us know what publishing company you signed with. Tell us about your intentions for the future and if you are a performing or a freelance songwriter. Tell us if you are collaborating on some or all of your songs. All songwriters who creatively contributed to a song must sign the cover letter authorizing the review. Copyrighting the songs in your submission with The U.S. Library of Congress is essential before sending them to us. We do not review uncopyrighted original songs. Songwriter's must officially own the exclusive rights to their songs by copyrighting them. As soon as you have mailed the Copyright Form PA to the Library of Congress, the songs are "Copyright Pending," and you can send them. Submit 1 CD or several CDs, requesting a "body of work review" by snail-mail. You may present up to 15 songs on each CD you submit. Unsolicited submissions are OK. We prefer a CD with up to 15 songs and typed 8 ½ × 11 lyric sheets, one song per sheet. Cassettes are limited to 3 songs. Responds in 4 months.

Music Mostly **mainstream** and **women's music**, **adult contemporary electric-acoustic**, **pop (cabaret, blues)** and **blues (R&B, country and folk)**; also **soft rock** (ballads), **New Age fusions** (instrumentals), **modern folk fusions** (environmental, socio-political), **children's music** and **light jazz**. Released "White House Worries" (single) from *Whitehouse Worries* (album), written and recorded by The Ramifications (progressive country-folk/socio-political-topical), released 2007 on Rustron Records; "Sanibel-Captiva and the Gulf of Mexico" (single—historical song) from *Song of Longboat Key* (album), recorded by Florida Rank & File (Florida folk); "Take the High Road" (single) from *Voting for Democracy* (album), recorded by The Panama City Pioneers (progressive-political-folk), released 2007 on Whimsong Records.

Tips "Find your own unique style; write well crafted songs with unpredictable concepts, strong hooks and definitive verse melody. New Age composers: evolve your themes and add multi-cultural diversity with instruments. Don't be predictable. Don't over-produce your demos and don't drown vocals. Carefully craft songs for single-song marketing. An album can have nine eclectic songs that are loosely crafted and not very commercially viable individually. It takes only one carefully crafted 'radio ready' song with the right arrangement to get your album the exposure it needs."

⬚ ⊘ SAHARA RECORDS AND FILMWORKS ENTERTAINMENT

10573 W. Pico Blvd., #352, Los Angeles CA 90064-2348. (310)948-9652. Fax: (310)474-7705. E-mail: info@edmsahara.com. Website: www.edmsahara.com. **Contact:** Edward De Miles, president. Record company, music publisher (EDM Music/BMI, Edward De Miles Music Company) and record producer (Edward De Miles). Estab. 1981. Releases 15-20 CD singles and 5-10 CDs/year. Pays 9½ × 11% royalty to artists on contract; statutory rate to publishers per song on record.

How to Contact *Does not accept unsolicited submissions.*

Music Mostly **R&B/dance**, **top 40 pop/rock** and **contemporary jazz**; also **TV-film themes, musical scores and jingles**. Released "Hooked on U," "Dance Wit Me" and "Moments" (singles), written and recorded by Steve Lynn (R&B) on Sahara Records. Other artists include Lost in Wonder, Devon Edwards and Multiple Choice.

Tips "We're looking for strong mainstream material. Lyrics and melodies with good hooks that grab people's attention."

⬚ SANDALPHON RECORDS

P.O. Box 29110, Portland OR 97296. (503)957-3929. E-mail: jackrabbit01@comcast.net. **Contact:** Ruth Otey, president. Record company, music publisher (Sandalphon Music/BMI), and management agency (Sandalphon Management). Estab. 2005. Staff size: 2. Pays negotiable royalty to artists on contract; statutory royalty to publisher per song on record.

Distributed By "We are currently negotiating for distribution."

How to Contact Submit demo packageby mail. Unsolicited submissions are OK. Prefers cassette or CD with 1-5 songs with lyric sheet and cover letter. Returns submissions if accompanied by a SASE or SAE and IRC for outside the United States. Responds in 6-8 weeks.

Music Mostly **rock**, **country**, and **alternative**; also **pop**, **gospel**, and **blues**.

SILVER WAVE RECORDS

P.O. Box 7943, Boulder CO 80306. (303)443-5617. Fax: (303)443-0877. E-mail: info@ silverwave.com. Website: www.silverwave.com. **Contact:** James Marienthal. Record company. Estab. 1986. Releases 3-4 CDs/year. Pays varying royalty to artists on contract and to publisher per song on record.

How to Contact *Call first and obtain permission to submit.* Prefers CD. Include SASE. Responds only if interested.

Music Mostly **Native American** and **world**.

SIMPLY GRAND MUSIC INC

P.O. Box 770208, Memphis TN 38177-0208. (901)763-4787. Fax: (901)763-4883. E-mail: wahani@aol.com. Website: www.simplygrandmusic.com. **Contact:** Linda Lucchesi, president. Record company (Memphis Town Music) and music publisher (Beckie Publishing Company). Estab. 1965. Staff size: 2. Released 7 CDs last year. Royalties are negotiable.

Distributed By Ace Records and various others.

How to Contact Contact first and obtain permission to submit a demo. Include CD with 1-3 songs and lyric sheet. Returns submissions if accompanied by an SASE with ample postage. Responds in 3 months.

Music Mostly interested in **country**, **soul/R&B**, **pop**; also interested in **top 40**, **soft rock**. Recently published "Can't Find Happiness" written by Charlie Chalmers and Paul Selph, Jr., recorded by Barbara & The Browns (soul) for *Can't Find Happiness* (album) on Ace Records; "Hooked on a Feeling" written by Mark James, recorded by The Ovations feat. Louis Williams (soul) for *One In a Million* (album) on Ace Records; "Love Made a Fool of Me" written by Gary McEwan and Elmo Paul, Jr., recorded by Bettye LaVette (soul/R&B) for *Take Another Little Piece of My Heart* (album) on Varese Sarabande Records.

SKELETON CREW

NJ.E-mail: info@skeletoncrewonline.com. Website: www.skeletoncrewonline.com.

How to Contact E-mail or send message through MySpace page for directions on sending material.

Music Punk, indie, rock, alternative. Artists include David Costa, Architects, New Tomorrow, The Mean Reds, and more.

Record Companies

⊘ SONY BMG

550 Madison Ave., New York NY 10022. Website: www.sonymusic.com.

• Sony BMG is one of the primary "Big 4" major labels.

How to Contact For specific contact information see the listings in this section for Sony subsidiaries Columbia Records, Epic Records, Sony Nashville, RCA Records, J Records, Arista, and American Recordings.

⊘ SONY MUSIC NASHVILLE

8 Music Square W., Nashville TN 37203-3204. (615)726-8300. Labels include Columbia Nashville, Arista Nashville, RCA, BNA, and Provident Music Group.

• Sony Music Nashville is a subsidiary of Sony BMG, one of the "Big 4" major labels.

How to Contact *Sony Music Nashville does not accept unsolicited submissions.*

Ⓝ ⊘ SUGAR HILL RECORDS

E-mail: info@sugarhillrecords.com. Website: www.sugarhillrecords.com. Record company. Estab. 1978.

• Welk Music Group acquired Sugar Hill Records in 1998.

How to Contact *No unsolicited submissions.* "If you are interested in having your music heard by Sugar Hill Records or the Welk Music Group, we suggest you establish a relationship with a manager, publisher, or attorney that has an ongoing relationship with our company. We do not have a list of such entities."

Music Mostly **Americana**, **bluegrass**, and **country**. Artists include Nickel Creek, Allison Moorer, The Duhks, Sonny Landreth, Scott Miller, Reckless Kelly, Tim O'Brien, The Gibson Brothers, and more.

☐ TANGENT® RECORDS

P.O. Box 383, Reynoldsburg OH 43068-0383. (614)751-1962. Fax: (614)751-6414. E-mail: info@tangentrecords.com. Website: www.tangentrecords.com. **Contact:** Andrew Batchelor, president. Director of Marketing: Elisa Batchelor. Record company and music publisher (ArcTangent Music/BMI). Estab. 1986. Staff size: 3. Releases 10-12 CDs/year. Pays negotiable royalty to artists on contract; statutory rate to publisher per song on record.

How to Contact Submit demo package by mail. Unsolicited submissions are OK. Prefers CD, with minimum of 3 songs and lead sheet if available. "Please include a brief biography/ history of artist(s) and/or band, including musical training/education, performance experience, recording studio experience, discography and photos (if available)." Does not return material. Responds if interested.

Music Mostly **artrock** and **contemporary instrumental/rock instrumental**; also **contemporary classical**, **world beat**, **jazz/rock**, **ambient**, **electronic**, and **New Age**.

Tips "Take the time to pull together a quality CD or cassette demo with package/

portfolio, including such relevant information as experience (on stage and in studio, etc.), education/training, biography, career goals, discography, photos, etc. Should be typed. We are not interested in generic sounding or 'straight ahead' music. We are seeking music that is innovative, pioneering and eclectic with a fresh, unique sound."

☑ TEXAS MUSIC CAFE

P.O. Box 50273, Austin TX 78763. E-mail: booking@texasmusiccafe.com. Website: www. texasmusiccafe.com. **Contact:** Aubin Hagelstein, booking. Television show. Estab. 1997. Staff size: 10. Releases 26 TV programs/year. Pays opportunity to perform on national television. Original music only.

Distributed By PBS in high definition and surround sound.

How to Contact Submit demo by mail or e-mail a link. Unsolicited submissions are OK. Prefers CD, videocassette (VHS/DVD) with sample songs. Does not return material. Responds only if interested.

Tips "Must be willing to travel to Texas at your expense to be taped. Let us know if you are traveling near central Texas."

☑ TEXAS ROSE RECORDS

2002 Platinum St., Garland TX 75042. (972)272-3131. Fax: (972)272-3155. E-mail: txrr1@ aol.com. Website: www.texasroserecords.com. **Contact:** Nancy Baxendale, president. Record company, music publisher (Yellow Rose of Texas Publishing) and record producer (Nancy Baxendale). Estab. 1994. Staff size: 3. Releases 3 CDs/year. Pays negotiable royalty to artists on contract; statutory rate to publisher per song on record.

Distributed By Self distribution.

How to Contact *Write or e-mail first for permission to submit.* Submit maximum of 2 songs on CD and lyrics. Does not return material. Responds only if interested.

Music Mostly **country**, **soft rock** and **blues**; also **pop**. Does not want hip-hop, rap, heavy metal. Released *Flyin' High Over Texas* (album), recorded by Dusty Martin (country); *High On The Hog* (album), recorded by Steve Harr (country); *Time For Time to Pay* (album), recorded by Jeff Elliot (country); *Double XXposure* (album), recorded by Jeff Elliott and Kim Neeley (country), and "Cowboy Super Hero" (single) written and recorded by Robert Mauldin.

Tips "We are interested in songs written for today's market with a strong musical hook. No home recordings, please."

☑ TOMMY BOY ENTERTAINMENT LLC

120 Fifth Avenue, 7th Floor, New York NY 10011. (212)388-8300. Fax: (212)388-8431. E-mail: info@tommyboy.com. Website: www.tommyboy.com. Record company. Labels include Penalty Recordings, Outcaste Records, Timber and Tommy Boy Gospel.

Distributed By WEA.

How to Contact E-mail to obtain current demo submission policy.

Music Artists include Chavela Vargas, Afrika Bambaataa, Biz Markie, Kool Keith, and INXS.

☐ TON RECORDS

4474 Rosewood Ave., Los Angeles CA 90004. E-mail: tonmusic@earthlink.net. Website: www.tonrecords.com or www.myspace.com/tonrecords. Vice President: Jay Vasquez. Labels include 7" collectors series and Ton Special Projects. Record company and record producer (RJ Vasquez). Estab. 1992. Releases 6-9 LPs, 1-2 EPs and 10-11 CDs/year. Pays negotiable royalty to artists on contract; statutory rate to publisher per song on record.

Distributed By MS, Com Four, Rotz, Subterranean, Revelation, Get Hip, Impact, Page Canada and Disco Dial.

How to Contact Not signing at present time.

Music Mostly **new music**; also **hard new music**. Released *Intoxicated Birthday Lies* (album), recorded by shoegazer (punk rock); *The Good Times R Killing Me* (album), recorded by Top Jimmy (blues); and *Beyond Repair* (album), recorded by Vasoline Tuner (space rock), all on Ton Records. Other artists include Why? Things Burn, Hungry 5, and the Ramblers.

Tips "Work as hard as we do."

☑ TOPCAT RECORDS

P.O. Box 670234, Dallas TX 75367. (972)484-4141. Fax: (972)620-8333. E-mail: info@topcatrecords.com. Website: www.topcatrecords.com or www.myspace.com/topcatrecords. President: Richard Chalk. Record company and record producer. Estab. 1991. Staff size: 3. Releases 4-6 CDs/year. Pays 10-15% royalty to artists on contract; statutory rate to publisher per song on record.

Distributed By City Hall.

How to Contact *Call first and obtain permission to submit.* Prefers CD. Does not return material. Responds in 1 month.

Music Mostly **blues**, **swing**, **rockabilly**, **Americana**, **Texana** and **R&B**. Released *If You Need Me* (album), written and recorded by Robert Ealey (blues); *Texas Blueswomen* (album by 3 Female Singers), recorded by various (blues/R&B); and *Jungle Jane* (album), written and recorded by Holland K. Smith (blues/swing), all on Topcat. Released CDs: *Jim Suhler & Alan Haynes—Live*; Bob Kirkpatrick *Drive Across Texas*; *Rock My Blues to Sleep* by Johnny Nicholas; *Walking Heart Attack*, by Holland K. Smith; *Dirt Road* (album), recorded by Jim Suhler; *Josh Alan Band* (album), recorded by Josh Alan; *Bust Out* (album), recorded by Robin Sylar. Other artists include Grant Cook, Muddy Waters, Big Mama Thornton, Big Joe Turner, Geo. "Harmonica" Smith, J.B. Hutto and Bee Houston. "View our Web site for an up-to-date listing of releases."

Tips "Send me blues (fast, slow, happy, sad, etc.) or good blues oriented R&B. No pop, hip-hop, or rap."

⊠ TOUCH AND GO/QUARTERSTICK RECORDS

P.O. Box 25520, Chicago IL 60625. (773)388-8888. Fax: (773)388-8888. E-mail: info@ tgrec.com. Website: www.touchandgorecords.com. Quarterstick Records: P.O. Box 25342, Chicago, IL 60625.

How to Contact Mail to one or the other (staffed by same people, no need to send to both labels). "Demos are listened to by any and all staffers who want to or have time to listen to them. Do not call or e-mail us about your demo." Do not e-mail mp3s or web URLs.

Music All Styles. Artists include Therapy?, TV on the Radio, Pinback, Naked Raygun, Blonde Redhead, Henry Rollins, Yeah Yeah Yeahs, Girls Against Boys, and more.

⊡ UAR RECORDS

P.O. Box 1264, 6020 W. Pottstown Rd., Peoria IL 61654-1264. (309)673-5755. Fax: (309)673-7636. E-mail: uarltd@A5.com. Website: www.unitedcyber.com. Contact: Jerry Hanlon, A&R director. Record company and music publisher (Jerjoy Music/BMI and Katysarah Music/ASCAP). Estab. 1978. Staff size: 2. Releases 3 or more CDs/year.

- Also see the listings for Kaysarah Music (ASCAP) and Jerjoy Music (BMI) in the Music Publishers section of this book.

How to Contact "If you are an artist seeking a record deal, please send a sample of your vocal and/or songwriting work-guitar and vocal is fine, no more than 4 songs. Fully produced demos are NOT necessary. Also send brief information on your background in the business, your goals, etc. If you are NOT a songwriter, please send 4 songs maximum of cover tunes that we can use to evaluate your vocal ability. If you wish a reply, please send a SASE, otherwise, you will not receive an answer. If you want a critique of your vocal abilities, please so state as we do not routinely offer critiques. Unsolicited submissions are OK. If you wish all of your material returned to you, be sure to include mailing materials and postage. WE DO NOT RETURN PHONE CALLS."

Music Mostly **American** and **Irish country**. Released "When Jackie Sang The Walking Talking Dolly," "Far Side Banks of Jordan," "There's You," all recorded by Jerry Hanlon. "Lisa Dance With Me," "Philomena From Ireland," "Rainbow," "I'd Better Stand Up," all recorded by the Heggarty Twins from Northern Ireland and Jerry Hanlon. "An Ordinary Woman," "All Your Little Secrets," recorded by Anne More.

Tips "We are a small independent company, but our belief is that every good voice deserves a chance to be heard and our door is always open to new and aspiring artists."

⊠ UNIVERSAL RECORDS

1755 Broadway, 7th Floor, New York NY 10019. (212)841-8000. Fax: (212)331-2580. Website: www.universalrecords.com. **Universal City office:** 70 Universal City Plaza, 3rd Floor, Universal City CA 91608. (818)777-1000. Vice Presidents A&R: Bruce Carbone, Tse Williams. Labels include Uptown Records, Mojo Records, Republic Records, Bystorm Records and Gut Reaction Records. Record company.

- Universal Records is a subsidiary of Universal Music Group, one of the "Big 4" major labels.

How to Contact *Universal Records in California does not accept unsolicited submissions. The New York office only allows you to call first and obtain permission to submit.*

Music Artists include India Arie, Erykah Bad, Godsmack, Kaiser Chiefs, and Lindsey Lohan.

⊠ ⊛ VAGRANT

2118 Wilshire Blvd. #361, Santa Monica CA 90403. E-mail: publicity@vagrant.com. Website: www.vagrant.com. United Kingdom: 3rd Floor, 1a Adpar St., London W2 1DE. E-mail: vagrantuk@vagrant.com.

How to Contact Send demos to: Demos c/o Vagrant Records at US mailing address.

Music Rock, alternative. Artists include Ace Enders, Waylon Jennings, The Bled, Placebo, Thrice, The Get Up Kids, Face to Face, Dashboard Confessional, Reggie and the Full Effect, Senses Fail, and more.

⊠ ⊘ THE VERVE MUSIC GROUP

1755 Broadway, 3rd Floor, New York NY 10019. (212)331-2000. Fax: (212)331-2064. E-mail: contact@vervemusicgroup.com. Website: www.vervemusicgroup.com. A&R Director: Dahlia Ambach. A&R Coordinator: Heather Buchanan. Los Angeles: 100 N. First St., Burbank CA 91502. (818)729-4804 Fax: (818)845-2564. Vice President A&R: Bud Harner. A&R Assistant: Heather Buchanan. Record company. Labels include Verve, GRP, Blue Thumb and Impulse! Records.

- Verve Music Group is a subsidiary of Universal Music Group, one of the "Big 4" major labels.

How to Contact *The Verve Music Group does not accept unsolicited submissions.*

Music Artists include Roy Hargrove, Diana Krall, George Benson, Al Jarreau, John Scofield, Natalie Cole, and David Sanborn.

⊠ VICTORY RECORDS

346 N. Justine St., Suite 504, Chicago IL 60607. (312)666-8661. Fax: (312)666-8665. Website: www.victoryrecords.com.

How to Contact Send press kit by mail.

Music Alternative, metal, rock. Artists include The Audition, Bayside, Catch 22, Funeral For A Friend, Otep, Hawthorne Heights, Ringworm, Secret Lives of the Freemasons, Silverstein, The Tossers, Voodoo Glow Skulls, William Control, Streetlight Manifesto, and more.

◙ VIRGIN RECORDS

1750 Vine St., Los Angeles CA 90028. (323)692-1100. Fax: (310)278-6231. Website: www.virginrecords.com. New York office: 150 5th Ave., 3rd Floor, New York NY 10016. (212)786-8200 Fax:(212)786-8343. Labels include Rap-A-Lot Records, Pointblank Records, SoulPower Records, AWOL Records, Astralwerks Records, Cheeba Sounds and Noo Trybe Records. Record company.

- Virgin Records is a subsidiary of the EMI Group, one of the "Big 4" major labels.

Distributed By EMD.

How to Contact *Virgin Records does not accept recorded material or lyrics unless submitted by a reputable industry source.* "If your act has received positive press or airplay on prior independent releases, we welcome your written query. Send a letter of introduction accompanied by all pertinent artist information. Do not send a tape until requested. All unsolicited materials will be returned unopened."

Music Mostly **rock** and **pop**. Artists include Lenny Kravitz, Placebo, The Rolling Stones, Joss Stone, Ben Harper, Iggy Pop, and Boz Scaggs.

⬇ ◙ WARNER BROS. RECORDS

3300 Warner Blvd., 3rd Floor, Burbank CA 91505. (818)846-9090. Fax: (818)953-3423. Website: www.wbr.com. **New York:** 75 Rockefeller Plaza, New York NY 10019. (212)275-4500 Fax:(212)275-4596. A&R: James Dowdall, Karl Rybacki. **Nashville:** 20 Music Square E., Nashville TN 37203. (615)748-8000 Fax:(615)214-1567. Labels include American Recordings, Eternal Records, Imago Records, Mute Records, Giant Records, Malpaso Records and Maverick Records. Record company.

- Warner Bros. Records is a subsidiary of Warner Music Group, one of the "Big 4" major labels.

Distributed By WEA.

How to Contact *Warner Bros. Records does not accept unsolicited material.* "All unsolicited material will be returned unopened. Those interested in having their tapes heard should establish a relationship with a manager, publisher or attorney that has an ongoing relationship with Warner Bros. Records."

Music Released *Van Halen 3* (album), recorded by Van Halen; *Evita* (soundtrack); and *Dizzy Up the Girl* (album), recorded by Goo Goo Dolls, both on Warner Bros. Records. Other artists include Faith Hill, Tom Petty & the Heartbreakers, Jeff Foxworthy, Porno For Pyros, Travis Tritt, Yellowjackets, Bela Fleck and the Flecktones, Al Jarreau, Joshua Redmond, Little Texas, and Curtis Mayfield.

◙ WINCHESTER RECORDS

25 Troubadour Lane, Berkeley Springs WV 25411. (304)258-8314. E-mail: mccoytroubadour@aol.com. Website: www.troubadourlounge.com. **Contact:** Jim or Bertha McCoy, owners. Labels include Master Records and Real McCoy Records. Record

company, music publisher (Jim McCoy Music, Clear Music, New Edition Music/BMI), record producer (Jim McCoy Productions) and recording studio. Releases 20 singles and 10 LPs/year. Pays standard royalty to artists; statutory rate to publisher for each record sold.

How to Contact *Write first and obtain permission to submit.* Prefers CD with 5-10 songs and lead sheet. Include SASE. Responds in 1 month.

Music Mostly **bluegrass**, **church/religious**, **country**, **folk**, **gospel**, **progressive** and **rock**. Released "Runaway Girl" (single by Earl Howard/Jim McCoy) from *Earl Howard Sings His Heart Out* (album), recorded by Earl Howard (country), released 2002 on Winchester; *Jim McCoy and Friends Remember Ernest Tubb* (album), recorded by Jim McCoy (country), released January 2003 on Winchester; *The Best of Winchester Records* (album), recorded by RileeGray/J.B. Miller/Jim McCoy/Carroll County (country), released 2002 on Winchester.

⊘ WIND-UP ENTERTAINMENT

79 Madison Ave., 7th Floor, New York NY 10016. (212)895-3100. Website: www. winduprecords.com. **Contact:** A&R. Record company. Estab. 1997. Releases 6-7 CDs/year. Pays negotiable royalty to artists on contract; statutory rate to publisher per song on record.

Distributed By BMG.

How to Contact *Write first and obtain permission to submit.* Prefers CD or DVD. Does not return material or respond to submissions.

Music Mostly **rock**, **folk** and **hard rock**. Artists include Seether, Evanescence, Finger Eleven, and People In Planes.

Tips "We rarely look for songwriters as opposed to bands, so writing a big hit single would be the rule of the day."

☑ XEMU RECORDS

609 Kappock Street, Suite 1A, Bronx NY 10463. (212)807-0290. Fax: (212)807-0583. E-mail: xemu@xemu.com. Website: www.xemu.com. **Contact:** Sulphin Marx, A&R. Record company. Estab. 1992. Staff size: 4. Releases 4 CDs/year. Pays negotiable royalty to artists on contract; statutory rate to publisher per song on record.

Distributed By Redeye Distribution.

How to Contact *Write first and obtain permission to submit.* Prefers CD with 3 songs. Does not return material. Responds in 2 months.

Music Mostly **alternative**. Released *Happy Suicide, Jim!* (album) by The Love Kills Theory (alternative rock); *Howls From The Hills* (album) by Dead Meadow; *The Fall* (album), recorded by Mikki James (alternative rock); *A is for Alpha* (album), recorded by Alpha Bitch (alternative rock); *Hold the Mayo* (album), recorded by Death Sandwich (alternative rock); *Stockholm Syndrome* (album), recorded by Trigger Happy (alternative rock) all released on Xemu Records. Other artists include Malvert P. Redd, The Fifth Dementia, and the Neanderthal Spongecake.

N ⊕ XL RECORDINGS

Beggar's Group, One Codrington Mews, London W11 2EH United Kingdom. Website: www.xlrecordings.com. US: 304 Hudson St., 7th Floor, New York NY 10013.

Music Alternative rock. Artists include Adele, Basement Jaxx, Be Your Own Pet, Beck, Dizzee Rascal, M.I.A, Peaches, Radiohead, Sigur Ros, The Horrors, The Raconteurs, The White Stripes, Thom Yorke, Vampire Weekend, and more.

Record Companies

ADDITIONAL RECORD COMPANIES

The following companies are also record companies, but their listings are found in other sections of the book. Read the listings for submission information.

A

ACR Productions 198

Awal.com 155

B

Backstreet Booking 220

Blues Alley Records 199

C

California Country Music 104

D

DaVinci's Notebook Records 201

Demi Monde Records & Publishing Ltd. 109

E

Earthscream Music Publishing Co. 111

F

Fifth Avenue Media, Ltd. 114

Final Mix Inc. 202

First Time Music (Publishing) U.K. 114

Fresh Entertainment 115

G

Glad Music Co. 115

H

Hailing Frequency Music Productions 203

Happy Melody 117

Hardison International Entertainment Corporation 227

Heart Consort Music 203

Heupferd Musikverlag GmbH 117

I

Island Culture Music Publishers 119

J

Ja/Nein Musikverlag GmbH 120

Jerjoy Music 120

K

Kaupps & Robert Publishing Co. 121

Kaysarah Music 121

L

L.A. Entertainment, Inc. 205

Levy Management, Rick 229

Lilly Music Publishing 122

M

Makers Mark Gold Music Productions 207

McCoy Music, Jim 125

Mega Truth Records 209

Montina Music 127

N

Neu Electro Productions 210

New Experience Records/Faze 4 Records 211

O

Orchid Publishing 130

P

Pegasus Music 130

Pollybyrd Publications Limited 132

Record Producers

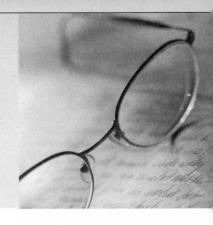

The independent producer can best be described as a creative coordinator. He's often the one with the most creative control over a recording project and is ultimately responsible for the finished product. Some record companies have in-house producers who work with the acts on that label (although, in more recent years, such producer-label relationships are often non-exclusive). Today, most record companies contract out-of-house, independent record producers on a project-by-project basis.

WHAT RECORD PRODUCERS DO

Producers play a large role in deciding what songs will be recorded for a particular project and are always on the lookout for new songs for their clients. They can be valuable contacts for songwriters because they work so closely with the artists whose records they produce. They usually have a lot more freedom than others in executive positions and are known for having a good ear for potential hit songs. Many producers are songwriters and musicians themselves. Since they wield a great deal of influence, a good song in the hands of the right producer at the right time stands a good chance of being cut. And even if a producer is not working on a specific project, he is well-acquainted with record company executives and artists and can often get material through doors not open to you.

SUBMITTING MATERIAL TO PRODUCERS

It can be difficult to get your tapes to the right producer at the right time. Many producers write their own songs and even if they don't write, they may be involved in their own publishing companies so they have instant access to all the songs in their catalogs. Also, some genres are more dependent on finding outside songs than others. A producer working with a rock group or a singer-songwriter will rarely take outside songs.

It's important to understand the intricacies of the producer/publisher situation. If you pitch your song directly to a producer first, before another publishing company publishes the song, the producer may ask you for the publishing rights (or a percentage thereof) to your song. You must decide whether the producer is really an active publisher who will try to get the song recorded again and again or whether he merely wants the publishing because it means extra income for him from the current recording project. You may be able to work out a co-publishing deal, where you and the producer split the publishing of the song. That means he will still receive his percentage of the publishing income, even if you secure a cover recording of the song by other artists in the future. Even though you would be giving up a little bit initially, you may benefit in the future.

Some producers will offer to sign artists and songwriters to "development deals." These can range from a situation where a producer auditions singers and musicians with the intention of building a group from the ground up, to development deals where a producer signs a band or singer-songwriter to his production company with the intention of developing the act and producing an album to shop to labels (sometimes referred to as a "baby record deal").

You must carefully consider whether such a deal is right for you. In some cases, such a deal can open doors and propel an act to the next level. In other worst-case scenarios, such a deal can result in loss of artistic and career control, with some acts held in contractual bondage for years at a time. Before you consider any such deal, be clear about your goals, the producer's reputation, and the sort of compromises you are willing to make to reach those goals. If you have any reservations whatsoever, don't do it.

The listings that follow outline which aspects of the music industry each producer is involved in, what type of music he is looking for, and what records and artists he's recently produced. Study the listings carefully, noting the artists each producer works with, and consider if any of your songs might fit a particular artist's or producer's style. Then determine whether they are open to your level of experience (see the A Sample Listing Decoded on page 12).

Consult the Category Index on page 370 to find producers who work with the type of music you write, and the Geographic Index at the back of the book to locate producers in your area.

ADDITIONAL RECORD PRODUCERS

There are **more record producers** located in other sections of the book! On page 216 use the list of Additional Record Producers to find listings within other sections who are also record producers.

Icons

For More Info

For more instructional information on the listings in this book, including explanations of symbols ( ), read the article *How To Use Songwriter's Market* on page 7.

⚡ ☑ "A" MAJOR SOUND CORPORATION

RR #1, Kensington PE COB 1MO Canada. (902)836-4571. E-mail: info@amajorsound.com. Website: www.amajorsound.com. **Contact:** Paul C. Milner, producer. Record producer and music publisher. Estab. 1989. Produces 8 CDs/year. Fee derived in part from sales royalty when song or artist is recorded, and/or outright fee from recording artist or record company, or investors.

How to Contact Submit demo package by mail. Unsolicited submissions are OK. Prefers CD with 5 songs and lyric sheet (lead sheet if available). Does not return material. Responds only if interested in 3 months.

Music Mostly **rock**, **A/C**, **alternative** and **pop**; also **Christian** and **R&B**. Produced *COLOUR* (album written by J. MacPhee/R. MacPhee/C. Buchanan/D. MacDonald), recorded by The Chucky Danger Band (pop/rock), released 2006; Winner of ECMA award; *Something In Between* (album, written by Matt Andersen), recorded by Matt Andersen and Friends (Blues), released 2008 on Weatherbox / Andersen; *In A Fever In A Dream* (album,written by Pat Deighan), recorded by Pat Deighan and The Orb Weavers (Rock), released in 2008 on Sandbar Music; *Saddle River String Band* (album, written by Saddle River Stringband), recorded by Saddle River Stringband (Blue Grass) released 2007 on Save As Music; Winner of ECMA award.

☐ ACR PRODUCTIONS

P.O. Box 5636, Midland TX 79704. (432)687-2702. E-mail: dwainethomas@sbcglobal.net. **Contact:** Dwaine Thomas, owner. Record producer, music publisher (Joranda Music/BMI) and record company (ACR Records). Estab. 1986. Produces 120 singles, 8-15 12" singles, 25 LPs, 25 EPs and 25 CDs/year. Fee derived from sales royalty when song or artist is recorded. "We charge for in-house recording only. Remainder is derived from royalties."

How to Contact Submit demo package by mail. Unsolicited submissions are OK. Prefers CD/DVD with 5 songs and lyric sheet. Does not return material. Responds in 6 weeks if interested.

Music Mostly **country swing**, **pop**, and **rock**; also **R&B** and **gospel**. Produced *Bottle's Almost Gone* (album) and "Black Gold" (single), written and recorded by Mike Nelson (country), both released 1999 on ACR Records; and *Nashville Series* (album), written and recorded by various (country), released 1998 on ProJam Music.

Tips "Be professional. No living room tapes!"

☑ ADR STUDIOS

(formerly Stuart J. Allyn), 250 Taxter Rd., Irvington NY 10533. (914)591-5616. Fax: (914)591-5617. E-mail: jackd@adrinc.org. Website: www.adrinc.org. Associate: Jack Walker. **Contact:** Jack Davis, general manager. President: Stuart J. Allyn. Record producer. Estab. 1972. Produces 6 singles and 3-6 CDs/year. Fee derived from sales royalty and outright fee from recording artist and record company.

How to Contact *Does not accept unsolicited submissions.*

Music Mostly **pop**, **rock**, **jazz**, and **theatrical**; also **R&B** and **country**. Produced *Thad Jones Legacy* (album), recorded by Vanguard Jazz Orchestra (jazz), released 2000 on New World Records. Other artists include Billy Joel, Aerosmith, Carole Demas, Michael Garin, The Magic Garden, Bob Stewart, The Dixie Peppers, Nora York, Buddy Barnes and various video and film scores.

ALLRS MUSIC PUBLISHING CO. (ASCAP)

P.O. Box 1545, Smithtown NY 11787. (718)767-8995. E-mail: allrsmusic@aol.com. Website: www.geocities.com/allrsmusic. **Contact:** Renee Silvestri, president. F.John Silvestri, founder. Music publisher, record company (MIDI Track Records), music consultant, artist management, record producer. Voting member of NARAS (The Grammy Awards), Voting member of the Country Music Association (The CMA Awards), SGMA, Songwriters Guild of America (Diamond Member). Estab. 1994. Staff size: 5. Publishes 3 songs/year; publishes 2 new songwriters/year. Pays standard royalty. Affiliate(s) Midi-Track Publishing Co. (BMI).

How to Contact "Write or e-mail first to obtain permission to submit. We do not accept unsolicited submissions." Prefers CD or cassette with 3 songs, lyric sheet and cover letter. "Make sure your CD or cassette tape is labeled with your name, mailing address, telephone number, and e-mail address. We do not return material." Responds via e-mail in 6 months.

Music Mostly **country**, **gospel**, **top 40**, **R&B**, **MOR** and **pop**. Does not want showtunes, jazz, classical or rap. Published "Why Can't You Hear My Prayer" (single by F. John Silvestri/Leslie Silvestri), recorded by eight-time Grammy nominee Huey Dunbar of the group DLG (Dark Latin Groove), released on Trend Records (other multiple releases, also recorded by Iliana Medina and released 2002 on MIDI Track Records); "Chasing Rainbows" (single by F. John Silvestri/Leslie Silvestri), recorded by Tommy Cash (country), released on MMT Records (including other multiple releases); "Because of You" (single by F. John Silvestri/Leslie Silvestri), recorded by Iliana Medina, released 2002 on MIDI Track Records, also recorded by three-time Grammy nominee Terri Williams, released on KMA Records; also recorded by Grand Ole Opry member Ernie Ashworth, released 2004 on KMA Records; "My Coney Island" (single by F. John Silvestri/Leslie Silvestri), recorded by eight-time Grammy nominee Huey Dunbar, released 2005 on MIDI Track Records.

Tips "Attend workshops, seminars, join songwriters organizations, and keep writing. You will achieve your goal."

□ BLUES ALLEY RECORDS

Rt. 1, Box 288, Clarksburg WV 26301. (304)598-2583. E-mail: info@bluesalleymusic.com. Website: www.bluesalleymusic.com. **Contact:** Joshua Swiger, producer. Record producer, record company and music publisher (Blues Alley Publishing/BMI). Produces 4-6 LPs and 2 EPs/year. Fee derived from sales royalty when song or artist is recorded.

How to Contact Submit demo package by mail. Unsolicited submissions are OK. Will only accept CDs with lead sheets and typed lyrics. Does not return material. Responds in 6 weeks.

Music Mostly **country, pop, Christian,** and **rock**. Produced *Monongalia*, recorded by The New Relics (country), 2009; *Chasing Venus*, recorded by The New Relics (acoustic rock), 2006; *Sons of Sirens*, recorded by Amity (rock), 2004; and *It's No Secret*, recorded by Samantha Caley (pop country), 2004.

☐ COACHOUSE MUSIC

P.O. Box 1308, Barrington IL 60011. (847)382-7631. Fax: (847)382-7651. E-mail: coachouse1@aol.com. **Contact:** Michael Freeman, president. Record producer. Estab. 1984. Produces 6-8 CDs/year. Fee derived from flat fee and/or sales royalty when song or artist is recorded.

How to Contact *Write or e-mail first and obtain permission to submit.* Prefers CD with 3-5 songs and lyric sheet. Include SASE. Responds in 6 weeks.

Music Mostly **rock**, **pop** and **blues**; also **alternative rock** and **country/Americana/roots**. Produced *Casque Nu* (album), written and recorded by Charlelie Couture on Chrysalis EMI France (contemporary pop); *Time Will Tell* (album), recorded by Studebaker John on Blind Pig Records (blues); *Where Blue Begins* (album by various/D. Coleman), recorded by Deborah Coleman on Blind Pig Records (contemporary blues); *A Man Amongst Men* (album), recorded by Bo Diddley (blues); *and Voodoo Menz (album), recorded by Corey Harris and Henry Butler. Two WC Handy nominations;* produced *Pinetop Perkins & Friends* on Telarc recorded by Pinetop Perkins—Grammy nominated. Other artists include Paul Chastain, Candi Station, Eleventh Dream Day, Magic Slim, The Tantrums, The Pranks, The Bad Examples, Mississippi Heat and Sherri Williams.

Tips "Be honest, be committed, strive for excellence."

☑ CREATIVE SOUL

Nashville TN 37179. (615)400-3910. Website: www.creativesoulonline.com. **Contact:** Eric Copeland, producer/writer. Record producer. Produces 5-10 singles and 8-15 albums/year. Fee derived from outright fee from recording artist or company. Other services include consulting/critique/review services.

Music Contemporary Christian, jazz, and **instrumental**; also **R&B** and **pop/rock**. "If you are a Christian jazz or instrumentalist, then all the better!" Produced Cedars Gray, recorded by Cedars Gray (contemporary Christian); It Is Of You, recorded by Matt Pitzl (contemporary Christian); Fairytale Life, recorded by Stephanie Newton (contemporary Christian); all released on Creative Soul Records. Other artists include Brett Rush, Frances Drost, Kristyn Leigh, Tom Dolan, and Canopy Red.

How to Contact *Contact first by e-mail to obtain permission to submit demo.* Prefers CD with 2-3 songs and lyric sheet and cover sheet. Does not return submissions. Responds only if interested.

Tips "Contact us first by e-mail, we are here in Nashville for you. We offer monthly information and special consults in Nashville for artists and writers. We want to meet you and talk with you about your dreams. E-mail us and let's start talking about your music and ministry!"

☑ JERRY CUPIT PRODUCTIONS

Box 121904, Nashville TN 37212. (615)731-0100. Fax: (615)731-3005. E-mail: dan@ cupitmusic.com. Website: www.cupitrecords.com. **Contact:** Dan Hagar, creative assistant. Record producer and music publisher (Cupit Music). Estab. 1984. Fee derived from sales royalty when song or artist is recorded or outright fee from artist.

- Also see the listing for Cupit Music Group in the Music Publishers section of this book.

How to Contact *Visit Web site for policy.* Prefers CD with bio and photo. Include SASE. Responds in 2 months.

Music Mostly **traditional and contemporary uptempo country**, **Southern rock, bluegrass,** and **gospel**. Produced "Make A wish" (single) from *Kevin Sharp* (album), recorded by Kevin Sharp (country), released 2007 on Cupit Records; "Working for the Weekend" (single) from *Ken Mellons* (album), recorded by Ken Mellons, released 1994 on Sony. Other artists include Michelle Cupit, Ben Gregg, Mustang Creek, Jerry Burkhart, and Bobby Seals.

Tips "Be prepared to work hard and be able to take constructive/professional criticism."

☑ DAVINCI'S NOTEBOOK RECORDS

69 Rockwood Ave., St. Catharines ON L2P 1E8 Canada. E-mail: admin@davincismusic. com. Website: www.davincismusic.com. Owner: Kevin Richard. Record producer, record company, music publisher, distributor and recording studio (The Sound Kitchen). Estab. 1992. Produces 1 CD/year. Fee derived from outright fee from artist or commission on sales. "Distribution is on consignment basis. Artist is responsible for all shipping, taxes, and import/export duties."

How to Contact *"E-mail first for postal details then submit demo CD by mail."* Unsolicited submissions are OK. Prefers CD and bio. Does not return material. Responds in 6 weeks.

Music Mostly **rock, instrumental rock, New Age** and **progressive-alternative**; also **R&B, pop** and **jazz**. Produced *Windows* (album by Kevin Hotte/Andy Smith), recorded by Musicom on DaVinci's Notebook Records (power New Age); *Inventing Fire, Illumination, A Different Drum* (albums) written and recorded by Kevin Richard on DNR/Independent (instrumental rock); and *The Cunninghams* (album), written and recorded by The

Cunninghams on Independent (gospel).

Tips "DNR is an artist-run label. Local bands and performers will receive priority. You should be more interested in getting a-foot-in-the-door exposure as opposed to making a fortune. Be satisfied with conquering the world using 'baby steps.' Indie labels don't have large corporate budgets for artist development. For non-local artists, we are more about online distribution than artist development. Being a local act means that you can perform live to promote your releases. For indie artist, selling from the stage is probably going to bring you the biggest volume of sales."

⊠ ⊘ THE EDWARD DE MILES MUSIC COMPANY

10573 W. Pico Blvd., #352, Los Angeles CA 90064-2348. (310)948-9652. Fax: (310)474-7705. E-mail: info@edmsahara.com. Website: www.edmsahara.com. **Contact:** Edward De Miles, president. Record producer, music publisher (Edward De Miles Music Co./ BMI) and record company (Sahara Records and Filmworks Entertainment). Estab. 1981. Produces 5-10 CDs/year. Fee derived from sales royalty when song or artist is recorded.

- Also see the listing for Edward De Miles in the Music Publishers and Managers & Booking Agents sections, as well as Sahara Records and Filmworks Entertainment in the Record Companies section of this book.

How to Contact Does not accept unsolicited submissions.

Music Mostly **R&B/dance**, **top 40 pop/rock** and **contemporary jazz**; also **country**, **TV and film themes—songs and jingles**. **Produced** "Moments" and "Dance Wit Me" (singles) (dance), both written and recorded by Steve Lynn; and "Games" (single), written and recorded by D'von Edwards (jazz), all on Sahara Records. Other artists include Multiple Choice.

Tips "Copyright all material before submitting. Equipment and showmanship a must."

⊙ FINAL MIX INC.

(formerly Final Mix Music), 2219 W. Olive Ave., Suite 102, Burbank CA 91506. (818)970-8717. E-mail: finalmix@aol.com. **Contact:** Theresa Frank, A&R. Record producer/remixer/ mix engineer, independent label (3.6 Music, Inc.) and music publisher (Ximlanif Music Publishing). Estab. 1989. Releases 12 singles and 3-5 LPs and CDs/year. Fee derived from sales royalty when song or artist is recorded.

How to Contact *Does not accept unsolicited submissions.*

Music Mostly **pop**, **rock**, **dance**, **R&B** and **rap**. Produced and/or mixer/remixer for Mary Mary, LeAnn Rimes, Charice, Train, Aaliyah, Hilary Duff, Jesse McCartney, Christina Aguilera, American Idol, Ray Charles, Quincy Jones, Michael Bolton, K-Ci and Jo Jo (of Jodeci), Will Smith, and/or mixer/remixer for Janet Jackson, Ice Cube, Queen Latifah, Jennifer Paige, and The Corrs.

☑ HAILING FREQUENCY MUSIC PRODUCTIONS

7438 Shoshone Ave., Van Nuys CA 91406. (818)881-9888. Fax: (818)881-0555. E-mail: blowinsmokeband@ktb.net. Website: www.blowinsmokeband.com. President: Lawrence Weisberg. Vice President: Larry Knight. Record producer, record company (Blowin' Smoke Records), management firm (Blowin' Smoke Productions) and music publisher (Hailing Frequency Publishing). Estab. 1992. Produces 3 LPs and 3 CDs/year. Fee derived from sales royalty when song or artist is recorded or outright fee from artist.

- Also see the listing for Blowin' Smoke Productions/Records in the Managers & Booking Agents section of this book.

How to Contact *Write or call first and obtain permission to submit.* Prefers cassette or VHS 1/2" videocassette. "Write or print legibly with complete contact instructions." Include SASE. Responds in 1 month.

Music Mostly **contemporary R&B**, **blues** and **blues-rock**; also **songs for film**, **jingles for commercials** and **gospel (contemporary)**. Produced "Beyond the Blues Horizon" (single), recorded by Blowin' Smoke Rhythm & Blues Band, released 2004. Other artists include the Fabulous Smokettes. New division creates songs and music tracks for both the mainstream and adult film industries.

☑ HEART CONSORT MUSIC

410 First St. SW., Mt. Vernon IA 52314. E-mail: mail@heartconsortmusic.com. Website: www.heartconsortmusic.com. **Contact:** Catherine Lawson, manager. Record producer, record company and music publisher. Estab. 1980. Produces 2-3 CDs/year. Fee derived from sales royalty when song or artist is recorded.

How to Contact Submit demo package by mail. Unsolicited submissions are OK. Prefers CD or cassette with 3 songs and 3 lyric sheets. Include SASE. Responds in 3 months.

Music Mostly **jazz**, **New Age** and **contemporary**. Produced *New Faces* (album), written and recorded by James Kennedy on Heart Consort Music (world/jazz).

Tips "We are interested in jazz/New Age artists with quality demos and original ideas. We aim for an international audience."

☐ HUMAN FACTOR PRODUCTIONS

P.O. Box 3742, Washington DC 20027. E-mail: info@hfproductions.com. Website: www.hfproductions.com and www.humanfactor.net. **Contact:** Blake Althen or Paula Bellenoit, producers/owners. Estab. 2001. Record producer and music publisher. "Human Factor Productions is a full service music production team offering a range of music production services, including composition, arranging, recording, remixing, and more. Human Factor also places music in television, film, and video."

How to Contact *Please e-mail to get permission to submit.* Original material only.

Music Mostly **adult contemporary**, **pop**, **singer/songwriter**, **rock (all types)**, **world/ethnic**, **techno/electronica**, **rap** and **soundtrack/film score**. Produced dance remixes of "No Bomb Is Smart" (single), written and recorded by SONiA of disappear fear (contemporary folk); "Fall Down," and "Without Light" (by S. Bitz), recorded by Abby Someone (heartland rock). Other artists include Jennifer Cutting's Ocean Orchestra (contemporary folk rock, celtic), Rachel Panay (dance), Pale Beneath the Blue (adult contemporary/singer/songwriter), Paul Kawabori (classical crossover), and Michelangelo (adult contemporary), and more.

Tips "Always include a cover letter clearly describing what you'd like the recipient to do for you as well as what you have to offer them. When you're recording songs, never leave the studio without 3 mixes: a full version, an instrumental-only version for TV, and a vocal-only version to make future remixes."

⦿ INTEGRATED ENTERTAINMENT

1815 JFK Blvd., #1612, Philadelphia PA 19103. (215)563-7147. E-mail: gelboni@aol.com. **Contact:** Gelboni, president. Record producer. Estab. 1991. Produces 6 EPs and 6 CDs/year. Fee derived from sales royalty when song or artist is recorded or outright fee from recording artist or record company.

How to Contact Submit demo package by mail. Solicited submissions only. CD only with 3 songs. "Draw a guitar on the outside of envelope so we'll know it's from a songwriter." Will respond if interested.

Music Mostly **rock** and **pop**. Produced *Gold Record* (album), written and recorded by Dash Rip Rock (rock) on Ichiban Records and many others.

▦ ▢ JUMP PRODUCTIONS

31 Paul Gilsonstraat, 8200 St-Andries Belgium. (050)31-63-80. E-mail: happymelody@skynet.be. **Contact:** Eddy Van Mouffaert, general manager. Record producer and music publisher (Jump Music). Estab. 1976. Produces 25 singles and 2 CDs/year. Fee derived from sales royalty when song or artist is recorded.

• Also see the listing for Happy Melody in the Music Publishers section of this book.

How to Contact Submit demo CD or tape by mail. Unsolicited submissions are OK. Prefers CD. Does not return material. Responds in 2 weeks.

Music Mostly **ballads**, **up-tempo**, **easy listening**, **disco** and **light pop**; also **instrumentals**. Produced "De Club Is Kampioen" (single by H. Spider/E. Govert), recorded by Benny Scott (light pop), released 2005 on Scorpion; *A Christmas of Hope* (album), recorded by Chris Clark (pop), released 2004 on 5 Stars; and *The Best of Le Grand Julot* (album), recorded by Le Grand Julot (accordion), released 2000 on Happy Melody.

▦ ⦿ JUNE PRODUCTIONS LTD.

The White House, 6 Beechwood Lane, Warlingham, Surrey CR6 9LT England. Phone: 44(0) 1883 622411 Fax: 44(0)1883 652457. E-mail: david@mackay99.plus.com. **Contact:** David Mackay, producer. Record producer and music producer (Sabre Music). Estab.

1970. Produces singles, CDs, and live stage show recordings. Fee derived from sales royalty.

How to Contact Submit demo CD or mp3 by mail. Unsolicited submissions are OK. Prefers CD or cassette with 1-2 songs and lyric sheet. SAE and IRC. Responds in 2 months.

Music Mostly **MOR**, **rock** and **top 40/pop**. Produced *Web of Love* (by various), recorded by Sarah Jory on Ritz Records (country rock). Other artists include Bonnie Tyler, Cliff Richard, Frankie Miller, Johnny Hallyday, Dusty Springfield, Charlotte Henry and Barry Humphries.

Tips "I am currently producing the music for a proposed musical in America. I am happy to review songs, but on the understanding that I am only producing occasionally because of theatre commitments."

L.A. ENTERTAINMENT, INC.

7095 Hollywood Blvd., #826, Hollywood CA 90028. 1-800-579-9157. Fax: (323)924-1095. E-mail: info@warriorrecords.com. Website: www.WarriorRecords.com. **Contact:** Jim Ervin, A&R. Record producer, record company (Warrior Records) and music publisher (New Entity Music/ASCAP, New Copyright Music/BMI, New Euphonic Music/SESAC). Estab. 1988. Fee derived from sales royalty when song or artist is recorded.

How to Contact Submit demo package by mail. Unsolicited submissions are OK. Prefers CD and/or videocassette with original songs, lyric and lead sheet if available. "We do not review Internet sites. Do not send MP3s, unless requested. All written submitted materials (e.g., lyric sheets, letter, etc.) should be typed." Does not return material unless SASE is included. Responds in 2 months only via e-mail or SASE.

Music All styles. "All genres are utilized with our music supervision company for Film & TV, but our original focus is on **alternative rock** and **urban genres** (e.g., **R&B**, **rap**, **gospel**).

LARK TALENT & ADVERTISING

P.O. Box 35726, Tulsa OK 74153. (918)786-8896. Fax: (918)786-8897. E-mail: janajae@ janajae.com. Website: www.janajae.com. **Contact:** Kathleen Pixley, vice president. Owner: Jana Jae. Record producer, music publisher (Jana Jae Music/BMI) and record company (Lark Record Productions, Inc.). Estab. 1980. Fee derived from sales royalty when song or artist is recorded.

- Also see the listings for Jana Jae Music in the Music Publishers section, Lark Record Productions in the Record Companies section, and Jana Jae Enterprises in the Managers & Booking Agents section of this book.

How to Contact Submit demo by mail. Unsolicited submissions are OK. Prefers CD or DVD with 3 songs and lead sheet. Does not return material. Responds in 1 month only if interested.

Music Mostly **country**, **bluegrass** and **classical**; also **instrumentals**. Produced "Bussin'

Ditty" (single by Steve Upfold); "Mayonnaise" (single by Steve Upfold); and "Flyin' South" (single by Cindy Walker), all recorded by Jana Jae on Lark Records (country). Other artists include Sydni, Hotwire and Matt Greif.

☐ LINEAR CYCLE PRODUCTIONS

P.O. Box 2608, Sepulveda CA 91393-2608. E-mail: LCP@wgn.net. Website: www. westworld.com/lcp/. **Contact:** Manny Pandanceski, producer. Record producer. Estab. 1980. Produces 15-25 singles, 6-10 12" singles, 15-20 LPs and 10 CDs/year. Fee derived from sales royalty when song or artist is recorded.

How to Contact Submit demo tape by mail. Unsolicited submissions are OK. Prefers cassette, 7 3/8 ips reel-to-reel or DVD. Only hard copies of recorded demos will be accepted. Demos submitted via mp3/AIFF must include an mp3 player in order for our firm to review the demos. Include SASE. Responds in 6 months.

Music Mostly **rock/pop**, **R&B/blues** and **country**; also **gospel** and **comedy**. Produced *"Not of This Lite"* (single by Hitte.), recorded by Gil Gal (pop/dance), released 2008 on Tozic Googh Records. *"If I Flop"* (single by Robert Stiffe) from his self titled album, recorded and released 2008 on "Swip" brand MP3's; and *"Don't Wanna F"* (single by Brite/Warmewartre) from *The Fone Rings 2 Much* (album), recorded by Sir Gagolatte, released 2008 on Too Kool Recordings.

Tips "We only listen to songs and other material recorded on quality tapes and CDs. We will not accept anything that sounds distorted, muffled and just plain bad! If you cannot afford to record demos on quality stock, or in some high aspects, shop somewhere else!"

☐ MAC-ATTACK PRODUCTIONS

868 NE 81 St., Miami FL 33138. (305)949-1422. E-mail: GoMacster@aol.com. **Contact:** Michael McNamee, engineer/producer. Record producer and music publisher (Mac-Attack Publishing/ASCAP). Estab. 1986. Fee derived from outright fee from recording artist or record company.

How to Contact Submit demo by mail. Unsolicited submissions are OK. Prefers CD or cassette or VHS videocassette with 3-5 songs, lyric sheet and bio. Does not return material. Responds in up to 3 months.

Music Mostly **pop**, **alternative rock** and **dance**. Engineered Compositions (album), written and recorded by Paul Martin (experimental), released 2006 on PMR Music. Produced and engineered *Tuscan Tongue* (album by Caution Automatic), recorded by Caution Automatic (rock), released 2005 on C.A. Records; Produced and engineered "Never Gonna Let You Go" (single by Bruce Jordan/John Link/Michael McNamee), recorded by Bruce Jordan (pop), released 2002 on H.M.S. Records. Other artists include Blowfly, Tally Tal, Nina Llopis, The Lead, Girl Talk, Tyranny of Shaw, and Jacobs Ladder.

☑ MAKERS MARK GOLD MUSIC PRODUCTIONS

534 W. Queen Lane, Philadelphia PA 19144. (215)849-7633. E-mail: Makers.Mark@ verizon.net. Website: www.mp3.com/paulhopkins. **Contact:** Paul E. Hopkins, producer/ publisher. Record producer, music publisher and record company (Prolific Records). Estab. 1991. Produces 15 singles, 5 12" singles and 4 LPs/year. Fee derived from outright fee from recording artist or record company. "We produce professional music videos in VHS and DVD format."

- Also see the listing for Makers Mark Gold in the Music Publishers section of this book.

How to Contact Submit demo tape or CD with bio by mail. Unsolicited submissions are OK. "No need to call or send SASE. Explain concept of your music and/or style, and your future direction as an artist or songwriter." Does not return material. No need to call or send SASE. Responds in 6 weeks if interested. See Prolific Records in label section.

Music "Our publishing and productions has changed to total Christian/Inspirational. gospel/Christian only. All genres contemporary, traditional, pop, dance, hip-hop gospel." Historically mostly R&B, hip-hop, gospel, pop and house. Published "Silent Love," "Why You Want My Love" and "Something for Nothing," (singles), written and recorded by Elaine Monk, released on Black Sands Records/Metropolitan Records; "Get Funky" (single), written and recorded by Larry Larr, released on Columbia Records; and "He Made A Way" (single by Kenyatta Arrington), "We Give All Praises Unto God" (single by Jacqueline D. Pate), "I Believe He Will" (single by Pastor Alyn E. Waller), and "Psalms 146" (single by Rodney Roberson), all songs recorded by The Enon Tabernacle Mass Choir from *Pastor Alyn E. Waller Presents: The Enon Tabernacle Mass Choir*, released on ECDC Records. (www.enontab.org). Also produces and publishes music for Bunim/ Murray productions network television, MTV's *Real World, Road Rules, Rebel Billionaire, Simple Life*, and movie soundtracks worldwide. Also produced deep soul remixes for Brian McKnight, Musiq Souchild, Jagged Edge, John Legend, and Elaine Monk.

☑ COOKIE MARENCO

P.O. Box 874, Belmont CA 94002. E-mail: sonic@acousticartsinternational.com. (650)591-6857. Record producer/engineer. "Over 20 years experience, 5 Grammy nominations, 2 gold records, proprietary surround recording technique. Estab. 1981. Produces 10 CDs/ year. $2,000 per day payable in advance.

How to Contact *Contact only if interested in production. Does not accept unsolicited material*. Must have budget.

Music Mostly **alternative modern rock**, **country**, **folk**, **rap**, **ethnic** and **avante-garde**; also **classical**, **pop** and **jazz**. Produced *Winter Solstice II* (album), written and recorded by various artists; *Heresay* (album by Paul McCandless); and *Deep At Night* (album by Alex DeGrassi), all on Windham Hill Records (instrumental). Other artists include Tony Furtado Band, Praxis, Oregon, Mary Chapin Carpenter, Max Roach and Charle Haden & Quartet West.

Tips "Specialist in high quality ANALOG recording. Mixing to 1/2" or DSD digital. Full service mastering and dynamic Web site development."

☑ PETE MARTIN/VAAM MUSIC PRODUCTIONS

P.O. Box 29550, Hollywood CA 90029-0550. (323)664-7765. E-mail: pmarti3636@aol. com. Website: www.VaamMusic.com. **Contact:** Pete Martin, president. Record producer, music publisher (Vaam Music/BMI and Pete Martin Music/ASCAP) and record company (Blue Gem Records). Estab. 1982.

- Also see the listings for Vaam Music Group in the Music Publishers section of this book and Blue Gem Records in the Record Companies section of this book.

How to Contact Send CD or cassette with 2 songs and a lyric sheet. Send small packages only. Include SASE. Responds in 1 month.

Music Mostly **top 40/pop**, **country** and **R&B**.

Tips "Study the market in the style that you write. Songs must be capable of reaching top 5 on charts."

☑ ☐ SCOTT MATHEWS, D/B/A HIT OR MYTH PRODUCTIONS INC.

246 Almonte Blvd., Mill Valley CA 94941. Fax: (415)389-9682. E-mail: scott@scottmathews. com. Website: www.ScottMathews.com. Contact: Mary Ezzell, A&R Director. President: Scott Mathews. Assistant: Tom Luekens. Record producer, song doctor, studio owner and music publisher (Hang On to Your Publishing/BMI). Estab. 1990. Produces 6-9 CDs/year. Fee derived from recording artist or record company (with royalty points).

- Scott Mathews has several gold and platinum awards for sales of nearly 15 million records. He has worked with more than 60 Rock & Roll Hall of Fame inductees and on several Grammy and Oscar-winning releases. He is currently working primarily with emerging artists while still making music with his legendary established artists.

How to Contact "No phone calls or publishing submissions, please." Submit demo CD by mail or an mp3 by email. "Unsolicited submissions are often the best ones and readily accepted. Include SASE if e-mail is not an option. Also include your e-mail address on your demo CD." Responds in 2 months.

Music Mostly rock/pop, alternative and singer/songwriters of all styles. Produced 4 tracks on Anthology (Best of), recorded by John Hiatt (rock/pop), released 2001 on Hip-O. Has produced Elvis Costello, Roy Orbison, Rosanne Cash, Jerry Garcia, Huey Lewis, and many more. Has recorded records with everyone from Barbra Streisand to John Lee Hooker, including Keith Richards, George Harrison, Mick Jagger, Van Morrison, Bonnie Raitt, and Eric Clapton to name but a few.

Tips "These days if you are not independent, you are dependent. The new artists that are coming up and achieving success in the music industry are the ones that prove they have a vision and can make incredible records without the huge financial commitment of a major label. When an emerging artist makes great product for the genre they are in, they are in the driver's seat to be able to make a fair and equitable deal for distribution, be it with a major or independent label. My philosophy is to go where you are loved. The truth is, a smaller label that is completely dedicated to you and shares your vision may help your career far more than a huge label that will not keep you around if you don't sell millions of units. Perhaps no label is needed at all, if you are up for the challenge of wearing a lot of hats. I feel too much pressure is put on the emerging artist when they have to pay huge sums back to the label in order to see their first royalty check. We all know those records can be made for a fraction of that cost without compromising quality or commercial appeal. I still believe in potential and our company is in business to back up that belief. It is up to us as record makers/visionaries to take that potential into the studio and come out with music that can compete with anything else on the market. Discovering, developing and producing artists that can sustain long careers is our main focus at Hit or Myth Productions. We are proud to be associated with so many legendary and timeless artists and our track record speaks for itself. If you love making music, don't let anyone dim that light. We look forward to hearing from you. (Please check out www. ScottMathews.com for more info, and also www.allmusic.com-keyword; Scott Mathews.) Accept no substitutes!"

☑ MEGA TRUTH RECORDS

P.O. Box 4988, Culver City CA 90231. E-mail: jonbare@aol.com. Website: www.jonbare. net. **Contact:** Jon Bare, CEO. Record producer and record company. Estab. 1994. Produces 2 CDs/year. Fee negotiable.

How to Contact Submit demo package by mail. Unsolicited submissions are OK. Prefers CD. "We specialize in recording world-class virtuoso musicians and bands with top players." Does not return material. Responds in 2 weeks only if interested.

Music Mostly **rock**, **blues** and **country rock**; also **swing**, **dance** and **instrumental**. Produced Party Platter recorded by Hula Monsters (swing); and Killer Whales, Shredzilla and Orcastra (by Jon Bare and the Killer Whales) (rock), all on Mega Truth Records. Other artists include The Rich Harper Blues Band, Aeon Dream & the Dream Machine and Techno Dudes.

Tips "Create a unique sound that blends great vocals and virtuoso musicianship with a beat that makes us want to get up and dance."

☒ ☑ MONTICANA PRODUCTIONS

P.O. Box 702, Snowdon Station, Montreal QC H3X 3X8 Canada. **Contact:** David Leonard, executive producer. Record producer, music publisher (Montina Music) and record company (Monticana Records). Estab. 1963. Fee derived from sales royalty when song or artist is recorded.

• Also see the listings for Monticana Records in the Record Companies section and Montina Music in the Music Publishers section of this book.

How to Contact Submit demo package by mail. Unsolicited submissions are OK. Prefers CD with maximum 4 songs. "Demos should be as tightly produced as a master." Include SASE.

Music Mostly **top 40**; also **bluegrass, blues, country, dance-oriented, easy listening, folk, gospel, jazz, MOR, progressive, R&B, rock** and **soul**.

Tips "Work creatively and believe passionately in what you do and aspire to be. Success comes to those who persevere, have talent, develop their craft and network."

☑ MUSTROCK PRODUCTIONZ WORLDWIDE

E-mail: recordmode@hotmail.com. President: Ivan "Doc" Rodriguez. Record producer and recording/mixing/mastering engineer. Estab. 1987. Produces various singles and CDs/year. Fee derived from sales royalty and advance payment when song or artist is recorded. " We are not a record company. We provide services for a fee—we do not sign or represent artists. We are a work-for-hire company."

How to Contact *E-mail first and obtain permission to submit.* Prefers mp3, CD, DVD and lyric sheet. Does not return material. Responds in 2 months. "Unless booking our services, only opinion will be given."

Music Mostly **hip-hop, R&B** and **pop**; also **soul, ballads** and **soundtracks**. Produced "Poor Georgie" (by MC Lyte/DJ DOC), recorded by MC Lyte on Atlantic Records (rap). Other artists include Caron Wheeler, The Hit Squad, The Awesome II, Black Steel Music, Underated Productions, EPMD, Redman, Dr. Dre & Ed-Lover, Das-EFX, Biz Markie, BDP, Eric B & Rakim, The Fugees, The Bushwackass, Shai and Pudgee, Alisha Keys, 50 cent, Tiro de Garcia, etc.

Tips "Services provided include ProTools production (pre/post/co), digital tracking, mixing, remixing, live show tapes, jingles, etc. For additional credits, go to www.allmusic. com, type 'Ivan Doc Rodriguez' under 'artist' and enter, or send e-mail."

☐ NEU ELECTRO PRODUCTIONS

P.O. Box 1582, Bridgeview IL 60455. (630)257-6289. E-mail: neuelectro@email.com. Website: www.neuelectro.com. **Contact:** Bob Neumann, owner. Record producer and record company. Estab. 1984. Produces 16 singles, 16 12" singles, 20 LPs and 4 CDs/year. Fee derived from outright fee from record company or recording artist.

How to Contact Submit demo package by mail. Unsolicited submissions are OK. Prefers CD with 3 songs and lyric sheet or lead sheet. "Provide accurate contact phone numbers and addresses, promo packages and photos." Include SASE for reply. Responds in 2 weeks. "A production fee estimate will be returned to artist."

Music Mostly **dance, house, techno, rap** and **rock**; also **experimental, New Age** and **top 40**. Produced "Juicy" (single), written and recorded by Juicy Black on Dark Planet International Records (house); "Make Me Smile" (single), written and recorded by Roz Baker (house); *Reactovate-6* (album by Bob Neumann), recorded by Beatbox-D on N.E.P.

Records (dance); and *Sands of Time* (album), recorded by Bob Neumann (New Age). Other artists include Skid Marx and The Deviants.

☑ NEW EXPERIENCE RECORDS/FAZE 4 RECORDS

P.O. Box 683, Lima OH 45802. E-mail: just_chilling_2002@yahoo.com. Website: www. faze4records.com. **Contact:** A&R Department. Music Publisher: James L. Milligan Jr. Record producer, music publisher (A New Rap Jam Publishing/ASCAP), management firm (Creative Star Management) and record company (New Experience Records, Grand-Slam Records and Pump It Up Records). Estab. 1989. Produces 15-20 12" singles, 2 LPs, 3 EPs and 2-5 CDs/year. Fee derived from sales royalty when song or artist is recorded or outright fee from record company, "depending on services required." Distributed by IODA, Distribution/Doodlebug Media.

- Also see the listings for A New Rap Jam Publishing in the Music Publishers section of this book.

How to Contact Write first to arrange personal interview. Address material to A&R Dept. or Talent Coordinator. Prefers CD with a minimum of 3 songs and lyric or lead sheet (if available). "If tapes are to be returned, proper postage should be enclosed and all tapes and letters should have SASE for faster reply." Responds in 6-8 weeks.

Music Mostly **pop**, **R&B** and **rap**; also **gospel**, **soul, contemporary gospel** and **rock**. Produced "The Son of God" (single by James Milligan/Anthony Milligan/Melvin Milligan) from *The Final Chapter* (album), recorded by T.M.C. Milligan Connection (R&B, Gospel), released 2002 on New Experience/Pump It Up Records. Other artists include Dion Mikel, Paulette Mikel, Melvin Milligan and Venesta Compton.

Tips "Do your homework on the music business. Be aware of all the new sampling laws. There are too many sound alikes. Be yourself. I look for what is different, vocal ability, voice range and sound stage presence, etc. Be on the look out for our new blues label Rough Edge Records/Rough Edge Entertainment. Blues material is now being reviewed. Send your best studio recorded material. Also be aware of the new digital downloading laws. People are being jailed and fined for recording music that has not been paid for. Do your homework. We have also signed Diamond Sound Productions, located in Fresno, CA and Ground Breakers Records. Now we can better serve our customers on the East and West Coast. You can also visit our Web site at www.faze4records.com for further information on our services. We are reviewing hip-hop and rap material that is positive, clean, and commercial; please no Gangsta rap if you want a deal with us as well as airplay. Also reviewing gospel music, gospel rap and anything with commercial appeal."

☐ NIGHTWORKS RECORDS

355 W. Potter Dr., Anchorage AK 99518. (907)562-3754. Fax: (907)561-4367. E-mail: kurt@surrealstudios.com. Website: www.surrealstudios.com. Owner: Kurt Riemann. Record producer. Produces 16 CDs/year. Fees derived from sales royalty when song or

artist is recorded.

How to Contact Submit demo package by mail. Unsolicited submissions are OK. Prefers CD with 2-3 songs "produced as fully as possible. Send jingles and songs on separate CDs." Does not return material. Responds in 1 month.

Music Produces a variety of music from **native Alaskan** to **Techno** to **Christmas**.

☐ THE PRESCRIPTION CO.

P.O. Box 222249, Great Neck NY 11021. (415)553-8540. E-mail: therxco@yahoo.com. **Contact:** David F. Gasman, president. San Francisco office: 525 Ashbury St., San Francisco CA 94117. (415)553-8540. VP Sales (West Coast warehouse): Bruce Brennan. Record producer and music publisher. Fee derived from sales royalty when artist or song is recorded or outright fee from record company.

• Also see the listing for Prescription Company in the Music Publishers section of this book.

How to Contact *Write or call first about your interest then submit demo.* Prefers cassette with any number of songs and lyric sheet. Include SASE. "Does not return material without SASE and sufficient postage."

Music Mostly **bluegrass**, **blues**, **children's**, **country**, **dance**, **easy listening**, **jazz**, **MOR**, **progressive**, **R&B**, **rock**, **soul** and **top 40/pop**. Produced "The World's Most Dangerous Man," "Here Comes Trouble" and "Automated People" (singles by D.F. Gasman) from *Special EP No. 1* (album), all recorded by Medicine Mike (rock), all released 2003 on Prescription.

☑ SPHERE GROUP ONE, LLC

795 Waterside Dr., Marco Island FL 34145. (239)398-6800. Fax: (239)394-9881. E-mail: spheregroupone@att.net. **Contact:** Tony Zarrella, president. Talent Manager: Janice Salvatore. Record producer, artist development and management firm. Estab. 1986.

How to Contact Submit CD/video by mail. Unsolicited submissions are OK. Prefers CD or DVD with strongest material and lyric sheets. "Must include: photos, press, résumé, goals and specifics of project submitted, etc." Does not return material.

Music Mostly **pop/rock (mainstream)**, **progressive/rock**, **New Age** and **crossover country/pop**; also **film soundtracks**. Produced Machine, "Rock to the Rescue," "Sunset At Night," "Double Trouble," "Take This Heart," "It's Our Love," and "You and I" (produced by T. Zarrella), recorded by 4 of Hearts (pop/rock) on Sphere Records and/or various labels. Other associated artists include Frontier 9, Oona Falcon, Myth, Survivor, and Wicked Lester/Kiss.

Tips "Be you. Take direction, have faith in yourself, producer and manager. Currently seeking artists/groups incorporating various styles into a focused mainstream product. Groups with a following are a plus. Artist development is our expertise and we listen! In the pocket, exceptional songs, experienced performers necessary."

☐ SRS PRODUCTIONS/HIT RECORDS NETWORK

P.O. Box 6235, Santa Barbara CA 93160. (805)705-3539. E-mail: cmswain@cox.net.
Contact: Greg Lewolt, Ernie Orosco and J.C. Martin, producers. Record producer, record company (Night City Records, Warrior Records and Tell International Records), radio and TV promotion and music publisher. Estab. 1984. Produces 4 singles, 2 12" singles, 4 LPs, 2 EPs and 2-4 CDs/year. Fee derived from outright fee from record company.
How to Contact Submit demo package by mail. Unsolicited submissions are OK. Prefers CD, cassette, or DVD videocassette with 4-8 songs, photos, bio and lyric sheet. Does not return material. Include SASE. Responds in 2 months.
Music Mostly **pop-rock**, **country** and **top 40**; also **top 40 funk**, **top 40 rock**, **dance rock** and **top 40 country**. Produced "A Love Divine" 4 song EP feat. Bobby Harris (The Drifters); Cornelius Bumpus (Doobie Brothers; Steely Dan); Mailia Mathis (Buffy the Vampire Slayer); Nick St. Nicholas (Steppinwolf); Kenny Cetera (Chicago); Jamie "Sitar" Shane (Canned Heat); I.C.U. by ICU's with Jimmy Le Roy and special guests.
Tips "Keep searching for the infectious chorus hook and don't give up."

☐ STUDIO SEVEN/LUNACY RECORDS

417 N. Virginia, Oklahoma City OK 73106. (405)236-0643. Fax: (405)236-0686. E-mail: cope@okla.net. **Contact:** Dave Copenhaver, Producer. Record producer, record label (Lunacy Records) and music publisher (Lunasong Music). Estab. 1990. Produces 10-12 CDs/year. Fee is derived from sales royalty when song or artist is recorded or outright fee from recording artist or record company. "All projects are on a customized basis."
How to Contact *Contact first and obtain permission to submit.* Prefers CD or cassette with lyric sheet. Include SASE. Responds in 6 weeks.
Music Mostly **rock**, **jazz-blues**, **country**, and **Native American**. Releases in 2009: Morris McCraven, Ben Treffer (What Would You Do?), Scott King (Let's Get Something Straight) Bailey Wilton (Bailey), Lorraine Worth (The Greatest Hero); Curt Shoemaker, The Boys of the Fort, Jack Hughes, Les Gilliam, Frosty, Jeff Fenholt, Joe Merrick, Ronnie and Imods, Leroy Jones.

☑ WESTWIRES RECORDING USA

(formerly Westwires Digital USA), 1042 Club Ave., Allentown PA 18109. (610)435-1924. E-mail: info@westwires.com. Website: www.westwires.com. **Contact:** Wayne Becker, owner/producer. Record producer and production company. Fee derived from outright fee from record company or artist retainer.
How to Contact *Contact via e-mail for permission to submit.* "No phone calls, please." Submit demo by mail or mp3 by e-mail. Unsolicited submissions are OK. Prefers mp3 with lyrics in MS Word or Adobe PDF file format, or CD, DVD, or VHS videocassette with 3 songs and lyric sheet. Does not return material. Responds in 1 month.
Music Mostly **rock**, **R&B**, **dance**, **alternative**, **folk** and **eclectic**. Produced Ye Ren (Dimala

Records), Weston (Universal/Mojo), Zakk Wylde (Spitfire Records). Other artists include Ryan Asher, Paul Rogers, Anne Le Baron, and Gary Hassay

Tips "We are interested in singer/songwriters and alternative artists living in the mid-Atlantic area. Must have steady gig schedule and established fan base."

☑ FRANK WILLSON

P.O. Box 2297, Universal City TX 78148. (210)653-3989. E-mail: bswr@netscape.com. Website: www.bsw-records.com. **Contact:** Frank Willson, producer. Record producer, management firm (Universal Music Marketing) and record company (BSW Records/Universal Music Records). Estab. 1987. Produces 20-25 albums/year. Fee derived from sales royalty when song or artist is recorded.

- Also see the listings for Universal Music Marketing in the Managers & Booking Agents section of this book.

How to Contact Submit demo package by mail. Unsolicited submissions are OK. Prefers CD with 3-4 songs and lyric sheets. Include SASE. Responds in 1 month.

Music Mostly **country**, **blues**, **jazz** and **soft rock**. Other artists include Candee Land, Dan Kimmel, Brad Lee, John Wayne, Sonny Marshall, Bobby Mountain and Crea Beal. "Visit our website for an up-to-date listing of artists."

☑ WLM MUSIC/RECORDING

2808 Cammie St., Durham NC 27705-2020. (919)471-3086. Fax: (919)471-4326. E-mail: wlm-musicrecording@nc.rr.com or wlm-band@nc.rr.com. **Contact:** Watts Lee Mangum, owner. Record producer. Estab. 1980. Fee derived from outright fee from recording artist. "In some cases, an advance payment requested for demo production."

How to Contact Submit demo by mail. Unsolicited submissions are OK. Prefers CD with 2-4 songs and lyric or lead sheet (if possible). Include SASE. Responds in 6 months.

Music Mostly **country**, **country/rock** and **blues/rock**; also **pop**, **rock**, **blues**, **gospel** and **bluegrass**. Produced "911," and "Petals of an Orchid" (singles), both written and recorded by Johnny Scoggins (country); and "Renew the Love" (single by Judy Evans), recorded by Bernie Evans (country), all on Independent. Other artists include Southern Breeze Band and Heart Breakers Band.

☑ WORLD RECORDS

5798 Deer Trail Dr., Traverse City MI 49684. E-mail: jack@worldrec.org. Website: www.worldrec.org. **Contact:** Jack Conners, producer. Record producer, engineer/technician and record company (World Records). Estab. 1984. Produces 1 CD/year. Fee derived from outright fee from recording artist.

How to Contact *Write first and obtain permission to submit.* Prefers CD with 1 or 2 songs. Include SASE. Responds in 6 weeks.

Music Mostly **classical**, **folk**, and **jazz**. Produced *Mahler, Orff, Collins* (album), recorded by Traverse Symphony Orchestra (classical), released 2006; *Reflections on Schubert* (album) recorded by Michael Coonrod (classical), released 2007. Other artists include Jeff Haas and The Camerata Singers.

◪ ZIG PRODUCTIONS

P.O. Box 120931, Arlington TN 76012. (214)354-8401. E-mail: billyherzig@hotmail. com. Website: www.zigproductions.com. **Contact:** Billy Herzig or Wendy Mazur. Record producer. Music publisher (Thistle Hill/BMI). Estab. 1998. "Occasionally I produce a single that is recorded separate from a full CD project." Produces 6-10 albums. Fee derived from sales royalty when song or artist is recorded and/or outright fee from recording artist. "Sometimes there are investors."

How to Contact Submit a demo by mail. Unsolicited submissions are OK. We do not return submissions. Responds only if interested.

Music Mostly **country**, **Americana**, and **rock**; also **pop**, **r&b**, and **alternative**. Produced "Ask Me to Stay" (single by King Cone/Josh McDaniel) from *Gallery*, recorded by King Cone (Texas country/Americana), released 2007 on King Cone; "A Cure for Awkward Silence" (single), recorded by Tyler Stock (acoustic rock), released 2007 on Payday Records; "Take Me Back" (single) from *Peace, Love & Crabs*, written and recorded by Deanna Dove (folk-rock), released 2007 on Island Girl. Also produced Robbins & Jones (country), Jordan Mycoskie (country), Carla Rhodes (comedy), Four Higher (alternative), Charis Thorsell (country), Shane Mallory (country), Rachel Rodriguez (blues-rock), Jessy Daumen (country), Frankie Moreno (rock/r&b), Shawna Russell (country), and many others.

ADDITIONAL RECORD PRODUCERS

The following companies are also record producers, but their listings are found in other sections of the book. Read the listings for submission information.

Managers & Booking Agents

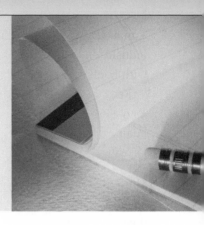

Before submitting to a manager or booking agent, be sure you know exactly what you need. If you're looking for someone to help you with performance opportunities, the booking agency is the one to contact. They can help you book shows either in your local area or throughout the country. If you're looking for someone to help guide your career, you need to contact a management firm. Some management firms may also handle booking; however, it may be in your best interest to look for a separate booking agency. A manager should be your manager—not your agent, publisher, lawyer or accountant.

MANAGERS

Of all the music industry players surrounding successful artists, managers are usually the people closest to the artists themselves. The artist manager can be a valuable contact, both for the songwriter trying to get songs to a particular artist and for the songwriter/performer. A manager and his connections can be invaluable in securing the right publishing deal or recording contract if the writer is also an artist. Getting songs to an artist's manager is yet another way to get your songs recorded, since the manager may play a large part in deciding what material his client uses. For the performer seeking management, a successful manager should be thought of as the foundation for a successful career.

The relationship between a manager and his client relies on mutual trust. A manager works as the liaison between you and the rest of the music industry, and he must know exactly what you want out of your career in order to help you achieve your goals. His handling of publicity, promotion and finances, as well as the contacts he has within the industry, can make or break your career. You should never be afraid to ask questions about any aspect of the relationship between you and a prospective manager.

Always remember that a manager works *for the artist*. A good manager is able to communicate his opinions to you without reservation, and should be willing to explain any confusing terminology or discuss plans with you before taking action.

A manager needs to be able to communicate successfully with all segments of the music industry in order to get his client the best deals possible. He needs to be able to work with booking agents, publishers, lawyers and record companies.

Keep in mind that y_____ _____king together toward a common goal: success for you and yo_____ _____ty, professionalism and a drive to succeed are qualiti_____ _____rtist—and a songwriter.

_____ performance venues for their clients. They _____ _____nager does, and have less contact with _____ on for his services, as does a manager. _____ on an act's earnings; booking agents _____ s and booking agents, more successful _____ ones set forth above.

_____AGERS & BOOKING AGENTS

_____ have provided information about the types of music they _____es of acts they represent. You'll want to refer to the Category Index _____ find out which companies deal with the type of music you write, and the _____aphic Index at the back of the book to help you locate companies near where you live. Then determine whether they are open to your level of experience (see A Sample Listing Decoded on page 12). Each listing also contains submission requirements and information about what items to include in a press kit and will also specify whether the company is a management firm or a booking agency. Remember that your submission represents you as an artist, and should be as organized and professional as possible.

ADDITIONAL MANAGERS & BOOKING AGENTS

There are **more managers & booking agents** located in other sections of the book! On page 242 use the list of Additional Managers & Booking Agents to find listings within other sections who are also managers/booking agents.

Managers & Agents

◪ BILL ANGELINI ENTERPRISES/BOOKYOUREVENT.COM

(formerly Management Plus), P.O. Box 132, Seguin TX 78155. (830)401-0061. Fax: (830)401-0069. E-mail: bill@bookyourevent.com. Website: www.bookyourevent.com. **Contact:** Bill Angelini, owner. Management firm and booking agency. Estab. 1980. Represents individual artists and groups from anywhere; currently handles 6 acts. Receives 10-15% commission. Reviews material for acts.

How to Contact Submit demo package by mail or EPK. Unsolicited submissions are OK. Press kit should include pictures, bio, and discography. Does not return material. Responds in 1 month.

Music Mostly **Latin American**, **Tejano** and **international**; also **Norteno** and **country**. Current acts include Jay Perez (Tejano), Ram Herrera (Tejano), Michael Salgado (Tejano), Flaco Jimenez (Tex-Mex), Electric Cowboys (tex-mex), Los Palominos (Tejano), Grupo Vida (Tejano), and Texmaniacs (Tex-Mex).

◪ ARTIST REPRESENTATION AND MANAGEMENT

1257 Arcade St., St. Paul MN 55106. (651)483-8754. Fax: (651)776-6338. E-mail: ra@armentertainment.com. Website: www.armentertainment.com. **Contact:** Roger Anderson, agent/manager. Management firm and booking agency. Estab. 1983. Represents artists from anywhere; currently handles 10 acts. Receives 15% commission. Reviews material for acts.

How to Contact Submit CD and video by mail. Unsolicited submissions are OK. Please include minimum 3 songs. If seeking management, references, current schedule, bio, photo, press clippings should also be included. "Priority is placed on original artists with product who are currently touring." Does not return material. Responds only if interested within 30 days.

Music Mostly **melodic rock**. Current acts include Warrant, Firehouse, Jesse Lang, Scarlet Haze, Head East, Frank Hannon of Tesla, LA Guns, Dokken, and Bret Michaels of Poison.

◪ BACKSTREET BOOKING

700 West Pete Rose Way, PMB 18 Cincinnati OH 45203. (513)442-4405. Fax: (513)834-9390. E-mail: info@backstreetbooking.com. Website: www.backstreetbooking.com. **Contact:** James Sfarnas, president. Booking agency. Estab. 1992. Represents individual artists and groups from anywhere; currently handles 30 acts. Receives 10-15% commission. Reviews material for acts.

How to Contact *Call first and obtain permission to submit.* Accepts only signed acts with product available nationally and/or internationally.

Music Mostly **niche-oriented music**. Current acts include Acumen (progressive jam rock), Niacin (fusion), John Novello (Fusion), Novello B3 Soul (Urban Jazz), Alex Skolnick Trio (progressive jazz), Jeff Berlin (Jazz), Greg Howe (Fusion), American English (Beatles

Tribute), The Van Dells (50s-60s Review).

Tips "Build a base on your own."

☑ BARNARD MANAGEMENT SERVICES (BMS)

2916 Main Street, Suite 200, Santa Monica CA 90405 (310) 392-2916. E-mail: bms@barnardus.com. **Contact:** Russell Barnard, president. Management firm. Estab. 1979. Represents artists, groups and songwriters; currently handles 2 acts. Receives 10-20% commission. Reviews material for acts.

How to Contact *Write first and obtain permission to submit.* Prefers CD with 3-10 songs and lead sheet. Artists may submit DVD (15-30 minutes) by permission only. If seeking management, press kit should include cover letter, bio, photo, demo DVD/CD, lyric sheets, press clippings, video and résumé. Does not return material. Responds in 2 months.

Music Mostly **country crossover**, **blues**, **country**, **R&B**, **rock** and **soul**. Current acts include Mark Shipper (songwriter/author) and Sally Rose (R&B band).

☑ BLANK & BLANK

One Belmont Ave., Suite 602, Bala Cynwyd PA 19004. (610)667-9900. Fax: (610)667-9901. **Contact:** E. Robert Blank, manager. Management firm. Represents individual artists and groups. Reviews material for acts.

How to Contact *Contact first and obtain permission to submit.* Prefers CD, DVD, or videocassette. If seeking management, press kit should include cover letter, demo tape/CD and video. Does not return material.

☑ THE BLUE CAT AGENCY

E-mail: bluecat_agency@yahoo.com. Website: www.geocities.com/bluecat_agency. **Contact:** Karen Kindig, owner/agent. Management firm and booking agency. Estab. 1989. Represents established individual artists and/or groups from anywhere; currently handles 5 acts. Receives 10-15% commission. Reviews material for acts.

How to Contact *E-mail only for permission to submit.* Prefers cassette or CD. If seeking management, press kit should include, CD or tape, bio, press clippings and photo. SASE. Responds in 2 months.

Music Mostly **rock/pop "en espanol"** and **jazz/latin jazz**. Works primarily with bands (established performers only). Current acts include Ylonda Nickell, Kai Eckhardt, Alejandro Santos, Ania Paz, Gabriel Rosati.

☐ BREAD & BUTTER PRODUCTIONS

P.O. Box 1539, Wimberley TX 78676. (512)301-7117. E-mail: sgladson@gmail.com. **Contact:** Steve Gladson, managing partner. Management firm and booking agency. Estab. 1969. Represents individual artists, songwriters and groups from anywhere; currently handles 6 acts. Receives 10-20% commission. Reviews material for acts.

How to Contact Submit demo package by mail. Unsolicited submissions OK. Prefers DVD or CD and lyric sheet. If seeking management, press kit should include cover letter, demo tape/CD, lyric sheets, press clippings, video, résumé, picture and bio or a list of your social networking sites. Does not return material. Responds in 1 month.

Music Mostly **alternative rock**, **country** and **R&B**; also **classic rock**, **folk** and **Americana**. Works primarily with singer/songwriters and original bands. Current acts include Lou Cabaza (songwriter/producer/manager), Duck Soup (band) and Gaylan Ladd (songwriter/singer/producer).

Tips "Remember why you are in this biz. The art comes first."

☑ BROTHERS MANAGEMENT ASSOCIATES

141 Dunbar Ave., Fords NJ 08863. (732)738-0880. Fax: (732)738-0970. E-mail: bmaent@ yahoo.com. Website: www.bmaent.com. **Contact:** Allen A. Faucera, president. Management firm and booking agency. Estab. 1972. Represents artists, groups and songwriters; currently handles 25 acts. Receives 15-20% commission. Reviews material for acts.

How to Contact *Write first and obtain permission to submit.* Prefers CD or DVD with 3-6 songs and lyric sheets. Include photographs and résumé. If seeking management, include photo, bio, tape and return envelope in press kit. Include SASE. Responds in 2 months.

Music Mostly **pop**, **rock**, **MOR** and **R&B**. Works primarily with vocalists and established groups. Current acts include Nils Lofgren.

Tips "Submit very commercial material—make demo of high quality."

🌐 ☑ CIRCUIT RIDER TALENT & MANAGEMENT CO.

123 Walton Ferry Rd., Hendersonville TN 37075. (615)824-1947. Fax: (615)264-0462. E-mail: dotwool@bellsouth.net. **Contact:** Linda S. Dotson, president. Consultation and deal negotiation firm, booking agency and music publisher (Channel Music, Cordial Music, Dotson & Dotson Music Publishers, Shalin Music Co.). Represents individual artists, songwriters and actors; currently handles 10 acts. Works with a large number of recording artists, songwriters, actors, and producers. (Includes the late multi-Grammy-winning producer/writer Skip Scarborough.) Receives 10-15% commissions booking agent (union rates). Reviews material for acts (free of charge) as publisher.

How to Contact *E-mail or call first and obtain permission to submit.* Prefers DVD or CD with 3 songs and lyric sheet. If seeking consultation, press kit should include bio, cover letter, résumé, lyric sheets if original songs, photo and CD or DVD with 3 songs. "Full press kit or EPK to my e-mail address required of artist's submissions." Include SASE. Responds "ASAP, sometimes 8 weeks, but if by EPK or internet, will be more timely."

Music Mostly **Latin blues**, **pop**, **country** and **gospel**; also **R&B** and **comedy**. Works primarily with vocalists, special concerts, movies and TV. Current acts include Razzy Bailey (award winning blues artist/writer), Clint Walker (actor/recording artist), Ben

Colder (comedy/novelty), and Freddy Weller (formerly Paul Revere & The Raiders/hit songwriter), and Dickie Lee.

Tips "Artists, have your act together. Have a full press kit, videos and be professional. Attitudes are a big factor in my agreeing to work with you (no egotists). This is a business, and we will be building your career."

☑ CLASS ACT PRODUCTIONS/MANAGEMENT

P.O. Box 55252, Sherman Oaks CA 91413. (818)980-1039. E-mail: peter.kimmel@ sbcglobal.net. **Contact:** Peter Kimmel, president. Management firm. Estab. 1985. Currently represents songwriters and music artists. Receives percentage of commission.

How to Contact Submit material via mail or e-mail. Unsolicited submissions are OK. For mail, include CD, cover letter, lyric sheets (essential) or submit electronic press kit by e-mail. Responds in 1 month.

Music All styles. Represents select first rate music material to music supervisors of films, television, commercials, etc.

Tips "We are also affiliated with Sound Image Entertainment recording studios and video production. See Web site at www.soundimage.us and www.soundimagevideo.com."

☑ CLOUSHER PRODUCTIONS

P.O. Box 1191, Mechanicsburg PA 17055. (717)766-7644. Fax: (717)766-1490. E-mail: cpinfo@msn.com. Website: www.clousher.com. **Contact:** Fred Clousher, owner. Booking agency and production company. Estab. 1972. Represents groups from anywhere; currently handles over 100 acts.

How to Contact Submit demo package by mail. Please, no electronic press kits. Unsolicited submissions are OK. Prefers CDs or DVD. Press kit should include bio, testimonials, credits, glossies, song list, references, and your contact information. Does not return material. "Performer should check back with us!"

Music Mostly **country**, **old rock** and **ethnic** (German, Hawaiian, etc.); also **dance bands** (regional), **Dixieland**, and **classical musicians**. "We work mostly with country, old time R&R, regional variety dance bands, tribute acts, and all types of variety acts." Current acts include Jasmine Morgan (country/pop vocalist), Robin Right (country vocalist and Tammy Wynette tribute artist) and Stanky & The Coalminers (polka band).

Tips "The songwriters we work with are entertainers themselves, which is the aspect we deal with. They usually have bands or do some sort of show, either with tracks or live music. We engage them for stage shows, concerts, etc. We DO NOT review songs you've written. We do not publish music, or submit performers to recording companies for contracts. We strictly set up live performances for them."

☑ THE EDWARD DE MILES MUSIC COMPANY

10573 W. Pico Blvd., #352, Los Angeles CA 90064-2348. (310)948-9652. Fax: (310)474-

7705. E-mail: info@edmsahara.com. Website: www.edmsahara.com. **Contact:** Edward de Miles, president. Management firm, booking agency, entertainment/sports promoter and TV/radio broadcast producer. Estab. 1984. Represents film, television, radio and musical artists; currently handles 15 acts. Receives 10-20% commission. Reviews material for acts. Regional operations in Chicago, Dallas, Houston and Nashville through marketing representatives. Licensed A.F. of M. booking agent.

- Also see listings for Edward De Miles in the Music Publishers and Record Producers sections, and Sahara Records and Filmworks Entertainment in the Record Companies section of this book.

How to Contact *Does not accept unsolicited materials.* Prefers CD with 3-5 songs, 8 × 10 b&w photo, bio and lyric sheet. "Copyright all material before submitting." If seeking management, include cover letter, bio, demo CD with 3-5 songs, 8 × 10 b&w photo, lyric sheet, press clippings and video if available in press kit. Include SASE. Does not return material. Responds in 1 month.

Music Mostly **country, dance, R&B/soul, rock, top 40/pop** and **urban contemporary**; also looking for material for **television, radio and film** productions. Works primarily with dance bands and vocalists. Current acts include Steve Lynn (R&B/dance), Multiple Choice (rap) and Devon Edwards (jazz).

Tips "Performers need to be well prepared with their presentations (equipment, showmanship a must)."

JOHN ECKERT ENTERTAINMENT CONSULTANTS

(formerly Pro Talent Consultants), 7723 Cora Dr., Lucerne CA 95458. (707)349-1809 or (310)499-8948 (Mar Vista/Beverly Hills, CA). E-mail: talentconsultants@gmail.com. **Contact:** John Eckert, coordinator or Rich Clark. MarVista/Santa Monica management firm and booking agency. Estab. 1979. Represents individual artists and groups; currently handles 12 acts. Receives 15% commission. Reviews material for acts.

How to Contact Submit demo package by mail. Unsolicited submissions are OK. "We prefer CD (4 songs). Submit videocassette with live performance only." If seeking management, press kit should include an 8 × 10 photo, a cassette or CD of at least 4-6 songs, a bio on group/artist, references, cover letter, press clippings, video and business card, or a phone number with address. Does not return material. Responds in 5 weeks.

Music Mostly **country, country/pop** and **rock**. Works primarily with vocalists, show bands, dance bands, and bar bands. Current acts include Ronny and the Daytonas (pop/rock-top 40 band), The Royal Guardsmen (pop/rock/top 40), Gary Lewis & the Playboys (top 40), The Chantays (Surf Group), Don Grady, (singer/songwriter, actor) and The Trashmen (Top 40 band).

SCOTT EVANS PRODUCTIONS

P.O. Box 814028, Hollywood FL 33081-4028. (954)963-4449. E-mail: evansprod@aol.

com. Website: www.theentertainmentmall.com. **Contact:** Ted Jones, new artists, or Jeanne K., Internet marketing and sales. Management firm and booking agency. Estab. 1979. Represents local, regional or international individual artists, groups, songwriters, comedians, novelty acts and dancers; currently handles over 200 acts. Receives 10-50% commission. Reviews material for acts.

How to Contact New artists can make submissions through the 'auditions' link located on the Web site. Unsolicited submissions are OK. "Please be sure that all submissions are copyrighted and not your original copy as we do not return material."

Music Mostly **pop**, **R&B** and **Broadway**. Deals with "all types of entertainers; no limitations." Current acts include Scott Evans and Company (variety song and dance), Dorit Zinger (female vocalist), Jeff Geist, Actors Repertory Theatre, Entertainment Express, Perfect Parties, Joy Deco (dance act), Flashback 2000 Revue (musical song and dance), Everybody Salsa (Latin song and dance) and Around the World (international song and dance).

Tips "Submit a neat, well put together, organized press kit."

☐ EXCLESISA BOOKING AGENCY

716 Windward Rd., Jackson MS 39206. (601)366-0220. E-mail: exclesis@bellsouth. net. Website: www.exclesisa-booking.com. **Contact:** Roy and Esther Wooten, booking managers/owners. Booking agency. Estab. 1989. Represents groups from anywhere; currently handles 9 acts. Receives 15% commission. Reviews material for acts.

How to Contact *Call first and obtain permission to submit.* Submit demo package by mail. Unsolicited submissions are OK. Prefers CD or videocassette. If seeking management, press kit should include CD or cassette, videocassette, pictures, address and telephone contact, and bio. Does not return material. Responds in 2 months.

Music Gospel only. Current acts include The Canton Spirituals, Darrell McFadden & The Disciples, The Jackson Southernaires, Slim & The Supreme Angels, The Pilgrim Jubilees, Spencer Taylor & the Highway Q'cs, The Annointed Jackson Singers, The Southern Sons, Jewel & Converted, and Ms. B & Tha' Band.

Tips "Make sure your demo is clear with a good sound so the agent can make a good judgment."

⬛ ☑ S.L. FELDMAN & ASSOCIATES & MACKLAM FELDMAN MANAGEMENT

1505 W. Second Ave. #200, Vancouver BC V6H 3Y4 Canada. (604)734-5945. Fax: (604)732-0922. E-mail: feldman@slfa.com. Website: www.slfa.com. Booking agency and artist management firm. Estab. 1970. Agency represents mostly established Canadian recording artists and groups; currently handles over 200 acts.

How to Contact *Write or call first to obtain permission to submit a demo.* Prefers CD, photo and bio. If seeking management, contact Watchdog for consideration and include video in press kit. SAE and IRC. Responds in 2 months.

Music Current acts include Elvis Costello, The Chieftains, Joni Mitchell, Diana Krall, Norah Jones, Susan Tedeschi, Ry Cooder, Pink Martini, Tracy Chapman, James Taylor, and Melody Gardot.

▦ ☑ FIRST TIME MANAGEMENT

Sovereign House, 12 Trewartha Rd., Praa Sands-Penzance, Cornwall TR20 9ST England (01736)762826. Fax: (01736)763328. E-mail: panamus@aol.com. Website: www. songwriters-guild.co.uk and www.myspace.com/guildofsongwriters. **Contact:** Roderick G. Jones, managing director. Management firm, record company (Digimax Records Ltd www.digimaxrecords.com, Rainy Day Records, Mohock Records, Pure Gold Records) and music publisher (Panama Music Library, Melody First Music Library, Eventide Music Library, Musik' Image Music Library, Promo Sonor International Music Library, Caribbean Music Library, ADN Creation Music Library, Piano Bar Music Library, Corelia Music Library, PSI Music Library,Scamp Music Publishing, First Time Music (Publishing) U.K. (www.panamamusic.co.uk and www.myspace.com/scampmusicpublishing) —registered members of The Mechanical Copyright Protection Society (MCPS) and The Performing Right Society (PRS)). Estab. 1986. Represents local, regional and international individual aritsts, groups, composers, DJs and songwriters. Receives 15-25% commission. Reviews material for acts.

- Also see the listings for First Time Music (Publishing) in the Music Publishers section of this book.

How to Contact Submit demo package by mail. Unsolicited submissions are OK. Prefers CD with 3 songs, lyric sheets and also complete album projects where writer/performer has finished masters. If seeking management, press kit should include cover letter, bio, photo, demo tape/CD, press clippings and anything relevant to make an impression. Does not return material. Responds in 1 month.

Music All styles. Works primarily with songwriters, composers, DJs, rappers, vocalists, bands, groups and choirs. Current acts include Willow (pop), Bram Stoker (gothic rock group), Kevin Kendle (New Age) Peter Arnold (folk/roots), David Jones (urban/R&B), Shanelle (R&B/dance), AudioJunkie & Stylus (dance/hardcore/funky house/electro house) Ray Guntrip (jazz).

Tips "Become a member of the Guild of International Songwriters and Composers (www. songwriters-guild.co.uk). Keep everything as professional as possible. Be patient and dedicated to your aims and objectives."

☑ BILL HALL ENTERTAINMENT & EVENTS

138 Frog Hollow Rd., Churchville PA 18966-1031. (215)357-5189. Fax: (215)357-0320. E-mail: Billhallevents@verizon.net. **Contact:** William B. Hall III, owner/president. Booking agency and production company. Represents individuals and groups; currently handles 20-25 acts. Receives 15% commission. Reviews material for acts.

How to Contact Submit demo package by mail. Unsolicited submissions are OK. Prefers CD, cassette, or videocassette of performance with 2-3 songs "and photos, promo material, and CD, record, or tape. We need quality material, preferably before a 'live' audience." Does not return material. Responds only if interested.

Music Marching band, **circus** and **novelty**. Works primarily with "unusual or novelty attractions in musical line, preferably those that appeal to family groups." Current acts include Fralinger and Polish-American Philadelphia Championship Mummers String Bands (marching and concert group), "Mr. Polynesian" Show Band and Hawaiian Revue (ethnic group), the "Phillies Whiz Kids Band" of Philadelphia Phillies Baseball team, Mummermania Musical Quartet, Philadelphia German Brass Band (concert band), Vogelgesang Circus Calliope, Kromer's Carousel Band Organ, Reilly Raiders Drum & Bugle Corps, Hoebel Steam Calliope, Caesar Rodney Brass Band, Philadelphia Police & Fire Pipes Band, Tim Laushey Pep & Dance Band, Larry Stout (show organist/keyboard player), Jersey Surf Drum & Bugle Corp, Caesar Rodney Brass Marching Band, Corporales San Simon Bolivian Dancers, Robinson's Grandmaster Concert Band Organ, and Bobby Burnett, vocalist/comedian.

Tips "Please send whatever helps us to most effectively market the attraction and/or artist. Provide something that gives you a clear edge over others in your field!"

☐ HARDISON INTERNATIONAL ENTERTAINMENT CORPORATION

P.O. Box 1732, Knoxville TN 37901-1732. (865)688-8680. E-mail: dennishardinson@ bellsouth.net. Website: www.myspace.com/hardison_music07 and http://www. hardisoninternational.netfirms.com. **Contact:** Dennis K. Hardison, CEO/founder. Dennis K. Hardison II, president; Travis J. Hardison, president, Denlatrin Record, a division of Hardison International Entertainment Corp. Contact: Management firm, booking agency, music publisher (Denlatrin Music) BMI, record label (Denlatrin Records) and record producer. Estab. 1984. Represents individual artists from anywhere; currently handles 3 acts. Receives 20% commission. Reviews material for acts. "We are seeking level-minded and patient individuals. Our primary interests are established recording acts with prior major deals."

- This company has promoted many acts in show business for over 30 years, including New Edition, Freddie Jackson, M.C. Lyte, Kool Moe Dee, Biz Markie, and Surface, to name a few.

How to Contact Submit demo package by mail. Unsolicited submissions are OK. Prefers CD with 3 songs only. If seeking management, press kit should include bio, promo picture and CD. Does not return materials. Responds in 6 weeks to the best material. Critiques available through MySpace, so enclose your MySpace address.

Music Mostly **R&B**, **hip-hop** and **rap**. Current acts include Dynamo (hip-hop), The Nafro Queens of Lagos, Nigeria, and Triniti (record producer, Public Enemy, Dynamo, among others, current studio and sound engineer for Chuck D).

Tips "We respond to the hottest material, so make it hot!"

Managers & Agents

☑ INTERNATIONAL ENTERTAINMENT BUREAU

3612 N. Washington Blvd., Indianapolis IN 46205-3592. (317)926-7566. E-mail: ieb@ prodigy.net. Booking agency. Estab. 1972. Represents individual artists and groups from anywhere; currently handles 151 acts. Receives 20% commission.

How to Contact *No unsolicited submissions.*

Music Mostly **rock**, **country**, and **A/C**; also **jazz**, **nostalgia**, and **ethnic**. Works primarily with bands, comedians and speakers. Current acts include Five Easy Pieces (A/C), Scott Greeson (country), and Cool City Swing Band (variety).

☑ JANA JAE ENTERPRISES

P.O. Box 35726, Tulsa OK 74153. (918)786-8896. Fax: (918)786-8897. E-mail: janajae@ janajae.com. Website: www.janajae.com. **Contact:** Kathleen Pixley, agent. Booking agency, music publisher (Jana Jae Publishing/BMI) and record company (Lark Record Productions, Inc.). Estab. 1979. Represents individual artists and songwriters; currently handles 12 acts. Receives 15% commission. Reviews material for acts.

- Also see the listings for Jana Jae Music in the Music Publishers section, Lark Record Productions in the Record Companies section and Lark Talent & Advertising in the Record Producers section of this book.

How to Contact Submit demo by mail. Unsolicited submissions are OK. Prefers CD or DVD of performance. If seeking management, press kit should include cover letter, bio, photo, demo tape/CD, lyric sheets and press clippings. Does not return material.

Music Mostly **country**, **classical** and **jazz instrumentals**; also **pop**. Works with vocalists, show and concert bands, solo instrumentalists. Represents Jana Jae (country singer/ fiddle player), Matt Greif (classical guitarist), Sydni (solo singer) and Hotwire (country show band).

☑ BOB KNIGHT AGENCY

185 Clinton Ave., Staten Island NY 10301. (718)448-8420. **Contact:** Bob Knight, president. Management firm, booking agency, music publisher and royalty collection firm. Estab. 1971. Represents artists, groups and songwriters; currently handles 7 acts. Receives 10-20% commission. Reviews material for acts and for submission to record companies and producers.

How to Contact Submit demo by mail. Unsolicited submissions are OK. Prefers cassette, CD, DVD, or videocassette (if available) with 5 songs and lead sheet "with bio and references." If seeking management, press kit should include bio, DVD, videocassette, CD, or audio cassette, as well as photo. Include SASE. Responds in 2 months.

Music Mostly **top 40/pop**; also **easy listening**, **MOR**, **R&B**, **soul**, **rock (nostalgia '50s and '60s)**, **alternative**, **country**, and **country/pop**. Works primarily with recording and name groups and artists—'50s, '60s and '70s acts, bands, high energy dance and show groups. Current acts include Delfonics (R&B nostalgia), B.T. Express (R&B),

Brass Construction (R&B), Main Ingredient (R&B), Denny Carmella's Review, Denny Carmella's Booty Shack, Carl Thomas (R&B), Santa Esmeralda starring Leroy Gomez (disco), Motown Magic (R&B/tribute), and Skyy (funk/R&B), "Elvis—That's the Way It Was" by Rick Alviti; Beatles tribute by the 4 Fabs; and Temptations Lead Singer 1971-75 by Damon Harris.

Tips "We're seeking artists and groups with completed albums/demos. Also seeking male and female solo artists with powerful and dynamic voice—top 40, pop, R&B, and rock, country, and opera for recording and live performances."

LEVINSON ENTERTAINMENT VENTURES INTERNATIONAL, INC.

1440 Veteran Ave., Suite 650, Los Angeles CA 90024. (323)663-6940. E-mail: leviinc@aol. com. President: Bob Levinson. **Contact:** Jed Leland, Jr. Management firm. Estab. 1978. Represents national individual artists, groups and songwriters; currently handles 4 acts. Receives 15-25% commission. Reviews material for acts.

How to Contact *Write first and obtain permission to submit.* Prefers CD, DVD, cassette, or VHS videocassette with 6 songs and lead sheet. If seeking management, press kit should include bio, pictures and press clips. Include SASE. Responds in 1 month.

Music Mostly **rock**, **MOR**, **R&B** and **country**. Works primarily with rock bands and vocalists.

Tips "Should be a working band, self-contained and, preferably, performing original material."

RICK LEVY MANAGEMENT

4250 A1AS, D-11, St. Augustine FL 32080. (904)806-0817. Fax: (904)460-1226. E-mail: rick@ricklevy.com. Website: www.ricklevy.com. **Contact:** Rick Levy, president. Management firm, music publisher (Flying Governor Music/BMI) and record company (Luxury Records). Estab. 1985. Represents local, regional or international individual artists and groups; currently handles 5 acts. Receives 15-20% commission. Reviews material for acts.

How to Contact *Write or call first and obtain permission to submit.* Prefers CD or DVD with 3 songs and lyric sheet. If seeking management, press kit should include cover letter, bio, demo tape/CD, DVD demo, photo and press clippings. Include SASE. Responds in 2 weeks.

Music Mostly **R&B** (no rap), **pop**, **country** and **oldies**; also **children's** and **educational videos** for schools. Current acts include Jay & the Techniques ('60s hit group), The Original Box Tops ('60s), The Limits (pop), Freddy Cannon ('60s), The Fallin Bones (Blues/rock), Tommy Roe ('60s), The Bushwhackers (country).

Tips "If you don't have 200% passion and commitment, don't bother. Be sure to contact only companies that deal with your type of music."

◘ LOGGINS PROMOTION

5018 Franklin Pike, Nashville TN 37220 E-mail: staff@LogginsPromotion.com. Website: www.logginspromotion.com. **Contact:** Paul Loggins, CEO. Management firm and radio promotion. Represents individual artists, groups and songwriters from anywhere; currently handles 6 acts. Receives 20% commission. Reviews material for acts.

How to Contact If seeking management, press kit should include picture, short bio, cover letter, press clippings and CD (preferred). "Mark on CD which cut you, as the artist, feel is the strongest." Does not return material. Responds in 2 weeks.

Music Mostly **adult**, **top 40** and **AAA**; also **urban**, **rap**, **alternative**, **college**, **smooth jazz** and **Americana**. Works primarily with bands and solo artists.

◙ MANAGEMENT BY JAFFE

68 Ridgewood Ave., Glen Ridge, NJ 07028. (973)743-1075. Fax: (973)743-1075. E-mail: jerjaf@aol.com. President: Jerry Jaffe. Management firm. Estab. 1987. Represents individual artists and groups from anywhere; currently handles 2 acts. Receives 20% commission. Reviews material for acts "rarely." Reviews for representation "sometimes."

How to Contact *Write or call first to arrange personal interview.* Prefers CD or DVD with 3-4 songs and lyric sheet. Does not return material. Responds in 2 months.

Music Mostly **rock/alternative**, **pop** and **Hot AC**. Works primarily with groups and singers/songwriters.

Tips "If you are influenced by Jesus & Mary Chain, please e-mail. Create some kind of 'buzz' first."

◙ PHIL MAYO & COMPANY

P.O. Box 304, Bomoseen VT 05732. (802)468-2554. Fax: (802)468-2554. E-mail: pmcamgphil@aol.com. **Contact:** Phil Mayo, President. Management firm and record company (AMG Records). Estab. 1981. Represents individual artists, groups and songwriters from anywhere; currently handles 4 acts. Receives 15-20% commission. Reviews material for acts.

How to Contact *Contact first and obtain permission to submit.* Prefers CD with 3 songs (professionally recorded) and lyric or lead sheet. If seeking management, include bio, photo and lyric sheet in press kit. Does not return material. Responds in 2 months.

Music Mostly **contemporary Christian pop**. Current and past acts have included John Hall, Guy Burlage, Jonell Mosser, Pam Buckland, Orleans, Gary Nicholson, and Jon Pousette-Dart.

◙ MEDIA MANAGEMENT

9P.O. Box 3773, San Rafael CA 94912-3773. (415)898-7474. Fax: (415)898-9191. E-mail: mediamanagement9@aol.com. **Contact:** Eugene, proprietor. Management firm. Estab. 1990. Represents international individual artists, groups and songwriters; currently handles 5 acts. Receives 15% commission. Reviews material for acts.

How to Contact Submit demo by mail. Unsolicited submissions are OK. Prefers CD or DVD with lyric sheet. If seeking management, include lyric sheets, demo CD, photo and bio. Does not return material.

Music R&B, **blues**, **rock**, **country**, and **pop**. Works primarily with songwriting performers/bands. Current acts include The John Lee Hooker Estate—management consultant, (blues); Peter Walker—management, (world folk guitar virtuoso); Zakiya Hooker—management, (blues and R&B) Greg Anton/ZERO II/Cast of Clowns (rock).

Tips "Write great radio-friendly songs with great musical and lyrical hooks."

☐ MERRI-WEBB PRODUCTIONS

P.O. Box 5474, Stockton CA 95205. (209)948-8186. Fax: (209)942-2163. Website: www.makingmusic4u.com. **Contact:** Kristy Ledford, A&R coordinator. Management firm, music publisher (Kaupp's & Robert Publishing Co./BMI) and record company (Kaupp Records). Represents regional (California) individual artists, groups and songwriters; currently handles 7 acts. Receives 10-15% commission. Reviews material for acts.

• Also see the listing for Kaupp & Robert Publishing Company in the Music Publishers section and Kaupp Records in the Record Companies section of the book.

How to Contact *Write first and obtain permission to submit or to arrange personal interview.* Prefers CDs with 3 songs maximum and lyric sheet. Include SASE. Responds in 3 months.

Music Mostly **country**, **A/C rock** and **R&B**; also **pop**, **rock** and **gospel**. Works primarily with vocalists, bands and songwriters. Current acts include Bruce Bolin (rock/pop singer), Nanci Lynn (country/pop singer) and Rick Webb (country/pop singer).

☐ MIDCOAST, INC.

1002 Jones Rd., Hendersonville TN 37075. (615)400-4664. E-mail: mid-co@ix.netcom.com. Managing Director: Bruce Andrew Bossert. Management firm and music publisher (MidCoast, Inc./BMI). Estab. 1984. Represents individual artists, groups and songwriters; currently handles 2 acts. Reviews material for acts.

How to Contact Submit demo package by mail. Unsolicited submissions are OK. Prefers CD, cassette, VHS videocassette or DAT with 2-4 songs and lyric sheet. If seeking management, press kit should include cover letter, "short" bio, tape, video, photo, press clippings and announcements of any performances in Nashville area. Does not return material. Responds in 6 weeks if interested.

Music Mostly **rock**, **pop** and **country**. Works primarily with original rock and country bands and artists. Current acts include Room 101 (alternative rock).

◨ NOTEWORTHY PRODUCTIONS

124½ Archwood Ave., Annapolis MD 21401. (410)268-8232. Fax: (410)268-2167. E-mail:

mcshane@mcnote.com. Website: www.mcnote.com. **Contact:** McShane Glover, president. Management firm and booking agency. Estab. 1985. Represents individual artists, groups and songwriters from everywhere; currently handles 6 acts. Receives 15-20% commission. Reviews material for acts.

How to Contact *Write first and obtain permission to submit.* Prefers CD/CDR with lyric sheet. If seeking management, press kit should include CD, photo, bio, venues played and press clippings (preferably reviews). "Follow up with a phone call 3-5 weeks after submission." Does not return material. Responds in 2 months.

Music Mostly **Americana**, **folk**, and **Celtic**. Works primarily with performing singer/ songwriters. Current acts include toby Walker (blues) and Pat Wictor (roots).

☐ PM MUSIC GROUP, INC.

(formerly Precision Management), 957 W. Marietta St. NW, Suite D, Atlanta GA 30318. (800)275-5336, ext. 0381042. E-mail: precisionmanagement@netzero.com. Website: www.pmmusicgroup.com. **Contact:** St. Paul Williams, operations director. Management firm and music publisher (Mytrell/BMI). Estab. 1990. Represents individual artists and/ or groups and songwriters from anywhere; currently handles 3 acts. Receives 20% commission. Reviews material for acts.

How to Contact Submit demo package by mail. Unsolicited submissions are OK. Prefers cassette or VHS videocassette with 3-4 songs and lyric sheet. If seeking management, press kit should include photo, bio, demo tape/CD, lyric sheets, press clippings and all relevant press information. Include SASE. Responds in 6 weeks.

Music Mostly **R&B**, **rap** and **gospel**; also **all types**.

☑ RAINBOW TALENT AGENCY, LLC

146 Round Pond Lane, Rochester NY 14626. (585)723-3334. Fax: (585)720-6172. E-mail: rtalent@frontiernet.net. Website: www.rainbowtalentagency.com. **Contact:** Carl Labate, President. Management firm and booking agency. Represents artists and groups; currently handles 4 acts. Receives 15-25% commission.

How to Contact Submit demo package by mail. Unsolicited submissions are OK. Prefers CD with minimum 3 songs. May send DVD if available; "a still photo and bio of the act; if you are a performer, it would be advantageous to show yourself or the group performing live. Theme videos are not helpful." If seeking management, include photos, bio, markets established, CD/DVD. Does not return material. Responds in 1 month.

Music Mostly **blues**, **rock**, and **R&B**. Works primarily with touring bands and recording artists. Current acts include Back to the Future (classical, jazz, worldbeat); Classic Albums Live (classic rock symphony); Hard Logic (high energy jazz fusion), and Spanky Haschmann Swing Orchestra (high energy swing).

Tips "My main interest is with groups or performers that are currently touring and have some product. And are at least 50% percent original. Strictly songwriters should apply elsewhere."

☐ RASPBERRY JAM MUSIC

(formerly Endangered Species Artist Management), 4 Berachah Ave., South Nyack NY 10960-4202. (845)353-4001. Fax: (845)353-4332. E-mail: muzik@verizon.net. Website: www.musicandamerica.com or www.anyamusic.com President: Fred Porter. Vice President: Suzanne Buckley. Management firm. Estab. 1979. Represents individual artists, groups and songwriters from anywhere; currently handles 3 acts. Receives 20% commission. Reviews material for acts.

How to Contact *Call first and obtain permission to submit.* Prefers CD with 3 or more songs and lyric sheet. "Please include a demo of your music, a clear, recent photograph as well as any current press, if any. A cover letter indicating at what stage in your career you are and expectations for your future. Please label the cassette and/or CD with your name and address as well as the song titles." If seeking management, press kit should include cover letter, bio, photo, demo/CD, lyric sheet and press clippings. Include SASE. Responds in 6 weeks.

Music Mostly **pop**, **rock** and **world**; also **Latin/heavy metal**, **R&B**, **jazz** and **instrumental**. Current acts include Jason Wilson & Tabarruk (pop/reggae, nominated for Juno award 2001), and Anya (teen singer).

Tips "Listen to everything, classical to country, old to contemporary, to develop an understanding of many writing styles. Write with many other partners to keep the creativity fresh. Don't feel your style will be ruined by taking a class or a writing seminar. We all process moods and images differently. This leads to uniqueness in the music."

☐ REIGN MUSIC AND MEDIA, LLC

(formerly Bassline Entertainment, Inc.), P.O. Box 2394, New York NY 10185. E-mail: talent@reignmm.com. Website: www.reignmm.com. **Contact:** Talent Relations Dept. Multi-media/Artist Development firm. Estab. 1993 as Bassline Entertainment. Promotes/ develops primarily local and regional vocalists, producers, and songwriters. Receives 20-25% commission. Reviews material for artists.

How to Contact Submit demo package by mail or e-mail. Unsolicited submissions are OK. Prefers CD, mp3, or video. Standard hard copy press kit or EPK should include cover letter, press clippings and/or reviews, bio, demo (in appropriate format), picture and accurate contact telephone number. Include SASE. Usually responds in 3 weeks.

Music Mostly **pop**, **R&B**, **club/dance** and **hip-hop/rap**; some **Latin**. Works primarily with singer/songwriters, producers, rappers and bands. Current acts include Calel (pop/ R&B/Christian hip hop) and Iceman (hip hop).

⊘ DIANE RICHARDS WORLD MANAGEMENT, INC.

E-mail: drworldmgm@aol.com. **Contact:** Diane Richards, president. Management firm. Estab. 1994. Represents individual artists, groups, songwriters and producers from anywhere; currently handles 8 acts. Receives 20% commission. Reviews material for acts.

How to Contact *Write first (via e-mail) and obtain permission to submit.* If seeking management, press kit should include cover letter, photograph, biography, cassette tape, telephone number and address. Does not return material. Responds in 1 month.

Music Mostly **dance**, **pop** and **rap**; also **New Age**, **A/C** and **jazz**. Works primarily with pop and dance acts, and songwriters who also are recording artists. Current acts include Sappho (songwriter/artist), Menace (songwriter/producer/artist) and Babygirl (R&B/rap artist).

▢ RUSTRON/WHIMSONG MUSIC PRODUCTIONS

Send all artist song submissions to: 1156 Park Lane, West Palm Beach FL 33417-5957. (561)686-1354. E-mail: RMP_WMP@bellsouth.net. **Contact:** Sheelah Adams, office administrator. Main Office in Connecticut. ("Main office does not review artist submissions—only South Florida Branch office does.") Executive Director: Rusty Gordon. Artist Consultants: Rusty Gordon and Davilyn Whims. Composition Management: Ron Caruso. Management firm, booking agency, music publisher (Rustron Music Publishers/BMI and Whimsong Publishing/ASCAP), record company and record producer. Estab. 1970. Represents individuals, groups and songwriters; currently handles 20 acts. Receives 10-30% commission. Reviews material for acts.

- Also see listing for Rustron Music in the Record Companies and section of this book.

How to Contact *Call to discuss submission.* Send CD or cassette with 10-15 songs (CD produced to sell at gigs with up to 15 songs on each CD preferred). Provide 8 1/2X11 typed lyric sheets for every song in the submission. If seeking management, send press kit including: cover letter, bio, demo CD(s), typed lyric sheets and press clippings. "SASE or International Reply Coupon (IRC)required for all correspondence." Responds in 4 months.

Music Mostly **adult contemporary electric-acoustic**, **blues (country folk/urban, Southern)**, **country (rock, blues, progressive)**, **easy listening**, **Cabaret**, **soft rock & pop (ballads)**, **women's music**, **R&B**, **folk/rock**; also **New Age instrumentals** and **New Age folk fusion**. Current acts include Jayne Margo-Reby (folk rock), Star Smiley (country), Robin Plitt (historical folk), Boomslang Swampsinger (Florida folk), Continental Divide (topical folk), Tracie Mitchell & Ivory Coast (folk rock/blues), Florida Rank & File (socio-political/folk/world music).

Tips "Carefully mix demo, don't drown the vocals, 10-15 songs in a submission. Prefer a for-sale CD made to sell at gigs with up to 15 songs on each. Send photo if artist is seeking marketing and/or production assistance. Very strong hooks, definitive verse melody, evolved concepts, unique and unpredictable themes. Flesh out a performing sound and style. The presentation should be unique to the artist. Stage presence a must!"

☑ SA'MALL MANAGEMENT

P.O. Box 261488, Encino CA 91426. (818)506-8533. Fax: (818)506-8534. E-mail: samusa@aol.com. Website: www.pplentertainmentgroup.com. **Contact:** Ted Steele, vice president of talent. Management firm, music publisher (Pollybyrd Publications) and record company (PPL Entertainment Group). Estab. 1990. Represents individual artists, groups and songwriters worldwide; currently handles 10 acts. Receives 10-25% commission. Reviews material for acts.

- Also see the listings for Pollybyrd Publications Limited in the Music Publishers section of this book.

How to Contact *E-mail first and obtain permission to submit.* "Only professional full-time artists who tour and have a fan base need apply. No weekend warriors, please." Prefers CD or cassette. If seeking management, press kit should include picture, bio and tape. Include SASE. Responds in 2 months.

Music All types. Current acts include Riki Hendrix (rock), Buddy Wright (blues), Fhyne, Suzette Cuseo, The Band AKA, LeJenz, B.D. Fuoco, Juz-cuz, Donato, MoBeatz, and Kapital P.

Ⓝ ☐ SANDALPHON MANAGEMENT

P.O. Box 29110, Portland OR 97296. (503)957-3929. E-mail: jackrabbit01@comcast.net. **Contact:** Ruth Otey, president. Management firm, music publisher (Sandalphon Music Publishing/BMI), and record company (Sandalphon Records). Estab. 2005. Represents individual artists, groups, songwriters; works with individual artists and groups from anywhere. Currently handles 0 acts. Receives negotiable commission. Reviews material for acts.

How to Contact Submit demo by mail. Unsolicited submissions are OK. Prefers cassette or CD with 1-5 songs and lyric sheet, cover letter. "Include name, address, and contact information." Include SASE or SAE and IRC for outside the United States. Responds in 6-8 weeks.

Music Mostly **rock**, **country**, and **alternative**; also **pop**, **gospel**, and **blues**. "We are looking for singers, bands, and singer/songwriters who are original but would be current in today's music markets. We help singers, bands, and singer-songwriters achieve their personal career goals."

Tips "Submit material you feel best represents you, your voice, your songs, or your band. Fresh and original songs and style are a plus. We are a West Coast management company looking for singers, bands, and singer-songwriters who are ready for the next level. We are looking for those with talent who are capable of being national and international contenders."

⌨ ✅ SERGE ENTERTAINMENT GROUP

P.O. Box 2760, Acworth GA 30102. (678)445-0006. Fax: (678)494-9289. E-mail: sergeent@ aol.com. Website: www.sergeentertainmentgroup.com. **Contact:** Sandy Serge, president. Management and PR firm and song publishers. Estab. 1987. Represents individual artists, groups, songwriters from anywhere; currently handles 20 acts. Receives 20% commission for management. Monthly fee required for PR acts.

How to Contact *E-mail first for permission to submit.* Submit demo package by mail. Unsolicited submissions are OK. Prefers CD or cassette with 4 songs and lyric sheet. If seeking management, press kit should include 8 × 10 photo, bio, cover letter, lyric sheets, max of 4 press clips, DVD, performance schedule and CD. "All information submitted must include name, address and phone number on each item." Does not return material. Responds in 6 weeks if interested.

Music Mostly **rock**, **pop** and **country**; also **New Age**. Works primarily with singer/ songwriters and bands. Current acts include Kevin Carlson (folk), ASIA featuring John Payne (classic rock), Erik Norlander (prog rock), and Chocolate Thunder (blues/jazz).

⌨ ◻ SILVER BOW MANAGEMENT

Box 5, 720 6th St., New Westminster BC V3L 3C5 Canada. (604)523-9309. Fax: (604)395-6316. E-mail: saddlestone@shaw.ca. Website: www.saddlestone.net. President: Grant Lucas. CEO: Candice James. Management firm, music publisher (Saddlestone Publishing, Silver Bow Publishing), record company (Saddlestone Records) and record producer (Silver Bow Productions, Krazy Cat Productions). Estab. 1988. Represents individual artists, groups, songwriters internationally; currently handles 6 acts. Receives standard commission. Reviews material for acts.

- Also see the listings for Saddlestone Publishing in the Music Publishers section and Silver Bow Productions in the Record Producers section of this book.

How to Contact Submit demo package by mail. Unsolicited submissions are OK. Prefers CDs with lyric sheets. If seeking management, press kit should include 8 × 10 photo, bio, cover letter, CD with lyric sheets, press clippings, video, résumé and current itinerary. "Visuals are everything—submit accordingly." Does not return material. Responds in 2 months.

Music Mostly **jazz**, **country**, **pop** and **rock**; also **R&B**, **Christian** and **alternative**. Works primarily with bands, vocalists and singer/songwriters. Current acts include The Soulmates (pop/euro dance), Rick Valiant (jazz), Lane Swan (MOR).

◻ T. SKORMAN PRODUCTIONS, INC.

5156 S. Orange Ave., Orlando FL 32809. (407)895-3000. Fax: (407)895-1422. E-mail: ted@tskorman.com. Website: www.tskorman.com. **Contact:** Ted Skorman, president. Management firm and booking agency. Estab. 1983. Represents groups; currently handles 40 acts. Receives 10-25% commission. Reviews material for acts.

How to Contact *E-mail first for permission to submit.* Prefers CD with 2 songs, or videocassette of no more than 6 minutes. "Live performance—no trick shots or editing tricks. We want to be able to view act as if we were there for a live show." If seeking management, press kit should include cover letter, bio, photo and demo CD or video. Does not return material. Responds only if interested.

Music Mostly **top 40**, **dance**, **pop**, and **country**. Works primarily with high-energy dance acts, recording acts, and top 40 bands. Current acts include Steph Carse (pop).

Tips "We have many pop recording acts and are looking for commercial material for their next albums."

☐ GARY SMELTZER PRODUCTIONS

603 W. 13th #2A, Austin TX 78701. (512)478-6020. Fax: (512)478-8979. E-mail: gsptalent@ aol.com. Website: www.GarySmeltzerProductions.com **Contact:** Gary Smeltzer, president. Management firm and booking agency. Estab. 1967. Represents individual artists and groups from anywhere. Currently handles 20 acts. "We book about 100 different bands each year—none are exclusive." Receives 20% commission. Reviews material for acts.

How to Contact Submit demo package by mail. Unsolicited submissions are OK. Prefers CD or DVD. If seeking management, press kit should include cover letter, résumé, CD/ DVD, bio, picture, lyric sheets, press clippings and video. Does not return material. Responds in 1 month.

Music Mostly **alternative**, **R&B** and **country**. Current acts include Ro Tel & the Hot Tomatoes (nostalgic '60s showband).

Tips "We prefer performing songwriters who can gig their music as a solo or group."

☑ SOUTHEASTERN ATTRACTIONS

1025 23rd St. South, Suite 302, Birmingham AL 35205. (205)307-6790. Fax: (205)942-7700. E-mail: staff@seattractions.com. Website: www.seattractions.com. **Contact:** Agent. Booking agency. Estab. 1967. Represents groups from anywhere; currently handles 200 acts. Receives 20% commission.

How to Contact Submit demo package by mail. Unsolicited submissions are OK. Prefers CD or DVD. Does not return material. Responds in 2 months.

Music Mostly **rock**, **alternative**, **oldies**, **country** and **dance**. Works primarily with bands. Current acts include Leaderdog (rock), Undergrounders (variety to contemporary), Style Band (Motown/dance), The Connection (Motown/dance), Rollin' in the Hay(bluegrass).

☑ STARKRAVIN' MANAGEMENT

11135 Weddington St., #424, N. Hollywood, CA 91601. (818)587-6801. Fax: (818)587-6802. E-mail: bcmclane@aol.com. Website: www.benmclane.com. **Contact:** B.C. McLane, Esq. Management and law firm. Estab. 1994. Represents individual artists, groups and songwriters. Receives 20% commission (management); $300/hour as attorney.

How to Contact Submit demo package by mail. Unsolicited submissions are OK. Prefers cassette. Does not return material. Responds in 1 month if interested.

Music Mostly **rock**, **pop** and **R&B**. Works primarily with bands.

☐ ST. JOHN ARTISTS

P.O. Box 619, Neenah WI 54957-0619. (920)722-2222. Fax: (920)725-2405. E-mail: jon@ stjohn-artists.com. Website: www.stjohn-artists.com/. **Contact:** Jon St. John and Gary Coquoz, agents. Booking agency. Estab. 1968. Represents local and regional individual artists and groups; currently handles 20 acts. Receives 15-20% commission. Reviews material for acts.

How to Contact *Call first and obtain permission to submit.* Prefers CD or DVD. If seeking management, press kit should include cover letter, bio, photo, demo tape/CD, video and résumé. Include SASE.

Music Mostly **rock** and **MOR**. Current acts include Tribute (variety/pop/country), Boogie & the Yo-Yo's ('60s to 2000s), Vic Ferrari (Top 40 '80s-2000's), Little Vito and the Torpedoes(variety '50s-2000's), Center Stage Variety Show Band (variety '60s-2000's) and Da Yoopers (musical comedy/novelty).

☑ TAS MUSIC CO./DAVE TASSE ENTERTAINMENT

N2467 Knollwood Dr., Lake Geneva WI 53147-9731. E-mail: david@baybreezerecords. com. Website: www.baybreezerecords.com. **Contact:** David Tasse. Booking agency, record company and music publisher. Represents artists, groups and songwriters; currently handles 21 acts. Receives 10-20% commission. Reviews material for acts.

How to Contact Submit demo tape by mail. Unsolicited submissions are OK. Prefers cassette with 2-4 songs and lyric sheet. Include performance videocassette if available. If seeking management, press kit should include tape, bio and photo. Does not return material. Responds in 3 weeks.

Music Mostly **pop** and **jazz**; also **dance**, **MOR**, **rock**, **soul** and **top 40**. Works primarily with show and dance bands. Current acts include Max Kelly (philosophic rock) and L.J. Young (rap).

☑ T.L.C. BOOKING AGENCY

37311 N. Valley Rd., Chattaroy WA 99003. (509)292-2201. Fax: (509)292-2205. E-mail: tlcagent@ix.netcom.com. Website: www.tlcagency.com. **Contact:** Tom or Carrie Lapsansky, agent/owners. Booking agency. Estab. 1970. Represents individual artists and groups from anywhere; currently handles 17 acts. Receives 10-15% commission. Reviews material for acts.

How to Contact *Call first and obtain permission to submit.* Prefers CD with 3-4 songs. Does not return material. Responds in 3 weeks.

Music Mostly **rock**, **country** and **variety**; also **comedians** and **magicians**. Works primarily with bands, singles and duos. Current acts include Nobody Famous (variety/classic rock), Mr. Happy (rock), Mad Rush (rock), Dixie Dandies (dixieland), and The Charm (variety/top 40).

⊘ UMBRELLA ARTISTS MANAGEMENT, INC.

2612 Erie Ave., P.O. Box 8369, Cincinnati OH 45208. (513)871-1500. Fax: (513)878-2240. E-mail: shertzman@cinci.rr.com. Website: www.stanhertzman.com. **Contact:** Stan Hertzman, president. Management firm. Represents artists and groups for specific circumstances.

How to Contact E-mail or specify website. Positive response only.

Music Mostly **contemporary country**, **rock** and **top 40/pop**. Works with contemporary/progressive pop/rock artists and writers on a per project basis. All deals in writing — no writing, no deal.

❑ UNIVERSAL MUSIC MARKETING

P.O. Box 2297, Universal City TX 78148. (210)653-3989. E-mail: bswrl8@wmconnect.net Website: www.bsw-records.com. **Contact:** Frank Willson, president. Management firm, record company (BSW Records), booking agency, music publisher and record producer (Frank Wilson). Estab. 1987. Represents individual artists and groups from anywhere; currently handles 12 acts. Receives 15% commission. Reviews material for acts.

• Also see the listings for BSW Records in the Music Publishers and Record Companies sections and Frank Wilson in the Record Producers section of this book.

How to Contact Submit demo package by mail. Unsolicited submissions are OK. Prefers CD or DVD with 3 songs and lyric sheet. If seeking management, include tape/CD, bio, photo and current activities. Include SASE. Responds in 6 weeks.

Music Mostly **country** and **light rock**; also **blues** and **jazz**. Works primarily with vocalists, singer/songwriters and bands. Current acts include Candee Land, Darlene Austin, Larry Butler, John Wayne, Sonny Marshall, Bobby Mountain, Crea Beal and Butch Martin (country). "Visit our website for an up-to-date listing of current acts."

☑ CHERYL K. WARNER PRODUCTIONS

P.O. Box 179, Hermitage TN 37076. (615)429-7849. E-mail: cherylkwarner@comcast. net. Website: www.cherylkwarner.com. **Contact:** Warner Productions, Inc. Recording and stage production, music consulting, music publisher, record label. Currently works with 2 acts. Reviews material for acts.

How to Contact Submit demo package by mail. Unsolicited submissions are OK. Prefers CD or DVD, but will accept CD with 3 best songs, lyric or lead sheet, bio and picture. Press kit should include CD, DVD with up-to-date bio, cover letter, lyric sheets, press clippings, and picture. Does not return material. Responds in 6 weeks if interested.

Music Mostly **country/traditional and contemporary**, **Christian/gospel** and **A/C/pop**. Works primarily with singer/songwriters and bands with original and versatile style. Current acts include Cheryl K. Warner (recording artist/entertainer) and Cheryl K. Warner Band (support/studio).

⚄ ◻ WINTERLAND ENTERTAINMENT MANAGEMENT & PUBLISHING

(formerly T.J. Booker Ltd.), P.O. Box 969, Rossland BC VOG 1YO Canada. (250)362-7795. E-mail: winterland@netidea.com. **Contact:** Tom Jones, owner. Management firm, booking agency and music publisher. Estab. 1976. Represents individual artists, groups and songwriters from anywhere; currently handles 6 acts. Receives 15% commission. Reviews material for acts.

How to Contact Submit demo package by mail. Unsolicited submissions are OK. Prefers CD, cassette or videocassette with 3 songs. If seeking management, include demo tape or CD, picture, cover letter and bio in press kit. Does not return material. Responds in 1 month.

Music Mostly **MOR**, **crossover**, **rock**, **pop**, and **country**. "Only book on an occasional basis. If you wish to submit, you are welcome. If I can I will review and critique your material. It is a changing world musically, but if it works, it works. There is no replacement for excellence."

⚄ WORLDSOUND, LLC

17837 1st Ave. South Suite 3, Seattle WA 98148. (206)444-0300. Fax: (206)244-0066. E-mail: music@worldsound.com. Website: www.worldsound.com. **Contact:** Warren Wyatt, A&R manager. Management firm. Estab. 1976. Represents individual artists, groups and songwriters from anywhere; currently handles 8 acts. Receives 20% commission. Reviews material for acts.

How to Contact "Online, send us an e-mail containing a link to your Web site where your songs can be heard and the lyrics are available—PLEASE DO NOT E-MAIL SONG FILES! By regular mail, unsolicited submissions are OK." Prefers CD with 2-10 songs and lyric sheet. "If seeking management, please send an e-mail with a link to your Web site—your site should contain song samples, band biography, photos, video (if available), press and demo reviews. By mail, please send the materials listed above and include SASE." Responds in 1 month.

Music Mostly **rock**, **pop**, and **world**; also **heavy metal**, **hard rock**, and **top 40**. Works primarily with pop/rock/world artists. Current acts include Makana (world music), Treble (pop), La Neo (contemporary/Hawaiian), and Keith Olsen (music producer).

Tips "Always submit new songs/material, even if you have sent material that was previously rejected; the music biz is always changing."

❑ D. ZIRILLI MANAGEMENT

P.O. Box 255, Cupertino CA 95015-0255. (408)257-2533. Fax: (408)252-8938. E-mail: donzirilli@aol.com. Website: www.zirilli.com. Owner: Don Zirilli. Management firm. Estab. 1965. Represents groups from anywhere; currently handles 1 act. Receives 20% commission or does fee-based consulting. Varies by project. Reviews material for acts.

How to Contact Submit demo package by mail. Unsolicited submissions are OK. Prefers CD, videocassette or DVD. If seeking management, press kit should include video. Does not return material. Responds in 2 weeks.

Music Mostly **rock**, **surf** and **MOR**. Current acts include Papa Doo Run Run (band).

Tips "Less is more."

ADDITIONAL MANAGERS & BOOKING AGENTS

The following companies are also managers/booking agents, but their listings are found in other sections of the book. Read the listings for submission information.

Music Firms

Advertising, Audiovisual & Commercial

I t's happened a million times—you hear a jingle on the radio or television and can't get it out of your head. That's the work of a successful jingle writer, writing songs to catch your attention and make you aware of the product being advertised. But the field of commercial music consists of more than just memorable jingles. It also includes background music that many companies use in videos for corporate and educational presentations, as well as films and TV shows.

SUBMITTING MATERIAL

More than any other market listed in this book, the commercial music market expects composers to have made an investment in the recording of their material before submitting. A sparse, piano/vocal demo won't work here; when dealing with commercial music firms, especially audiovisual firms and music libraries, high quality production is important. Your demo may be kept on file at one of these companies until a need for it arises, and it may be used or sold as you sent it. Therefore, your demo tape or reel must be as fully produced as possible.

The presentation package that goes along with your demo must be just as professional. A list of your credits should be a part of your submission, to give the company an idea of your experience in this field. If you have no experience, look to local television and radio stations to get your start. Don't expect to be paid for many of your first jobs in the commercial music field; it's more important to get the credits and exposure that can lead to higher-paying jobs.

Commercial music and jingle writing can be a lucrative field for the composer/songwriter with a gift for writing catchy melodies and the ability to write in many different music styles. It's a very competitive field, so it pays to have a professional presentation package that makes your work stand out.

Three different segments of the commercial music world are listed here: advertising agencies, audiovisual firms and commercial music houses/music libraries. Each looks for a different type of music, so read these descriptions carefully to see where the music you write fits in.

ADVERTISING AGENCIES

Ad agencies work on assignment as their clients' needs arise. Through consultation and input from the creative staff, ad agencies seek jingles and music to stimulate the consumer to identify with a product or service.

When contacting ad agencies, keep in mind they are searching for music that can capture and then hold an audience's attention. Most jingles are short, with a strong, memorable hook. When an ad agency listens to a demo, it is not necessarily looking for a finished product so much as for an indication of creativity and diversity. Many composers put together a reel of excerpts of work from previous projects, or short pieces of music that show they can write in a variety of styles.

AUDIOVISUAL FIRMS

Audiovisual firms create a variety of products, from film and video shows for sales meetings, corporate gatherings and educational markets, to motion pictures and TV shows. With the increase of home video use, how-to videos are a big market for audiovisual firms, as are spoken word educational videos. All of these products need music to accompany them. For your quick reference, companies working to place music in movies and TV shows (excluding commercials) have a preceding their listing (also see the Film & TV Index on page 417 for a complete list of these companies).

Like ad agencies, audiovisual firms look for versatile, well-rounded songwriters. When submitting demos to these firms, you need to demonstrate your versatility in writing specialized background music and themes. Listings for companies will tell what facet(s) of the audiovisual field they are involved in and what types of clients they serve. Your demo tape should also be as professional and fully produced as possible; audiovisual firms often seek demo tapes that can be put on file for future use when the need arises.

COMMERCIAL MUSIC HOUSES & MUSIC LIBRARIES

Commercial music houses are companies contracted (either by an ad agency or the advertiser) to compose custom jingles. Since they are neither an ad agency nor an audiovisual firm, their main concern is music. They use a lot of it, too—some composed by inhouse songwriters and some contributed by outside, freelance writers.

Music libraries are different in that their music is not custom composed for a specific client. Their job is to provide a collection of instrumental music in many different styles that, for an annual fee or on a per-use basis, the customer can use however he chooses.

In the following listings, commercial music houses and music libraries, which are usually the most open to works by new composers, are identified as such by **bold** type.

The commercial music market is similar to most other businesses in one aspect: experience is important. Until you develop a list of credits, pay for your work may not be high. Don't pass up opportunities if a job is non- or low-paying. These assignments will add to your list of credits, make you contacts in the field, and improve your marketability.

Money & rights

Many of the companies listed in this section pay by the job, but there may be some situations where the company asks you to sign a contract that will specify royalty payments. If this happens, research the contract thoroughly, and know exactly what is expected of you and how much you'll be paid.

Depending on the particular job and the company, you may be asked to sell one-time rights or all rights. One-time rights involve using your material for one presentation only. All rights means the buyer can use your work any way he chooses, as many times as he likes. Be sure you know exactly what you're giving up, and how the company may use your music in the future.

In the commercial world, many of the big advertising agencies have their own publishing companies where writers assign their compositions. In these situations, writers sign contracts whereby they do receive performance and mechanical royalties when applicable.

ADDITIONAL LISTINGS

For additional names and addresses of ad agencies that may use jingles and/or commercial music, refer to the *Standard Directory of Advertising Agencies* (National Register Publishing). For a list of audiovisual firms, check out the latest edition of *AV Marketplace* (R.R. Bowker). Both these books may be found at your local library. To contact companies in your area, see the Geographic Index at the back of this book.

THE AD AGENCY

P.O. Box 470572, San Francisco CA 94147. **Contact:** Michael Carden, creative director. **Advertising agency and jingle/commercial music production house.** Clients include business, industry and retail. Estab. 1971. Uses the services of music houses, independent songwriter/composers and lyricists for scoring of commercials, background music for video production, and jingles for commercials. Commissions 20 composers and 15 lyricists/year. Pays by the job or by the hour. Buys all or one-time rights.

How to Contact Submit demo tape of previous work. Prefers cassette with 5-8 songs and lyric sheet. Include SASE. Responds in 3 weeks.

Music Uses variety of musical styles for commercials, promotion, TV, video presentations.

Tips "Our clients and our needs change frequently."

ADVERTEL, INC.

P.O. Box 18053, Pittsburgh PA 15236-0053. (412)344-4700. Fax: (412)344-4712. E-mail: pberan@advertel.com. Website: www.advertel.com. **Contact:** Paul Beran, president/CEO. **Telephonic/Internet production company.** Clients include small and multi-national companies. Estab. 1983. Uses the services of music houses and independent songwriters/composers for scoring of instrumentals (all varieties) and telephonic production. Commissions 3-4 composers/year. Pay varies. Buys all rights and phone exclusive rights.

How to Contact Submit demo of previous work. Prefers CD. "Most compositions are 2 minutes strung together in 6, 12, 18 minute length productions." Does not return material; prefers to keep on file. Responds "right away if submission fills an immediate need."

Music Uses all varieties, including unusual; mostly subdued music beds. Radio-type production used exclusively in telephone and Internet applications.

Tips "Go for volume. We have continuous need for all varieties of music in 2 minute lengths."

◪ CANTRAX RECORDERS

Dept. CM, 2119 Fidler Ave., Long Beach CA 90815. (562)498-4593. Fax: (562)498-4852. E-mail: cantrax@earthlink.net. **Contact:** Richard Cannata, owner. Recording studio. Clients include anyone needing recording services (i.e., industrial, radio, commercial). Estab. 1980. Uses the services of independent songwriters/composers and lyricists for scoring of independent features and films and background music for radio, industrials and promotions, commercials for radio and TV and jingles for radio. Commissions 10 composers/year. Pays fees set by the artist. "We take 15%."

How to Contact *"No phone calls, please."* Query with résumé of credits or submit demo CD of previous work. Prefers CD—no cassettes. Does not return material. Responds in 2 weeks if SASE is provided.

Music Uses jazz, New Age, rock, easy listening and classical for slide shows, jingles and soundtracks.

Tips "You must have a serious, professional attitude."

CEDAR CREST STUDIO

#17 CR 830, Henderson AR 72544. Website: www.cedarcreststudio.com. **Contact:** Bob Ketchum, owner. **Audiovisual firm and jingle/commercial music production house.** Clients include corporate, industrial, sales, music publishing, training, educational, legal, medical, music and Internet. Estab. 1973. Sometimes uses the services of independent songwriters/composers for background music for video productions, jingles for TV spots and commercials for radio and TV. Pays by the job or by royalties. Buys all rights or one-time rights.

How to Contact Query with résumé of credits or submit demo tape of previous work. Prefers CD, cassette, or DVD. Does not return material. "We keep it on file for future reference." Responds in 2 months.

Music Uses up-tempo pop (not too "rocky"), unobtrusive—no solos for commercials and background music for video presentations.

Tips "Hang, hang, hang. Be open to suggestions. Improvise, adapt, overcome."

COMMUNICATIONS FOR LEARNING

395 Massachusetts Ave., Arlington MA 02474. (781)641-2350. E-mail: comlearn@thecia. net. Website: www.communicationsforlearning.com. **Contact:** Jonathan L. Barkan, executive producer/director. Video, multimedia, exhibit and graphic design firm. Clients include multi-nationals, industry, government, institutions, local, national and international nonprofits. Uses services of music houses and independent songwriters/composers as theme and background music for videos and multimedia. Commissions 1-2 composers/year. Pays $2,000-5,000/job and one-time use fees. Rights purchased vary.

How to Contact Submit demo and work available for library use. Prefers CD to Web links. Does not return material; prefers to keep on file. "For each job we consider our entire collection." Responds in 3 months.

Music Uses all styles of music for all sorts of assignments.

Tips "Please don't call. Just send your best material available for library use on CD. We'll be in touch if a piece works and negotiate a price. Make certain your name and contact information are on the CD itself, not only on the cover letter."

DBF A MEDIA COMPANY

9683 Charles St., LaPlata MD 20646. (301)645-6110. Fax: (301)392-6111. E-mail: service@ dbfmedia.com. Website: www.dbfmedia.com. **Contact:** Randy Runyon, general manager. Video Production. Estab. 1981. Uses the services of music houses for background music for industrial, training, educational and promo videos, jingles and commercials for radio and TV. Buys all rights.

Music "All genre for MOH, industrial, training, video/photo montages and commercials."

How to Contact Submit demo CD of previous work. Prefers CD or DVD with 5-8 songs and lead sheet. Include SASE, but prefers to keep material on file. Responds in 6 months.

DISK PRODUCTIONS

1100 Perkins Rd., Baton Rouge LA 70802. Fax: (225)343-0210. E-mail: disk_productions@ yahoo.com. **Contact:** Joey Decker, director. **Jingle/production house.** Clients include advertising agencies and film companies. Estab. 1982. Uses the services of music houses, independent songwriters/composers and lyricists for scoring and background music for TV spots, films and jingles for radio and TV. Commissions 7 songwriters/composers and 7 lyricists/year. Pays by the job. Buys all rights.

How to Contact Submit demo of previous work. Prefers DVD, CD, cassette or DAT. Does not return material. Responds in 2 weeks.

Music Needs all types of music for jingles, music beds or background music for TV and radio, etc.

Tips "Advertising techniques change with time. Don't be locked in a certain style of writing. Give me music that I can't get from pay needle-drop."

FINE ART PRODUCTIONS/RICHIE SURACI PICTURES, MULTIMEDIA, INTERACTIVE

67 Maple St., Newburgh NY 12550-4034. (914)527-9740. Fax: (845)561-5866. E-mail: rs7fap@bestweb.net. Website: www.idsi.net/~rs7fap/tentsales.htm. **Contact:** Richard Suraci, owner. Advertising agency, audiovisual firm, scoring service, **jingle/commercial music production house**, motion picture production company (Richie Suraci Pictures) and **music sound effect library**. Clients include corporate, industrial, motion picture and broadcast firms. Estab. 1987. Uses services of independent songwriters/composers for scoring, background music and jingles for various projects and commercials for radio and TV. Commissions 1-2 songwriters or composers and 1-2 lyricists/year. Pays by the job, royalty or by the hours. Buys all rights.

How to Contact Submit demo tape of previous work or tape demonstrating composition skills, query with résumé of credits or write or call first to arrange personal interview. Prefers CD, DVD, cassette (or ½", ¾", or 1" videocassette) with as many songs as possible and lyric or lead sheets. Include SASE, but prefers to keep material on file. Responds in 1 year.

Music Uses all types of music for all types of assignments.

HOME, INC.

165 Brookside Avenue Extension, Jamaica Plain MA 02130. E-mail: alanmichel@homeinc.

org. Director: Alan Michel. Audiovisual firm and video production company. Clients include cable television, nonprofit organizations, pilot programs, entertainment companies and industrial. Uses the services of music houses and independent songwriters/composers for scoring of music videos, background music and commercials for TV. Commissions 2-5 songwriters/year. Pays up to $200-600/job. Buys all rights and one-time rights.

How to Contact Submit demo tape of previous work. Prefers CD or Web site URL with 6 pieces. Does not return material; prefers to keep on file. Responds as projects require.

Music Mostly synthesizer. Uses all styles of music for educational videos.

Tips "Have a variety of products available and be willing to match your skills to the project and the budget."

K&R ALL MEDIA PRODUCTIONS LLC

(formerly K&R's Recording Studios), 28533 Greenfield, Southfield MI 48076. (248)557-8276. E-mail: recordav@knr.net. Website: www.knr.net. **Contact:** Ken Glaza. Scoring service and **jingle/commercial music production house**. Clients include commercial and industrial firms. Services include sound for pictures (music, dialogue). Uses the services of independent songwriters/composers and lyricists for scoring of film and video, commercials and industrials and jingles and commercials for radio and TV. Commissions 1 composer/month. Pays by the job. Buys all rights.

How to Contact Submit demo tape of previous work. Prefers CD or VHS videocassette with 5-7 short pieces. "We rack your tape for client to judge." Does not return material.

Tips "Keep samples short. Show me what you can do in five minutes. Go to knr.net 'free samples' and listen to the sensitivity expressed in emotional music."

NOVUS

121 E. 24th St., 12 Floor, New York NY 10010. (212)487-1377. Fax: (212)505-3300. E-mail: novuscom@aol.com. **Contact:** Robert Antonik, president/creative director. Marketing and communications company. Clients include corporations and interactive media. Estab. 1986. Uses the services of music houses, independent songwriters/composers and lyricists for scoring, background music for documentaries, commercials, multimedia applications, website, film shorts, and commercials for radio and TV. Commissions 2 composers and 4 lyricists/year. Pay varies per job. Buys one-time rights.

How to Contact *Request a submission of demo.* Query with résumé. Submit demo of work. Prefers CD with 2-3 songs. "We prefer to keep submitted material on file, but will return material if SASE is enclosed. Responds in 6 weeks.

Music Uses **all styles** for a variety of different assignments.

Tips "Always present your best and don't add quantity to your demo. Novus is a creative marketing and communications company. We work with various public relations, artists managements and legal advisors. We create multimedia events."

OMNI COMMUNICATIONS

Dept. SM, P.O. Box 302, Carmel IN 46082-0302. (317)846-2345. E-mail: omni@ omniproductions.com. Website: www.omniproductions.com. President: W. H. Long. Creative Director: S.M. Long. Production Manager: Jim Mullet. Television, digital media production and audiovisual firm. Estab. 1978. Serves industrial, commercial and educational clients. Uses the services of music houses and songwriters for scoring of films and television productions, DVD's, CD-ROMs and internet streams; background music for voiceovers; lyricists for original music and themes. Pays by the job. Buys all rights.

How to Contact Submit demo tape of previous work. Prefers CD or DVD. Does not return material. Responds in 2 weeks.

Music Varies with each and every project; from classical, contemporary to commercial industrial.

Tips "Submit good demo tape with examples of your range to command the attention of our producers."

QUALLY & COMPANY INC.

2 E. Oak, Suite 2903, Chicago IL 60611. (312)280-1898. **Contact:** Michael Iva, creative director. **Advertising agency.** Uses the services of music houses, independent songwriters/ composers and lyricists for scoring, background music and jingles for radio and TV commercials. Commissions 2-4 composers and 2-4 lyricists/year. Pays by the job. Buys various rights depending on deal.

How to Contact Submit demo CD of previous work or query with résumé of credits. Include SASE, but prefers to keep material on file.

Music Uses all kinds of music for commercials.

⊠ UTOPIAN EMPIRE CREATIVEWORKS

P.O. Box 9, Traverse City MI 49685-0009 or P.O. Box 458, Kapa 'a (Kaua'i) HI 96746-0458. (231)943-5050 or (231)943-4000. E-mail: creativeservices@UtopianEmpire.com. Website: www.UtopianEmpire.com. **Contact:** Ms. M'Lynn Hartwell, president. Web design, multimedia firm and motion picture/video production company. Primarily serves commercial, industrial and nonprofit clients. We provide the following services: advertising, marketing, design/packaging, distribution and booking. Uses services of music houses, independent songwriters/composers for jingles and scoring of and background music for multi-image/multimedia, film and video. Negotiates pay. Buys all or one-time rights.

How to Contact Submit CD of previous work, demonstrating composition skills or query with resume of credits. Prefers CD. Does not return material; prefers to keep on file. Responds only if interested.

Music Uses mostly industrial/commercial themes.

VIDEO I-D, INC.

Dept. SM, 105 Muller Rd., Washington IL 61571. (309)444-4323. Fax: (309)444-4333. E-mail: videoid@videoid.com. Website: www.VideoID.com. **Contact:** Gwen Wagner, manager, operations. Post production/teleproductions. Clients include law enforcement, industrial and business. Estab. 1977. Uses the services of music houses and independent songwriters/composers for background music for video productions. Pays per job. Buys one-time rights.

How to Contact Submit demo of previous work. Prefers CD or VHS videocassette with 5 songs and lyric sheet. Does not return material. Responds in 1 month.

Play Producers
& Publishers

Finding a theater company willing to invest in a new production can be frustrating for an unknown playwright. But whether you write the plays, compose the music or pen the lyrics, it is important to remember not only where to start but how to start. Theater in the U.S. is a hierarchy, with Broadway, Off Broadway and Off Off Broadway being pretty much off limits to all but the Stephen Sondheims of the world.

Aspiring theater writers would do best to train their sights on nonprofit regional and community theaters to get started. The encouraging news is there are a great number of local theater companies throughout the U.S. with experimental artistic directors who are looking for new works to produce, and many are included in this section. This section covers two segments of the industry: theater companies and dinner theaters are listed under Play Producers (beginning on page 254), and publishers of musical theater works are listed under the Play Publishers heading (beginning on page 259). All these markets are actively seeking new works of all types for their stages or publications.

BREAKING IN

Starting locally will allow you to research each company carefully and learn about their past performances, the type of musicals they present, and the kinds of material they're looking for. When you find theaters you think may be interested in your work, attend as many performances as possible, so you know exactly what type of material each theater presents. Or volunteer to work at a theater, whether it be moving sets or selling tickets. This will give you valuable insight into the day-to-day workings of a theater and the creation of a new show. On a national level, you will find prestigious organizations offering workshops and apprenticeships covering every subject from arts administration to directing to costuming. But it could be more helpful to look into professional internships at theaters and attend theater workshops in your area. The more knowledgeable you are about the workings of a particular company or theater, the easier it will be to tailor your work to fit its style and the more responsive they will be to you and your work. (See the Workshops & Conferences section on page 325 for more information.) As a composer for the stage, you need to know as much as possible about a theater and how it works, its history and the different roles played by the people involved in it. Flexibility is the key to successful productions, and knowing how a theater works will only help you in cooperating and collaborating with the director, producer, technical people and actors.

If you're a playwright looking to have his play published in book form or in theater publications, see the listings under the Play Publishers section (page 259). To find play producers and publishers in your area, consult the Geographic Index at the back of this book.

Play Producers

PLAY PRODUCERS

BAILIWICK REPERTORY

Bailiwick Arts Center, 2936 N. Southport, Chicago IL 60657. (773)883-1090. Fax: (773)883-2017. E-mail: david@bailiwick.org. Website: www.bailiwick.org. **Director:** David Zak. Producer: Rusty Hernandez. Play producer. Estab. 1982. Produces 5 mainstage, 5 one-act plays and 1-2 new musicals/year. "We do Chicago productions of new works on adaptations that are politically or thematically intriguing and relevant. We also do an annual director's festival which produces 50-75 new short works each year." Pays 5-8% royalty.

How to Contact "Review our manuscript submission guidelines or the professional page of our Web site." Responds in 6 months.

Musical Theater "We want innovative, dangerous, exciting material."

Productions *The Christmas Schooner*, by John Reeger and Julie Shannon (holiday musical); *The Hunchback of Notre Dame* (Dennis DeYoung); *Jerry Springer—The Opera*, American Premiere; *Parade, Dr. Sex* (World Premiere), etc.

Tips "Be creative. Be patient. Be persistent. Make me believe in your dream."

BARTER THEATRE

P.O. Box 867, Abingdon VA 24212. (276)628-3991. Fax: (276)619-3335. E-mail: barterinfo@bartertheatre.com. Website: www.bartertheatre.com. **Contact:** Richard Rose, Producing Artistic Director. Play/musical producer. Estab. 1933. Produces app. 10-12 plays and 6-8 musicals (at least 1 new musical)/year. Audience: tourist and local mix, mid-American/Southern, diverse, all ages. Two spaces: 507-seat proscenium stage, 167-seat thrust stage.

How to Contact : Query with synopsis, character breakdown, set description, and CD of the songs. Be sure CDs will play back properly. Include SASE. Responds in 1 year.

Musical Theater "We investigate all types. We are not looking for any particular standard. Prefer sellable titles with unique use of music. Prefer small cast musicals, although have done large-scale projects with marketable titles or subject matter. We do not accept one-act or juke-box musicals. We use original music in many of our plays. Does not wish to see very urban material, or material with very strong language."

Productions 2009 season includes: *The Wizard of Oz,* Jimmy Rodgers: America's Blue Yodeller; Joseph and the Amazing Technicolor Dreamcoat; The Fantastiks; several children's musicals, and Little Shop of Horrors.

Tips "Be patient. Be talented. Be original and make sure subject matter fits our audience. And, please, make sure your CD will play before you send it in."

WILLIAM CAREY UNIVERSITY DINNER THEATRE

William Carey University, Hattiesburg MS 39401-5499. (601)318-6218. E-mail: thecom@

wmcarey.edu. **Contact:** O.L. Quave, managing director. Play producer. Produces 2 musicals/year. "Our dinner theater operates only in summer and plays to family audiences." Payment negotiable.

How to Contact Query with synopsis, character breakdown and set description. Does not return material. Responds in 1 month.

Musical Theater "Plays should be simply-staged, have small casts (8-10 maximum), and be suitable for family viewing; two hours maximum length. Score should require piano only, or piano, synthesizer."

Productions *Smoke on the Mountain*; *Spitfire Grill*; and *Pump Boys and Dinettes*.

THE DIRECTORS COMPANY

311 W. 43rd St., Suite 307, New York NY 10036. (212)246-5877. E-mail: directorscompany@gmail.com. Website: www.directorscompany.org. **Contact:** Leah Michalos, general manager. Artistic/Producing Director: Michael Parva. Play producer. Estab. 1980. Produces 1-2 new musicals/year. Performance space is a 99-seat theatre located in the heart of Manhattan's Theatre District. "It is beautifully equipped with dressing rooms, box office and reception area in the lobby." Pays negotiable rate.

How to Contact Query first by mail or e-mail. Include SASE. Responds in 1 year.

• We are not currently accepting submissions.

Musical Theater "The Harold Prince Musical Theatre Program develops new musicals by incorporating the director in the early stages of collaboration. The program seeks cutting edge material that works to break boundaries in music theatre. We produce workshops or developmental productions. The emphasis is on the material, not on production values, therefore, we do not limit cast sizes. However, there are limits on props and production values." No children's musicals or revues.

Productions *Jubilee*, by Kelly Dupuis/Marc Smollin (an absurdly magical exploration of fate, family, and fish); *Tales of Tinseltown* (reading), by Michael Colby/Paul Katz (a sardonic parody of 1930s Hollywood); and *Nightmare Alley* (reading), by Jonathan Brielle (about a drifter in 1932 looking for a way to begin a life in hard times).

ENSEMBLE THEATRE OF CINCINNATI

1127 Vine St., Cincinnati OH 45202. (513)421-3555. Fax: (513)562-4104. E-mail: administration@cincyetc.com. Website: www.cincyetc.com. **Contact:** D. Lynn Meyers, producing artistic director. Play producer. Estab. 1986. Produces 6 plays and at least 1 new musical/year. Audience is multi-generational and multi-cultural. 191 seats, proscenium stage. Pays 5-8% royalty (negotiable).

How to Contact Please call or write to inquire if ETC is accepting new scripts.

Musical Theater "All types of musicals are acceptable. Cast not over ten; minimum set, please."

Productions *Hedwig & the Angry Inch*, by John Cameron Mitchel (rock star/transgender/

Play Producers

love story); *Alice in Wonderland*, by David Kisor and Joe McDonough (update of the classic tale); and *The Frog Princess*, by Joe McDonough and David Kisor (family retelling of classic tale).

Tips Looking for "creative, inventive, contemporary subjects or classic tales. If we ask you to send your script, please send materials as complete as possible, including a SASE."

LOS ANGELES DESIGNERS' THEATRE

P.O. Box 1883, Studio City CA 91614-0883. (323)650-9600. Fax: (323)654-3210. E-mail: ladesigners@juno.com. **Contact:** Richard Niederberg, artistic director. Play producer. Estab. 1970. Produces 20-25 plays and 8-10 new musicals/year. Audience includes Hollywood production executives in film, TV, records and multimedia. Plays are produced at several locations, primarily Studio City, California. Pay is negotiable.

How to Contact Query first. Does not return material. Responds only if interested. *Send proposals only.*

Musical Theater "We seek out controversial material. Street language OK, nudity is fine, religious themes, social themes, political themes are encouraged. Our audience is very 'jaded' as it consists of TV, motion picture and music publishing executives who have 'seen it all'." Does not wish to see bland, 'safe' material. We like first productions. In the cover letter state in great detail the proposed involvement of the songwriter, other than as a writer (i.e., director, actor, singer, publicist, designer, etc.). Also, state if there are any liens on the material or if anything has been promised."

Productions *St. Tim*, by Fred Grab (historical '60s musical); *Slipper and the Rose* (gang musical); and *1593—The Devils Due* (historical musical).

Tips "Make it very 'commercial' and inexpensive to produce. Allow for non-traditional casting. Be prepared with ideas as to how to transform your work to film or videotaped entertainment."

PLAYWRIGHTS HORIZONS

416 W. 42nd St., New York NY 10036. (212)564-1235. Fax: (212)594-0296. E-mail: literary@ playwrightshorizons.org. Website: www.playwrightshorizons.org. **Contact:** Kent Nicholson, Director of Musical Theater. Estab. 1971. Produces about 5 plays and 1 new musical/year. "Adventurous New York City theater-going audience." Pays general Off-Broadway contract.

How to Contact Submit complete manuscript and tape or CD of songs. Attn: Kent Nicholson. Include SASE. Responds in 8 months.

Musical Theater American writers. "No revivals, one-acts or children's shows; otherwise we're flexible. We have a particular interest in scores with a distinctively contemporary and American flavor. We generally develop work from scratch; we're open to proposals for shows and scripts in early stages of development."

Productions *Grey Gardens, Saved, Floyd and Clea Under the Western Sky, Assassins, Sunday in the Park with George*

SHAKESPEARE SANTA CRUZ

Theater Arts Center, U.C.S.C., 1156 High Street, Santa Cruz CA 95064. (831)459-5810. E-mail: iago@ucsc.edu. Website: www.shakespearesantacruz.org. **Contact:** Marco Barricelli, artistic director. Play producer. Estab. 1982. Produces 4 plays/year. Performance spaces are an outdoor redwood grove; and an indoor 540-seat thrust. Pay is negotiable.
How to Contact Query first. Include SASE. Responds in 2 months.
Musical Theater "Shakespeare Santa Cruz produces musicals in its Winter Holiday Season (Oct-Dec). We are also interested in composers' original music for pre-existing plays—including songs, for example, for Shakespeare's plays."
Productions *Cinderella*, by Kate Hawley (book and lyrics) and Gregg Coffin (composer); and *Gretel and Hansel*, by Kate Hawley (book and lyrics) and composer Craig Bohmler; *The Princess and the Pea*, by Kate Hawley (book and lyrics) and composer Adam Wernick; *Sleeping Beauty*, by Kate Hawley (book and lyrics) and composer Adam Wernick.
Tips "Always contact us before sending material."

THE TEN-MINUTE MUSICALS PROJECT

P.O. Box 461194, West Hollywood CA 90046. E-mail: info@tenminutemusicals.org. Website: www.tenminutemusicals.org. **Contact:** Michael Koppy, producer. Play producer. Estab. 1987. All pieces are new musicals. Pays $250 advance.
How to Contact Submit complete manuscript, score and CD of songs. Include SASE. Responds in 3 months.Musical Theater Seeks complete short stage musicals of 8-15 minutes in length. Maximum cast: 9. "No parodies—original music only."
Productions Away to Pago Pago, by Jack Feldman/Barry Manilow/John PiRoman/Bruce Sussman; The Bottle Imp, by Kenneth Vega (from the story of the same title by Robert Louis Stevenson); and The Furnished Room, by Saragail Katzman (from the story of the same title by O. Henry), and many others.
Tips "Start with a solid story—either an adaptation or an original idea—but with a solid beginning, middle and end (probably with a plot twist at the climax). We caution that it will surely take much time and effort to create a quality work. (Occasionally a clearly talented and capable writer and composer seem to have almost 'dashed' something off, under the misperception that inspiration can carry the day in this format. Works selected in previous rounds all clearly evince that considerable deliberation and craft were invested.) We're seeking short contemporary musical theater material, in the style of what might be found on Broadway, Off-Broadway or the West End. Think of shows like *Candide* or *Little Shop of Horrors*, pop operas like *Sweeney Todd* or *Chess*, or chamber musicals like *Once on this Island* or *Falsettos*. (Even small accessible operas like *The Telephone* or *Trouble in Tahiti* are possible models.) All have solid plots, and all rely on sung material to advance them. Of primary importance is to start with a strong story, even if it means postponing work on music and lyrics until the dramatic foundation is complete."

THUNDER BAY THEATRE

400 N. Second Ave., Alpena MI 49707. (989)354-2267. Website: www.thunderbaytheatre.com. Artistic Director: Mark S. Butterfuss. Play producer. Estab. 1967. Produces 12 productions/year including 5 musicals and 7 plays. Performance space is thrust stage. Pays variable royalty or per performance.

How to Contact Submit complete manuscript, score and tape of songs. Include SASE.

Musical Theater Small cast. Not equipped for large sets. Considers original background music for use in a play being developed or for use in a pre-existing play.

Productions 2009 Musicals *Brigadoon, The Producers, The Rat Pack Lounge, White Christmas, Beauty and the Beast.*

WEST END ARTISTS

c/o St. Luke's Theatre, 308 West 46th St., New York NY 10036. (212)947-3499. Fax: (212)265-4074. **West Coast:** 18034 Ventura Blvd. #291, Encino CA 91316. (818)623-0040. Fax: (818)623-0202. E-mail: egaynes@aol.com. **Contact:** Pamela Hall, associate artistic director. Artistic Director: Edmund Gaynes. Play producer. Estab. 1983. "We operate St. Luke's Theatre, Actors Temple Theatre, and Theatres at 45 Bleecker St. in New York City, and Whitmore-Lindley Theatre Center in Los Angeles." Produces 5 plays and 3 new musicals/year. Audience "covers a broad spectrum, from general public to heavy theater/film/TV industry crowds. Pays 6% royalty.

How to Contact Submit complete manuscript, score and tape of songs. Include SASE. Responds in 3 months.

Musical Theater "Prefer small-cast musicals and revues. Full length preferred. Interested in children's shows also." Cast size: "Maximum 12; exceptional material with larger casts will be considered."

Productions Off-Broadway: *Picon Pie* - Lambs Theatre (2004-05); *Trolls* - Actors Playhouse, (2005); *The Big Voice: God or Merman?* - Actors Temple Theatre (2006-07); Danny and Sylvia: The Danny Kaye Musical — St. Luke's Theatre (2009).

Tips "If you feel every word or note you have written is sacred and chiseled in stone and are unwilling to work collaboratively with a professional director, don't bother to submit."

PLAY PUBLISHERS

BAKER'S PLAYS

45 W. 25th St., New York, NY 10010. (212)206-8990. Fax: (212)206-1429. E-mail: info@ bakersplays.com. Website: www.bakersplays.com. **Contact:** Roxane Heinze-Bradshaw, Managing Editor. Play publisher. Estab. 1845. Publishes 25-30 plays and 5-10 new musicals/year. Plays are used by children's theaters, junior and senior high schools, colleges and community theaters. Pays negotiated book and production royalty.

> • See the listing for Baker's Plays High School Playwriting Contest in the Contests & Awards section.

How to Contact Submit complete manuscript and CD. Include SASE. Also accepts online submission—see Web site for more information. Responds in 4 months.

Musical Theater "Seeking musicals for teen production and children's theater production. We prefer large cast, contemporary musicals which are easy to stage and produce. Plot your shows strongly, keep your scenery and staging simple, your musical numbers and choreography easily explained and blocked out. Music must be camera-ready."

Productions *Stone Soup,* by Anne Glasner & Betty Hollinger (children's musical); *A Walk in the Sky,* book and lyrics by Dale Wasserman, music by Allan Jay Friedman (family musical); *Beanstalk! The Musical!* book by Ross Mihalko and Donna Swift, music by Linda Berg, lyrics by Ross Mihalko (children's musical).

CONTEMPORARY DRAMA SERVICE

885 Elkton Dr., Colorado Springs CO 80907. (719)594-4422. E-mail: editor@meriwether. com. Website: www.contemporarydrama.com. **Contact:** Arthur Zapel, associate editor. Play publisher. Estab. 1979. Publishes 40-50 plays and 4-6 new musicals/year. "We publish for young children and teens in mainstream Christian churches and for teens and college level in the secular market. Our musicals are performed in churches, schools and colleges." Pays 10-50% book and performance royalty.

How to Contact *Query first* then submit complete manuscript, score and tape of songs. Include SASE. Responds in 1 month.

Musical Theater "For churches we publish musical programs for children and teens to perform at Easter, Christmas or some special occasion. Our school musicals are for teens to perform as class plays or special entertainments. Cast size may vary from 15-25 depending on use. We prefer more parts for girls than boys. Music must be written in the vocal range of teens. Staging should be relatively simple but may vary as needed. We are not interested in elementary school material. Elementary level is OK for church music but not public school elementary. Music must have full piano accompaniment and be professionally scored for camera-ready publication."

Publications *Lucky, Lucky Hudson and the 12th Street Gang*, by Tim Kelly, book, and Bill Francoeur, music and lyrics (spoof of old time gangster movies); *Is There A Doctor in the House?*, by Tim Kelly, book, and Bill Francoeur, music and lyrics (adapted from Moliere comedy); and *Jitterbug Juliet* , by Mark Dissette, book, and Bill Francoeur, music and lyrics (spoof of *Romeo and Juliet*).

Tips "Familiarize yourself with our market. Send $1 postage for catalog. Try to determine what would fit in, yet still be unique."

ELDRIDGE PUBLISHING CO., INC.

P.O. Box 14367, Tallahassee FL 32317. Phone/Fax: (850)385-2463. E-mail: info@histage. com. Website: www.histage.com. **Contact:** Susan Shore, musical editor. Play publisher. Estab. 1906. Publishes 50 plays and 1-2 musicals/year. Seeking "large cast musicals which appeal to students. We like variety and originality in the music, easy staging and costuming. Also looking for children's theater musicals which have smaller casts and are easy to tour. We serve the school market (6th grade through 12th); and church market (Christmas musicals)." Pays 50% royalty and 10% copy sales in school market.

How to Contact Submit manuscript, score or lead sheets and CD of songs. Include SASE. Responds in 1 month.

Publications *The Bard is Back*, by Stephen Murray ("a high school's production of Romeo & Juliet is a disaster!"); and *Boogie-Woogie Bugle Girls*, book by Craig Sodaro, music and lyrics by Stephen Murray (WWII themed musical).

Tips "We're always looking for talented composers but not through individual songs. We're only interested in complete school or church musicals. Lead sheets, CDs, and script are best way to submit. Let us see your work!"

ENCORE PERFORMANCE PUBLISHING

P.O. Box 14367, Tallahassee FL 32317. (850)385-2463. E-mail: info@encoreplay.com. Website: www.encoreplay.com. **Contact:** Meredith Edwards, senior editor. Drama publisher. "We publish complete musicals, not single songs." Estab. 1978. Publishes 1-2 musicals/year. Pays standard royalty.

How to Contact See website for submission guidelines. Materials should include complete musical including libretto, lyrics, lead sheets, and demo CD. Responds in 2 months.

Musical Theater "We are especially interested in musicals for schools (from grade school through high school)."

Publications *Elephans*, music by Larrance Fingerhut, books and lyrics by Jeff Goode; *Anne With An "e": The Green Gables Musical*, books and lyrics by Neil K. Newell and C. Michael Perry.

SAMUEL FRENCH, INC.

45 W. 25th St., New York NY 10010. (212)206-8990. Fax: (212)206-1429. Website: www. samuelfrench.com. Hollywood office: 7623 Sunset Blvd., Hollywood CA 90046. (323)876-0570. Fax: (323)876-6822. President: Leon Embry. **Contact:** Roxane Heinze-Bradshaw, managing editor. Play publisher. Estab. 1830. Publishes approximately 100 plays and 10-

20 new musicals/year. Amateur and professional theaters.

How to Contact *Query first.* Include SASE. Online query form is available. Responds in 10 weeks.

Musical Theater "We publish primarily successful musicals from the NYC, London and regional stage."

Publications *Evil Dead: The Musical,* by George Reinblatt—lyrics/book, and Frank Cipolla, Christopher Bond, Melissa Morris, George Reinblatt - music (Horror Movie parody); *Hats! The Musical*, book by Marcia Milgrom Dodge & Anthony Dodge, additional material by Rob Bartlett, Lynne Taylor-Corbett & Sharon Vaughn. Songs by Grammy, Golden Globe, and Tony winning songwriters (musical celebration of turning 50); *Adding Machine: A Musical*, composed by Joshua Schmidt, Libretto by Jason Loewith and Joshua Schmidt (dark comic of *The Adding Machine* by Elmer Rice).

PIONEER DRAMA SERVICE

P.O. Box 4267, Englewood CO 80155. (800)333-7262. Fax: (303)779-4315. Website: www. pioneerdrama.com. **Contact:** Lori Conary, assistant editor. Play publisher. Estab. 1963. "Plays are performed by junior high and high school drama departments, church youth groups, college and university theaters, semi-professional and professional children's theaters, parks and recreation departments." Playwrights paid 50% royalty (10% sales) split when there are multiple authors/composers.

How to Contact Query with character breakdown, synopsis and set description or submit full manuscript and CD of music. Include SASE. Responds in 6 months.

Musical Theater "We seek full length children's musicals, high school musicals and one act children's musicals to be performed by children, secondary school students, and/or adults. We want musicals easy to perform, simple sets, many female roles and very few solos. Must be appropriate for educational market. We are not interested in profanity, themes with exclusively adult interest, sex, drinking, smoking, etc. Several of our full-length plays are being converted to musicals. We edit them, then contract with someone to write the music and lyrics."

Publications *The Big Bad Musical,* by Alec Strum, music and lyrics by Bill Francoeur; *Nottingham: a Totally Teen Musical Book,* by Flip Kobler and Cincy Marcus, music by Dennis Poore, lyrics by Flip Kobler; *The Elves and the Shoemaker—the musical,* by Katen Boettcher-Tate, music and lyrics by Bill Francoeur.

Tips "Research and learn about our company. Our Web site and catalog provide an incredible amount of information."

PLAYERS PRESS, INC.

P.O. Box 1132, Studio City CA 91614. Associate Editor: Karen Flathers. Vice President: Robert W. Gordon. Play publisher, music book publisher, educational publisher. Estab. 1965. Publishes 20-70 plays and 1-3 new musicals/year. Full line of plays for all audiences:

classics, modern, contemporary, religious and children. Pays variable royalty and variable amount/performance.

How to Contact Query first. Include SASE. Responds in 3-6 months (3 weeks on queries).

Musical Theater "We will consider all submitted works. Presently musicals for adults and high schools are in demand. When cast size can be flexible (describe how it can be done in your work) it sells better."

Publications *The Revolution Machine*, by Donna Marie Swajéoki (American Revolution musical); *The Best of Times*, by Steven Porter (musical adaptation of *A Tale of Two Cities*); *Peter n' the Wolf*, by William-Alan Landes (musical theatre version of the famed Russian Classic by the same name).

Tips "For plays and musicals, have your work produced at least twice. Be present for rehearsals and work with competent people. Then submit material asked for in good clear copy with good audio and/or video tapes."

Classical Performing Arts

Finding an audience is critical to the composer of orchestral music. Fortunately, baby boomers are swelling the ranks of classical music audiences and bringing with them a taste for fresh, innovative music. So the climate is fair for composers seeking their first performance.

Finding a performance venue is particularly important because once a composer has his work performed for an audience and establishes himself as a talented newcomer, it can lead to more performances and commissions for new works.

BEFORE YOU SUBMIT

Be aware that most classical music organizations are nonprofit groups, and don't have a large budget for acquiring new works. It takes a lot of time and money to put together an orchestral performance of a new composition, therefore these groups are quite selective when choosing new works to perform. Don't be disappointed if the payment offered by these groups is small or even non-existent. What you gain is the chance to have your music performed for an appreciative audience. Also realize that many classical groups are understaffed, so it may take longer than expected to hear back on your submission. It pays to be patient, and employ diplomacy, tact and timing in your follow-up.

In this section you will find listings for classical performing arts organizations throughout the U.S. But if you have no prior performances to your credit, it's a good idea to begin with a small chamber orchestra, for example. Smaller symphony and chamber orchestras are usually more inclined to experiment with new works. A local university or conservatory of music, where you may already have contacts, is a great place to start.

All of the groups listed in this section are interested in hearing new works from contemporary classical composers. Pay close attention to the music needs of each group, and when you find one you feel might be interested in your music, follow submission guidelines carefully. To locate classical performing arts groups in your area, consult the Geographic Index at the back of this book.

ACADIANA SYMPHONY ORCHESTRA

412 Travis St., Lafayette LA 70503. (337)232-4277. Fax: (337)237-4712. E-mail: information@acadianasymphony.org. Website: www.acadianasymphony.org. **Contact**: Geraldine Hubbel, executive director. Symphony orchestra. Estab. 1984. Members are amateurs and professionals. Performs 20 concerts/year, including 1 new work. Commissions 1 new work/year. Performs in 2,230-seat hall with "wonderful acoustics." Pays "according to the type of composition."

How to Contact Call first. Does not return material. Responds in 2 months.

Music Full orchestra: 10 minutes at most. Reduced orchestra, educational pieces: short, up to 5 minutes.

Performances Quincy Hilliard's *Universal Covenant* (orchestral suite); James Hanna's *In Memoriam* (strings/elegy); and Gregory Danner's *A New Beginning* (full orchestra fanfare).

THE AMERICAN BOYCHOIR

19 Lambert Dr., Princeton NJ 08540. (609)924-5858. Fax: (609)924-5812. E-mail: admissions@americanboychoir.org. Website: www.americanboychoir.org. General Manager: Janet B. Kaltenbach. Music Director: Fernando Malvar-Ruiz. Professional boychoir. Estab. 1937. Members are musically talented boys in grades 4-8. Performs 150 concerts/year. Commissions 1 new work approximately every 3 years. Actively seeks high quality arrangements. Performs national and international tours, orchestral engagements, church services, workshops, school programs, local concerts, and at corporate and social functions.

How to Contact Submit complete score. Include SASE. Responds in 1 year.

Music Choral works in unison, SA, SSA, SSAA or SATB division; unaccompanied and with piano or organ; occasional chamber orchestra or brass ensemble. Works are usually sung by 28 to 60 boys. Composers must know boychoir sonority.

Performances *Four Seasons*, by Michael Torke (orchestral-choral); *Garden of Light*, by Aaron Kernis (orchestral-choral); *Reasons for Loving the Harmonica*, by Libby Larsen (piano); and *Songs Eternity*, by Steven Paulus (piano).

AMERICAN OPERA MUSICAL THEATRE CO.

400 W. 43rd St. #19D, New York NY 10036. (212)594-1839. Fax: (646)290-8471. E-mail: aomtc@mindspring.com. Website: www.americanoperacompany.com/aomtc.htm. **Contact:** Diana Corto, artistic director. Opera and musical theatre producing/presenting organization. Estab. 1995. Members are professionals with varying degrees of experience. Performs 2 operas, many concerts/year and 1 musical theatre production each year. Audience is sophisticated and knowledgeable about music and theatre. "We rent performance spaces in New York, and are either sponsored by a presenter, or are paid performance fees for opera and concerts."

How to Contact "We are only accepting photos and resumes at this time—no CDs or DVDs."

Music "Must be vocal (for opera or for music theatre). Cast should not exceed 10. Orchestration should not exceed 30, smaller groups preferred. No rock 'n' roll, brassy pop."

Performances Nationally and internationally: Puccini's *La Boheme*; Verdi's *Rigoletto*; *The Jewel Box*; *Iolanta*; *La Molinara* and *The World Goes Round*.

ANDERSON SYMPHONY ORCHESTRA

1124 Meridian Plaza, Anderson IN 46016. (765)644-2111. Fax: (765)644-7703. E-mail: aso@andersonsymphony.org. Website: www.andersonsymphony.org. **Contact:** Dr. Richard Sowers, conductor. Executive Director: George W. Vinson. Symphony orchestra. Estab. 1967. Members are professionals. Performs 7 concerts/year. Performs for typical mid-western audience in a 1,500-seat restored Paramount Theatre. Pay negotiable.

How to Contact Query first. Include SASE. Responds in several months.

Music "Shorter lengths better; concerti OK; difficulty level: mod high; limited by typically 3 full service rehearsals."

◪ ARCADY

P.O. Box 955, Simcoe ON N3Y 5B3 Canada. (519)428-3185. E-mail: info@arcady.ca. Website: www.arcady.ca. **Contact:** Ronald Beckett, director. Professional chorus and orchestra. Members are professionals, university music majors and recent graduates from throughout Ontario. "Arcady forms the bridge between the student and the professional performing career." Performs 12 concerts/year including 1 new works. Pay negotiable.

How to Contact Submit complete score and tape of piece(s). Does not return material. Responds in 3 months.

Music "Compositions appropriate for ensemble accustomed to performance of chamber works, accompanied or unaccompanied, with independence of parts. Specialize in repertoire of 17th, 18th and 20th centuries. Number of singers does not exceed 30. Orchestra is limited to strings, supported by a professional quartet. No popular, commercial or show music."

Performances Ronald Beckett's *I Am...* (opera); Ronald Beckett's *John* (opera); and David Lenson's *Prologue to Dido and Aeneas* (masque).

Tips "Arcady is a touring ensemble experienced with both concert and stage performance."

THE ATLANTA YOUNG SINGERS OF CALLANWOLDE

980 Briarcliff Rd. N.E., Atlanta GA 30306. (404)873-3365. Fax: (404)873-0756. E-mail: info@aysc.org. Website: www.aysc.org. **Contact:** Paige F. Mathis, music director. Children's chorus. Estab. 1975. Performs 3 major concerts/year as well as invitational

performances and co-productions with other Atlanta arts organizations. Audience consists of community members, families, alumni, and supporters. Performs most often at churches. Pay is negotiable.

How to Contact Submit complete score and tape of piece(s). Include SASE. Responds in accordance with request.

Music "Subjects and styles appealing to 3rd-12th grade boys and girls. Contemporary concerns of the world of interest. Unusual sacred, folk, classic style. Internationally and ethnically bonding. Medium difficulty preferred, with or without keyboard accompaniment."

Tips "Our mission is to promote service and growth through singing."

AUGSBURG CHOIR

Augsburg College, 2211 Riverside Avenue S., Minneapolis MN 55454. (612)330-1000. E-mail: hendricp@augsburg.edu. Website: www.augsburg.edu. **Director of Choral Activities:** Peter A. Hendrickson. Vocal ensemble (SATB choir). Members are amateurs. Performs 25 concerts/year, including 1-6 new works. Commissions 0-2 composers or new works/year. Audience is all ages, "sophisticated and unsophisticated." Concerts are performed in churches, concert halls and schools. Pays for outright purchase.

How to Contact Query first. Include SASE. Responds in 1 month.

Music Seeking "sacred choral pieces, no more than 5-7 minutes long, to be sung a cappella or with obbligato instrument. Can contain vocal solos. We have 50-60 members in our choir."

Performances Carol Barnett's *Spiritual Journey*; Steven Heitzeg's *Litanies for the Living* (choral/orchestral); and Morton Lanriclsen's *O Magnum Mysteries* (a cappella choral).

BILLINGS SYMPHONY

2721 2nd Ave N., Suite 350, Billings MT 59101-1936. (406)252-3610. Fax: (406)252-3353. E-mail: symphony@billingssymphony.org. Website: www.billingssymphony.org. **Contact:** Dr. Uri Barnea, music director. Symphony orchestra, orchestra and chorale. Estab. 1950. Members are professionals and amateurs. Performs 12-15 concerts/year, including 6-7 new works. Traditional audience. Performs at Alberta Bair Theater (capacity 1,416). Pays by outright purchase (or rental).

How to Contact Query first. Include SASE. Responds in 2 weeks.

Music Any style. Traditional notation preferred.

Performances Jim Cockey's *Symphony No. 2 (Parmly's Dream)* (symphony orchestra with chorus and soloists); Ilse-Mari Lee's *Cello Concerto* (concerto for cello solo and orchestra); and Jim Beckel's *Christmas Fanfare* (brass and percussion).

Tips "Write what you feel (be honest) and sharpen your compositional and craftsmanship skills."

THE BOSTON PHILHARMONIC

295 Huntington Ave., #210, Boston MA 02115. (617)236-0999. Fax: (617)236-8613. E-mail: info@bostonphil.org. Website: www.bostonphil.org. **Music Director:** Benjamin Zander. Symphony orchestra. Estab. 1979. Members are professionals, amateurs and students. Performs 2 concerts/year. Audience is ages 30-70. Performs at New England Conservatory's Jordan Hall, Boston's Symphony Hall and Sanders Theatre in Cambridge. Both Jordan Hall and Sanders Theatre are small (approximately 1,100 seats) and very intimate.

How to Contact *Does not accept new music at this time.*

Music Full orchestra only.

Performances Dutilleuxs' *Tout un monde lointain* for cello and orchestra (symphonic); Bernstein's *Fancy Free* (symphonic/jazzy); Copland's *El Salon Mexico* (symphonic); Gershwin's *Rhapsody in Blue*; Shostakovitch's *Symphony No. 10*; Harbison's *Concerto for Oboe*; Holst's *The Planet Suite*; Schwantner's *New Morning for the World*; Berg's *Seven Early Songs*; and Ive's *The Unanswered Question*.

BRAVO! L.A.

16823 Liggett St., North Hills CA 91343. (818)892-8737. Fax: (818)892-1227. E-mail: info@bravo-la.com. Website: www.bravo-la.com. **Contact:** Cellist Dr. Janice Foy, director. An umbrella organization of recording/touring musicians, formed in 1994. Includes the following musical ensembles: the New American Quartet (string quartet); The Ascending Wave (harp/cello duo); Celllissimo! L.A. (cello ensemble); Sierra Chamber Players (includes piano with strings or other combos), the Happy Band and the World Peace Orchestra (jazz groups playing all styles). The latest combo is solo cello with flamenco dancer, Jani Quintero.

How to Contact Submit scores/tape of pieces. Include SASE. Responds in a few months. "We also record DEMOS for those needing entry into various situations and we use a DEMO rate through the Musicians Union Local 47 as our contract for that. If you want to do a Limited Pressing recording, that also goes through the Union with an appropriate contract."

Music "We do all styles from classical to jazz. You can hear examples of most of the above ensembles on the site. You may also read about the latest musical antics of these musicians at the site."

Tips "Let Bravo! L.A. know about your latest or upcoming performances and if you have a tape/CD of it, please forward or send an audio clip! If you have trouble getting through the spam blocker, let me know! We do not provide funding but there are many different grants out there for different situations. Good luck!"

⚅ CANADIAN OPERA COMPANY

227 Front St. E., Toronto ON M5A 1E8 Canada. (416)363-6671. Fax: (416)363-5584. E-mail: sandrag@coc.ca. Website: www.coc.ca. **Contact:** Sandra J. Gavinchuk, music administrator.

Classical Arts

Opera company. Estab. 1950. Members are professionals. 68-72 performances, including a minimum of 1 new work/year. Pays by contract.

How to Contact Submit complete score and tapes of vocal and/or operatic works. "Vocal works please." Include SASE. Responds in 5 weeks.

Music Vocal works, operatic in nature. "Do not submit works which are not for voice. Ask for requirements for the Composers-In-Residence program."

Performances Dean Burry's *Brothers Grimm* (children's opera, 50 minutes long); Paul Ruders' *Handmaid's Tale* (full length opera, 2 acts, epilogue); Dean Burry's Isis and the Seven Scorpions (45-minute opera for children); Berg's *Wozzek*; James Rolfe's *Swoon*: James Rolfe's *Donna* (work title for forthcoming work).

Tips "We have a Composers-In-Residence program which is open to Canadian composers or landed immigrants."

CARMEL SYMPHONY ORCHESTRA

P.O. Box 761, Carmel IN 46082-0761. (317)844-9717. Fax: (317)844-9916. E-mail: info@ carmelsymphony.org. Website: www.carmelsymphony.org. **Contact**: Allen Davis, executive director. Symphony orchestra. Estab. 1976. Members are professionals and amateurs. Performs 15 concerts/year, including 1-2 new works. Audience is "40% senior citizens, 85% white." Performs in a 1,500-seat high school performing arts center. Pay is negotiable.

How to Contact *Query first*. Include SASE. Responds in 3 months.

Music "Full orchestra works, 10-20 minutes in length. Can be geared toward 'children's' or 'Masterworks' programs. 65-70 piece orchestra, medium difficulty."

Performances Jim Beckel's *Glass Bead Game* (full orchestra); Percy Grainger's *Molly on the Shore* (full orchestra); and Frank Glover's *Impressions of New England* (full orchestra and jazz quartet).

CARSON CITY SYMPHONY

P.O. Box 2001, Carson City NV 89701-6532, Carson City NV 89702-2001. (775)883-4154. Fax: (775)883-4371. E-mail: dcbugli@aol.com. Website: www.ccsymphony.com. **Contact:** David C. Bugli, music director/conductor. Amateur community orchestra. Estab. 1984. Members are amateurs. Performs 5 concerts, including 2 new works/year. Audience is largely Carson City/Reno area residents, many of them retirees. "Most concerts are performed in the Carson City Community Center Auditorium, which seats 800." Pay varies for outright purchase.

How to Contact Submit complete score and tape or CD of works. Does not return material. Responds in 2 months.

Music "We want classical, pop orchestrations, orchestrations of early music for modern orchestras, concertos for violin or piano, holiday music for chorus and orchestra (children's choirs and handbell ensemble available), music by women, music for brass choir. Most performers are amateurs, but there are a few professionals who perform with us. Available winds and percussion: 2 flutes and flute/piccolo, 2 oboes (E.H. double sometimes), 2 clarinets, 1 bass clarinet, 2 bassoons, 4 horns, 3 trumpets, 3 trombones, 1 tuba, timpani, and percussion. Harp and piano. Strings: 8-8-5-6-3 (or fewer). Avoid music that lacks melodic appeal. Composers should contact us first. Each concert has a different emphasis. Note: Associated choral group, Carson Chamber Singers, performs several times a year with the orchestra and independently."

Performances Thomas Svoboda's *Overture of the Season* (minimalist overture); Gwyneth Walker's *A Concerto of Hymns and Spirituals for Trumpet and Orchestra;* and Jim Cockey's *A Land of Sage and Sun.*

Tips "It is better to write several short movements well than to write long, unimaginative pieces, especially when starting out. Be willing to revise after submitting the work, even if it was premiered elsewhere."

CHATTANOOGA GIRLS CHOIR

P.O. Box 6036, Chattanooga TN 37401. (423)629-6188. E-mail: office@chattanoogagirlschoir. com. Website: http://chattanoogagirlschoir.com. **Contact**: LuAnne Holden, artistic director. Vocal ensemble. Estab. 1986. Members are amateurs. Performs 2 concerts/year including at least 1 new work. Audience consists of cultural and civic organizations and national and international tours. Performance space includes concert halls and churches. Pays for outright purchase or per performance.

How to Contact Query first. Include SASE. Responds in 6 weeks.

Music Seeks renaissance, baroque, classical, romantic, twentieth century, folk and musical theatre for young voices of up to 8 minutes. Performers include 5 treble choices: 4th grade (2 pts.); 5th grade (2 pts.) (SA); grades 6-9 (3 pts.) (SSA); grades 10-12 (3-4 pts.) (SSAA); and a combined choir: grades 6-12 (3-4 pts.) (SSAA). Medium level of difficulty. "Avoid extremely high Tessitura Sop I and extremely low Tessitura Alto II."

Performances Jan Swafford's *Iphigenia Book: Meagher* (choral drama); Penny Tullock's *How Can I Keep from Singing* (Shaker hymn).

CHEYENNE SYMPHONY ORCHESTRA

P.O. Box 851, Cheyenne WY 82003. (307)778-8561. Fax: (307)634-7512. E-mail: director@ cheyennesymphony.org. Website: www.cheyennesymphony.org. **Contact:** Chloe Illoway, executive director. Symphony orchestra. Estab. 1955. Members are professionals. Performs 5-6 concerts/year. "Orchestra performs for a conservative, mid-to-upper income audience of 1,200 season members."

How to Contact Query first to music director William Intriligator. Does not return material.

CIMARRON CIRCUIT OPERA COMPANY

P.O. Box 1085, Norman OK 73070. (405)364-8962. E-mail: info@ccocopera.org. Website: www.ccocopera.org. **Contact:** Kevin Smith, music director. Opera company. Estab. 1975. Members are semi professional. Performs 75 concerts/year including 1-2 new works. Commissions 1 or less new work/year. "CCOC performs for children across the state of Oklahoma and for a dedicated audience in central Oklahoma. As a touring company, we adapt to the performance space provided, ranging from a classroom to a full raised stage." Pay is negotiable.

How to Contact Query first. Does not return material. Responds in 6 months.

Music "We are seeking operas or operettas in English only. We would like to begin including new, American works in our repertoire. Children's operas should be no longer than 45 minutes and require no more than a synthesizer for accompaniment. Adult operas should be appropriate for families, and may require either full orchestration or synthesizer. CCOC is a professional company whose members have varying degrees of experience, so any difficulty level is appropriate. There should be a small to moderate number of principals. Children's work should have no more than four principals. Our slogan is 'Opera is a family thing to do.' If we cannot market a work to families, we do not want to see it."

Performances Menotti's *Amahl & the Night Visitors*; and Barab's *La Pizza Con Funghi*.

Tips "45-minute fairy tale-type children's operas with possibly a 'moral' work well for our market. Looking for works appealing to K-8 grade students. No more than four principles."

CONNECTICUT CHORAL ARTISTS/CONCORA

52 Main St., New Britain CT 06051. (860)224-7500. Fax: (860) 827-8890. E-mail: contact@concora.org. Website: www.concora.org. **Contact:** Laura Oliver, executive director. Richard Coffey, artistic director. Professional concert choir, also an 18-voice ensemble dedicated to contemporary a cappella works. Estab. 1974. Members are professionals. Performs 15 concerts/year, including 3-5 new works. "Mixed audience in terms of age and background; performs in various halls and churches in the region." Payment "depends upon underwriting we can obtain for the project."

How to Contact Query first. "No unsolicited submissions accepted." Include SASE. Responds in 1 year.

Music Seeking "works for mixed chorus of 36 singers; unaccompanied or with keyboard and/or small instrumental ensemble; text sacred or secular/any language; prefers suites or cyclical works, total time not exceeding 15 minutes. Performance spaces and budgets prohibit large instrumental ensembles. Works suited for 750-seat halls are preferable. Substantial organ or piano parts acceptable. Scores should be very legible in every way."

Performances Don McCullough's *Holocaust Contata* (choral with narration); Robert Cohen's *Sprig of Lilac: Peter Quince at the Clavier* (choral); Greg Bartholomew's *The 21st*

Century: A Girl Born in Afghanistan (choral).

Tips "Use conventional notation and be sure manuscript is legible in every way. Recognize and respect the vocal range of each vocal part. Work should have an identifiable rhythmic structure."

DUO CLASICO

4 Essex St., Clifton NJ 07014. (973)655-4379. E-mail: wittend@mail.montclair.edu. Website: www.davidwitten.com. **Contact:** David Witten. Chamber music ensemble. Estab. 1986. Members are professionals. Performs 16 concerts/year including 4 new works. Commissions 1 composer or new work/year. Performs in small recital halls. Pays 10% royalty.

How to Contact Query first. Include SASE. Responds in 6 weeks.

Music "We welcome scores for flute solo, piano solo or duo. Particular interest in Latin American composers."

Performances Diego Luzuriaga's *La Muchica* (modern, with extended techniques); Robert Starer's *Yizkor & Anima Aeterna* (rhythmic); and Piazzolla's *Etudes Tanguistiques* (solo flute).

Tips "Extended techniques, or with tape, are fine!"

⊕ EUROPEAN UNION CHAMBER ORCHESTRA

Hollick, Yarnscombe EX31 3LQ United Kingdom. (44)1271 858249. Fax: (44)1271 858375. E-mail: eucorchl@aol.com. Website: www.etd.gb.com. **Contact:** Ambrose Miller, general manager. Chamber orchestra. Members are professionals. Performs 70 concerts/year, including 6 new works. Commissions 2 composers or new works/year. Performs regular tours of Europe, Americas and Asia, including major venues. Pays per performance or for outright purchase, depending on work.

How to Contact Query first. Does not return material. Responds in 6 weeks.

Music Seeking compositions for strings, 2 oboes and 2 horns with a duration of about 8 minutes.

Performances Peeter Vahi "Prayer Wheel"; James MacMillan "Kiss on Wood", arr Karkof.

Tips "Keep the work to less than 15 minutes in duration, it should be sufficiently 'modern' to be interesting but not too difficult as this could take up rehearsal time. It should be possible to perform without a conductor."

FONTANA CONCERT SOCIETY

359 S. Kalamazoo Mall, Suite 200, Kalamazoo MI 49007. (269)382-7774. Fax: (269)382-0812. E-mail: info@fontanachamberarts.org. Website: www.fontanachamberarts.org/history.html. **Contact:** Mr. Ab Sengupta, executive and artistic director. Chamber music ensemble presenter. Estab. 1980. Members are professionals. Fontana Chamber Arts

presents over 45 events, including the 6-week Summer Festival of Music and Art, which runs from mid-July to the end of August. Regional and guest artists perform classical, contemporary, jazz and nontraditional music. Commissions and performs new works each year. Fontana Chamber Arts presents 7 classical and 2 jazz concerts during the Fall/Winter season. Audience consists of well-educated individuals who accept challenging new works, but like the traditional as well. Summer—180 seat hall; Fall/winter—various venues, from 400 to 1,500 seats.

How to Contact Submit complete score, resume and tapes of piece(s). Include SASE. Responds in approximately 1 month.

Music Chamber music—any combination of strings, winds, piano. No "pop" music, new age type. Special interest in composers attending premiere and speaking to the audience.

Performances 2010—Juiliard String Quartet; Ben Allison and Man Size Safe; Esperanza Spalding; Cyro Baptista *Banquet of the Spirits*; Tord Gustavsen Trio; eighth blackbird; 2008—Imani Winds Josephine Baker: *A Life of Le Jazz Hot!;* Mitsuko Uchida & Friends; 2007—Billy Child's *The Path Among the Trees* (Billy Child's Jazz Chamber Ensemble with Ying Quartet)

Tips "Provide a résumé and clearly marked tape of a piece played by live performers."

FORT WORTH CHILDREN'S OPERA

1300 Gendy St., Fort Worth TX 76107. (817)731-0726, ext. 19. Fax: (817)731-0835. E-mail: kwolfe@fwopera.org. Website: www.fwopera.org. **Contact:** Tony Kostecki, director of education. Opera company. Estab. 1946. Members are professionals. Performs over 180 in-school performances/year." Audience consists of elementary school children; performs in major venues for district-wide groups and individual school auditoriums, cafetoriums and gymnasiums. Pays $40/performance.

How to Contact Submit complete score and tape of piece(s). Include SASE. Responds in 6 months.

Music "Familiar fairy tales or stories adapted to music of opera composers, or newly-composed music of suitable quality. Ideal length: 40-45 minutes. Piano or keyboard accompaniment. Should include moral, safety or school issues. Can be ethnic in subject matter and must speak to pre-K and grade 1-6 children. Prefer pieces with good, memorable melodies. Performed by young, trained professionals on 9-month contract. Requires work for four performers, doubled roles OK, SATB plus accompanist/narrator. Special interest in biligual (Spanish/English) works."

GREATER GRAND FORKS SYMPHONY ORCHESTRA

3350 Campus Rd., Mail Stop 7084, Grand Forks ND 58202-7084. (701)777-3359. Fax: (701)777-3320. E-mail: ggfso@und.edu. Website: www.ggfso.org. **Contact:** James Hannon, music director. Symphony orchestra. Estab. 1908. Members are professionals and/or amateurs. Performs 6 concerts/year. "New works are presented in 2-4 of our programs." Audience is "a mix of ages and musical experience. In 1997-98 we moved into a renovated, 420-seat theater." Pay is negotiable, depending on licensing agreements.

How to Contact Submit complete score or complete score and tape of pieces. Include SASE. Responds in 6 months.

Music "Style is open, instrumentation the limiting factor. Music can be scored for an ensemble up to but not exceeding: 3,2,3,2/4,3,3,1/3 perc./strings. Rehearsal time limited to 3 hours for new works."

Performances Michael Harwood's *Amusement Park Suite* (orchestra); Randall Davidson's *Mexico Bolivar Tango* (chamber orchestra); and John Corigliano's *Voyage* (flute and orchestra); Linda Tutas Haugen's *Fable of Old Turtle* (saxophone concerto); Michael Wittgraf's *Landmarks*; Joan Tower's *Made in America*.

HEARTLAND MEN'S CHORUS

P.O. Box 32374, Kansas City MO 64171-5374. (816)931-3338. Fax: (816)531-1367. E-mail: hmc@hmckc.org. Website: www.hmckc.org. **Contact:** Joseph Nadeau, artistic director. Men's chorus. Estab. 1986. Members are professionals and amateurs. Performs 3 concerts/year; 9-10 are new works. Commissions 1 composer or new works/year. Performs for a diverse audience at the Folly Theater (1,100 seats). Pay is negotiable.

How to Contact Query first. Include SASE. Responds in 2 months.

Music "Interested in works for male chorus (ttbb). Must be suitable for performance by a gay male chorus. We will consider any orchestration, or a cappella."

Performances Mark Hayes' *Two Flutes Playing* (commissioned song cycle); Alan Shorter's *Country Angel Christmas* (commissioned chidren's musical); Kevin Robinson's *Life is a Cabaret: The Music of Kander and Ebb* (commissioned musical).

Tips "Find a text that relates to the contemporary gay experience, something that will touch peoples' lives."

HELENA SYMPHONY

P.O. Box 1073, Helena MT 59624. (406)442-1860. E-mail: boxoffice@helenasymphony. org. Website: www.helenasymphony.org. **Contact:** Allan R. Scott, music director and conductor. Symphony orchestra. Estab. 1955. Members are professionals and amateurs. Performs 7-10 concerts/year including new works. Performance space is an 1,800 seat concert hall. Payment varies.

How to Contact Query first. Include SASE. Responds in 3 months.

Music "Imaginative, collaborative, not too atonal. We want to appeal to an audience of all ages. We don't have a huge string complement. Medium to difficult okay—at frontiers of professional ability we cannot do."

Performances Eric Funk's *A Christmas Overture* (orchestra); Donald O. Johnston's *A Christmas Processional* (orchestra/chorale); and Elizabeth Sellers' *Prairie* (orchestra/short ballet piece).

Classical Arts

Tips "Try to balance tension and repose in your works. New instrument combinations are appealing."

HENDERSONVILLE SYMPHONY ORCHESTRA

P.O. Box 1811, Hendersonville NC 28739. (828)697-5884. Fax: (828)697-5765. E-mail: hso1@bellsouth.net. Website: www.hendersonvillesymphony.org. **Contact:** Sandie Salvaggio-Walker, general manager. Symphony orchestra. Estab. 1971. Members are professionals and amateurs. Performs 6 concerts/year. "We would welcome a new work per year." Audience is a cross-section of retirees, professionals and some children. Performance space is a 857-seat high school audiorium.

How to Contact Query first. Include SASE. Responds in 1 month.

Music "We use a broad spectrum of music (classical concerts and pops)."

Performances Nelson's *Jubilee* (personal expression in a traditional method); Britten's "The Courtly Dances" from Glorina (time-tested); and Chip Davis' arrangement for Mannheim Steamroller's *Deck the Halls* (modern adaptation of traditional melody).

Tips "Submit your work even though we are a community orchestra. We like to be challenged. We have the most heavily patronized fine arts group in the county. Our emphasis is on education."

HERMANN SONS GERMAN BAND

P.O. Box 162, Medina TX 78055. (830)589-2268. E-mail: herbert@festmusik.com. Website: www.festmusik.com. **Contact:** Herbert Bilhartz, music director. Community band with German instrumentation. Estab. 1990. Members are both professionals and amateurs. Performs 4 concerts/year including 2 new works. Commissions no new composers or new works/year. Performs for "mostly older people who like German polkas, waltzes and marches. We normally play only published arrangements from Germany."

How to Contact Query first; then submit full set of parts and score, condensed or full. Include SASE. Responds in 6 weeks.

Music "We like European-style polkas or waltzes (Viennese or Missouri tempo), either original or arrangements of public domain tunes. Arrangements of traditional American folk tunes in this genre would be especially welcome. Also, polkas or waltzes featuring one or two solo instruments (from instrumentation below) would be great. OK for solo parts to be technically demanding. Although we have no funds to commission works, we will provide you with a cassette recording of our performance. Also, we would assist composers in submitting works to band music publishers in Germany for possible publication. Polkas and waltzes generally follow this format: Intro; 1st strain repeated; 2nd strain repeated; DS to 1 strain; Trio: Intro; 32 bar strain; 'break-up' strain; Trio DS. Much like military march form. Instrumentation: Fl/Picc, 3 clars in Bb, 2 Fluegelhorns in Bb; 3 Tpts in Bb, 2 or 4 Hns in F or Eb, 2 Baritones (melody/countermelody parts; 1 in Bb TC, 1 in BC), 2 Baritones in Bb TC (rhythm parts), 3 Trombones, 2 Tubas (in octaves, mostly), Drum set, Timpani optional. We don't use saxes, but a German publisher would want 4-5 sax parts. Parts should be medium to medium difficult. All brass parts should be considered one player to the part; woodwinds, two to the part. No concert type pieces; no modern popular or rock styles. However, a 'theme and variations' form with contrasting jazz, rock, country, modern variations would be clever, and our fans might go for such a piece (as might a German publisher)."

Performances New music performed in 2005: Stefan Rundel's *Mein Gluecksstern ("My Lucky Star")*.

Tips "German town bands love to play American tunes. There are many thousands of these bands over there and competition among band music publishers in Germany is keen. Few Americans are aware of this potential market, so few American arrangers get published over there. Simple harmony is best for this style, but good counterpoint helps a lot. Make use of the dark quality of the Fluegelhorns and the bright, fanfare quality of the trumpets. Give the two baritones (one in TC and one in BC) plenty of exposed melodic material. Keep them in harmony with each other (3rds and 6ths), unlike American band arrangements, which have only one Baritone line. If you want to write a piece in this style, give me a call, and I will send you some sample scores to give you a better idea."

HUDSON VALLEY PHILHARMONIC

35 Market St., Poughkeepise NY 12601. (845)473-2072. Fax: (845)473-4259. E-mail: slamarca@bardavon.org. Website: www.bardavon.org. **Contact:** Stephen LaMarca, production manager. Symphony orchestra. Estab. 1969. Members are professionals. Performs 20 concerts/year including 1 new work. "Classical subscription concerts for all ages; Pops concerts for all ages; New Wave concerts—crossover projects with a rock 'n' roll artist performing with an orchestra. HVP performs in three main theatres which are concert auditoriums with stages and professional lighting and sound." Pay is negotiable.

How to Contact Query first. Include SASE. Responds only if interested.

Music "HVP is open to serious classical music, pop music and rock 'n' roll crossover projects. Desired length of work between 10-20 minutes. Orchestrations can be varied by should always include strings. There is no limit to difficulty since our musicians are professional. The ideal number of musicians to write for would include up to a Brahms-size orchestra 2222, 4231, T, 2P, piano, harp, strings."

Performances Joan Tower's *Island Rhythms* (serious classical work); Bill Vanaver's *P'nai El* (symphony work with dance); and Joseph Bertolozzi's *Serenade* (light classical, pop work).

Tips "Don't get locked into doing very traditional orchestrations or styles. Our music director is interested in fresh, creative formats. He is an orchestrator as well and can offer good advice on what works well. Songwriters who are into crossover projects should definitely submit works. Over the past four years, HVP has done concerts featuring the works of Natalie Merchant, John Cale, Sterling Morrison, Richie Havens, and R. Carlos

Naka (Native American flute player), all reorchestrated by our music director for small orchestra with the artist."

INDIANA UNIVERSITY NEW MUSIC ENSEMBLE

Indiana University Bloomington, School of Music, Bloomington IN 47405-2200. E-mail: ddzubay@indiana.edu. Website: www.indiana.edu/~nme. **Contact**: David Dzubay, director. Performs solo, chamber and large ensemble works. Estab.1974. Members are students. Presents 4 concerts/year.

Music Peter Lieberson's *Free and Easy Wanderer*; Sven-David Sandstrom's *Wind Pieces*; Atar Arad's *Sonata*; and David Dzubay's *Dancesing in a Green Bay*.

KENTUCKY OPERA

323 West Broadway, Louisville KY 40202. (502)584-4500. Fax: (502)584-7484. E-mail: info@ kyopera.org. Website: www.kyopera.org. **Contact**: Alise Oliver, artistic administration. Opera. Estab. 1952. Members are professionals. Performs 3 main stage/year. Performs at Brown Theatre, 1,400. Pays by royalty, outright purchase or per performance.

How to Contact *Write or call first before submitting. No unsolicited submissions.* Submit complete score. Include SASE. Responds in 6 months.

Music Seeks opera—1 to 3 acts with orchestrations. No limitations.

Performances *Traviata, Of Mice and Men, Hansel and Gretel, Pirates of Penzance, Werther, Iolanta.*

LAMARCA AMERICAN VARIETY SINGERS

2655 W. 230th Place, Torrance CA 90505. (310)325-8708. E-mail: lamarcamusic@lycos.com. Website: www.cdbaby.com/cd/plkandel1. **Contact**: Priscilla LaMarca-Kandell, director. Composer of children's songs for home and school use, educational and entertaining. Also, vocal, ear training, and sight-singing exercises to help other songwriters improve their singing demo techniques.

How to Contact Query first. Include SASE. Responds in 2 weeks.

Music "Seeks 3-10 or 15 minute medleys; a variety of musical styles from Broadway—pop styles to humorous specialty songs. Top 40 dance music, light rock and patriotic themes. No rap or anything not suitable for family audiences."

Performances *Disney Movie Music* (uplifting); *Children's Music* (educational/positive); and *Beatles Medley* (love songs).

LIMA SYMPHONY ORCHESTRA

133 Elizabeth St., Lima OH 45801. (419)222-5701. Fax: (419)222-6587. Website: www. limasymphony.com. **Contact**: Crafton Beck, music conductor. Symphony orchestra. Estab. 1953. Members are professionals. Performs 17-18 concerts including at least 1 new work/

year. Commissions at least 1 composer or new work/year. Middle to older audience; also Young People's Series. Mixture for stage and summer productions. Performs in Veterans' Memorial Civic & Convention Center, a beautiful hall seating 1,670; various temporary shells for summer outdoors events; churches; museums and libraries. Pays $2,500 for outright purchase (Anniversary commission) or grants $1,500-5,000.

How to Contact Submit complete score if not performed; otherwise submit complete score and tape of piece(s). Include SASE. Responds in 3 months.

Music "Good balance of incisive rhythm, lyricism, dynamic contrast and pacing. Chamber orchestra to full (85-member) symphony orchestra." Does not wish to see "excessive odd meter changes."

Performances Frank Proto's *American Overture* (some original music and fantasy); Werner Tharichen's *Concerto for Timpani and Orchestra*; and James Oliverio's *Pilgrimage—Concerto for Brass* (interesting, dynamic writing for brass and the orchestra).

Tips "Know your instruments, be willing to experiment with unconventional textures, be available for in depth analysis with conductor, be at more than one rehearsal. Be sure that individual parts are correctly matching the score and done in good, neat calligraphy."

LYRIC OPERA OF CHICAGO

20 N. Wacker Dr., Chicago IL 60606. (312)332-2244 ext. 3500. Fax: (312)419-8345. E-mail: jgriffin@lyricopera.org. Website: www.lyricopera.org. **Contact:** Julie Griffin-Meadors, music administrator. Opera company. Estab. 1953. Members are professionals. Performs 80 operas/year including 1 new work in some years. Commissions 1 new work every 4 or 5 years. "Performances are held in a 3,563 seat house for a sophisticated opera audience, predominantly 30+ years old." Payment varies.

How to Contact Query first. Does not return material. Responds in 6 months.

Music "Full-length opera suitable for a large house with full orchestra. No musical comedy or Broadway musical style. We rarely perform one-act operas. We are only interested in works by composers and librettists with extensive theatrical experience. We have few openings for new works, so candidates must be of the highest quality. Do not send score or other materials without a prior contact."

Performances William Bolcom's *View from the Bridge*; John Corigliano's *Ghosts of Versailles*; and Leonard Bernstein's *Candide*.

Tips "Have extensive credentials and an international reputation."

MILWAUKEE YOUTH SYMPHONY ORCHESTRA

325 West Walnut St., Milwaukee WI 53212. (414)267-2950. Fax: (414)267-2960. E-mail: general@myso.org. Website: www.myso.org. **Contact:** Frances Richman, executive director. Multiple youth orchestras and other instrumental ensembles. Estab. 1956. Members are students. Performs 12-15 concerts/year including 1-2 new works. "Our groups perform in Uihlein Hall at the Marcus Center for the Performing Arts in Milwaukee plus area sites.

The audiences usually consist of parents, music teachers and other interested community members, with periodic reviews in the Milwaukee Journal Sentinel." Payment varies.

How to Contact Query first. Include SASE. Does not return material. Responds in 1 month.

Performances James Woodward's *Tuba Concerto*.

Tips "Be sure you realize you are working with *students* (albeit many of the best in southeastern Wisconsin) and not professional musicians. The music needs to be on a technical level students can handle. Our students are 8-18 years of age, in 2 full symphony orchestras, a wind ensemble and 2 string orchestras, plus two flute choirs, advanced chamber orchestra and 15-20 small chamber ensembles."

MOORES OPERA CENTER

University of Houston, 120 Moores School of Music Building, Houston TX 77204-4201. (713)743-3009. E-mail: bross@uh.edu. Website: www.uh.edu/music/Mooresopera/. **Director of Opera:** Buck Ross. Opera/music theater program. Members are professionals, amateurs and students. Performs 12-14 concerts/year including 1 new work. Performs in a proscenium theater which seats 800. Pit seats approximately up to 75 players. Audience covers wide spectrum, from first time opera-goers to very sophisticated. Pays per performance.

How to Contact Submit complete score and tapes of piece(s). Include SASE. Responds in 6 months.

Music "We seek music that is feasible for high graduate level student singers. Chamber orchestras are very useful. No more than two and a half hours. No children's operas."

Performances John Corigliano's *The Ghosts of Versailles*; Carlisle Floyd's *Bilby's Doll*; Robert Nelson's *A Room With a View*; Conrad Susa's *The Dangerous Liaisons*; and Dominick Argento's *Casanova's Homecoming*.

OPERA MEMPHIS

6745 Wolf River Parkway, Memphis TN 38120. (901)257-3100. Fax: (901)257-3109. E-mail: info@operamemphis.org. Website: www.operamemphis.org. **Contact:** Michael Ching, artistic director. Opera company. Estab. 1955. Members are professionals. Performs 8-12 concerts/year including new works. Occasionally commissions composers. Audience consists of older, wealthier patrons, along with many students and young professionals. Pay is negotiable.

How to Contact Query first. Include SASE. Responds in 1 year or less.

Music Accessible practical pieces for educational or second stage programs. Educational pieces should not exceed 90 minutes or 4-6 performers. We encourage songwriters to contact us with proposals or work samples for theatrical works. We are very interested in crossover work.

Performances Mike Reid's *Different Fields* (one act opera); David Olney's *Light in August* (folk opera); and Sid Selvidge's *Riversongs* (one act blues opera).

Tips "Spend many hours thinking about the synopsis (plot outline)."

PALMETTO MASTERSINGERS

P.O. Box 7441, Columbia SC 29202. (803)765-0777. E-mail: info@palmettomastersingers. org. Website: www.palmettomastersingers.org. **Contact:** Walter Cuttino, music director. 80 voice male chorus. Estab. 1981 by the late Dr. Arpad Darasz. Members are professionals and amateurs. Performs 8-10 concerts/year. Commissions 1 composer of new works every other year (on average). Audience is generally older adults, "but it's a wide mix." Performance space for the season series is the Koger Center (approximately 2,000 seats) in Columbia, SC. More intimate venues also available. Fee is negotiable for outright purchase.

How to Contact Query first. Include SASE. Or e-mail to info@palmettomastersingers. org.

Music Seeking music of 10-15 minutes in length, "not too far out tonally. Orchestration is negotiable, but chamber size (10-15 players) is normal. We rehearse once a week and probably will not have more than 8-10 rehearsals. These rehearsals (2 hours each) are spent learning a 1½-hour program. Only 1-2 rehearsals (max) are with the orchestra. Piano accompaniments need not be simplified, as our accompanist is exceptional."

Performances Randal Alan Bass' *Te Deum* (12-minute, brass and percussion); Dick Goodwin's *Mark Twain Remarks* (40 minute, full symphony); and Randol Alan Bass' *A Simple Prayer* (a capella 6 minute).

Tips "Contact us as early as possible, given that programs are planned by July. Although this is an amateur chorus, we have performed concert tours of Europe, performed at Carnegie Hall, The National Cathedral and the White House in Washington, DC. We are skilled amateurs."

PICCOLO OPERA COMPANY INC.

24 Del Rio Blvd., Boca Raton FL 33432-4734. (800)282-3161. Fax: (561)394-0520. E-mail: leejon51@msn.com. **Contact:** Lee Merrill, executive assistant. Traveling opera company. Estab. 1962. Members are professionals. Performs 1-50 concerts/year including 1-2 new works. Commissions 0-1 composer or new work/year. Operas are performed for a mixed audience of children and adults. Pays by performance or outright purchase. Operas in English.

How to Contact *Query first.* Include SASE.

Music "Productions for either children or adults. Musical theater pieces, lasting about one hour, for adults to perform for adults and/or youngsters. Performers are mature singers with experience. The cast should have few performers (up to 10), no chorus or ballet, accompanied by piano or local orchestra. Skeletal scenery. All in English."

Performances Menotti's *The Telephone*; Mozart's *Cosi Fan Tutte*; and Puccini's *La Boheme* (repertoire of more than 22 productions).

PRINCETON SYMPHONY ORCHESTRA

P.O. Box 250, Princeton NJ 08542. (609)497-0020. Fax: (609)497-0904. E-mail: info@ princetonsymphony.org. Website: www.princetonsymphony.org. **Contact:** Mark Laycock, music director. Symphony orchestra. Estab. 1980. Members are professionals. Performs 6-10 concerts/year including some new works. Commissions 1 composer or new work/ year. Performs in a "beautiful, intimate 800-seat hall with amazing sound." Pays by arrangement.

Music "Orchestra usually numbers 40-60 individuals."

PRISM SAXOPHONE QUARTET

30 Seaman Av., #4M, New York NY 10034 or 257 Harvey St., Philadelphia PA 19144. (215)438-5282. E-mail: info@prismquartet.com. Website: www.prismquartet.com. President, New Sounds Music Inc. Prism Quartet: Matthew Levy. Chamber music ensemble. Estab. 1984. Members are professionals. Performs 80 concerts/year including 10-15 new works. Commissions 4 composers or new works/year. "Ours are primarily traditional chamber music audiences." Pays royalty per performance from BMI or ASCAP or commission range from $100 to $15,000.

How to Contact Submit complete score (with parts) and tape of piece(s). Does not return material. Responds in 3 months.

Music "Orchestration—sax quartet, SATB. Lengths—5-25 minutes. Styles—contemporary, classical, jazz, crossover, ethnic, gospel, avant-garde. No limitations on level of difficulty. No more than 4 performers (SATB sax quartet). No transcriptions. The Prism Quartet places special emphasis on crossover works which integrate a variety of musical styles."

Performances David Liebman's *The Gray Convoy* (jazz); Bradford Ellis's *Tooka-Ood Zasch* (ethnic-world music); and William Albright's *Fantasy Etudes* (contemporary classical).

SACRAMENTO MASTER SINGERS

P.O. Box 417997, Sacramento CA 95841. (916)971-3159. Fax: (916)788-7464. E-mail: smscbarb@aol.com. Website: www.mastersingers.org. **Contact:** Ralph Hughes, conductor/ artistic director. Vocal ensemble. Estab. 1984. Members are professionals and amateurs. Performs 9 concerts/year including 5-6 new works. Commissions 2 new works/year. Audience is made up of mainly college age and older patrons. Performs mostly in churches with 500-900 seating capacity. Pays $200 for outright purchase.

How to Contact Submit complete score and tape of piece(s). Include SASE. Responds in 5 weeks.

Music "A cappella works; works with small orchestras or few instruments; works based on classical styles with a 'modern' twist; multi-cultural music; shorter works probably preferable, but this is not a requirement. We usually have 38-45 singers capable of a high level of difficulty, but find that often simple works are very pleasing."

Performances Joe Jennings' *An Old Black Woman, Homeless and Indistinct* (SATB, oboe, strings, dramatic).

Tips "Keep in mind we are a chamber ensemble, not a 100-voice choir."

SINGING BOYS OF PENNSYLVANIA

P.O. Box 206, Wind Gap PA 18091. (610)759-6002. Fax: (610)759-6042. Website: www. singingboysofpennsylvania.org. **Contact:** K. Bernard Schade, Ed. D., director. Vocal ensemble. Estab. 1970. Members are professional children. Performs 100 concerts/year including 3-5 new works. "We attract general audiences: family, senior citizens, churches, concert associations, university concert series and schools." Pays $300-3,000 for outright purchase.

How to Contact *Query first.* Does not return material. Responds in 3 weeks.

Music "We want music for commercials, voices in the SSA or SSAA ranges, sacred works or arrangements of American folk music with accompaniment. Our range of voices are from G below middle C to A (13th above middle C). Reading ability of choir is good but works which require a lot of work with little possibility of more than one performance are of little value. We sing very few popular songs except for special events. We perform music by composers who are well-known and works by living composers who are writing in traditional choral forms. Works which have a full orchestral score are of interest. The orchestration should be fairly light, so as not to cover the voices. Works for Christmas have more value than some other, since we perform with orchestras on an annual basis."

Performances Don Locklair's *The Columbus Madrigals* (opera).

Tips "It must be appropriate music and words for children. We do not deal in pop music. Folk music, classics and sacred are acceptable."

ST. LOUIS CHAMBER CHORUS

P.O. Box 11558, Clayton MO 63105. (636)458-4343. E-mail: maltworm@inlink.com. Website: www.chamberchorus.org. **Contact:** Philip Barnes, artistic director. Vocal ensemble, chamber music ensemble. Estab. 1956. Members are professionals and amateurs. Performs 6 concerts/year including 5-10 new works. Commissions 3-4 new works/year. Audience is "diverse and interested in unaccompanied choral work and outstanding architectural/acoustic venues." Performances take place at various auditoria noted for their excellent acoustics—churches, synagogues, schools and university halls. Pays by arrangement.

How to Contact Query first. Does not return material. "Panel of 'readers' submit report to Artistic Director. Responds in 3 months. 'General Advice' leaflet available on request."

Music *"Only a cappella writing!* No contemporary 'popular' works; historical editions welcomed. No improvisatory works. Our programs are tailored for specific acoustics—composers should indicate their preference."

Performances Sir Richard Rodney Bennett's *A Contemplation Upon Flowers* (a cappella madrigal); Ned Rorem's *Ode to Man* (a cappella chorus for mixed voices); and Sasha Johnson Manning's *Requiem* (a cappella oratorio).

Tips "We only consider a cappella works which can be produced in five rehearsals. Therefore pieces of great complexity or duration are discouraged. Our seasons are planned 2-3 years ahead, so much lead time is required for programming a new work. We will accept hand-written manuscript, but we prefer typeset music."

SUSQUEHANNA SYMPHONY ORCHESTRA

P.O. Box 963, Abingdon, MD 21009. E-mail: sheldon.bair@ssorchestra.org. Website: www.ssorchestra.org. **Contact:** Sheldon Bair, music director. Symphony orchestra. Estab. 1978. Members are amateurs. Performs 6 concerts/year including 1-2 new works. Composers paid depending on the circumstances. "We perform in 1 hall, 600 seats with fine acoustics. Our audience encompasses all ages."

How to Contact Query first. Include SASE. Responds in 3 or more months.

Music "We desire works for large orchestra, any length, in a 'conservative 20th and 21st century' style. Seek fine music for large orchestra. We are a community orchestra, so the music must be within our grasp. Violin I to 7th position by step only; Violin II—stay within 5th position; English horn and harp are OK. Full orchestra pieces preferred."

Performances *Angelus and Vocalise, The Gift of the Magi, Ascent to Victory, Romance*.

⚅ TORONTO MENDELSSOHN CHOIR

60 Simcoe St., Toronto ON M5J 2H5 Canada. (416)598-0422. Fax: (416)598-2992. E-mail: manager@tmchoir.org or admin@tmchoir.org. Website: www.tmchoir.org. **Contact:** Eileen Keown, executive director. Vocal ensemble. Members are professionals and amateurs. Performs 25 concerts/year including 1-3 new works. "Most performances take place in Roy Thomson Hall. The audience is reasonably sophisticated, musically knowledgeable but with moderately conservative tastes." Pays by commission and ASCAP/SOCAN.

How to Contact Query first or submit complete score and tapes of pieces. Include SASE. Responds in 6 months.

Music All works must suit a large choir (180 voices) and standard orchestral forces or with some other not-too-exotic accompaniment. Length should be restricted to no longer than 1/2 of a nocturnal concert. The choir sings at a very professional level and can sight-read almost anything. "Works should fit naturally with the repertoire of a large choir which performs the standard choral orchestral repertoire."

Performances Holman's *Jezebel*; Orff's *Catulli Carmina*; and Lambert's *Rio Grande*.

⚅ VANCOUVER CHAMBER CHOIR

1254 W. Seventh Ave., Vancouver BC V6H 1B6 Canada. E-mail: info@vancouverchamberchoir.com. Website: www.vancouverchamberchoir.com. **Contact:** Jon Washburn, artistic director. Vocal ensemble. Members are professionals. Performs 40 concerts/year including 5-8 new works. Commissions 2-4 composers or new works/year. Pays SOCAN royalty or negotiated fee for commissions.

How to Contact Submit complete score and tape of piece(s). Does not return material. Responds in 6 months if possible.

Music Seeks "choral works of all types for small chorus, with or without accompaniment and/or soloists. Concert music only. Choir made up of 20 singers. Large or unusual instrumental accompaniments are less likely to be appropriate. No pop music."

Performances The VCC has commissioned and premiered over 200 new works by Canadian and international composers, including Alice Parker's *That Sturdy Vine* (cantata for chorus, soloists and orchestra); R. Murray Schafer's *Magic Songs* (SATB a cappella); and Jon Washburn's *A Stephen Foster Medley* (SSAATTBB/piano).

Tips "We are looking for choral music that is performable yet innovative, and which has the potential to become 'standard repertoire.' Although we perform much new music, only a small portion of the many scores which are submitted can be utilized."

VANCOUVER YOUTH SYMPHONY ORCHESTRA SOCIETY

3214 West 10th Ave., Vancouver BC V6K 2L2 Canada. (604)737-0714. Fax: (604)737-0739. E-mail: vyso@telus.net. Website: www.vyso.com. **Music Directors:** Roger Cole (artistic director and senior orchestra conductor), Jin Zhang (intermediate orchestra conductor), and Margitta Krebs (debut and junior orchestra conductor). Youth orchestra. "Four divisions consisting of musicians ranging in age from 8-22 years old." Estab. 1930. Members are amateurs. Performs 10-15 concerts/year in various lower mainland venues. Concert admission by donation.

Music "Extensive and varied orchestral repertoire is performed by all divisions. Please contact the VYSO for more information."

VIRGINIA OPERA

P.O. Box 2580, Norfolk VA 23501. (757)627-9545. E-mail: info@vaopera.com. Website: www.vaopera.org. **Director of Education:** Jeff Corrirean. Artistic Director: Peter Mark. Opera company. Estab. 1974. Members are professionals. Performs more than 560 concerts/year. Commissions vary on number of composers or new works/year. Concerts are performed for school children throughout Virginia, grades K-5, 6-8 and 9-12 at the Harrison Opera House in Norfolk, and at public/private schools in Virginia. Pays on commission.

How to Contact Query first. Include SASE. Response time varies.

Music "Audience accessible style approximately 45 minutes in length. Limit cast list to three vocal artists of any combination. Accompanied by piano and/or keyboard. Works are performed before school children of all ages. Pieces must be age appropriate both aurally and dramatically. Musical styles are encouraged to be diverse, contemporary as well as traditional. Works are produced and presented with sets, costumes, etc."

Limitations: "Three vocal performers (any combination). One keyboardist. Medium to difficult acceptable, but prefer easy to medium. Seeking only pieces which are suitable for presentation as part of an opera education program for Virginia Opera's education and outreach department. Subject matter must meet strict guidelines relative to Learning Objectives, etc. Musical idiom must be representative of current trends in opera, musical theater. Extreme dissonance, row systems not applicable to this environment."

Performances Seymour Barab's *Cinderella*; John David Earnest's *The Legend of Sleepy Hollow*; and Seymour Barab's *The Pied Piper of Hamelin*.

Tips "Theatricality is very important. New works should stimulate interest in musical theater as a legitimate art form for school children with no prior exposure to live theatrical entertainment. Composer should be willing to create a product which will find success within the educational system."

WHEATON SYMPHONY ORCHESTRA

344 Spring Ave., Glen Ellyn IL 60137. (630)858-5552. Fax: (630)790-9703. E-mail: dmattob@aol.com. **Contact:** Don Mattison, manager. Symphony orchestra. Estab. 1959. Members are professionals and amateurs. Performs 6 concerts/year including a varying number of new works. "No pay for performance but can probably record your piece."

How to Contact Query first. Include SASE. Responds in 1 month.

Music "This is a good amateur orchestra that wants pieces in a traditional idiom. Large scale works for orchestra only. No avant garde, 12-tone or atonal material. Pieces should be 20 minutes or less and must be prepared in 3 rehearsals. Instrumentation needed for woodwinds in 3s, full brass 4-3-3-1, 4 percussion and strings—full-instrumentation only. Selections for full orchestra only. No pay for reading your piece, but we will record it at our expense. We will rehearse and give a world premiere of your piece if it is in the stated orchestration, probably with keyboard added."

Performances Richard Williams's *Symphony in G Minor* (4 movement symphony); Dennis Johnson's *Must Jesus Bear the Cross Alone, Azon* (traditional); and Michael Diemer's *Skating* (traditional style).

Contests & Awards

Participating in contests is a great way to gain exposure for your music. Prizes vary from contest to contest, from cash to musical merchandise to studio time, and even publishing and recording deals. For musical theater and classical composers, the prize may be a performance of your work. Even if you don't win, valuable contacts can be made through contests. Many times, contests are judged by music publishers and other industry professionals, so your music may find its way into the hands of key industry people who can help further your career.

HOW TO SELECT A CONTEST

It's important to remember when entering any contest to do proper research before signing anything or sending any money. We have confidence in the contests listed in *Songwriter's Market*, but it pays to read the fine print. First, be sure you understand the contest rules and stipulations once you receive the entry forms and guidelines. Then you need to weigh what you will gain against what they're asking you to give up. If a publishing or recording contract is the only prize a contest is offering, you may want to think twice before entering. Basically, the company sponsoring the contest is asking you to pay a fee for them to listen to your song under the guise of a contest, something a legitimate publisher or record company would not do. For those contests offering studio time, musical equipment or cash prizes, you need to decide if the entry fee you're paying is worth the chance to win such prizes.

Be wary of exorbitant entry fees, and if you have any doubts whatsoever as to the legitimacy of a contest, it's best to stay away. Songwriters need to approach a contest, award or grant in the same manner as they would a record or publishing company. Make your submission as professional as possible; follow directions and submit material exactly as stated on the entry form.

Contests in this section encompass all types of music and levels of competition. Read each listing carefully and contact them if the contest interests you. Many contests now have Web sites that offer additional information and even entry forms you can print. Be sure to read the rules carefully and be sure you understand exactly what a contest is offering before entering.

AGO AWARD IN ORGAN COMPOSITION

American Guild of Organists, 475 Riverside Dr., Suite 1260, New York NY 10115. (212)870-2310. Fax: (212)870-2163. E-mail: info@agohq.org. Website: www.agohq.org. **Contact:** Harold Calhoun, competitions administrator. For composers and performing artists. Biennial award.

Requirements Organ solo, no longer than 8 minutes in duration. Specifics vary from year to year. Deadline: TBA, but usually early spring of odd-numbered year. Go to the Web site for application.

Awards $2,000; publication by Hinshaw Music Inc.; performance at the biennial National Convention of the American Guild of Organists.

AGO/ECS PUBLISHING AWARD IN CHORAL COMPOSITION

American Guild of Organists, 475 Riverside Dr., Suite 1260, New York NY 10115. (212)870-2310. Fax: (212)870-2163. E-mail: info@agohq.org. Website: www.agohq.org. **Contact:** Harold Calhoun, competitions administrator. Biannual award.

Requirements Composers are invited to submit a work for SATB choir and organ in which the organ plays a significant and independent role. Work submitted must be unpublished and are usually 3.5 to 5 minutes in length. There is no age restriction. Deadline: TBA, "but usually late fall in even numbered years." Application information on the website.

Awards $2,000 cash prize, publication by ECS Publishing and premier performance at the AGO National Convention.

ALEA III INTERNATIONAL COMPOSITION PRIZE

855 Commonwealth Ave., Boston MA 02215. (617)353-3340. E-mail: aleaiii@bu.edu. Website: www.aleaiii.com. For composers. Annual award.

Purpose To promote and encourage young composers in the composition of new music.

Requirements Composers born after January 1, 1980 may participate; 1 composition per composer. Works may be for solo voice or instrument or for chamber ensemble up to 15 members lasting between 6 and 15 minutes. Available instruments are: one flute (doubling piccolo or alto), one oboe (doubling English horn), one clarinet (doubling bass clarinet), one bassoon, one horn, one trumpet, one trombone, one tuba, two percussion players, one harp, one keyboard player, one guitar, two violins, one viola, one cello, one bass, tape and one voice. "One of the 15 performers could play an unusual, exotic or rare instrument, or be a specialized vocalist. For more info and guidelines, please refer to our Web site." All works must be unpublished and must not have been publicly performed or broadcast, in whole or in part or in any other version before the announcement of the prize in late September or early October of 2010. Works that have won other awards are not eligible. Deadline: March 15, 2010. Send for application. Submitted work required with application. "Real name should not appear on score; a nom de plume should be signed instead. Sealed envelope with entry form should be attached to each score."

Awards ALEA III International Composition Prize: $2,500. Awarded once annually. Between 6-8 finalists are chosen and their works are performed in a competition concert by the ALEA III contemporary music ensemble. At the end of the concert, one piece will be selected to receive the prize. One grand prize winner is selected by a panel of judges.

Tips "Emphasis placed on works written in 20th century compositional idioms."

AMERICAN SONGWRITER LYRIC CONTEST

1303 16th Avenue S., 2nd Floor, Nashville TN 37212. (615)321-6096. Fax: (615)321-6097. E-mail: info@americansongwriter.com. Website: www.americansongwriter.com. **Contact:** Matt Shearon. Estab. 1984. For songwriters and composers. Award for each bimonthly issue of American Songwriter magazine, plus grand prize winner at year-end.

Purpose To promote and encourage the craft of lyric writing.

Requirements Lyrics must be typed and a check for $10 (per entry) must be enclosed. Deadlines: January 22, March 23, May 23, July 24, September 25, November 16. Submit online through American Songspace or Sonicbids.com. Lyrics only. "If you enter two or more lyrics, you automatically receive a 1-year subscription to *American Songwriter* magazine (Canada: 3 or more; Other Countries: 4 or more)."

Awards A DX1 Martin guitar valued at $700 to bi-monthly contest winner. Grand prize winner receives airfare to Nashville and a demo session; and top 5 winning lyrics reprinted in each magazine, and 12 Honorable Mentions. One entrant interviewed each issue. Also: Grand Prize Winner gets to choose his/her "Dream Co-Writing Session" with either Bobby Braddock ("He Stopped Loving Her Today") or Kent Blazy ("If Tomorrow Never Comes"). Lyrics judged by independent A&R, PRO representatives, songwriters, publishers, and *American Songwriter* staff.

Tips "You do not have to be a subscriber to enter or win. You may submit as many entries as you like. All genres of music accepted."

ARTISTS' FELLOWSHIPS

New York Foundation for the Arts, 20 Jay St., 7th Floor, Brooklyn NY 11201. (212)366-6900. Fax: (212)366-1778. E-mail: nyfaafp@nyfa.org. Website: www.nyfa.org. To receive an application, or contact the fellowship's department, call: (212)366-6900, ext. 219. **Contact:** Margie Lempert, senior officer. For songwriters, composers and musical playwrights. Annual award, but each category funded biennially. Estab. 1984.

Purpose "Artists' Fellowships are $7,000 grants awarded by the New York Foundation for the Arts to individual originating artists living in New York State. The Foundation is committed to supporting artists from all over New York State at all stages of their professional careers. Fellows may use the grant according to their own needs; it should not be confused with project support."

Requirements Must be 18 years of age or older; resident of New York State for 2 years prior to application; and cannot be enrolled in any graduate or undergraduate degree program. Applications will be available in July. Deadline: October. Samples of work are required with application. 1 or 2 original compositions on separate audiotapes or audio CDs and at least 2 copies of corresponding scores or fully harmonized lead sheets.

Awards All Artists' Fellowships awards are for $7,000. Payment of $6,300 upon verification of NY State residency, and remainder upon completion of a mutually agreed upon public service activity. Nonrenewable. "Fellowships are awarded on the basis of the quality of work submitted. Applications are reviewed by a panel of 5 composers representing the aesthetic, ethnic, sexual and geographic diversity within New York State. The panelists change each year and review all allowable material submitted."

Tips "Please note that musical playwrights may submit only if they write the music for their plays--librettists must submit in our playwriting category."

BILLBOARD SONG CONTEST

P.O. Box 1000, Mounds, OK 74047. (918)624-2100. Fax: (918)827-6533. E-mail: mark@ jimhalsey.com. Website: www.billboardsongcontest.com. **Contact:** Mark Furnas, Director. Estab. 1988. For songwriters, composers and performing artists. Annual international contest.

Purpose "To reward deserving songwriters and performers for their talent."

Requirements Entry fee: $30.

Awards To be announced. For entry forms and additional information send SASE to the above address or visit website.

Tips "Participants should understand popular music structure."

THE BLANK THEATRE COMPANY YOUNG PLAYWRIGHTS FESTIVAL

P.O. Box 38756, Los Angeles CA 90038. (323)662-7734. Fax: (323)661-3903. E-mail: submissions@youngplaywrights.com. Website: www.youngplaywrights.com. Estab. 1993. For both musical and non-musical playwrights. Annual award.

Purpose "To give young playwrights an opportunity to learn more about playwriting and to give them a chance to have their work mentored, developed, and presented by professional artists."

Requirements Playwrights must be 19 years old or younger on March 15, 2010. Send legible, original plays of any length and on any subject (co-written plays are acceptable provided all co-writers meet eligibility requirements). Submissions must be postmarked by March 15 and must include a cover sheet with the playwright's name, date of birth, school (if any), home address, home phone number, e-mail address and production history. Pages must be numbered and submitted unbound (unstapled). For musicals, a tape or CD of a selection from the score should be submitted with the script. Manuscripts will not be returned. Please do not send originals. Semi-finalists and winners will be contacted in May.

Awards Winning playwrights receive a workshop presentation of their work.

CMT/NSAI ANNUAL SONG CONTEST

1710 Roy Acuff Place, Nashville TN 37203. (615)256-3354. E-mail: songcontest@ nashvillesongwriters.com. Website: www.nashvillesongwriters.com. **Contact:** David Petrelli, NSAI Event Director.

Purpose "A chance for aspiring songwriters to be heard by music industry decision makers."

Requirements Entry fee: $35 per song (NSAI member); $45 per song (non-member). Submissions accepted beginning August 1, 2009. In order to be eligible contestants must not be receiving income from any work submitted--original material only. Mail-in submissions must be in CD form and include both lyrics and melody. Online submissions available through sonicbids.com. Visit Web site for complete list of rules and regulations. Deadline is different each year; check website or send for application. Samples are required with application in the format of cassette or CD.

Awards Grand Prize winner receives a one-on-one mentoring session with music superstar, Jewel. CMT Listener's Choice award gives fans a chance to vote for their favorite song entry. Visit Web site for complete list of prizes.

COLUMBIA ENTERTAINMENT COMPANY'S JACKIE WHITE MEMORIAL PLAYWRITING CONTEST

309 Parkade Blvd., Columbia MO 65202. (573)874-5628. Website: www.cectheatre.org. **Contact:** Betsy Phillips, contest director, CEC contest. For musical playwrights. Annual award.

Purpose "We are looking for top-notch scripts suitable for family audiences with 7 or more fully-developed roles."

Requirements "May be adaptations or plays with original story lines and cannot have been previously published. Please write or call for complete rules." Send SASE or visit Web site for application; then send scripts to address above. Full-length play, neatly typed. No name on title page, but name, address and name of play on a 3 × 5 index card and lead sheets, as well as tape of musical numbers. $25 entry fee.

Awards $500 1st Prize. Play may or may not be produced at discretion of CEC. "The judging committee is taken from members of Columbia Entertainment Company's Executive and Advisory boards, and from theater school parents. Readings by up to eight members, with at least three readings of all entries, and winning entries being read by entire committee. All plays will receive a written evaluation."

Tips "We especially like plays that deal with current day problems and concerns. However, if the play is good enough, any suitable subject matter is fine."

COMPOSERS GUILD ANNUAL COMPOSITION CONTEST

P.O. Box 586, Farmington UT 84025-0586. (801)451-2275. **Contact:** Ruth B. Gatrell, president. Estab. 1963. For songwriters, musical playwrights and composers. Annual award.

Purpose "To stimulate musical composition and help composers through judge's comments on each composition submitted. Composers can broaden their creative skills by entering different categories. Categories: Arrangements (original in public domain or with composer's permission); Music for Children; Choral; Instrumental; Jazz/New Age; Keyboard; Orchestra/Band; Popular (all types); Vocal Solo; Young Composer (18 or under on August 31)."

Requirements Score and/or cassette or CD. Entry fee: $20 for work 7 minutes or more in length (may include multimovements on compositions), $15 for work less than 7 minutes. Dues are $25/year. Member entry fees: $10 for work 7 minutes or more, $5 less than 7 minutes. Deadline: August 31. Send or call for application.

Awards Award of Excellence $500; 1st Prize in each category except Award of Excellence category $100; 2nd Prize in each category $50; 3rd Prize in each category $25; Honorable Mention certificates. Age Group Certificates A (16-18); B (13-15); C (10-12); D (7-9); E (6 & under) also awarded in Young Composer category. Any winning entry is eligible for inclusion on the Composers Guild Spectacular concert held the last Saturday in January, subject to limitation of reasonable program length, but composer must furnish at least one well-qualified live performer (recorded accompaniments may be used). Judge has a doctorate in music, plus compositions published and performed (usually has vast teaching experience). Same judge never used in successive years.

Tips "Submit good clear copies of score. Have cassette cued up. Only one composition per cassette/CD (each entry requires separate cassette/CD). No composer names to appear on score or cassette/CD. Enter as many categories and compositions as you wish. Separate entry fee for each. One check can cover all entries and dues."

CRS NATIONAL COMPOSERS COMPETITION

724 Winchester Rd., Broomall PA 19008. (610)544-5920. E-mail: crsnews@verizon.net. Website: www.crsnews.org. **Contact:** Caroline Hunt, administrative assistant. Senior Representative: Jack Shusterman. Estab. 1981. For songwriters, composers and performing artists. College faculty and gifted artists. Annual award.

Requirements For composers, songwriters, performing artists and ensembles. Each category requires a separate application fee. The work submitted must be non-published (prior to acceptance) and not commercially recorded on any label. The work submitted must not exceed nine performers. Each composer/performer may submit one work for each application submitted. (Taped performances by composers are additionally encouraged.) Composition must not exceed sixteen minutes in length. CRS reserves the right not to accept a First Prize Winner. Write with SASE for application or visit website. Add $3.50 for postage and handling. Deadline: December 10. Must send a detailed résumé with application form available on our Web page under "Events" category. Samples of work required with application. Send score and parts with optional CD or DAT. Application fee: $50.

Awards 1st Prize: Commercial recording grant for winning composition/performance. Applications are judged by panel of judges determined each year.

CUNNINGHAM COMMISSION FOR YOUTH THEATRE

(formerly Cunningham Prize for Playwriting), The Theatre School at DePaul University, 2135 N. Kenmore Ave., Chicago IL 60614. (773)325-7938. Fax: (773)325-7920. E-mail: aables@depaul.edu. Website: http://theatreschool.depaul.edu. **Contact:** Anna Ables. Estab. 1990. For playwrights. Annual award.

Purpose "The purpose of the Commission is to encourage the writing of dramatic works for young audiences that affirm the centrality of religion, broadly defined, and the human quest for meaning, truth, and community. The Theatre School intends to produce the plays created through this commission in its award-winning Chicago Playworks for Families and Young Audiences series at the historic Merle Reskin Theatre. Each year Chicago Playworks productions are seen by 35,000 students and families from throughout the Chicago area."

Requirements "Candidates for the commission must be writers whose residence is in the Chicago area, defined as within 100 miles of the Loop. Playwrights who have won the award within the last five years are not eligible. Deadline: annually by December 1. Candidates should submit a résumé, a 20 page sample of their work, and a brief statement about their interest in the commission. The submission should not include a proposal for a project the playwright would complete if awarded the commission. The writing sample may be from a play of any genre for any audience."

Awards $6,000. "Winners will be notified by May 1. The Selection Committee is chaired by the Dean of The Theatre School and is composed of members of the Cunningham Commission advisory committee and faculty of The Theatre School."

DELTA OMICRON INTERNATIONAL COMPOSITION COMPETITION

12297 W. Tennessee Place, Lakewood CO 80228. (303)989-2871. E-mail: rbzdx@webtv.net Website: www.delta-omicron.org **Composition Competition Chair:** Judith L. Eidson. For composers. Triennial award. Next contest: 2012.

Purpose "To encourage composers worldwide to continually add to our wonderful heritage of musical creativity instrumentally and/or vocally."

Requirements People from college age on (or someone younger who is enrolled in college). Work must be unpublished and unperformed in public. "View our website (www.delta-omicron.org) for specific submission guidelines such as instrument selection and deadline Click on 'Composition Competition' on homepage." Manuscripts should be legibly written in ink or processed, signed with *nom de plume*, and free from any marks that would identify the composer to the judges. Entry fee: $25 per composition. Send for application. Composition is required with application. A total of three copies of composition are required, one for each judge. Music copies should *not* be spiral bound.

Awards 1st Place: $1,000 and world premiere at Delta Omicron Triennial Conference. Judged by 2-3 judges (performers, conductors, and/or composers).

EUROPEAN INTERNATIONAL COMPETITION FOR COMPOSERS/IBLA FOUNDATION

226 East 2nd St., Loft 1B, New York NY 10009. (212)387-0111. E-mail: iblanyc@aol.com. Website: www.ibla.org. **Contact:** Mr. Michael Yasenak, executive director. Chairman: Dr. S. Moltisanti. Estab. 1995. For songwriters and composers. Annual award.

Purpose "To promote the winners' career through exposure, publicity, recordings with Athena Records and nationwide distribution with the Empire Group."

Requirements Deadline: April 30. Send for application. Music score and/or recording of one work are required with application. Application fee is refunded if not admitted into the program.

Awards Winners are presented in concerts in Europe-Japan, USA.

FULBRIGHT SCHOLAR PROGRAM, COUNCIL FOR INTERNATIONAL EXCHANGE OF SCHOLARS

3007 Tilden St. NW, Suite 5L, Washington DC 20008-3009. (202)686-4000. E-mail: scholars@cies.iie.org. Website: www.cies.org. Estab. 1946. For composers and academics. Annual award.

Purpose "Awards for university lecturing and advanced research abroad are offered annually in virtually all academic disciplines including musical composition."

Requirements "U.S. citizenship at time of application; M.F.A., Ph.D. or equivalent professional qualifications; for lecturing awards, university teaching experience (some awards are for professionals non-academic)." Applications become available in March each year, for grants to be taken up 1½ years later. Application deadlines: August 1, all world areas. Write or call for application. Samples of work are required with application.

Awards "Benefits vary by country, but generally include round-trip travel for the grantee and for most full academic-year awards, one dependent; stipend in U.S. dollars and/or local currency; in many countries, tuition allowance for school age children; and book and baggage allowance. Grant duration ranges from 3 months-1 academic year."

HARVEY GAUL COMPOSITION CONTEST

The Pittsburgh New Music Ensemble, Inc., 527 Coyne Ter., Pittsburgh PA 15207. E-mail: pnme@pnme.org. Website: www.pnme. org. **Contact:** Jeffrey Nytch, DMA, managing director. For composers. Biennial.

Purpose Objective is to encourage composition of new music.

Requirements "Must be citizen of the US. Please submit score and recording, if available

(CDs only) of a representative instrumental score." Next contest 2011. Send SASE for application or download from www.pnme.org. Samples of work are required with application. Entry fee: $20.

Awards Harvey Gaul Composition Contest: $6,000. Winner will receive commission for new work to be premiered by the PNME.

GRASSY HILL KERRVILLE NEW FOLK COMPETITION

(formerly New Folk Concerts For Emerging Songwriters), P.O. Box 291466, Kerrville TX 78029. (830)257-3600. Fax: (830)257-8680. E-mail: info@kerrville-music.com. Website: www.kerrvillefolkfestival.com. Contact: Dalis Allen, producer. For songwriters. Annual award.

• Also see the listing for Kerrville Folk Festival in the Workshops section of this book.

Purpose "To provide an opportunity for emerging songwriters to be heard and rewarded for excellence."

Requirements Songwriter enters 2 original songs burned to CD (cassettes no longer accepted), or uploaded to SonicBids, with entry fee; no more than one submission may be entered; 6-8 minutes total for 2 songs. Application online, no lyric sheets or press material needed. Submissions accepted between December 1-March 15 or first 800 entries received prior to that date. Call or e-mail to request rules. Entry fee: $25.

Awards New Folk Award Winner. 32 finalists invited to sing the 2 songs entered during The Kerrville Folk Festival in May. 6 writers are chosen as award winners. Each of the 6 receives a cash award of $450 or more and performs at a winner's concert during the Kerrville Folk Festival in June. Initial round of entries judged by the Festival Producer. 32 finalists judged by panel of 3 performer/songwriters.

Tips "Do not allow instrumental accompaniment to drown out lyric content. Don't enter without complete copy of the rules. Former winners and finalists include Lyle Lovett, Nanci Griffith, Hal Ketchum, John Gorka, David Wilcox, Lucinda Williams and Robert Earl Keen, Tish Hinojosa, Carrie Newcomer, Jimmy Lafave, etc."

GREAT AMERICAN SONG CONTEST

PMB 135, 6327-C SW Capitol Hill Hwy., Portland OR 97239-1937. E-mail: info@ GreatAmericanSong.com. Website: www.GreatAmericanSong.com. **Contact:** Carla Starrett, event coordinator. Estab. 1998. For songwriters, composers and lyricists. Annual award.

• Also see the listing for Songwriters Resource Network in the Organizations section of this book.

Purpose To help songwriters get their songs heard by music-industry professionals; to generate educational and networking opportunities for participating songwriters; to help songwriters open doors in the music business.

Requirements Entry fee: $25. "Annual deadline. Check our website for details or send

SASE along with your mailed request for information."

Awards Winners receive a mix of cash awards and prizes. The focus of the contest is on networking and educational opportunities. (All participants receive detailed evaluations of their songs by industry professionals.) Songs are judged by knowledgeable music-industry professionals, including prominent hit songwriters, producers and publishers.

Tips "Focus should be on the song. The quality of the demo isn't important. Judges will be looking for good songwriting talent. They will base their evaluations on the song--not the quality of the recording or the voice performance."

HENRICO THEATRE COMPANY ONE-ACT PLAYWRITING COMPETITION

P.O. Box 90775, Richmond VA 23273. (804)501-5115. Fax: (804)501-5284. E-mail: per22@ co.henrico.va.us. **Contact:** Amy A. Perdue, cultural arts senior coordinator. For musical playwrights, songwriters, composers and performing artists. Annual award.

Purpose Original one-act musicals for a community theater organization.

Requirements "Only one-act plays or musicals will be considered. The manuscript should be a one-act original (not an adaptation), unpublished, and unproduced, free of royalty and copyright restrictions. Scripts with smaller casts and simpler sets may be given preference. Controversial themes and excessive language should be avoided. Standard play script form should be used. All plays will be judged anonymously; therefore, there should be two title pages; the first must contain the play's title and the author's complete address and telephone number. The second title page must contain only the play's title. The playwright must submit two excellent quality copies. Receipt of all scripts will be acknowledged by mail. Scripts will be returned if SASE is included. No scripts will be returned until after the winner is announced. The HTC does not assume responsibility for loss, damage or return of scripts. All reasonable care will be taken." Deadline: July 1st.

Awards 1st Prize $300; 2nd Prize $200; 3rd Prize $200.

IAMA (INTERNATIONAL ACOUSTIC MUSIC AWARDS)

2881 E. Oakland Park Blvd, Suite 414, Fort Lauderdale, FL 33306. (954)537-3127. **Contact:** Jessica Brandon, artist relations. Established 2004. E-mail: info@inacoustic.com. Website: http://www.inacoustic.com. For singer-songwriters, musicians, performing musicians in the acoustic genre.

Purpose "The purpose is to promote the excellence in Acoustic music performance and songwriting." Genres include: Folk, Alternative, Bluegrass, etc.

Requirements Visit Web site for entry form and details. "All songs submitted must be original. There must be at least an acoustic instrument (voice) in any song. Electric and Electronic instruments, along with loops is allowed but acoustic instruments (or voice) must be clearly heard in all songs submitted. Contestants may enter as many songs in as many categories as desired but each entry requires a separate CD, entry form, lyric sheet and entry fee. CDs and lyrics will not be returned. Winners will be chosen by a

Blue Ribbon Judging Committee comprised of music industry professionals including A&R managers from record labels, publishers and producers. Entries are judged equally on music performance, production, originality, lyrics, melody and composition. Songs may be in any language. Winners will be notified by e-mail and must sign and return an affidavit confirming that winner's song is original and he/she holds rights to the song. Entry fee: $35/entry.

Awards Prizes: Overall Grand Prize receives $11,000.00 worth of merchandise, First Prizes in all categories win $900.00 worth of merchandise and services, Runner-Up prizes in all categories receive $600.00 worth of merchandise and services. All first prizes and runner-up winners will receive a track on IAMA compilation CD which goes out to radio stations.

Tips "Judging is based on music performance, music production, songwriting and originality/artistry."

L.A. DESIGNERS' THEATRE MUSIC AWARDS

P.O. Box 1883, Studio City CA 91614-0883. (323)650-9600. Fax: (323)654-3210. E-mail: ladesigners@juno.com. Artistic Director: Richard Niederberg. For songwriters, composers, performing artists, musical playwrights and rights holders of music.

Purpose To produce new musicals, operettas, opera-boufes and plays with music, as well as new dance pieces with new music scores.

Requirements Submit nonreturnable cassette, tape, CD or any other medium by first or 4th class mail. "We prefer proposals to scripts." Acceptance: continuous. Submit nonreturnable materials with cover letter. No application form or fee is necessary.

Awards Music is commissioned for a particular project. Amounts are negotiable. Applications judged by our artistic staff.

Tips "Make the material 'classic, yet commercial' and easy to record/re-record/edit. Make sure rights are totally free of all 'strings,' 'understandings,' 'promises,' etc. ASCAP/BMI/SESAC registration is OK, as long as 'grand' or 'performing rights' are available."

THE JOHN LENNON SONGWRITING CONTEST

180 Brighton Rd., Suite 801, Clifton NJ 07012. E-mail: info@jlsc.com. Website: www.jlsc.com. Estab. 1996. For songwriters. Open year-round.

Purpose "The purpose of the John Lennon Songwriting Contest is to promote the art of songwriting by assisting in the discovery of new talent as well as providing more established songwriters with an opportunity to advance their careers."

Requirements Each entry must consist of the following: completed and signed application; audio cassette, CD or mp3 containing one song only, 5 minutes or less in length; lyric sheet typed or printed legibly (English translation is required when applicable); $30 entry fee. Deadline: December 15, 2009. Applications can be found in various music-oriented magazines and on our website. Prospective entrants can send for an application or contact the contest via e-mail at info@jlsc.com.

Awards Entries are accepted in the following 12 categories: rock, country, jazz, pop, world, gospel/inspirational, R&B, hip-hop, Latin, electronic, folk and children's music. Winners will receive EMI Publishing Contracts, Studio Equipment from Brian Moore Guitars, Roland, Edirol and Audio Technica, 1,000 CDs in full color with premium 6-panel Digipaks courtesy of Discmakers, and gift certificates from Musiciansfriend.com. One entrant wil be chosen to TOUR and PERFORM for one week on Warped Tour '06. One Lennon Award winning song will be named "Maxell Song of the Year" and take home an additional $20,000 in cash courtesy of the Maxell Corporation.

MAXIM MAZUMDAR NEW PLAY COMPETITION

One Curtain Up Alley, Buffalo NY 14202-1911. (716)852-2600. Fax: (716)852-2266. E-mail: newplays@alleyway.com. Website: www.alleyway.com. **Contact:** Literary Manager. For musical playwrights. Annual award.

Purpose Alleyway Theatre is dedicated to the development and production of new works. Winners of the competition will receive production and royalties.

Requirements Unproduced full-length work not less than 90 minutes long with cast limit of 10 and unit or simple set, or unproduced one-act work less than 15 minutes long with cast limit of 6 and simple set; prefers work with unconventional setting that explores the boundaries of theatricality; limit of 1 submission in each category; guidelines available online, no entry form. $25 playwright entry fee. Script, résumé, SASE optional. CD or cassette mandatory. Deadline: July 1.

Awards Production for full-length play or musical with royalty and production for one-act play or musical.

Tips "Entries may be of any style, but preference will be given to those scripts which take place in unconventional settings and explore the boundaries of theatricality. No more than ten performers is a definite, unchangeable requirement."

MID-ATLANTIC SONG CONTEST

Songwriters' Association of Washington, PMB 106-137, 4200 Wisconsin Ave., NW, Washington DC 20016. E-mail: masc@saw.org. Website: www.saw.org. For songwriters and composers. Estab. 1982. Annual award.

• Also see the listing for Songwriters Association of Washington in the Organizations section.

Purpose This is one of the longest-running contests in the nation; SAW has organized twenty-six contests since 1982. The competition is designed to afford rising songwriters in a wide variety of genres the opportunity to receive awards and exposure in an environment of peer competition.

Requirements Amateur status is important. Applicants should request a brochure/application using the contact information above. Rules and procedures are clearly explained in that brochure. CD and 3 copies of the lyrics are to be submitted with an application form and fee for each entry, or submit mp3 entries by applying online or through Sonicbids. Beginning this year, online entries will also be accepted. Reduced entry fees are offered to members of Songwriters' Association of Washington; membership can be arranged simultaneously with entering. Multi-song discounts are also offered. Applications are mailed out and posted on their website around June 1; the submission deadline is mid-September; awards are typically announced late in the fall.

Awards The two best songs in each of ten categories win prize packages donated by the contest's corporate sponsors: BMI, Oasis CD Manufacturing, Omega Recording Studios, Mary Cliff and Sonic Bids. Winning songwriters are invited to perform in Washington, DC at the Awards Ceremony Gala, and the twenty winning songs are included on a compilation CD. The best song in each category is eligible for three grand cash prizes. Certificates are awarded to other entries meriting honorable mention.

Tips "Enter the song in the most appropriate category. Make the sound recording the best it can be (even though judges are asked to focus on melody and lyric and not on production.) Avoid clichés, extended introductions, and long instrumental solos."

THELONIOUS MONK INTERNATIONAL JAZZ COMPOSERS COMPETITION

(Sponsored by BMI) Thelonious Monk Institute of Jazz, 5225 Wisconsin Ave. NW, #605, Washington DC 20015. (202)364-7272. Fax: (202)364-0176. E-mail: info@monkinstitute. org. Website: www.monkinstitute.org. **Contact:** Leonard Brown, program director. Estab. 1993. For songwriters and composers. Annual award.

Purpose The award is given to an aspiring jazz composer who best demonstrates originality, creativity and excellence in jazz composition.

Requirements Deadline: July 17. Send for application. Submission must include application form, resume of musical experience, CD or cassette, entry, four copies of the full score, and a photo. The composition features a different instrument each year. Entry fee: $35.

Awards $10,000. Applications are judged by panel of jazz musicians. "The Institute will provide piano, bass, guitar, drum set, tenor saxophone, and trumpet for the final performance. The winner will be responsible for the costs of any different instrumentation included in the composition."

NACUSA YOUNG COMPOSERS' COMPETITION

Box 49256 Barrington Station, Los Angeles CA 90049. (818)274-6048. E-mail: nacusa@ music-usa.org. Website: www.music-usa.org/nacusa. **Contact:** Daniel Kessner, president, NACUSA. Estab. 1978. For composers. Annual award.

- Also see the National Association of Composers/USA (NACUSA) listing in the Organization section.

Purpose To encourage the composition of new American concert hall music.

Requirements Entry fee: $20 (membership fee). Deadline: October 30. Send for application. Samples are not required.

Awards 1st Prize: $400; 2nd Prize: $100; and possible Los Angeles performances. Applications are judged by a committee of experienced NACUSA composer members.

PULITZER PRIZE IN MUSIC

709 Journalism Building, Columbia University, New York NY 10027. (212)854-3841. Fax: (212)854-3342. E-mail: pulitzer@www.pulitzer.org. Website: www.pulitzer.org. **Contact:** Music Secretary. For composers and musical playwrights. Annual award.

Requirements "For distinguished musical composition by an American that has had its first performance or recording in the United States during the year." Entries should reflect current creative activity. Works that receive their American premiere between January 16, 2009 and December 31, 2009 are eligible. A public performance or the public release of a recording shall constitute a premiere. Deadline: December 31. Samples of work are required with application, biography and photograph of composer, date and place of performance, score or manuscript and recording of the work, entry form and $50 entry fee.

Awards "One award: $10,000. Applications are judged first by a nominating jury, then by the Pulitzer Prize Board."

ROCKY MOUNTAIN FOLKS FESTIVAL SONGWRITER SHOWCASE

Planet Bluegrass, ATTN: Songwriter Showcase, P.O. Box 769, Lyons CO 80540. (800)624-2422 or (303)823-0848. Fax: (303)823-0849. E-mail: brian@bluegrass.com. Website: www.bluegrass.com. **Contact:** Steve Szymanski, director. Estab. 1993. For songwriters, composers and performers. Annual award.

Purpose Award based on having the best song and performance.

Requirements Deadline: June 30. Finalists notified by July 14. Rules available on Web site. Samples of work are required with application. Send CD with $10/song entry fee. Can now submit online: www.sonicbids.com/rockymountainfolk06. Contestants cannot be signed to a major label or publishing deal. No backup musicians allowed.

Awards 1st Place is a 2006 Festival Main Stage set, custom Hayes Guitar, $100, and a free one song drumoverdubs (http://www.drumoverdubs.com) certificate (valued at $300); 2nd Place is $500 and a Baby Taylor Guitar; 3rd Place is $400 and a Baby Taylor Guitar; 4th Place is $300; 5th Place is $200; 6th to 10th Place is $100 each. Each finalist will also receive a complimentary three-day Folks Festival pass that includes onsite camping, and a Songwriter In The Round slot during the Festival on our workshop stage.

RICHARD RODGERS AWARDS

American Academy of Arts and Letters, 633 W. 155th St., New York NY 10032. (212)368-5900. **Contact:** Jane Bolster, coordinator. Estab. 1978. Deadline: November 2, 2009. "The Richard Rodgers Awards subsidize staged reading, studio productions, and full productions by nonprofit theaters in New York City of works by composers and writers who are not already established in the field of musical theater. The awards are only for musicals--songs by themselves are not eligible. The authors must be citizens or permanent residents of the United States." Guidelines for this award may be obtained by sending a SASE to above address or download from www.artsandletters.org.

ROME PRIZE COMPETITION FELLOWSHIP

American Academy in Rome, 7 E. 60th St., New York NY 10022-1001. (212)751-7200. Fax: (212)751-7220. E-mail: info@aarome.org. Website: www.aarome.org. **Contact:** Programs Department. For composers. Annual award.

Purpose "Through its annual Rome Prize Competition, the academy awards up to thirty fellowships in eleven disciplines, including musical composition. Winners of the Rome Prize pursue independent projects while residing at the Academy's eleven acre center in Rome."

Requirements "Applicants for 11-month fellowships must be US citizens and hold a bachelor's degree in music, musical composition or its equivalent." Deadline: November 1. Entry fee: $30. Application guidelines are available through the Academy's Web site.

Awards "Up to two fellowships are awarded annually in musical composition. Fellowship consists of room, board, and a studio at the Academy facilities in Rome as well as a stipend of $25,000. In all cases, excellence is the primary criterion for selection, based on the quality of the materials submitted. Winners are announced in mid-April and fellowships generally begin in early September."

TELLURIDE TROUBADOUR CONTEST

Planet Bluegrass, ATTN: Troubadour Competition, P.O. Box 769, Lyons CO 80540. (303)823-0848 or (800)624-2422. Fax: (303)823-0849. E-mail: brian@bluegrass.com. Website: www.bluegrass.com. **Contact:** Steve Szymanski, director. Estab. 1991. For songwriters, composers and performers. Annual award.

Purpose Award based on having best song and performance.

Requirements Deadline: must be postmarked by April 16; notified May 7, if selected. Rules available on website. Send CD and $10/song entry fee (limit of 2 songs). Can now submit music online at www.sonicbids.com/telluride2006. Contestants cannot be signed to a major label or publishing deal. No backup musicians allowed.

Awards 1st: custom Shanti Guitar, $200 and Festival Main Stage Set; 2nd: $400, "Limo" portable amplifier, and Little Martin guitar; 3rd: $300 and Little Martin guitar; 4th: $200 and Little Martin guitar; 5th: $100 and Baby Taylor guitar. Applications judged by panel of judges.

THE TEN-MINUTE MUSICALS PROJECT

P.O. Box 461194, West Hollywood CA 90046. Website: www.tenminutemusicals.org. **Contact:** Michael Koppy, producer. For songwriters, composers and musical playwrights. Annual award.

Purpose "We are building a full-length stage musical comprised of complete short musicals, each of which play for between 8-14 minutes. Award is $250 for each work chosen for development towards inclusion in the project, plus a share of royalties when produced."

Requirements Deadline: August 31. Responds by November 30. See Web site for guidelines. Final submission should include script, CD, and lead sheets.

Awards $250 for each work selected. "Works should have complete stories, with a definite beginning, middle and end."

U.S.A. SONGWRITING COMPETITION

2881 E. Oakland Park Blvd., Suite 414, Ft. Lauderdale FL 33306. (954)537-3127. Fax: (954)537-9690. E-mail: info@songwriting.net. Website: www.songwriting.net. **Contact:** Contest Manager. Estab. 1994. For songwriters, composers, performing artists and lyricists. Annual award.

Purpose "To honor good songwriters/composers all over the world, especially the unknown ones."

Requirements Open to professional and beginner songwriters. No limit on entries. Each entry must include an entry fee, a cassette tape of song(s) and lyric sheet(s). Judged by music industry representatives. Past judges have included record label representatives and publishers from Arista Records, EMI and Warner/Chappell. Deadline: To be announced. Entry fee: To be announced. Send SASE with request or e-mail for entry forms at any time. Samples of work are not required.

Awards Prizes include cash and merchandise in 15 different categories: pop, rock, country, Latin, R&B, gospel, folk, jazz, "lyrics only" category, instrumental and many others.

Tips "Judging is based on lyrics, originality, melody and overall composition. CD-quality production is great but not a consideration in judging."

U.S.-JAPAN CREATIVE ARTISTS EXCHANGE FELLOWSHIP PROGRAM

Japan-U.S. Friendship Commission, 1201 15th St. NW, Suite 330, Washington DC 20005. (202)653-9800. Fax: (202)653-9802. E-mail: jusfc@jusfc.gov. Website: www.jusfc.gov. **Contact:** Margaret Mihori, assistant executive director. Estab. 1980. For all creative artists. Annual award.

Purpose "For artists to go as seekers, as cultural visionaries, and as living liaisons to the traditional and contemporary life of Japan."

Requirements "Artists' works must exemplify the best in U.S. arts." Deadline: Feb. 1, 2010. Send for application and guidelines. Applications available via Internet. Samples of work are required with application. Requires 2 pieces on CD or DVD.

Awards Five artists are awarded a 5 month residency anywhere in Japan. Awards monthly stipend for living expenses, housing and professional support services; up to $6,000 for pre-departure costs, including such items as language training and economy class roundtrip airfare, plus 600,000 yen for monthly living expenses, housing allowance, and professional support services, as well as other arts professionals with expertise in Japanese culture.

Tips "Applicants should anticipate a highly rigorous review of their artistry and should have compelling reasons for wanting to work in Japan."

Y.E.S. FESTIVAL OF NEW PLAYS

Northern Kentucky University Dept. of Theatre, FA-205, Highland Heights KY 41099-1007. (859)572-6303. Fax: (859)572-6057. E-mail: forman@nku.edu. **Contact:** Sandra Forman, project director. Estab. 1983. For musical playwrights. Biennial award (odd numbered years).

Purpose "The festival seeks to encourage new playwrights and develop new plays and musicals. Three plays or musicals are given full productions."

Requirements "No entry fee. Submit a script with a completed entry form. Musicals should be submitted with a piano/conductor's score and/or a vocal parts score. Scripts may be submitted May 1 through Sept. 30, 2010, for the New Play Festival occurring April 2011. Send SASE for application."

Awards Three awards of $500. "The winners are brought to NKU at our expense to view late rehearsals and opening night." Submissions are judged by a panel of readers.

Tips "Plays/musicals which have heavy demands for mature actors are not as likely to be selected as an equally good script with roles for 18-30 year olds."

Organizations

One of the first places a beginning songwriter should look for guidance and support is a songwriting organization. Offering encouragement, instruction, contacts and feedback, these groups of professional and amateur songwriters can help an aspiring songwriter hone the skills needed to compete in the ever-changing music industry.

The type of organization you choose to join depends on what you want to get out of it. Local groups can offer a friendly, supportive environment where you can work on your songs and have them critiqued in a constructive way by other songwriters. They're also great places to meet collaborators. Larger, national organizations can give you access to music business professionals and other songwriters across the country.

Most of the organizations listed in this book are non-profit groups with membership open to specific groups of people—songwriters, musicians, classical composers, etc. They can be local groups with a membership of less than 100 people, or large national organizations with thousands of members from all over the country. In addition to regular meetings, most organizations occasionally sponsor events such as seminars and workshops to which music industry personnel are invited to talk about the business, and perhaps listen to and critique demo tapes.

Check the following listings, bulletin boards at local music stores and your local newspapers for area organizations. If you are unable to locate an organization within an easy distance of your home, you may want to consider joining one of the national groups. These groups, based in New York, Los Angeles and Nashville, keep their members involved and informed through newsletters, regional workshops and large yearly conferences. They can help a writer who feels isolated in his hometown get his music heard by professionals in the major music centers.

In the following listings, organizations describe their purpose and activities, as well as how much it costs to join. Before joining any organization, consider what they have to offer and how becoming a member will benefit you. To locate organizations close to home, see the Geographic Index at the back of this book.

ACADEMY OF COUNTRY MUSIC

5500 Balboa Blvd., #200, Encino CA 91316. (818)788-8000. Fax: (818)788-0999. E-mail: info@ acmcountry.com. Website: www.acmcountry.com. **Contact:** Bob Romeo, executive director. Estab. 1964. Serves country music industry professionals. Eligibility for professional members is limited to those individuals who derive some portion of their income directly from country music. Each member is classified by one of the following categories: artist/entertainer, club/venue operator, musician, on-air personality, manager, talent agent, composer, music publisher, public relations, publications, radio, TV/motion picture, record company, talent buyer or affiliated (general). The purpose of ACM is to promote and enhance the image of country music. The Academy is involved year-round in activities important to the country music community. Some of these activities include charity fund-raisers, participation in country music seminars, talent contests, artist showcases, assistance to producers in placing country music on television and in motion pictures and backing legislation that benefits the interests of the country music community. The ACM is governed by directors and run by officers elected annually. Applications are accepted throughout the year. Membership is $75/ year.

AMERICAN SOCIETY OF COMPOSERS, AUTHORS AND PUBLISHERS (ASCAP)

One Lincoln Plaza, New York NY 10023. (212)621-6000 (administration); (212)621-6240 (membership). E-mail: info@ascap.com. Website: www.ascap.com. President and Chairman of the Board: Marilyn Bergman. CEO: John LoFrumento. Executive Vice President/ Membership: Todd Brabec. **Contact:** Member Services at (800)95-ASCAP. **Regional offices-- West Coast:** 7920 Sunset Blvd., 3rd Floor, Los Angeles CA 90046, (323)883-1000; **Nashville:** 2 Music Square W., Nashville TN 37203, (615)742-5000; **Chicago:** 1608 N. Milwaukee Ave., Suite 1007, Chicago IL 60647, (773)394-4286; **Atlanta:** PMB 400-541 10th St. NW, Atlanta GA 30318, (404)351-1224; **Florida:** 420 Lincoln Rd., Suite 385, Miami Beach FL 33139, (305)673-3446; **United Kingdom:** 8 Cork St., London W1S 3LJ England, 011-44-207-439-0909; **Puerto Rico:** 654 Ave. Munoz Rivera, IBM Plaza Suite 1101 B, Hato Rey, Puerto Rico 00918, (787)281-0782. ASCAP is a membership association of over 240,000 composers, lyricists, songwriters, and music publishers, whose function is to protect the rights of its members by licensing and collecting royalties for the nondramatic public performance of their copyrighted works. ASCAP licensees include radio, television, cable, live concert promoters, bars, restaurants, symphony orchestras, new media, and other users of music. ASCAP is the leading performing rights society in the world. All revenues, less operating expenses, are distributed to members (about 86 cents of each dollar). ASCAP was the first US performing rights organization to distribute royalties from the Internet. Founded in 1914, ASCAP is the only society created and owned by writers and publishers. The ASCAP Board of Directors consists of 12 writers and 12 publishers, elected by the membership. ASCAP's Member Card provides exclusive benefits geared towards working music professionals. Among the benefits are health, musical instrument and equipment, tour and studio liability, term life and long term care insurance, discounts on musical instruments, equipment and supplies, access to a credit union, and much more. ASCAP hosts a wide array of showcases and workshops throughout the year, and offers grants, special awards, and networking opportunities in a variety of genres. Visit their Web site listed above for more information.

Resources

ARIZONA SONGWRITERS ASSOCIATION

428 E. Thunderbird Rd., #737, Phoenix AZ 85022. E-mail: azsongwriters@cox.net. **Contact**: Jon Iger, president. Estab. 1977. Members are all ages; all styles of music, novice to pro; many make money placing their songs in film and TV. Most members are residents of Arizona. Purpose is to educate about the craft and business of songwriting and to facilitate networking with business professionals and other songwriters, musicians, singers and studios. Offers instruction, e-newsletter, workshops, performance, and song pitching opportunities. Applications accepted year-round. Membership fee: $25/year.

ASSOCIATION OF INDEPENDENT MUSIC PUBLISHERS

Los Angeles Chapter: P.O. Box 69473, Los Angeles CA 90069. (818)771-7301. New York line: (212)391-2532. E-mail: LAinfo@aimp.org or NYinfo@aimp.org. Website: www.aimp.org. Estab. 1977. Purpose is to educate members on new developments in the music publishing industry and to provide networking opportunities. Offers monthly panels and networking events. Applications accepted year-round. Membership fee: NY: $75/year; LA: $76/year.

AUSTIN SONGWRITERS GROUP

P.O. Box 2578, Austin TX 78768. (512)203-1972. E-mail: info@austinsongwritersgroup.com. Website: www.austinsongwritersgroup.com. **Contact:** Lee Duffy, president. Vice President: Brent Allen. Estab. 1986. Serves all ages and all levels, from just beginning to advanced. "Prospective members should have an interest in the field of songwriting, whether it be for profit or hobby. The main purpose of this organization is to educate members in the craft and business of songwriting; to provide resources for growth and advancement in the area of songwriting; and to provide opportunities for performance and contact with the music industry." The primary benefit of membership to a songwriter is exposed to music industry professionals, which increases contacts and furthers the songwriter's education in both craft and business aspects. Offers competitions, instruction, lectures, library, newsletter, performance opportunities, evaluation services, workshops and contact with musi c industry professionals through special guest speakers at meetings, plus our yearly 'Austin Songwriters Symposium,' which includes instruction, song evaluations, and song pitching direct to those pros currently seeking material for their artists, publishing companies, etc." Applications accepted year-round. Membership fee: $100/year.

Tips Our newsletter is top-quality-packed with helpful information on all aspects of songwriting-craft, business, recording and producing tips, and industry networking opportunities. Go to our website and sign up for emails to keep you informed about on going and up coming events!"

BALTIMORE SONGWRITERS ASSOCIATION

P.O. Box 22496, Baltimore MD 21203. (410)669-1075. E-mail: info@baltimoresongwriters.org. Website: www.baltimoresongwriters.org. **Contact:** Ken Gutberlet, president. Estab. 1997. "The BSA is an inclusive organization with all ages, skill levels and genres of music welcome." Offers instruction, newsletter, lectures, workshops, performance opportunities. Applications accepted year-round; membership not limited to location or musical status. Membership fee: $25.

Tips "We are trying to build a musical community that is more supportive and less competitive.

We are dedicated to helping songwriters grow and become better in their craft."

THE BLACK ROCK COALITION

P.O. Box 1054, Cooper Station, New York NY 10276. (212)713-5097. E-mail: ldavis@ blackrockcoalition.org. Website: www.blackrockcoalition.org. **Contact**: LaRonda Davis, president. Estab. 1985. Serves musicians, songwriters--male and female ages 18-40 (average). Also engineers, entertainment attorneys and producers. Looking for members who are "mature and serious about music as an artist or activist willing to help fellow musicians. The BRC independently produces, promotes and distributes Black alternative music acts as a collective and supportive voice for such musicians within the music and record business. The main purpose of this organization is to produce, promote and distribute the full spectrum of black music along with educating the public on what black music is. The BRC is now soliciting recorded music by bands and individuals for Black Rock Coalition Records. Please send copyrighted and original material only." Offers instruction, newsletter, lectures, free seminars and workshops, monthly membership meeting, quarterly magazine, performing opportunities, evaluation services, business advice, full roster of all members. Applications accepted year-round. Bands must submit a tape, bio with picture and a self-addressed, stamped envelope before sending their membership fee. Membership fee: $25 per individual/$100 per band.

THE BOSTON SONGWRITERS WORKSHOP

(617)499-6932. Website: www.bostonsongwriters.org. Estab. 1988. "The Boston Songwriters Workshop is made up of a very diverse group of people, ranging in age from late teens to people in their sixties, and even older. The interest areas are also diverse, running the gamut from folk, pop and rock to musical theater, jazz, R&B, dance, rap and classical. Skill levels within the group range from relative newcomers to established veterans that have had cuts and/or songs published. By virtue of group consensus, there are no eligibility requirements other than a serious desire to pursue one's songwriting ventures, and availability and interest in volunteering for the various activities required to run the organization. The purpose of the BSW is to establish a community of songwriters and composers within the greater Boston area, so that its members may better help each other to make further gains in their respective musical careers." Offers performance opportunities, instruction, newsletter, workshops and bi-weekly critique sessions. Applications accepted year-round. Membership: $35/year; newsletter subscription only: $10/year; guest (nonmember) fees: free, limited to two meetings.

BROADCAST MUSIC, INC. (BMI)

320 W. 57th St., New York NY 10019. (212)586-2000. E-mail: newyork@bmi.com. Website: www.bmi.com. **Los Angeles:** 8730 Sunset Blvd., Los Angeles CA 90069. (310)659-9109. E-mail: losangeles@bmi.com. **Nashville:** 10 Music Square East, Nashville TN 37203. (615)401-2000. E-mail: nashville@bmi.com. **Miami:** 1691 Michigan Av., Miami FL 33139. (305)673-5148. E-mail: miami@bmi.com. **Atlanta:** Tower Place 100, 3340 Peachtree Rd., NE, Suite 570, Atlanta GA 30326. (404)261-5151. E-mail: atlanta@bmi.com. **Puerto Rico:** 1250 Av. Ponce de Leon, San Jose Building Santurce PR 00907. (787)754-6490. **United Kingdom:** 84 Harley House, Marylebone Rd., London NW1 5HN United Kingdom. 011-44-207-486-2036. E-mail: london@bmi.com. President and CEO: Del R. Bryant. Senior Vice Presidents, New York: Phillip Graham, Writer/Publisher Relations; Alison Smith, Performing Rights. Vice Presidents:

New York: Charlie Feldman; Los Angeles: Barbara Cane and Doreen Ringer Ross; Nashville: Paul Corbin; Miami: Diane J. Almodovar; Atlanta: Catherine Brewton. Senior Executive, London: Brandon Bakshi. BMI is a performing rights organization representing approximately 300,000 songwriters, composers and music publishers in all genres of music, including pop, rock, country, R&B, rap, jazz, Latin, gospel and contemporary classical. "Applicants must have written a musical composition, alone or in collaboration with other writers, which is commercially published, recorded or otherwise likely to be performed." Purpose: BMI acts on behalf of its songwriters, composers and music publishers by insuring payment for performance of their works through the collection of licensing fees from radio stations, Internet outlets, broadcast and cable TV stations, hotels, nightclubs, aerobics centers and other users of music. This income is distributed to the writers and publishers in the form of royalty payments, based on how the music is used. BMI also undertakes intensive lobbying efforts in Washington D.C. on behalf of its affiliates, seeking to protect their performing rights through the enactment of new legislation and enforcement of current copyright law. In addition, BMI helps aspiring songwriters develop their skills through various workshops, seminars and competitions it sponsors throughout the country. Applications accepted year-round. There is no membership fee for songwriters; a one-time fee of $150 is required to affiliate an individually-owned publishing company; $250 for partnerships, corporations and limited-liability companies. "Visit our Web site for specific contacts, e-mail addresses and additional membership information."

CALIFORNIA LAWYERS FOR THE ARTS

Fort Mason Center, Building C, Room 255, San Francisco CA 94123. (415)775-7200. Fax: (415)775-1143. E-mail: cla@calawyersforthearts.org. Website: www.calawyersforthearts.org. **Southern California:** 1641 18th St., Santa Monica CA 90404. (310)998-5590. Fax: (310)998-5594. E-mail: usercla@aol.com. **Sacramento Office:** 1127 11th St., Suite 214, Sacramento CA 95814. (916)442-6210. Fax: (916)442-6281. E-mail: clasacto@aol.com. **Oakland Office:** 1212 Broadway St., Suite 834, Oakland CA 94612. (510)444-6351. Fax: (510)444-6352. E-mail: oakcla@there.net. **Contact:** Alma Robinson, executive director. Systems Coordinator: Josie Porter. Estab. 1974. "For artists of all disciplines, skill levels, and ages, supporting individuals and organizations, and arts organizations. Artists of all disciplines are welcome, whether professionals or amateurs. We also welcome groups and individuals who support the arts. We work most closely with the California arts community. Our mission is to establish a bridge between the legal and arts communities so that artists and art groups may handle their creative activities with greater business and legal competence; the legal profession will be more aware of issues affecting the arts community; and the law will become more responsive to the arts community." Offers newsletter, lectures, library, workshops, mediation service, attorney referral service, housing referrals, publications and advocacy. Membership fee: $20 for senior citizens and full-time students; $25 for working artists; $40 for general individual; $60 for panel attorney; $100 to $1,000 for patrons. Organizations: $50 for small organizations (budget under $100,000); $90 for large organizations (budget of $100,000 or more); $100 to $1,000 for corporate sponsors.

◩ CANADA COUNCIL FOR THE ARTS/CONSEIL DES ARTS DU CANADA

350 Albert St., P.O. Box 1047, Ottawa ON K1P 5V8 Canada. (613)566-4414, ext. 5060. E-mail:

info@canadacouncil.ca. Website: www.canadacouncil.ca. **Contact:** Christian Mondor, information officer. Estab. 1957. An independent agency that fosters and promotes the arts in Canada by providing grants and services to professional artists including songwriters and musicians. "Individual artists must be Canadian citizens or permanent residents of Canada, and must have completed basic training and/or have the recognition as professionals within their fields. The Canada Council offers grants to professional musicians to pursue their individual artistic development and creation. There are specific deadline dates for the various programs of assistance. Visit our Web site at www.canadacouncil.ca/music for more details."

⊠ CANADIAN ACADEMY OF RECORDING ARTS & SCIENCES (CARAS)

345 Adelaide Street West, 2nd Floor, Toronto ON M5V 1R5 Canada. (416)485-3135. Fax: (416)485-4978. E-mail: info@junoawards.ca. Website: www.junoawards.ca. **Contact:** Meghan McCabe, office coordinator. President: Melanie Berry. Manager, Awards and Events: Leisa Peacock. Manager, Marketing and Communications: Tammy Kitchener. Membership is open to all employees (including support staff) in broadcasting and record companies, as well as producers, personal managers, recording artists, recording engineers, arrangers, composers, music publishers, album designers, promoters, talent and booking agents, record retailers, rack jobbers, distributors, recording studios and other music industry related professions (on approval). Applicants must be affiliated with the Canadian recording industry. Offers newsletter, nomination and voting privileges for Juno Awards and discount tickets to Juno Awards show. "CARAS strives to foster the development of the Canadian music and recording industries and to contribute toward higher artistic standards." Applications accepted year-round. Membership fee is $50/year (Canadian) + GST = $53.00. Applications accepted from individuals only, not from companies or organizations.

⊠ ☑ CANADIAN COUNTRY MUSIC ASSOCIATION

30-B Commercial Road, Toronto ON M4G 1Z4 Canada. (416)947-1331. Fax: (416)947-5924. E-mail: country@ccma.org. Website: www.ccma.org. **Contact:** Brandi Mills, communications & marketing. Estab. 1976. Members are artists, songwriters, musicians, producers, radio station personnel, managers, booking agents and others. Offers newsletter, workshops, performance opportunities and the CCMA awards every September. "Through our newsletters and conventions we offer a means of meeting and associating with artists and others in the industry. The CCMA is a federally chartered, nonprofit organization, dedicated to the promotion and development of Canadian country music throughout Canada and the world and to providing a unity of purpose for the Canadian country music industry." See website for membership information and benefits.

⊠ CANADIAN MUSICAL REPRODUCTION RIGHTS AGENCY LTD.

56 Wellesley St. W, #320, Toronto ON M5S 2S3 Canada. (416)926-1966. Fax: (416)926-7521. E-mail: inquiries@cmrra.ca. Website: www.cmrra.ca. **Contact:** Michael Mackie, membership services. Estab. 1975. Members are music copyright owners, music publishers, sub-publishers and administrators. Representation by CMRRA is open to any person, firm or corporation anywhere in the world, which owns and/or administers one or more copyrighted musical works. CMRRA is a music licensing agency--Canada's largest--which represents music copyright owners, publishers and administrators for the purpose of mechanical and synchronization

licensing in Canada. Offers mechanical and synchronization licensing. Applications accepted year-round.

CENTRAL CAROLINA SONGWRITERS ASSOCIATION (CCSA)

131 Henry Baker Road, Zebulon, NC 27597. (919) 269-6240. E-mail: ccsa_raleigh@yahoo. com. Website: www.ccsa-raleigh.com. **Contact:** Tony Dickens, president, or vice president Diana Dimsdale. Established in 1997, CCSA welcomes songwriters of all experience levels from beginner to professional within the local RDU/Triad/Eastern area of North Carolina to join our group. Our members' musical background varies, covering a wide array of musical genres. CCSA meets monthly in Raleigh, NC. We are unable to accept applications from incarcerated persons or those who do not reside in the local area as our group's primary focus is on songwriters who are able to attend the monthly meetings-to ensure members get the best value for their yearly dues. CCSA strives to provide each songwriter and musician a resourceful organization where members grow musically by networking and sharing with one another. Offers annual songwriters forum, periodic workshops, critiques at the monthly meetings, opportunities to perform and network with fellow members. Applications are accepted year round. Dues are $24/year (pro-rated for new members at $2/month by date of application) with annual renewal each January.

THE COLLEGE MUSIC SOCIETY

312 E. Pine St., Missoula MT 59802. (406)721-9616. Fax: (406)721-9419. E-mail: cms@music. org. Website: www.music.org. Estab. 1959. Serves college, university and conservatory professors, as well as independent musicians. "The College Music Society is a consortium of college, conservatory, university and independent musicians and scholars interested in all disciplines of music. Its mission is to promote music teaching and learning, musical creativity and expression, research and dialogue, and diversity and interdisciplinary interaction." Offers journal, newsletter, lectures, workshops, performance opportunities, job listing service, databases of organizations and institutions, music faculty and mailing lists. Applications accepted year-round. Membership fee: $65 (regular dues), $35 (student dues), $35 (retiree dues).

CONNECTICUT SONGWRITERS ASSOCIATION

P.O. Box 511, Mystic CT 06355. E-mail: info@ctsongs.com. Website: www.ctsongs.com. **Contact:** Bill Pere, Executive Director. Associate Director: Kay Pere. "We are an educational, nonprofit organization dedicated to improving the art and craft of original music. Founded in 1979, CSA has had almost 2,000 active members and has become one of the best known and respected songwriters' associations in the country. Membership in the CSA admits you to 12-18 seminars/workshops/song critique sessions per year at multiple locations in Connecticut. Out-of-state members may mail in songs for free critiques at our meetings. Noted professionals deal with all aspects of the craft and business of music including lyric writing, music theory, music technology, arrangement and production, legal and business aspects, performance techniques, song analysis and recording techniques. CSA offers song screening sessions for members and songs that pass are then eligible for inclusion on the CSA sampler anthology through various retail and online outlets and are brought to national music conferences. CSA is well connected in both the independent music scene and the traditional music industry.

CSA also offers showcases and concerts which are open to the public and designed to give artists a venue for performing their original material for an attentive, listening audience. CSA benefits help local soup kitchens, group homes, hospice, world hunger, libraries, nature centers, community centers and more. CSA shows encompass ballads to bluegrass and Bach to rock. Our monthly newsletter, Connecticut Songsmith, offers free classified advertising for members, and has been edited and published by Bill Pere since 1980. Annual dues: $40; senior citizen and full time students $30; organizations $80. Memberships are tax-deductible as business expenses or as charitable contributions to the extent allowed by law."

DALLAS SONGWRITERS ASSOCIATION

Sammons Center for the Arts, 3630 Harry Hines, Box 20, Dallas TX 75219. (214)750-0916. E-mail: info@dallassongwriters.org. Website: www.dallassongwriters.org. **Contact:** Paul Penrod, membership director. President: Steve Sullivan. Founding President Emeritis: Barbara McMillen. Estab. 1986. Serves songwriters and lyricists of Dallas/Ft. Worth metroplex. Members are adults ages 18-65, Dallas/Ft. Worth area songwriters/lyricists who are or aspire to be professionals. Purpose is to provide songwriters an opportunity to meet other songwriters, share information, find co-writers and support each other through group discussions at monthly meetings; to provide songwriters an opportunity to have their songs heard and critiqued by peers and professionals by playing cassettes and providing an open mike at monthly meetings and open mics, showcases, and festival stages, and by offering contests judged by publishers; to provide songwriters opportunities to meet other music business professionals by inviting guest speakers to monthly meetings and workshops; and to provide songwriters opportunities to learn more about the craft of songwriting and the business of music by presenting mini-workshops at each monthly meeting. "We offer a chance for the songwriter to learn from peers and industry professionals and an opportunity to belong to a supportive group environment to encourage the individual to continue his/her songwriting endeavors." Offers competitions (including the Annual Song Contest with over $5,000 in prizes, and the Quarterly Lyric Contest), field trips, instruction, lectures, newsletter, performance opportunities, social outings, workshops and seminars. "Our members are eligible for discounts at several local music stores and seminars." Applications accepted year-round. Membership fee: $50. "When inquiring by phone, please leave complete mailing address and phone number or e-mail address where you can be reached day and night."

THE DRAMATISTS GUILD OF AMERICA, INC.

(formerly The Dramatists Guild, Inc.), 1501 Broadway, Suite 701, New York NY 10036. (212)398-9366. Fax: (212)944-0420. E-mail: info@dramatistsguild.com. Website: www.dramatistsguild.com. **Contact:** Roland Tec, director of membership. "For over three-quarters of a century, The Dramatists Guild has been the professional association of playwrights, composers and lyricists, with more than 6,000 members across the country. All theater writers, whether produced or not, are eligible for Associate membership ($95/year); those who are engaged in a drama-related field but are not a playwright are eligible for Subscribing membership ($25/year); students enrolled in writing degree programs at colleges or universities are eligible for Student membership ($35/year); writers who have been produced on Broadway, Off-Broadway or on the main stage of a LORT theater are eligible for Active membership ($150/year). The Guild offers its members the following activities and services: use of the Guild's contracts (including the Approved Production Contract for Broadway, the Off-Broadway contract, the LORT contract, the collaboration agreements for both musicals and drama, the 99 Seat Theatre Plan contract, the Small Theatre contract, commissioning agreements, and the Underlying Rights Agreements contract; advice on all theatrical contracts including Broadway, Off-Broadway, regional, showcase, Equity-waiver, dinner theater and collaboration contracts); a nationwide toll-free number for all members with business or contract questions or problems; advice and information on a wide spectrum of issues affecting writers; free and/or discounted ticket service; symposia led by experienced professionals in major cities nationwide; access to health insurance programs; and a spacious meeting room which can accommodate up to 50 people for readings and auditions on a rental basis. The Guild's publications are: The Dramatist, a bimonthly journal containing articles on all aspects of the theater (which includes The Dramatists Guild Newsletter, with announcements of all Guild activities and current information of interest to dramatists); and an annual resource directory with up-to-date information on agents, publishers, grants, producers, playwriting contests, conferences and workshops, and an interactive Web site that brings our community of writers together to exchange ideas and share information.

THE FIELD

161 Sixth Ave., 14th Floor, New York NY 10013. (212)691-6969. Fax: (212)255-2053. E-mail: pele@thefield.org. Website: www.thefield.org. Contact: any staff member. Estab. 1986. "The Field gives independent performing artists the tools to develop and sustain their creative and professional lives, while allowing the public to have immediate, direct access to a remarkable range of contemporary artwork. The organization was started by eight emerging artists who shared common roots in contemporary dance and theater. Meeting regularly, these artists created a structure to help each other improve their artwork, and counter the isolation that often comes with the territory of an artistic career. The Field offers a comprehensive series of educational programs, resources, and services. Artists can participate in a broad array of programs and services including art development workshops, performance opportunities, career management training and development, fundraising consultations, fiscal sponsorship, a Resource Center, and artist residencies. The Field's goal is to help artists develop their best artwork by deepening the artistic process and finding effective ways to bring that art into the marketplace. Most Field programs cost between $35 and $150, and tickets to our performance events are $10. In addition, since 1992, The Field has coordinated a network of satellite sites in Atlanta, Chicago, Houston, Miami, Philadelphia, Phoenix, Rochester (NY), Salt Lake City, San Francisco, Seattle, Tucson, Richmond (VA), and Washington. The Field is the only organization in New York that provides comprehensive programming for independent performing artists on a completely non-exclusive basis. Programs are open to artists from all disciplines, aesthetic viewpoints, and levels of development." Offers workshops and performance opportunities on a seasonal basis. Applications accepted year-round. Membership fee: $100/year.

Tips "The Field's resource center is an artist-focused library/computer lab where artists can access office equipment and work in a quiet and supportive environment. Located at The Field's office, the Resource Center offers fund-raising resources and hands-on assistance, including databases such as the Foundation Directory Online, computer workstations, and a library of books, journals, and information directories. One-on-one assistance and consultations are also available to guide users through grant writing and other fund-raising endeavors. GoTour (www.gotour.org) is a free Web site offering independent artists the resources they need to take their show on the road. Visitors log on for free and access a national arts network where they can search for venues, network with artists nationwide, find media contacts, read advice from other artists and arts professionals, add information on their local arts community, post tour anecdotes, and list concert information and classified ads."

FORT WORTH SONGWRITERS ASSOCIATION

P.O. Box 162443, Fort Worth TX 76161. (817)654-5400. E-mail: info@fwsa.com. Website: www. fwsa.com. President: Judy Boots. Vice-Presidents: Rick Tate and John Terry. Secretary: Lynda Timmons Elvington. Treasurer: Rick Tate. Estab. 1992. Members are ages 18-83, beginners up to and including published writers. Interests cover gospel, country, western swing, rock, pop, bluegrass and blues. Purpose is to allow songwriters to become more proficient at songwriting; to provide an opportunity for their efforts to be performed before a live audience; to provide songwriters an opportunity to meet co-writers. "We provide our members free critiques of their efforts. We provide a monthly newsletter outlining current happenings in the business of songwriting. We offer competitions and mini workshops with guest speakers from the music industry. We promote a weekly open 'mic' for singers of original material, and hold invitational songwriter showcase events a various times throughout the year. Each year, we hold a Christmas Song Contest, judged by independent music industry professionals. We also offer free web pages for members or links to member Web sites." Applications accepted year-round. Membership fee: $35.

GOSPEL MUSIC ASSOCIATION

1205 Division St., Nashville TN 37203. (615)242-0303. E-mail: megan@gospelmusic.org. Website: www.gospelmusic.org. **Contact:** Megan Ledford, member and customer service representative. Estab. 1964. Serves songwriters, musicians and anyone directly involved in or who supports gospel music. Professional members include advertising agencies, musicians, songwriters, agents/managers, composers, retailers, music publishers, print and broadcast media, and other members of the recording industry. Associate members include supporters of gospel music and those whose involvement in the industry does not provide them with income. The primary purpose of the GMA is to expose, promote, and celebrate the Gospel through music. A GMA membership offers newsletters, performance experiences and workshops, as well as networking opportunities. Applications accepted year-round. Membership fee: $95/year (professional); $60/year (associate); and $25/year (college student).

THE GUILD OF INTERNATIONAL SONGWRITERS & COMPOSERS

Sovereign House, 12 Trewartha Road, Praa Sands, Penzance, Cornwall TR20 9ST England. (01736)762826. Fax: (01736)763328. email: songmag@aol.com. Website: www.songwriters-guild.com and www.myspace.com/guildofsongwriters. General Secretary: Carole Jones. The Guild of International Songwriters & Composers is an international music industry organisation based in England in the United Kingdom. Guild members are songwriters, composers, lyricists, poets, performing songwriters, musicians, music publishers, studio owners, managers, independent record companies, music industry personnel, etc., from many countries throughout the world. The Guild of International Songwriters & Composers has been publishing Songwriting and Composing Magazine since 1986, which is issued free to all Guild members throughout their membership. The Guild of International Songwriters and Composers offers advice, guidance, assistance, copyright protection service, information, encouragement, contact information, Intellectual property/copyright protection of members works through the Guild's Copyright Registration Centre along with other free services and more to Guild members with regard to helping members achieve their aims, ambitions, progression and advancement in respect to the many different aspects of the music industry. Information, advice and services available to Guild members throughout their membership includes assistance, advice and help on many matters and issues relating to the music industry in general. Annual membership fees: are £50. For further information please visit the Guild's Web site or MySpace page.

HAWAI'I SONGWRITERS ASSOCIATION

P.O. Box 231325, Las Vegas, NV, 89105. (702)897-9066. E-mail: stanrubens@aol.com. Website: www.stanrubens.com. **Contact:** Stan Rubens, secretary. Estab. 1972. "We have two classes of membership: Professional (must have had at least one song commercially published and for sale to general public) and Regular (any one who wants to join and share in our activities). Both classes can vote equally, but only Professional members can hold office. Must be 18 years old to join. Our members include musicians, entertainers and record producers. Membership is world-wide and open to all varieties of music, not just ethnic Hawaiian. President, Stan Rubens, has published 4 albums." Offers competitions, instruction, monthly newsletter, lectures, workshops, performance opportunities and evaluation services. Applications accepted year-round. Membership fee: $24. Stan Rubens teaches songwriting either privately or in group or school sessions.

INTERNATIONAL BLUEGRASS MUSIC ASSOCIATION (IBMA)

2 Music Circle South, Suite 100, Nashville TN 37203. 1(888)GET-IBMA. Fax: (615)256-0450. E-mail: info@ibma.org. Website: www.ibma.org. Member Services: Jill Snider. Estab. 1985. Serves songwriters, musicians and professionals in bluegrass music. "IBMA is a trade association composed of people and organizations involved professionally and semi-professionally in the bluegrass music industry, including performers, agents, songwriters, music publishers, promoters, print and broadcast media, local associations, recording manufacturers and distributors. Voting members must be currently or formerly involved in the bluegrass industry as full or part-time professionals. A songwriter attempting to become professionally involved in our field would be eligible. Our mission statement reads: "IBMA: Working together for high standards of professionalism, a greater appreciation for our music, and the success of the world-wide bluegrass music community." IBMA publishes a bimonthly International Bluegrass, holds an annual trade show/convention with a songwriters showcase in the fall, represents our field outside the bluegrass music community, and compiles and disseminates databases of bluegrass related resources and organizations. Market research on the bluegrass consumer is available and we offer Bluegrass in the Schools information and matching grants. The primary value in this organization for a songwriter is having current information about the bluegrass music field and contacts with other songwriters, publishers, musicians and record companies." Offers workshops, liability insurance, rental car discounts, consultation and databases of record companies, radio stations, press, organizations and gigs. Applications accepted year-round. Membership fee: for a non-voting patron $40/year; for an

individual voting professional $70/year; for an organizational voting professional $200/year.

🌐 INTERNATIONAL SONGWRITERS ASSOCIATION LTD.

P.O. Box 46, Limerick City, Ireland. E-mail: jliddane@songwriter.iol.ie. Website: www. songwriter.co.uk. Contact: Anna M. Sinden, membership department. Serves songwriters and music publishers. "The ISA headquarters is in Limerick City, Ireland, and from there it provides its members with assessment services, copyright services, legal and other advisory services and an investigations service, plus a magazine for one yearly fee. Our members are songwriters in more than 50 countries worldwide, of all ages. There are no qualifications, but applicants under 18 are not accepted. We provide information and assistance to professional or semi-professional songwriters. Our publication, Songwriter, which was founded in 1967, features detailed exclusive interviews with songwriters and music publishers, as well as directory information of value to writers." Offers competitions, instruction, library, newsletter and a weekly e-mail newsletter Songwriter Newswire. Applications accepted year-round. Membership fee for European writers is £19.95; for non-European writers, US $30.

JUST PLAIN FOLKS MUSIC ORGANIZATION

5327 Kit Dr., Indianapolis IN 46237. (317)513-6557. E-mail: info@jpfolks.com. Website: www. jpfolks.com. **Contact:** Brian Austin Whitney(brian@jpfolks.com), founder or Linda Berger (linda@jpfolks.com), projects director. Estab. 1998. "Just Plain Folks is among the world's largest Music Organizations. Our members cover nearly every musical style and professional field, from songwriters, artists, publishers, producers, record labels, entertainment attorneys, publicists and PR experts, performing rights organization staffers, live and recording engineers, educators, music students, musical instrument manufacturers, TV, Radio and Print Media and almost every major Internet Music entity. Representing all 50 US States and over 160 countries worldwide, we have members of all ages, musical styles and levels of success, including winners and nominees of every major music industry award, as well as those just starting out. A complete demographics listing of our group is available on our website. Whether you are a #1 hit songwriter or artist, or the newest kid on the block, you are welcome to join. Membership does require an active e-mail account." The purpose of this organization is "to share wisdom, ideas and experiences with others who have been there, and to help educate those who have yet to make the journey. Just Plain Folks provides its members with a friendly networking and support community that uses the power of the Internet and combines it with good old-fashioned human interaction. We help promote our members ready for success and educate those still learning." Offers special programs to members, including:

- *Just Plain Notes Newsletter:* Members receive our frequent e-mail newsletters full of expert info on how to succeed in the music business, profiles of members successes and advice, opportunities to develop your career and tons of first-person networking contacts to help you along the way. (Note: we send this out 2-3 times/month via e-mail only.)

Tips "Our motto is 'We're All In This Together!'"

LOS ANGELES MUSIC NETWORK

P.O. Box 2446, Toluca Lake CA 91610-2446. (818)769-6095. E-mail: info@lamn.com. Website: www.lamn.com. **Contact:** Tess Taylor, president. Estab. 1988. "Connections. Performance opportunities. Facts. Career advancement. All that is available with your membership in the

Los Angeles Music Network (LAMN). Our emphasis is on sharing knowledge and information, giving you access to top professionals and promoting career development. LAMN is an association of music industry professionals, i.e., artists, singers, songwriters, and people who work in various aspects of the music industry with an emphasis on the creative. Members are ambitious and interested in advancing their careers. LAMN promotes career advancement, communication and education among artists and creatives. LAMN sponsors industry events and educational panels held at venues in the Los Angeles area and now in other major music hubs around the country (New York, Las Vegas, Phoenix, and San Francisco). LAMN Jams are popular among our members. Experience LAMN Jams in L.A. or N.Y. by performing your original music in front of industry experts who can advance your career by getting your music in the hands of hard-to-reach music supervisors. the 'anti-American Idol' singer-songwriter contest gives artists an opportunity to perform in front of industry experts and receive instant feedback to their music, lyrics and performance. As a result of the exposure, Tim Fagan won the John Mayer Songwriting Contest and was invited to tour with the Goo Goo Dolls, Lifehouse, and recently, the platinum recording artist Colbie Caillat. This paired him with multi-platinum songwriter and recording artist John Mayer, with whom Fagan co-wrote 'Deeper.' Publisher Robert Walls has pitched music from LAMN Jam performers to hit TV shows like The OC and Gray's Anatomy, and the upcoming flick The Devil Wears Prada. Other performers have received offers including publishing and production deals and studio gigs. Offers performance opportunities, instruction, newsletter, lectures, seminars, music industry job listings, career counseling, resume publishing, mentor network, and many professional networking opportunities. See our Web site for current job listings and a calendar of upcoming events. Applications accepted year-round. Annual membership fee is $115.

◘ MANITOBA MUSIC

1-376 Donald St., Winnipeg MB R3B 2J2 Canada. (204)942-8650. Fax: (204)942-6083. E-mail: info@manitobamusic.com. Website: www.manitobamusic.com. **Contact:** Sara Stasiuk, Executive Director. Estab. 1987. Organization consists of "songwriters, producers, agents, musicians, managers, retailers, publicists, radio, talent buyers, media, record labels, etc. (no age limit, no skill level minimum). Must have interest in the future of Manitoba's music industry." The main purpose of Manitoba Music is to foster growth in all areas of the Manitoba music industry primarily through education, promotion and lobbying. Offers newsletter, extensive website, directory of Manitoba's music industry, workshops and performance opportunities. Manitoba Music is also involved with the Western Canadian Music Awards festival, conference and awards show. Applications accepted year-round. Membership fee: $50 (Canadian funds).

MEET THE COMPOSER

90 John St., Suite 312, New York NY 10038. (212)645-6949. Fax: (212)645-9669. E-mail: mtc@meetthecomposer.org. Website: www.meetthecomposer.org. Estab. 1974. "Meet The Composer serves composers working in all styles of music, at every career stage, through a variety of grant programs and information resources. A nonprofit organization, Meet The Composer raises money from foundations, corporations, individual patrons and government sources and designs programs that support all genres of music--from folk, ethnic, jazz, electronic, symphonic, and chamber to choral, music theater, opera and dance. Meet The

Composer awards grants for composer fees to non-profit organizations that perform, present, or commission original works. This is not a membership organization; all composers are eligible for support. Meet The Composer was founded in 1974 to increase artistic and financial opportunities for composers by fostering the creation, performance, dissemination, and appreciation of their music." Offers grant programs and information services. Deadlines vary for each grant program.

MEMPHIS SONGWRITERS' ASSOCIATION

4728 Spottswood, #191, Memphis TN 38117-4815. (901)577-0906. E-mail: admin@ memphissongwriters.org. Website: www.memphissongwriters.org and www.myspace. com/memphissongwriters. **Contact:** Phillip Beasley, MSA president. Estab. 1973. "MSA is a nonprofit songwriters organization serving songwriters nationally. Our mission is to dedicate our services to promote, advance, and help songwriters in the composition of music, lyrics and songs; to work for better conditions in our profession; and to secure and protect the rights of MSA songwriters. The Memphis Songwriters Association are organizational members of the Folk Alliance (FA.org). We also supply copyright forms. We offer critique sessions for writers at our monthly meetings. We also have monthly open mic songwriters night to encourage creativity, networking and co-writing. We host an annual songwriter's seminar and an annual songwriter's showcase, as well as a bi-monthly guest speaker series, which provide education, competition and entertainment for the songwriter. In addition, our members receive a bimonthly newsletter to keep them informed of MSA activities, demo services and opportunities in the songwriting field." Annual fee: $50; Student/Senior: $35.

MINNESOTA ASSOCIATION OF SONGWRITERS

P.O. Box 4262, Saint Paul MN 55104. E-mail: info@mnsongwriters.org. Website: www. mnsongwriters.org. "Includes a wide variety of members, ranging in age from 18 to 80; type of music is very diverse, ranging from alternative rock to contemporary Christian; skill levels range from beginning songwriters to writers with recorded and published material. Main requirement is an interest in songwriting. Although most members come from the Minneapolis-St. Paul area, others come in from surrounding cities, nearby Wisconsin, and other parts of the country. Some members are full-time musicians, but most represent a wide variety of occupations. MAS is a nonprofit community of songwriters which informs, educates, inspires and assists its members in the art and business of songwriting." Offers instruction, newsletter, lectures, workshops, performance opportunities and evaluation services. Applications accepted year-round. Membership fee: Individual: $25; Business: $65. **Tips** "Members are kept current on resources and opportunities. Original works are played at meetings and are critiqued by involved members. Through this process, writers hone their skills and gain experience and confidence in submitting their works to others."

⚡ MUSIC BC__PACIFIC MUSIC INDUSTRY ASSOCIATION

#530-425 Carrall St., Vancouver BC V6B 6E3 Canada. (604)873-1914. 1-888-866-8570 (Toll Free in BC). Fax: (604)873-9686. E-mail: info@musicbc.org. Website: www.musicbc.org. Estab. 1990. Music BC(formerly PMIA) is a non-profit society that supports and promotes the spirit, development, and growth of the BC music community provincially, nationally, and internationally. Music BC provides education, resources, advocacy, opportunities for funding, and a forum for communication. Visit Web site for membership benefits.

MUSICIANS CONTACT

P.O. Box 788, Woodland Hills CA 91365. (818)888-7879. E-mail: information@musicianscontact. com. Website: www.musicianscontact.com. **Contact:** Sterling Howard, president. Estab. 1969. "The primary source of paying jobs for musicians and vocalists nationwide. Job opportunities are posted daily on the Internet. Also offers exposure to the music industry for solo artists and complete acts seeking representation."

NASHVILLE SONGWRITERS ASSOCIATION INTERNATIONAL (NSAI)

1710 Roy Acuff Place, Nashville TN 37203. (615)256-3354 or (800)321-6008. Fax: (615)256-0034. E-mail: nsai@nashvillesongwriters.com. Website: www.nashvillesongwriters.com. Executive Director: Barton Herbison. Purpose: a not-for-profit service organization for both aspiring and professional songwriters in all fields of music. Membership: Spans the United States and several foreign countries. Songwriters may apply in one of four annual categories: Active ($150 U.S currency for songwriters are actively working to improve in the craft of writing and/or actively pursing a career within the songwriting industry); Student ($100 U.S for full-time college, high school, or middle school students); Professional ($100 U.S. currency for songwriters who are staff writers for a publishing company or earn 51 percent of their annual income from songwriting, whether from advances, royalties, or performances, or are generally regarded as a professional songwriter within the music industry); Lifetime (please contact NSAI for details). Membership benefits: music industry information and advice, song evaluations, eNews, access to industry professionals through weekly Nashville workshops and several annual events, regional workshops, use of office facilities, discounts on books and discounts on NSAI's three annual events. There are also "branch" workshops of NSAI. Workshops must meet certain standards and are accountable to NSAI. Interested coordinators may apply to NSAI.

- Also see the listing for NSAI Songwriters Symposium (formerly NSAI Spring Symposium) in the Workshops section of this book.

THE NATIONAL ASSOCIATION OF COMPOSERS/USA (NACUSA)

P.O. Box 49256, Barrington Station, Los Angeles CA 90049. E-mail: nacusa@music-usa.org. Website: www.music-usa.org/nacusa. **Contact:** Daniel Kessner, president. Estab. 1932. Serves songwriters, musicians and classical composers. "We are of most value to the concert hall composer. Members are serious music composers of all ages and from all parts of the country, who have a real interest in composing, performing, and listening to modern concert hall music. The main purpose of our organization is to perform, publish, broadcast and write news about composers of serious concert hall music--mostly chamber and solo pieces. Composers may achieve national notice of their work through our newsletter and concerts, and the fairly rare feeling of supporting a non-commercial music enterprise dedicated to raising the musical and social position of the serious composer." Offers competitions, lectures, performance opportunities, library and newsletter. Applications accepted year-round. Membership fee: National (regular): $25; National (students/seniors): $15.

- Also see the listing for NACUSA Young Composers' Competition in the Contests section of this book.

Tips "99% of the money earned in music is earned, or so it seems, by popular songwriters who might feel they owe the art of music something, and this is one way they might help support that art. It's a chance to foster fraternal solidarity with their less prosperous, but wonderfully interesting classical colleagues at a time when the very existence of serious art seems to be questioned by the general populace."

OKLAHOMA SONGWRITERS ASSOCIATION

P.O. Box 6298, Moore OK 73153. Website: www.oksongwriters.com. **Contact:** Tom Marshall. Estab. 1983. Serves songwriters, musicians, professional writers and amateur writers. "A nonprofit, all-volunteer organization providing educational and networking opportunities for songwriters, lyricists, composers and performing musicians. Co-sponsor of the Woody Guthrie Songwriting contest and open mics in conjunction with the Woody Guthrie Folk Festival. New programs in the works, watch the website for updates.

OPERA AMERICA

330 Seventh Ave., 16th Floor, New York NY 10001. (212)796-8620. Fax: (212)796-8631. E-mail: frontdesk@operaamerica.org. Website: www.operaamerica.org. **Contact:** Rebecca Ackerman, membership manager. Estab. 1970. Members are composers, librettists, musicians, singers, and opera/music theater producers. Offers conferences, workshops, and seminars for artists. Publishes online database of opera/music theater companies in the US and Canada, database of opportunities for performing and creative artists, online directory of opera and musical performances world-wide and US, and an online directory of new works created and being developed by current-day composers and librettists, to encourage the performance of new works. Applications accepted year-round. Publishes quarterly magazine and a variety of electronic newsletters. Membership fee is on a sliding scale by membership level.

OUTMUSIC

P.O. Box 376, Old Chelsea Station, New York NY 10113-0376. (914)595-6952. E-mail: feedback@outmusic.com. Website: www.outmusic.com. **Contact:** Ed Mannix, communications director. Estab. 1990. "OUTMUSIC is comprised of gay men, lesbians, bisexuals and transgenders. They represent all different musical styles from rock to classical. Many are writers of original material. We are open to all levels of accomplishment--professional, amateur, and interested industry people. The only requirement for membership is an interest in the growth and visibility of music and lyrics created by the LGBT community. We supply our members with support and networking opportunities. In addition, we help to encourage artists to bring their work 'OUT' into the world." Offers newsletter, lectures, workshops, performance opportunities, networking, industry leads and monthly open mics. Sponsors Outmusic Awards. Applications accepted year-round. For membership information go to www.outmusic.com.
Tips "OUTMUSIC has spawned *The Gay Music Guide*, The Gay and Lesbian American Music Awards (GLAMA), several compilation albums and many independent recording projects."

PACIFIC NORTHWEST SONGWRITERS ASSOCIATION

P.O. Box 98564, Seattle WA 98198. (206)824-1568. E-mail: pnsapals@hotmail.com. "PNSA is a nonprofit organization, serving the songwriters of the Puget Sound area since 1977. Members have had songs recorded by national artists on singles, albums, videos and network television specials. Several have released their own albums and the group has done an album together. For only $45 per year, PNSA offers monthly workshops, a quarterly newsletter and direct contact with national artists, publishers, producers and record companies. New members are welcome and good times are guaranteed. And remember, the world always needs another great song!"

PITTSBURGH SONGWRITERS ASSOCIATION

222 Pennsylvania Ave., California PA 15419. E-mail: vstragand@aol.com, jferreri@ zoominternet.net. Website: (under construction). **Contact:** Van Stragand (412)418-8647 or Joe Ferreri (724)640-0671. Estab. 1983. "We are a non-profit organization dedicated to helping its members develop and market their songs. Writers of any age and experience level welcome. Current members are from all age brackets. All musical styles and interests are welcome. Our organization wants to serve as a source of quality material for publishers and other industry professionals. We assist members in developing their songs and their professional approach. We provide meetings, showcases, collaboration opportunities, instruction, industry guests, library and social outings. Annual dues: $40 with discounts available for students and seniors. We have no initiation fee. Prospective members are invited to attend two free meetings. Interested parties please call contacts above."

PORTLAND SONGWRITERS ASSOCIATION

P.O. Box 42389, Portland OR 97242. E-mail: info@portlandongwriters.org. Website: www. portlandsongwriters.org. Estab. 1991. "The PSA is a nonprofit organization providing education and opportunities that will assist writers in creating and marketing their songs. The PSA offers an annual National Songwriting Contest, monthly workshops, songwriter showcases, special performance venues, quarterly newsletter, mail-in critique service, discounted seminars by music industry pros." Annual dues: $50 (no eligibility requirements).

Tips "Although most of our members are from the Pacific Northwest, we offer services that can assist songwriters anywhere. Our goal is to provide information and contacts to help songwriters grow artistically and gain access to publishing, recording and related music markets. For more information, please call, write or e-mail."

RHODE ISLAND SONGWRITERS' ASSOCIATION (RISA)

P.O. Box 367, Harmony RI 02829. E-mail: risongwriters@yahoo.com. Website: www. risongwriters.com. **Co-Chairs:** John Fuzek and Bill Furney. Estab. 1993. "Membership consists of novice and professional songwriters. RISA provides opportunities to the aspiring writer or performer as well as the established regional artists who have recordings, are published and perform regularly. The only eligibility requirement is an interest in the group and the group's goals. Non-writers are welcome as well." The main purpose is to "encourage, foster and conduct the art and craft of original musical and/or lyrical composition through education, information, collaboration and performance." Offers instruction, newsletter, lectures, workshops, performance opportunities and evaluation services. Applications accepted year-round. Membership fees: $25/year (individual); $40/year (family/band). "The group holds twice monthly critique sessions; twice monthly performer showcases (one performer featured) at a local coffeehouse; songwriter showcases (usually 6-8 performers); weekly open mikes; and a yearly songwriter festival called 'Hear In Rhode Island,' featuring approximately 50

Rhode Island acts, over two days."

SAN DIEGO SONGWRITERS GUILD

3368 Governor Dr., Suite F-326, San Diego CA 92122. E-mail: sdsongwriters@hotmail.com. Website: www.sdsongwriters.org. **Contact:** Joseph Carmel, membership/correspondence. Estab. 1982. "Members range from their early 20s to senior citizens with a variety of skill levels. Several members perform and work full time in music. Many are published and have songs recorded. Some are getting major artist record cuts. Most members are from San Diego county. New writers are encouraged to participate and meet others. All musical styles are represented." The purpose of this organization is to "serve the needs of songwriters and artists, especially helping them in the business and craft of songwriting through industry guest appearances." Offers competitions, newsletter, workshops, performance opportunities, discounts on services offered by fellow members, in-person song pitches and evaluations by publishers, producers and A&R executives. Applications accepted year-round. Membership dues: $55 full; $30 student; $125 corporate sponsorship. Meeting admission for non-members: $20 (may be applied toward membership if joining within 30 days).

Tips "Members benefit most from participation in meetings and concerts. Generally, one major meeting held monthly on a Monday evening, at the Doubletree Hotel, Hazard Center, San Diego. E-mail for meeting details. Can join at meetings."

SESAC INC.

55 Music Square East, Nashville TN 37203. (615)320-0055. Fax: (615) 329-9627. **New York:** 152 W. 57th St., 57th Floor, New York NY 10019. (212)586-3450. Fax: (212)489-5699. Website: www.sesac.com. **Los Angeles:** 501 Santa Monica Blvd., Suite 450, Santa Monica CA 90401. (310)393-9671. Fax: (310)393-6497; **Atlanta**: 981 Joseph E. Lowery Blvd NW, Ste 111, Atlanta, GA 30318. (404)867-1330. Fax: (404)897-1306; **Miami:** 420 Lincoln Rd, Ste 502, Miami FL 33139, (305)534-7500. Fax: (305)534-7578; **London:** 67 Upper Berkeley St., London WIH 7QX United Kingdom. (020)76169284. **Contact:** Trevor Gale, vice president writer/publisher relations. Chief Operating Officer: Pat Collins. "SESAC is a selective organization taking pride in having a repertory based on quality rather than quantity. Serves writers and publishers in all types of music who have their works performed by radio, television, nightclubs, cable TV, etc. Purpose of organization is to collect and distribute performance royalties to all active affiliates. As a SESAC affiliate, the individual may obtain equipment insurance at competitive rates. Music is reviewed upon invitation by the Writer/Publisher Relations dept."

⚄ SOCAN

(SOCIETY OF COMPOSERS, AUTHORS AND MUSIC PUBLISHERS OF CANADA) Head Office: 41 Valleybrook Dr., Toronto ON M3B 2S6 Canada. English Information Center: (866) (307)6226. French Information Center: (866) (800)55-SOCAN. Fax: (416)445-7108. Website: www.socan.ca. CEO: Andre LeBel. Vice President Member Relations & General Manager, West Coast Division: Kent Sturgeon. Vice President Member Services: Jeff King. Director, Member Relations: Lynne Foster. " SOCAN is the Canadian copyright collective for the communication and performance of musical works. We administer these rights on behalf of our members (composers, lyricists, songwriters, and their publishers) and those of affiliated international organizations by licensing this use of their music in Canada. The fees collected are distributed as royalties to our members and to affiliated organizations throughout the world. We also distribute royalties received from those organizations to our members for the use of their music worldwide. SOCAN has offices in Toronto, Montreal, Vancouver, Edmonton, and Dartmouth."

SOCIETY OF COMPOSERS & LYRICISTS

8447 Wilshire Blvd., Suite 401, Beverly Hills CA 90211. (310)281-2812. Fax: (310)284-4861. E-mail: execdir@thescl.com. Website: www.thescl.com. The professional nonprofit trade organization for members actively engaged in writing music/lyrics for films, TV, and/or video games, or are students of film composition or songwriting for film. Primary mission is to advance the interests of the film and TV music community. Offers an award-winning quarterly publication, educational seminars, screenings, special member-only events, and other member benefits. Applications accepted year-round. Membership fee: $135 Full Membership (composers, lyricists, songwriters--film/TV music credits must be submitted); $85 Associate/Student Membership for composers, lyricists, songwriters without credits only; $135 Sponsor/Special Friend Membership (music editors, music supervisors, music attorneys, agents, etc.).

▨ ▢ SODRAC INC.

Tower B, Suite 1010, 1470 Peel Montreal Quebec H3A 1T1 Canada. (514)845-3268. Fax: (514)845-3401. E-mail: sodrac@sodrac.ca. Website: www.sodrac.ca. \lang4105**Contact:** Jean-Francois Marquis, membership department (author, composer and publisher) or François Dell'Aniello, visual arts and crafts department (visual artist and rights owner). Estab. 1985. " SODRAC is a reproduction rights collective society facilitating since 1985 the clearing of rights on musical and artistic works based on the Copyright Board of Canada tariffs or through collective agreements concluded with any users and is responsible for the distribution of royalties to its national and international members. The Society counts over 5,000 Canadian members and represents musical repertoire originating from nearly 100 foreign countries and manages the right of over 25,000 Canadian and foreign visual artists. SODRAC is the only reproduction rights society in Canada where both songwriters and music publishers are represented, equally and directly." Serves those with an interest in songwriting and music publishing no matter what their age or skill level is. " Members must have written or published at least one musical work that has been reproduced on an audio (CD, cassette, or LP) or audio-visual support (TV, DVD, video), or published five musical works that have been recorded and used for commercial purposes. The new member will benefit from a society working to secure his reproduction rights (mechanicals) and broadcast mechanicals." Applications accepted year-round.

SONGWRITERS ASSOCIATION OF WASHINGTON

PMB 106-137, 4200 Wisconsin Ave. NW, Washington DC 20016. (301)654-8434. E-mail: membership@SAW.org. Website: www.saw.org. Estab. 1979. "SAW is a nonprofit organization operated by a volunteer board of directors. It is committed to providing its members opportunities to learn more about the art of songwriting, learn more about the music business, perform in public, and connect with fellow songwriters. SAW sponsors various events to achieve these goals: workshops, open mics, songwriter exchanges, and showcases. In addition,

SAW organizes the Mid-Atlantic Song Contest open to entrants nationwide each year; "the competition in 2008 will be the 25th contest SAW has adjudicated since 1982, making it one of the longest-running song contests in the nation." (Contest information masc@saw.org). As well as maintaining a Web site, SAW publishes a monthly e-newsletter for members containing information on upcoming local events, member news, contest information, and articles of interest, as well as a member directory, a valuable tool for networking. Joint membership with the Washington Area Music Association as well as a two-year membership are available at a savings. Use the contact information above for membership inquiries.

THE SONGWRITERS GUILD OF AMERICA

Los Angeles Office: New address to be announced. (323)462-1108. E-mail: la@songwritersguild. com. **Nashville Office**: 209 10th Ave. S., Suite 321, Nashville TN 37203. (615)742-9945. Fax: (615)742-9948. E-mail: nash@songwritersguild.com. SGA Administration: 209 10th Ave. S., Suite 321, Nashville TN 37203. (615)742-9945. Fax: (615)742-9948. E-mail: corporate@ songwritersguild.com. President: Rick Carnes. SGAF Director of Operations: Mark Saxon. Estab. 1931. "The Songwriters Guild of America Foundation offers a series of workshops with discounts for some to SGA members, including online classes and song critique opportunities. There is a charge for some songwriting classes and seminars; however, online classes and some monthly events may be included with an SGA membership. Charges vary depending on the class or event. Current class offerings and workshops vary. Visit Web site to sign up for the newsletter and e-events, and for more information on current events and workshops. Some current events in Nashville are the Ask-a-Pro and ProCritique sessions that give SGA members the opportunity to present their songs and receive constructive feedback from industry professionals. Various performance opportunities are also available to members, including an SGA Showcase at the Bluebird. The New York office hosts a weekly Pro-Shop, which is coordinated by producer/musician/award winning singer Ann Johns Ruckert. For each of six sessions an active publisher, producer or A&R person is invited to personally screen material from SGA writers. Participation is limited to 10 writers and an audit of one session. Audition of material is required. Various performance opportunities and critique sessions are also available from time to time. SGAF Week is held periodically and is a week of scheduled events and seminars of interest to songwriters that includes workshops, seminars and showcases."

SONGWRITERS HALL OF FAME (SONGHALL)

330 W. 58th St., Suite 411, New York NY 10019-1827. (212)957-9230. Fax: (212)957-9227. E-mail: info@songhall.org. Website: www.songhall.org. **Contact**: Managing Director: April Anderson. Estab. 1969. "SongHall membership consists of songwriters of all levels, music publishers, producers, record company executives, music attorneys, and lovers of popular music of all ages. There are different levels of membership, all able to vote in the election for inductees, except Associates who pay only $25 in dues, but are unable to vote. SongHall's mission is to honor the popular songwriters who write the soundtrack for the world, as well as providing educational and networking opportunities to our members through our workshop and showcase programs." Offers: newsletter, workshops, performance opportunities, networking meetings with industry pros and scholarships for excellence in songwriting. Applications accepted year-round. Membership fees: $25 and up.

SONGWRITERS OF WISCONSIN INTERNATIONAL

P.O. Box 1027, Neenah WI 54957-1027. (920)725-5129. E-mail: sowi@new.rr.com. Website: www.SongwritersOfWisconsin.org. **Contact:** Tony Ansems, president. Workshops Coordinator: Mike Heath. Estab. 1983. Serves songwriters. "Membership is open to songwriters writing all styles of music. Residency in Wisconsin is recommended but not required. Members are encouraged to bring tapes and lyric sheets of their songs to the meetings, but it is not required. We are striving to improve the craft of songwriting in Wisconsin. Living in Wisconsin, a songwriter would be close to any of the workshops and showcases offered each month at different towns. The primary value of membership for a songwriter is in sharing ideas with other songwriters, being critiqued and helping other songwriters." Offers competitions (contest entry deadline: June 15), field trips, instruction, lectures, newsletter, performance opportunities, social outings, workshops and critique sessions. Applications accepted year-round. Membership dues: $30/year.

Tips "Critique meetings every last Thursday of each month, January through October, 7 p.m.-10 p.m. at Sabre Lanes, 1330 Midway Road, Menasha WI. E-mail for more details."

SONGWRITERS RESOURCE NETWORK

PMB 135, 6327-C SW Capitol Hill Hwy, Portland OR 97239-1937. E-mail: info@SongwritersResourceNetwork.com. Website: www.SongwritersResourceNetwork.com. **Contact:** Steve Cahill, president. Estab. 1998. "For songwriters and lyricists of every kind, from beginners to advanced." No eligibility requirements. "Purpose is to provide free information to help songwriters develop their craft, market their songs, and learn about songwriting opportunities." Sponsors the annual Great American Song Contest, offers marketing tips and website access to music industry contacts. "We provide leads to publishers, producers and other music industry professionals." Visit website or send SASE for more information.

- Also see the listing for Great American Song Contest in the Contests section of this book.

SOUTHWEST VIRGINIA SONGWRITERS ASSOCIATION

P.O. Box 698, Salem VA 24153. Website: www.svsa.info. **Contact:** Greg Trafidlo. Estab. 1981. 80 members of all ages and skill all levels, mainly country, folk, gospel, contemporary and rock but other musical interests too. "The purpose of SVSA is to increase, broaden and expand the knowledge of each member and to support, better and further the progress and success of each member in songwriting and related fields of endeavor." Offers performance opportunities, evaluation services, instruction, newsletter, workshops, monthly meetings and monthly newsletter. Application accepted year-round. Membership fee: $20/year.

TEXAS MUSIC OFFICE

P.O. Box 13246, Austin TX 78711. (512)463-6666. Fax: (512)463-4114. E-mail: music@governor.state.tx.us. Website: www.enjoytexasmusic.com. **Contact:** Casey Monahan, director. Estab. 1990. "The Texas Music Office (TMO) is a state-funded business promotion office and information clearinghouse for the Texas music industry. The TMO assists more than 14,000 individual clients each year, ranging from a new band trying to make statewide business contacts to BBC journalists seeking information on Down South Hip hop. The TMO is the sister office to the Texas Film Commission, both of which are within the Office of the Governor. The

TMO serves the Texas music industry by using its Business Referral Network: Texas Music Industry (7,880 Texas music businesses in 96 music business categories); Texas Music Events (625 Texas music events); Texas Talent Register (8,036 Texas recording artists); Texas Radio Stations (942 Texas stations); US Music Contacts; Classical Texas (detailed information for all classical music organizations in Texas); and International (1,425 foreign businesses interested in Texas music). Provides referrals to Texas music businesses, talent and events in order to attract new business to Texas and/or to encourage Texas businesses and individuals to keep music business in-state. Serves as a liaison between music businesses and other government offices and agencies. Publicizes significant developments within the Texas music industry."

⊠ TORONTO MUSICIANS' ASSOCIATION

15 Gervais Dr., Suite 500, Toronto ON M3C 1Y8 Canada. (416)421-1020. Fax: (416)421-7011. E-mail: info@tma149.ca. Website: www.torontomusicians.org. Executive Director: Bill Skolnick. Estab. 1887. Serves musicians--All musical styles, background, areas of the industry. "Must be a Canadian citizen, show proof of immigration status, or have a valid work permit for an extended period of time." The purpose of this organization is "to unite musicians into one organization, in order that they may, individually and collectively, secure, maintain and profit from improved economic, working and artistic conditions." Offers newsletter. Applications accepted year-round. Joining fee: $225 (Canadian); student fee: $100 (Canadian). Student must have proof of school enrollment.

VOLUNTEER LAWYERS FOR THE ARTS

1 E. 53rd St., 6th Floor, New York NY 10022. (212)319-ARTS (2787), ext. 1 (Monday-Friday 9:30-12 and 1-4 EST). Fax: (212)752-6575. E-mail: epaul@vlany.org. Website: www.vlany.org. **Contact:** Elena M. Paul, esq., executive director. Estab. 1969. Serves songwriters, musicians and all performing, visual, literary and fine arts artists and groups. Offers legal assistance and representation to eligible individual artists and arts organizations who cannot afford private counsel and a mediation service. VLA sells publications on arts-related issues and offers educational conferences, lectures, seminars and workshops. In addition, there are affiliates nationwide who assist local arts organizations and artists. Call for information.

WASHINGTON AREA MUSIC ASSOCIATION

6263 Occoquan Forest Drive, Manassas VA 20112. (202)338-1134. Fax: (703)393-1028. E-mail: dcmusic@wamadc.com. Website: www.wamadc.com. **Contact:** Mike Schreibman, president. Estab. 1985. Serves songwriters, musicians and performers, managers, club owners and entertainment lawyers; "all those with an interest in the Washington music scene." The organization is designed to promote the Washington music scene and increase its visibility. Its primary value to members is its seminars and networking opportunities. Offers lectures, newsletter, performance opportunities and workshops. WAMA sponsors the annual Washington Music Awards (The Wammies) and The Crosstown Jam or annual showcase of artists in the DC area. Applications accepted year-round. Annual dues: $35 for one year; $60 for two years.

WEST COAST SONGWRITERS

(formerly Northern California Songwriters Association), 1724 Laurel St., Suite 120, San

Carlos CA 94070. (650)654-3966. E-mail: ian@westcoastsongwriters.org. Website: www. westcoastsongwriters.org. **Contact:** Ian Crombie, executive director. Serves songwriters and musicians. Estab. 1979. "Our 1,200 members are lyricists and composers from ages 16-80, from beginners to professional songwriters. No eligibility requirements. Our purpose is to provide the education and opportunities that will support our writers in creating and marketing outstanding songs. WCS provides support and direction through local networking and input from Los Angeles and Nashville music industry leaders, as well as valuable marketing opportunities. Most songwriters need some form of collaboration, and by being a member they are exposed to other writers, ideas, critiquing, etc." Offers annual West Coast Songwriters Conference, "the largest event of its kind in northern California. This 2-day event held the second weekend in September features 16 seminars, 50 screening sessions (over 1,200 songs listened to by industry professionals) and a sunset concert with hit songwriters performing their songs." Also offers monthly visits from major publishers, songwriting classes, competitions, seminars conducted by hit songwriters ("we sell audio tapes of our seminars-- list of tapes available on request"), mail-in song-screening service for members who cannot attend due to time or location, a monthly e-newsletter, monthly performance opportunities and workshops. Applications accepted year-round. Dues: $40/year, student; $75/year, regular membership; $99 band membership; $100+ contributing membership.

Tips "WCS's functions draw local talent and nationally recognized names together. This is of a tremendous value to writers outside a major music center. We are developing a strong songwriting community in Northern and Southern California. We serve the San Jose, Monterey Bay, East Bay, San Francisco, Los Angeles, Sacramento and Portland, WA areas and we have the support of some outstanding writers and publishers from both Los Angeles and Nashville. They provide us with invaluable direction and inspiration."

Workshops & Conferences

For a songwriter just starting out, conferences and workshops can provide valuable learning opportunities. At conferences, songwriters can have their songs evaluated, hear suggestions for further improvement and receive feedback from music business experts. They are also excellent places to make valuable industry contacts. Workshops can help a songwriter improve his craft and learn more about the business of songwriting. They may involve classes on songwriting and the business, as well as lectures and seminars by industry professionals.

Each year, hundreds of workshops and conferences take place all over the country. Songwriters can choose from small regional workshops held in someone's living room to large national conferences such as South by Southwest in Austin, Texas, which hosts more than 6,000 industry people, songwriters and performers. Many songwriting organizations—national and local—host workshops that offer instruction on just about every songwriting topic imaginable, from lyric writing and marketing strategy to contract negotiation. Conferences provide songwriters the chance to meet one on one with publishing and record company professionals and give performers the chance to showcase their work for a live audience (usually consisting of industry people) during the conference. There are conferences and workshops that address almost every type of music, offering programs for songwriters, performers, musical playwrights and much more.

This section includes national and local workshops and conferences with a brief description of what they offer, when they are held and how much they cost to attend. Write or call any that interest you for further information. To find out what workshops or conferences take place in specific parts of the country, see the Geographic Index at the end of this book.

APPEL FARM ARTS AND MUSIC FESTIVAL

P.O. Box 888, Elmer NJ 08318. (856)358-2472. Fax: (856)358-6513. E-mail: perform@ appelfarm.org. Website: www.appelfarm.org. **Contact:** Sean Timmons, artistic director. Estab Festival: 1989; Series: 1970. "Our annual open air festival is the highlight of our year-round Performing Arts Series which was established to showcase the finest contemporary songwriters. Festival includes a diversity of styles including rock, roots, folk, world music, blues, etc." Past performers have included Rufus Wainwright, Fountains of Wayne, Indigo Girls, Ani DiFranco, They Might Be Giants, Randy Newman, Jackson Browne, David Gray and more. Programs for songwriters and musicians include performance opportunities as part of Festival and Performing Arts Series. Programs for musical playwrights also include performance opportunities as part of Performing Arts Series. Festival is a one-day event held in June, and Performing Arts Series is held year-round. Both are held at the Appel Farm Arts and Music Center in Southern New Jersey. Up to 20 songwriters/musicians participate in each event. Participants are songwriters, individual vocalists, bands, ensembles, vocal groups, composers, individual instrumentalists and dance/mime/movement. Participants are selected by on line submissions. Applicants should forward links to their web sites, myspace pages etc. Application materials accepted year round. Faculty opportunities are available as part of residential Summer Arts Program for children, July/August.

⚏ ASCAP "I CREATE MUSIC" EXPO

One Lincoln Plaza, New York NY 10023.Estab. 2006. (212)621-6278. Fax: (212)621-6387. E-mail: pstack@ascap.com. Website: www.ascap.com. Contact: Paula Stack. 3-day event held in April.

ASCAP MUSICAL THEATRE WORKSHOP

1 Lincoln Plaza, New York NY 10023. (212)621-6234. Fax: (212)621-6558. E-mail: mkerker@ ascap.com. Website: www.ascap.com. **Contact:** Michael A. Kerker, director of musical theatre. Estab. 1981. Workshop is for musical theatre composers and lyricists only. Its purpose is to nurture and develop new musicals for the theatre. Offers programs for songwriters. Offers programs annually, usually April through May. Event took place in New York City. Four musical works are selected. Others are invited to audit the workshop. Participants are amateur and professional songwriters, composers and musical playwrights. Participants are selected by demo CD submission. Deadline: mid-March. Also available: the annual ASCAP/Disney Musical Theatre Workshop in Los Angeles. It takes place in January and February. Deadline is late November. Details similar to New York workshop as above.

ASCAP WEST COAST/LESTER SILL SONGWRITERS WORKSHOP

7920 Sunset Blvd., 3rd Floor, Los Angeles CA 90046. (323)883-1000. Fax: (323)883-1049. E-mail: info@ascap.com. Website: www.ascap.com. Annual workshop for advanced songwriters sponsored by the ASCAP Foundation. Re-named in 1995 to honor ASCAP's late Board member and industry pioneer Lester Sill, the workshop takes place over a four-week period and features prominent guest speakers from various facets of the music business. Workshop dates and deadlines vary from year to year; refer to www.ascap.com for updated info. Applicants must submit two songs on a CD (cassette tapes not accepted), lyrics, brief bio and short explanation as to why they would like to participate. Limited number of participants are selected each year.

BMI-LEHMAN ENGEL MUSICAL THEATRE WORKSHOP

320 W. 57th St., New York NY 10019. (212)586-2000. E-mail: musicaltheatre@bmi.com. Website: www.bmi.com. **Contact:** Jean Banks, senior director of musical theatre. Estab. 1961. " BMI is a music licensing company which collects royalties for affiliated writers and publishers. We offer programs to musical theatre composers, lyricists and librettists. The BMI-Lehman Engel Musical Theatre Workshops were formed if an effort to refresh and stimulate professional writers, as well as to encourage and develop new creative talent for the musical theatre." Each workshop meets 1 afternoon a week for 2 hours at BMI, New York. Participants are professional songwriters, composers and playwrights. BMI-Lehman Musical Theatre Workshop Showcase presents the best of the workshop to producers, agents, record and publishing company execs, press and directors for possible option and production. Go to BMI. com - click on Musical Theatre - for application. Tape and lyrics of 3 compositions required with applications" BMI also sponsors a jazz composers workshop. For more information contact Raette Johnson at rjohnson@bmi.com.

BROADWAY TOMORROW PREVIEWS

c/o Science of Light, Inc., 191 Claremont Ave., Suite 53, New York NY 10027. E-mail: solministry@juno.com. Website: www.solministry.com/bway_tom.html. **Contact:** Elyse Curtis, PhD, artistic director. Estab. 1983. Purpose is the enrichment of American theater by nurturing new musicals. Offers series in which composers living in New York city area present self-contained scores of their new musicals in concert. Submission is by audio cassette or CD of music, synopsis, cast breakdown, résumé, reviews, if any, acknowledgement postcard and SASE. Participants selected by screening of submissions. Programs are presented in fall and spring with possibility of full production of works presented in concert.

▣ CMJ MUSIC MARATHON, MUSICFEST & FILMFEST

100 Fifth Av., 11th Floor, New York NY 10011. (212)277-7120. Fax: (212)719-9396. Website: www.cmj.com/marathon/. **Contact:** Operations Manager. Estab. 1981. Premier annual alternative music gathering of more than 9,000 music business and film professionals. Fall, NYC. Features 4 days and nights of more than 50 panels and workshops focusing on every facet of the industry; exclusive film screenings; keynote speeches by the world's most intriguing and controversial voices; exhibition area featuring live performance stage; over 1,000 of music's brightest and most visionary talents (from the unsigned to the legendary) performing over 4 evenings at more than 50 of NYC's most important music venues. Participants are selected by submitting demonstration tape. Go to website for application.

CUTTING EDGE MUSIC BUSINESS CONFERENCE

1524 N. Claiborne Ave., New Orleans LA 70116. (504)945-1800. Fax: (504)945-1873. E-mail: cut_edge@bellsouth.net. Website: www.jass.com/cuttingedge. Executive Producer: Eric L. Cager. Showcase Producer: Nathaniel Franklin. Estab. 1993. "The conference is a five-day international conference which covers the business and educational aspects of the music industry. As part of the conference, the New Works showcase features over 200 bands and artists from around the country and Canada in showcases of original music. All music genres are represented." Offers programs for songwriters and performers. "Bands and artists should submit material for consideration of entry into the New Works showcase." Event takes place during August in New Orleans. 1,000 songwriters/musicians participate in each event. Participants are songwriters, vocalists and bands. Send for application. Deadline: June 1. "The Music Business Institute offers a month-long series of free educational workshops for those involved in the music industry. The workshops take place each October. Further information is available via our Web site."

FOLK ALLIANCE ANNUAL CONFERENCE

510 South Main, Memphis, TN 38103. (901) 522-1170. Fax: (901) 522-1172. E-mail: fa@ folk.org. Website: www.folk.org. **Contact**: Louis Meyers, Executive Director. Estab. 1989. Conference/workshop topics change each year. Conference takes place mid-February and lasts 4 days at a different location each year. 2,000 + attendees include artists, agents, arts administrators, print/broadcast media, folklorists, folk societies, merchandisers, presenters, festivals, recording companies, etc. Artists wishing to showcase should contact the office for a showcase application form. Closing date for official showcase application is November 19, 2009. Event is 17-21 February 2010. Costs vary.

HOLLYWOOD REPORTER/BILLBOARD FILM & TV MUSIC CONFERENCE

Sofitel LA, 8555 Beverly Blvd., Los Angeles CA 90048. (646)654-4626. E-mail: bbevents@ billboard.com. Website: www.billboardevents.com/. **Contact**: Lisa Kastner. Estab. 1995. Promotes all music for film and television. Offers programs for songwriters and composers. Held at the Directors Guild of America in October. More than 350 songwriters/musicians participate in each event. Participants are professional songwriters, composers, plus producers, directors, etc. Conference panelists are selected by invitation. For registration information, call the Special Events Dept. at Hollywood Reporter. Fee: $349-499/person.

KERRVILLE FOLK FESTIVAL

Kerrville Festivals, Inc., P.O. Box 291466, Kerrville TX 78029. (830)257-3600. E-mail: info@ kerrville-music.com. Website: www.kerrvillefolkfestival.com. **Contact:** Dalis Allen, producer. Estab. 1972. Hosts 3-day songwriters' school, a 4-day music business school and New Folk concert competition sponsored by Performing Songwriter magazine. Festival produced in late spring and late summer. Spring festival lasts 18 days and is held outdoors at Quiet Valley Ranch. 110 or more songwriters participate. Performers are professional songwriters and bands. Participants selected by submitting demo, by invitation only. Send cassette, or CD, promotional material and list of upcoming appearances. "Songwriter and music schools include lunch, experienced professional instructors, camping on ranch and concerts. Rustic facilities. Food available at reasonable cost. Audition materials accepted at above address. These three-day and four-day seminars include noon meals, handouts and camping on the ranch. Usually held during Kerrville Folk Festival, first and second week in June. Write or check the Web site for contest rules, schools and seminars information, and festival schedules. Also establishing a Phoenix Fund to provide assistance to ill or injured singer/songwriters who find themselves in distress."

LAMB'S RETREAT FOR SONGWRITERS

Presented by SPRINGFED ARTS, a nonprofit organization, P.O. Box 304, Royal Oak MI 48068-0304. (248)589-1594. Fax: (248)589-9981. E-mail: johndlamb@ameritech.net. Website: www.springfed.org. **Contact:** John D. Lamb, director. Estab. 1995. Offers programs for songwriters on annual basis; November 5-8, 2009 and November 12-15, 2009 at The Birchwood Inn, Harbor Springs, MI. 60 songwriters/musicians participate in each event. Participants are amateur and professional songwriters. Anyone can participate. Send for registration or e-mail. Deadline: two weeks before event begins. Fee: $275-495, includes all meals. Facilities are single/double occupancy lodging with private baths; 2 conference rooms and hospitality lodge. Offers song assignments, songwriting workshops, song swaps, open mic and one-on-one mentoring. Faculty are noted songwriters, such as Michael Smith, Chuck Brodsky, Stacey Earle, Idgy Vaughn, and Amy Speace. Partial scholarships may be available by writing: Blissfest Music Organization, Jim Gillespie, P.O. Box 441, Harbor Springs, MI 49740. Deadline: 2 weeks before event.

MANCHESTER MUSIC FESTIVAL

P.O. Box 33, Manchester VT 05254. (802)362-1956 or (800)639-5868. Fax: (802)362-0711. E-mail: mmfvt@comcast.net. Website: www.manchestermusicfestival.org. **Contact:** Robyn Madison, managing director. Estab. 1974. Offers classical music education and performances. Summer program for young professional musicians offered in tandem with a professional concert series in the mountains of Manchester VT. Up to 23 young professionals, age 19 and up, are selected by audition for the Young Artists Program, which provides instruction, performance and teaching opportunities, with full scholarship for all participants. Commissioning opportunities for new music, and performance opportunities for professional chamber ensembles and soloists for both summer and fall/winter concert series. "Celebrating 34 years of fine music."

MUSIC BUSINESS SOLUTIONS/CAREER BUILDING WORKSHOPS

P.O. Box 230266, Boston MA 02123-0266. (888)655-8335. E-mail: peter@mbsolutions.com. Website: www.mbsolutions.com. **Contact:** Peter Spellman, director. Estab. 1991. Workshop titles include "Discovering Your Music Career Niche," "How to Release an Independent Record" and "Promoting and Marketing Music in the 21st Century." Offers programs for music entrepreneurs, songwriters, musical playwrights, composers and performers. Offers programs year-round, annually and bi-annually. Event takes place at various colleges, recording studios, hotels, conferences. 10-100 songwriters/musicians participate in each event. Participants are both amateur and professional songwriters, vocalists, music business professionals, composers, bands, musical playwrights and instrumentalists. Anyone can participate. Fee: varies. "Music Business Solutions offers a number of other services and programs for both songwriters and musicians including: private music career counseling, business plan development and internet marketing; publication of Music Biz Insight: Power Reading for Busy Music Professionals, a bimonthly e-zine chock full of music management and marketing tips and resources. Free subscription with e-mail address."

⚡ NEW MUSIC WEST

1062 Homer St., #301, Vancouver BC V6B 2W9 Canada. (604)689-2910. Fax: (604)689-2912.

Website: www.newmusicwest.com. Estab. 1990. A four day music festival and conference held May each year in Vancouver BC. The conference offers songwriter intensive workshops; demo critique sessions with A&R and publishers; information on the business of publishing; master producer workshops: "We invite established hit record producers to conduct three-hour intensive hands-on workshops with 30 young producers/musicians in studio environments." The festival offers songwriters in the round and 250 original music showcases. Largest music industry event in the North Pacific Rim. Entry fee: Full Pass: $150; Student: $50; Registered Artists (not selected for showcase): $70. Check website for most recent festival dates.

NORFOLK CHAMBER MUSIC FESTIVAL

September-May address: Woolsey Hall, 500 College St., Suite 301, New Haven CT 06520. (203)432-1966. Fax: (203)432-2136. E-mail: norfolk@yale.edu. Website: www.yale.edu/norfolk. June-August address: Ellen Battell, Stoeckel Estate, Routes 44 and 272, Norfolk CT 06058. (860)542-3000. Fax: (860)542-3004. **Contact**: Deanne E. Chin, operations manager. Estab. 1941. Festival season of chamber music. Offers programs for composers and performers. Offers programs summer only. Approximately 45 fellows participate. Participants are up-and-coming composers and instrumentalists. Participants are selected by following a screening round. Auditions are held in New Haven, CT. Send for application. Deadline: January 16. Fee: $50. Held at the Ellen Battell Stoeckel Estate, the Festival offers a magnificent Music Shed with seating for 1,000, practice facilities, music library, dining hall, laundry and art gallery. Nearby are hiking, bicycling and swimming.

◪ NORTH BY NORTHEAST MUSIC FESTIVAL AND CONFERENCE

189 Church St., Lower Level, Toronto ON M5B 1Y7 Canada. (416)863-6963. Fax: (416)863-0828. E-mail: info@nxne.com. Website: www.nxne.com. **Contact:** Gillian Zulauf, conference and panel coordinator. Estab. 1995. "Our festival takes place mid-June at over 30 venues across downtown Toronto, drawing over 2,000 conference delegates, 500 bands and 50,000 music fans. Musical genres include everything from folk to funk, roots to rock, polka to punk and all points in between, bringing exceptional new talent, media front-runners, music business heavies and music fans from all over the world to Toronto." Participants include emerging and established songwriters, vocalists, composers, bands and instrumentalists. Festival performers are selected by submitting a CD and accompanying press kit or applying through sonicbids. com. Application forms are available by website or by calling the office. Submission period each year is from November 1 to the third weekend in January. Submissions "early bird" fee: $25. Conference registration fee: $149-249. "Our conference is held at the deluxe Holiday Inn on King and the program includes mentor sessions--15-minute one-on-one opportunities for songwriters and composers to ask questions of industry experts, roundtables, panel discussions, keynote speakers, etc. North By Northeast 2008 will be held June 12-15."

NSAI SONG CAMPS

1710 Roy Acuff Place, Nashville TN 37023. (800)321-6008 or (615)256-3354. Fax: (615)256-0034. E-mail: songcamps@nashvillesongwriters.com. Website: www.nashvillesongwriters. com. **Contact:** Deanie Williams, NSAI Events Director. Estab. 1992. Offers programs strictly for songwriters. Event held 4 times/year in Nashville. "We provide most meals and lodging is available. We also present an amazing evening of music presented by the faculty." Camps are 3 days long, with 36-112 participants, depending on the camp. "There are different levels of camps, some having preferred prerequisites. Each camp varies. Please call, e-mail or refer to Web site. It really isn't about the genre of music, but the quality of the song itself. Song Camp strives to strengthen the writer's vision and skills, therefore producing the better song. Song Camp is known as 'boot camp' for songwriters. It is guaranteed to catapult you forward in your writing! Participants are all aspiring songwriters led by a pro faculty. We do accept lyricists only and composers only with the hopes of expanding their scope." Participants are selected through submission of 2 songs with lyric sheet. Song Camp is open to NSAI members, although anyone can apply and upon acceptance join the organization. There is no formal application form. See Web site for membership and event information. •Also see the listing for Nashville Songwriters Association International (NSAI) in the Organizations section of this book.

NSAI SONGWRITERS SONGPOSIUM

1710 Roy Acuff Pl., Nashville TN 37203. (615)256-3354 OR 1-800-321-6008. Fax: (615)256-0034. E-mail: events@NashvilleSongwriters.com. Website: www.nashvillesongwriters.com. Covers "all types of music. Participants take part in publisher evaluations, as well as large group sessions with different guest speakers." Offers annual programs for songwriters. Event takes place in April in downtown Nashville. 300 amateur songwriters/musicians participate in each event. Send for application.

⚡ ORFORD FESTIVAL

Orford Arts Centre, 3165 Chemim DuParc, Orford QC J1X 7A2 Canada. (819)843-9871 or 1-800-567-6155. Fax: (819)843-7274. E-mail: centre@arts-orford.org. Website: www.arts-orford.org. **Contact:** Anne-Marie Dubois, registrar/information manager. Artistic Coordinator: Nicolas Bélanger. Estab. 1951. "Each year, the Orford Arts Centre produces up to 35 concerts in the context of its Music Festival. It receives artists from all over the world in classical and chamber music." Offers master classes for music students, young professional classical musicians and chamber music ensembles. New offerings include master classes for all instruments, voice, and opera. Master classes last 2 months and take place at Orford Arts Centre from the end of June to the middle of August. 350 students participate each year. Participants are selected by demo tape submissions. Send for application. Closing date for application is mid to late March. Check our website for specific dates and deadlines. Scholarships for qualified students.

THE SONGWRITERS GUILD OF AMERICA FOUNDATION

1560 Broadway, Suite #408, New York NY 10036. (212)221-6006. E-mail sgaf.msaxon@ mindspring.com. Website: www.songwritersguild.com. Director of Operations: Mark Saxon. The Foundation is in charge of many events, including workshops in the NY area.

SONGWRITERS PLAYGROUND®

75-A Lake Rd., #366, Congers NY 10920. (845)267-0001. E-mail: heavyhitters@earthlink.net. **Contact:** Barbara Jordan, director. Estab. 1990. "To help songwriters, performers and composers develop creative and business skills through the critically acclaimed programs Songwriters Playground[[PIRg]], The 'Reel' Deal on Getting Songs Placed in Film and Television, and the Mind Your Own Business Seminars. We offer programs year-round. Workshops last anywhere from 2-15 hours. Workshops are held at various venues throughout the United States. Prices vary according to the length of the workshop." Participants are amateur and professionals. Anyone can participate. Send or call for application.

SOUTH BY SOUTHWEST MUSIC CONFERENCE

SXSW Headquarters, P.O. Box 4999, Austin TX 78765. (512)467-7979. Fax: (512)451-0754. E-mail: sxsw@sxsw.com. Website: www.sxsw.com. **Contact:** Conference Organizer. **UK and Ireland:** Cill Ruan, 7 Ard na Croise, Thurles, Co. Tipperary Ireland. Phone: 353-504-26488. Fax: 353-504-26787. E-mail: una@sxsw.com. **Contact:** Una Johnston. **Europe**: Einsiedlerweg 6, D-72074 Tuebingen-Pfrondorf 72074, Germany. (49-7071-885-604. E-mail: mirko@sxsw.com. **Contact:** Mirko Whitfield. **Asia:** Meijidori Bldg. 403, 2-3-21 Kabuki-cho Shinjuku-ku, Tokyo 160-0021 Japan. Phone: +82 3-5292-5551. Fax: +82 3-5292-5552. E-mail: info@sxsw-asia.com. **Contact:** Hiroshi Asada. **Australia/New Zealand/Hawaii:** 20 Hordern St., Newtown NSW 2042 Australia. Phone: 61-2-9557-7766. Fax: 61-2-9557-7788. E-mail: tripp@sxsw.om. **Contact:** Phil Tripp. Estab. 1987. South by Southwest (SXSW) is a private company based in Austin, Texas, with a year-round staff of professionals dedicated to building and delivering conference and festival events for entertainment and related media industry professionals. Since 1987, SXSW has produced the internationally-recognized music and media conference and festival (SXSW). As the entertainment business adjusted to issues of future growth and development, in 1994, SXSW added conferences and festivals for the film industry (SXSW Film) as well as for the blossoming interactive media (SXSW Interactive Festival). Now three industry events converge in Austin during a Texas-sized week, mirroring the ever increasing convergence of entertainment/media outlets. The next SXSW Music Conference and Festival will be held March 17-21, 2010 at the Austin Convention Center in Austin, TX. Offers panel discussions, "Crash Course" educational seminars and nighttime showcases. SXSW Music seeks out speakers who have developed unique ways to create and sell music. With our Wednesday Crash Courses and introductory panels, the basics will be covered in plain English. From Thursday through Saturday, the conference includes over fifty sessions including a panel of label heads discussing strategy, interviews with notable artists, topical discussions, demo listening sessions and the mentor program. And when the sun goes down, a multitude of performances by musicians and songwriters from across the country and around the world populate the SXSW Music Festival, held in venues in central Austin." Write, e-mail or visit Web site for dates and registration instructions.

Tips "Go to the Web site in August to apply for showcase consideration. SXSW is also involved in North by Northeast (NXNE), held in Toronto, Canada in late Spring."

THE SWANNANOA GATHERING–CONTEMPORARY FOLK WEEK

Warren Wilson College, P.O. Box 9000, Asheville NC 28815-9000. E-mail: gathering@warren-wilson.edu. Website: www.swangathering.com. Director: Jim Magill. "For anyone who ever wanted to make music for an audience, we offer a comprehensive week in artist development, including classes in Songwriting, Performance, and Vocal Coaching, 2009 staff included Kathy Mattea, Peter Mulvey, Cliff Eberhardt, Sara Hickman, Anais Mitchell, Vance Gilbert, Kate Campbell, Jon Vezner, David Roth, Siobhan Quinn, and Ray Chesna." For a brochure or other info contact The Swannanoa Gathering at the phone number/address above. Takes place last week in July. 2009 Tuition: $430. Housing (including all meals): $ 340. Annual program of

Workshops & Conferences 333

The Swannanoa Gathering Folk Arts Workshops.

THE TEN-MINUTE MUSICALS PROJECT

P.O. Box 461194, West Hollywood CA 90046. E-mail: info@tenminutemusicals.org. Website: www.tenminutemusicals.org. **Contact:** Michael Koppy, producer. Estab. 1986. Promotes short complete stage musicals. Offers programs for songwriters, composers and musical playwrights. "Works selected are generally included in full-length 'anthology musical'--11 of the first 16 selected works are now in the show Stories 1.0, for instance." Awards a $250 royalty advance for each work selected. Participants are amateur and professional songwriters, composers and musical playwrights. Participants are selected by demonstration CD, script, lead sheets. Send Web site for submission guidelines. Deadline: August 31st annually.

UNDERCURRENTS

P.O. Box 94040, Cleveland OH 44101-6040. (440)331-0700. E-mail: music@undercurrents.com. Website: www.undercurrents.com. **Contact:** John Latimer, president. Estab. 1989. A music, event and art marketing and promotion network with online and offline exposure featuring music showcases, seminars, trade shows, networking forums. Ongoing programs and performances for songwriters, composers, and performers. Participants are selected by EPK, demo, biography and photo. Register at www.undercurrents.com.

WEST COAST SONGWRITERS CONFERENCE

(formerly Northern California Songwriters Association Conference), 1724 Laurel St., Suite 120, San Carlos CA 94070. (650)654-3966. E-mail: info@westcoastsongwriters.org. Website: www.westcoastsongwriters.org. **Contact:** Ian Crombie, executive director. Estab. 1980. "Conference offers opportunity and education. 16 seminars, 50 song screening sessions (1,500 songs reviewed), performance showcases, one on one sessions and concerts." Offers programs for lyricists, songwriters, composers and performers. "During the year we have competitive live Songwriter competitions. Winners go into the playoffs. Winners of the playoffs perform at the sunset concert at the conference." Event takes place second weekend in September at Foothill College, Los Altos Hills CA. Over 500 songwriters/musicians participate in this event. Participants are songwriters, composers, musical playwrights, vocalists, bands, instrumentalists and those interested in a career in the music business. Send for application. Deadline: September 1. Fee: $150-275. "See our listing in the Organizations section."

WESTERN WIND WORKSHOP IN ENSEMBLE SINGING

263 W. 86 St., New York NY 10024. (212)873-2848 or (800)788-2187. Fax: (212)873-2849. E-mail: workshops@westernwind.org. Website: www.westernwind.org. **Contact:** William Zukoff, executive producer. Estab. 1981. Participants learn the art of ensemble singing--no conductor, one on-a-part. Workshop focuses on blend, diction, phrasing and production. Offers programs for performers. Limited talent-based scholarship available. Offers programs annually. Takes place June, July and August in the music department at Smith College, Northampton MA. 70-80 songwriters/musicians participate in each event. Participants are amateur and professional vocalists. Anyone can participate. Send for application or register at their website. Workshop takes place in the Smith College music department. Arrangers' works are frequently studied and performed. Also offers additional workshops President's

Day weekend in Brattleboro VT and Columbus Day weekend in Woodstock VT.

WINTER MUSIC CONFERENCE INC.

3450 NE 12 Terrace, Ft. Lauderdale FL 33334. (954)563-4444. Fax: (954)563-1599. E-mail: info@wintermusicconference.com. Website: www.wintermusicconference.com. President: Margo Possenti. Estab. 1985. Features educational seminars and showcases for dance, hip hop, alternative and rap. Offers programs for songwriters and performers. Offers programs annually. Event takes place March of each year in Miami FL. 3,000 songwriters/musicians participate in each event. Participants are amateur and professional songwriters, composers, musical playwrights, vocalists, bands and instrumentalists. Participants are selected by submitting demo tape. Send SASE, visit website or call for application. Deadline: February. Event held at either nightclubs or hotel with complete staging, lights and sound.

Retreats & Colonies

This section provides information on retreats and artists' colonies. These are places for creatives, including songwriters, to find solitude and spend concentrated time focusing on their work. While a residency at a colony may offer participation in seminars, critiques or performances, the atmosphere of a colony or retreat is much more relaxed than that of a conference or workshop. Also, a songwriter's stay at a colony is typically anywhere from one to twelve weeks (sometimes longer), while time spent at a conference may only run from one to fourteen days.

Like conferences and workshops, however, artists' colonies and retreats span a wide range. Yaddo, perhaps the most well-known colony, limits its residencies to artists "working at a professional level in their field, as determined by a judging panel of professionals in the field." The Brevard Music Center offers residencies only to those involved in classical music. Despite different focuses, all artists' colonies and retreats have one thing in common: They are places where you may work undisturbed, usually in nature-oriented, secluded settings.

SELECTING A COLONY OR RETREAT

When selecting a colony or retreat, the primary consideration for many songwriters is cost, and you'll discover that arrangements vary greatly. Some colonies provide residencies as well as stipends for personal expenses. Some suggest donations of a certain amount. Still others offer residencies for substantial sums but have financial assistance available.

When investigating the various options, consider meal and housing arrangements and your family obligations. Some colonies provide meals for residents, while others require residents to pay for meals. Some colonies house artists in one main building; others provide separate cottages. A few have provisions for spouses and families. Others prohibit families altogether.

Overall, residencies at colonies and retreats are competitive. Since only a handful of spots are available at each place, you often must apply months in advance for the time period you desire. A number of locations are open year-round, and you may find planning to go during the "off-season" lessens your competition. Other colonies, however, are only available during certain months. In any case, be prepared to include a sample of your best work with your application. Also, know what project you'll work on while in residence and have alternative projects in mind in case the first one doesn't work out once you're there.

Each listing in this section details fee requirements, meal and housing arrangements, and space and time availability, as well as the retreat's surroundings, facilities and special activities. Of course, before making a final decision, send a SASE to the colonies or retreats that interest you to receive their most up-to-date details. Costs, application requirements and deadlines are particularly subject to change.

MUSICIAN'S RESOURCE

For other listings of songwriter-friendly colonies, see *Musician's Resource* (available from Watson-Guptill (www.watsonguptill.com), which not only provides information about conferences, workshops and academic programs but also residencies and retreats. Also check the Publications of Interest section in this book for newsletters and other periodicals providing this information.

THE HAMBIDGE CENTER

Attn: Residency Director, P.O. Box 339, Rabun Gap GA 30568. (706)746-5718. Fax: (706)746-9933 E-mail: director@hambidge.org. Website: www.hambidge.org. **Contact:** Rosemary Magee, residency chair. Estab. 1934 (Center); 1988 (residency). Offers 2-week to 2-month residencies year round. Open to all artists. Accommodates 8 at one time. Personal living quarters include a private cottage with kitchen, bath, and living/studio space. Offers composer/musical studio equipped with piano. Activities include communal dinners February through December and nightly or periodic sharing of works-in-progress.

Costs $150/week.

Requirements Send SASE for application forms and guidelines, or available on Web site. Accepts inquiries via fax and e-mail. Application fee: $30. Deadlines: January 15, April 15, and September 15.

ISLE ROYALE NATIONAL PARK ARTIST-IN-RESIDENCE PROGRAM

800 E. Lakeshore Dr., Houghton MI 49931. (906)482-0984. Fax: (906)482-8753. E-mail: ISRO_Parkinfo@nps.gov. Website: www.nps.gov/ISRO/. **Contact:** Greg Blust, coordinator. Estab. 1991. Offers 2-3 week residencies from mid-June to mid-September. Open to all art forms. Accommodates 1 artist with 1 companion at one time. Personal living quarters include cabin with shared outhouse. A canoe is provided for transportation. Offers a guest house at the site that can be used as a studio. The artist is asked to contribute a piece of work representative of their stay at Isle Royale, to be used by the park in an appropriate manner. During their residency, artists will be asked to share their experience (1 presentation per week of residency, about 1 hour/week) with the public by demonstration, talk, or other means.

Requirements Deadline: postmarked February 16, 2010. Send for application forms and guidelines. Accepts inquiries via fax or e-mail. A panel of professionals from various disciplines, and park representatives will choose the finalists. The selection is based on artistic integrity, ability to reside in a wilderness environment, a willingness to donate a finished piece of work inspired on the island, and the artist's ability to relate and interpret the park through their work.

KALANI OCEANSIDE RETREAT

VILLAGERR 2 Box 4500, Pahoa-Beach Road HI 96778-9724. (808)965-7828 or 800-800-6886. Fax: (808)965-0527. E-mail: kalani@kalani.com. Website: www.kalani.com. **Contact:** Richard Koob, director. Estab. 1980. Offers 2-week to 2-month residencies. Open to all artists who can verify professional accomplishments. Accommodates 120 at one time. Personal living quarters include private cottage or lodge room with private or shared bath. Full (3 meals/day) dining service. Offers shared studio/library spaces. Activities include opportunity to share works in progress, ongoing yoga, hula and other classes; beach, thermal springs, Volcanos National Park nearby; Olympic pool/spa on 120-acre facility.

Costs $84-240/night lodging with stipend, including 3 meals/day. Transportation by rental car from $45/day, Kalani service $65/trip, or taxi $90/trip.

Requirements Accepts inquiries via fax or e-mail.

THE MACDOWELL COLONY

100 High St., Peterborough NH 03458. (603)924-3886. Fax: (603)924-9142. E-mail: admissions@

macdowellcolony.org. Website: www.macdowellcolony.org. **Contact:** Admissions Director. Estab. 1907. Offers year-round residencies of up to 8 weeks. Open to writers and playwrights, composers, film/video makers, visual artists, architects and interdisciplinary artists. Personal living quarters include single rooms with shared baths. Offers private studios on 450-acre grounds. Travel assistance and artist grants awarded based on need.

Costs None (contributions accepted).

Requirements Visit Web site for application forms and guidelines (which include work sample requirements). Application deadline: January 15, April 15 and September 15.

SITKA CENTER FOR ART & ECOLOGY

P.O. Box 65, Otis OR 97368-0065. (541)994-5485. Fax: (541)994-8024. E-mail: info@sitkacenter. org. Website: www.sitkacenter.org. **Contact:** Eric Vines, executive director. Estab. 1971. Offers 4-month residencies in October through January or February through May; shorter residencies are available upon arrangement. Open to emerging, mid-career, or professional artists and naturalists. Residences include 3 living quarters, each self-contained with a sleeping area, kitchen and bathroom. Offers 4 studios. Workshops or presentations are encouraged; an exhibition/presentation to share residents' works is held in January and May.

Costs Residency and housing provided. The resident is asked to provide some form of community service on behalf of Sitka.

Requirements *Applications due by April 21 for a Fall or Spring residency.* Send completed application with résumé, 2 letters of recommendation, work samples and SASE.

VIRGINIA CENTER FOR THE CREATIVE ARTS

154 San Angelo Dr., Amherst VA 24521. (434)946-7236. Fax: (434)946-7239. E-mail: vcca@ vcca.com. Website: www.vcca.com. **Contact:** Sheila Gulley Pleasants, director of artists' services. Estab. 1971. Offers residencies year-round, typical residency lasts 2 weeks to 2 months. Open to originating artists: composers, writers and visual artists. Accommodates 25 at one time. Personal living quarters include 22 single rooms, 2 double rooms, bathrooms shared with one other person. All meals are served. Kitchens for fellows' use available at studios and residence. The VCCA van goes into town twice a week. Fellows share their work regularly. Four studios have pianos.

Costs No transportation costs are covered. "Artists are accepted into the VCCA without regard for their ability to contribute financially to their residency. The suggested daily contribution, if possible, is $35."

Requirements Send SASE for application form or download from Web site. Applications are reviewed by panelists. Application fee: $30. Deadline: May 15 for October-January residency; September 15 for February-May residency; January 15 for June-September residency.

State & Provincial Grants

A rts councils in the United States and Canada provide assistance to artists (including poets) in the form of fellowships or grants. These grants can be substantial and confer prestige upon recipients; however, **only state or province residents are eligible.** Because deadlines and available support vary annually, query first (with a SASE) or check Web sites for guidelines.

UNITED STATES ARTS AGENCIES

Alabama State Council on the Arts, 201 Monroe St., Montgomery AL 36130-1800. (334)242-4076. E-mail: staff@arts.alabama.gov. Web site: www.arts.state.al.us

Alaska State Council on the Arts, 411 W. Fourth Ave., Suite 1-E, Anchorage AK 99501-2343. (907)269-6610 or (888)278-7424. E-mail: aksca_info@eed.state. ak.us. Web site: www.eed. state.ak.us/aksca

Arizona Commission on the Arts, 417 W. Roosevelt St., Phoenix AZ 85003-1326. (602)771-6501. E-mail: info@azarts.gov. Web site: www.azarts.gov

Arkansas Arts Council, 1500 Tower Bldg., 323 Center St., Little Rock AR 72201. (501)324-9766. E-mail: info@arkansasarts.com. Web site: www.arkansasarts. com

California Arts Council, 1300 I St., Suite 930, Sacramento CA 95814. (916)322-6555. E-mail: info@caartscouncil.com. Web site: www.cac.ca.gov

Colorado Council on the Arts, 1625 Broadway, Suite 2700, Denver CO 80202. (303)892-3802. E-mail: online form. Web site: www.coloarts.state.co.us

Connecticut Commission on Culture & Tourism, Arts Division, One Financial Plaza, 755 Main St., Hartford CT 06103. (860)256-2800. Web site: www. cultureandtourism.org

Delaware Division of the Arts, Carvel State Office Bldg., 4th Floor, 820 N. French St., Wilmington DE 19801. (302)577-8278 (New Castle Co.) or (302)739-5304 (Kent or Sussex Counties). E-mail: delarts@state.de.us. Web site: www.artsdel.org

District of Columbia Commission on the Arts & Humanities, 410 Eighth St. NW, 5th Floor, Washington DC 20004. (202)724-5613. E-mail: cah@dc.gov. Web site: http://dcarts. dc.gov

Florida Arts Council, Division of Cultural Affairs, R.A. Gray Building, Third Floor, 500 S. Bronough St., Tallahassee FL 32399-0250. (850)245-6470. E-mail: info@florida-arts. org. Web site: http://dcarts.dc.gov

Georgia Council for the Arts, 260 14th St., Suite 401, Atlanta GA 30318. (404)685-2787. E-mail: gaarts@gaarts.org. Web site: www.gaarts.org

Guam Council on the Arts & Humanities Agency, P.O. Box 2950, Hagatna GU 96932. (671)646-2781. Web site: www.guam.net

Hawai'i State Foundation on Culture & the Arts, 2500 S. Hotel St., 2nd Floor, Honolulu HI 96813. (808)586-0300. E-mail: ken.hamilton@hawaii.gov. Web site: http.state.hi.us/ sfca

Idaho Commission on the Arts, 2410 N. Old Penitentiary Rd., Boise ID 83712. (208)334-2119 or (800)278-3863. E-mail: info@arts.idaho.gov. Web site: www.arts.idaho.gov

Illinois Arts Council, James R. Thompson Center, 100 W. Randolph, Suite 10-500, Chicago IL 60601. (312)814-6750. E-mail: iac.info@illinois.gov. Web site: www.state.il.us/ agency/iac

Indiana Arts Commission, 150 W. Market St., Suite 618, Indianapolis IN 46204. (317)232-1268. E-mail: IndianaArtsCommission@iac.in.gov. Web site: www.in.gov/arts

Iowa Arts Council, 600 E. Locust, Des Moines IA 50319-0290. (515)281-6412. Web site: www.iowaartscouncil.org

Kansas Arts Commission, 700 SW Jackson, Suite 1004, Topeka KS 66603-3761. (785)296-3335. E-mail: KAC@arts.state.ks.us. Web site: http://arts.state.ks.us

Kentucky Arts Council, 21st Floor, Capital Plaza Tower, 500 Mero St., Frankfort KY 40601-1987. (502)564-3757 or (888)833-2787. E-mail: kyarts@ky.gov. Web site: http://artscouncil.ky.gov

Louisiana Division of the Arts, Capitol Annex Bldg., 1051 N. 3rd St., 4th Floor, Room #420, Baton Rouge LA 70804. (225)342-8180. Web site: www.crt.state.la.us/arts

Maine Arts Commission, 193 State St., 25 State House Station, Augusta ME 04333-0025.

(207)287-2724. E-mail: MaineArts.info@maine.gov. Web site: www.mainearts.com

Maryland State Arts Council, 175 W. Ostend St., Suite E, Baltimore MD 21230. (410)767-6555. E-mail: msac@msac.org. Web site: www.msac.org

Massachusetts Cultural Council, 10 St. James Ave., 3rd Floor, Boston MA 02116-3803. (617)727-3668. E-mail: mcc@art.state.ma.us. Web site: www.massculturalcouncil.org

Michigan Council of History, Arts and Libraries, 702 W. Kalamazoo St., P.O. Box 30705, Lansing MI 48909-8205. (517)241-4011. E-mail: artsinfo@michigan.gov. Web site: www.michigan.gov/hal/0,1607,7-160-17445_19272---,00.html

Minnesota State Arts Board, Park Square Court, 400 Sibley St., Suite 200, St. Paul MN 55101-1928. (651)215-1600 or (800)866-2787. E-mail: msab@arts.state.mn.us. Web site: www.arts.state.mn.us

Mississippi Arts Commission, 501 N. West St., Suite 701B, Woolfolk Bldg., Jackson MS 39201. (601)359-6030. Web site: www.arts.state.ms.us

Missouri Arts Council, 815 Olive St., Suite 16, St. Louis MO 63101-1503. (314)340-6845 or (866)407-4752. E-mail: moarts@ded.mo.gov. Web site: www.missouriartscouncil.org

Montana Arts Council, 316 N. Park Ave., Suite 252, Helena MT 59620-2201. (406)444-6430. E-mail: mac@mt.gov. Web site: www.art.state.mt.us

National Assembly of State Arts Agencies, 1029 Vermont Ave. NW, 2nd Floor, Washington DC 20005. (202)347-6352. E-mail: nasaa@nasaa-arts.org. Web site: www.nasaa-arts.org

Nebraska Arts Council, 1004 Farnam St., Plaza Level, Omaha NE 68102. (402)595-2122 or (800)341-4067. Web site: www.nebraskaartscouncil.org

Nevada Arts Council, 716 N. Carson St., Suite A, Carson City NV 89701. (775)687-6680. E-mail: online form. Web site: http://dmla.clan.lib.nv.us/docs/arts

New Hampshire State Council on the Arts, 21/2 Beacon St., 2nd Floor, Concord NH 03301-4974. (603)271-2789. Web site: www.nh.gov/nharts

New Jersey State Council on the Arts, 225 W. State St., P.O. Box 306, Trenton NJ 08625. (609)292-6130. Web site: www.njartscouncil.org

New Mexico Arts, Dept. of Cultural Affairs, P.O. Box 1450, Santa Fe NM 87504-1450. (505)827-6490 or (800)879-4278. Web site: www.nmarts.org

Resources

New York State Council on the Arts, 175 Varick St., New York NY 10014. (212)627-4455. Web site: www.nysca.org

North Carolina Arts Council, 109 East Jones St., Cultural Resources Building, Raleigh NC 27601. (919)807-6500. E-mail: ncarts@ncmail.net. Web site: www.ncarts.org

North Dakota Council on the Arts, 1600 E. Century Ave., Suite 6, Bismarck ND 58503. (701)328-7590. E-mail: comserv@state.nd.us. Web site: www.state.nd.us/arts

Commonwealth Council for Arts and Culture (Northern Mariana Islands), P.O. Box 5553, CHRB, Saipan MP 96950. (670)322-9982 or (670)322-9983. E-mail: galaidi@vzpacifica.net. Web site: www.geocities.com/ccacarts/ccacwebsite.html

Ohio Arts Council, 727 E. Main St., Columbus OH 43205-1796. (614)466-2613. Web site: www.oac.state.oh.us

Oklahoma Arts Council, Jim Thorpe Building, 2101 N. Lincoln Blvd., Suite 640, Oklahoma City OK 73105. (405)521-2931. E-mail: okarts@arts.ok.gov. Web site: www.arts.state.ok.us

Oregon Arts Commission, 775 Summer St. NE, Suite 200, Salem OR 97301-1280. (503)986-0082. E-mail: oregon.artscomm@state.or.us. Web site: www.oregonartscommission.org

Pennsylvania Council on the Arts, 216 Finance Bldg., Harrisburg PA 17120. (717)787-6883. Web site: www.pacouncilonthearts.org

Institute of Puerto Rican Culture, P.O. Box 9024184, San Juan PR 00902-4184. (787)724-0700. E-mail: www@icp.gobierno.prWeb site: www.icp.gobierno.pr

Rhode Island State Council on the Arts, One Capitol Hill, Third Floor, Providence RI 02908. (401)222-3880. E-mail: info@arts.ri.gov. Web site: www.arts.ri.gov

South Carolina Arts Commission, 1800 Gervais St., Columbia SC 29201. (803)734-8696. E-mail: info@arts.state.sc.us. Web site: www.southcarolinaarts.com

South Dakota Arts Council, 711 E. Wells Ave., Pierre SD 57501-3369. (605)773-3301. E-mail: sdac@state.sd.us. Web site: www.artscouncil.sd.gov

Tennessee Arts Commission, 401 Charlotte Ave., Nashville TN 37243-0780. (615)741-1701. Web site: www.arts.state.tn.us

Texas Commission on the Arts, E.O. Thompson Office Building, 920 Colorado, Suite 501, Austin TX 78701. (512)463-5535. E-mail: front.desk@arts.state.tx.us. Web site: www.arts.state.tx.us

Utah Arts Council, 617 E. South Temple, Salt Lake City UT 84102-1177. (801)236-7555. Web site: http://arts.utah.gov

Vermont Arts Council, 136 State St., Drawer 33, Montpelier VT 05633-6001. (802)828-3291. E-mail: online form. Web site: www.vermontartscouncil.org

Virgin Islands Council on the Arts, 5070 Norre Gade, St. Thomas VI 00802-6872. (340)774-5984. Web site: http://vicouncilonarts.org

Virginia Commission for the Arts, Lewis House, 223 Governor St., 2nd Floor, Richmond VA 23219. (804)225-3132. E-mail: arts@arts.virginia.gov. Web site: www.arts.state.va.us

Washington State Arts Commission, 711 Capitol Way S., Suite 600, P.O. Box 42675, Olympia WA 98504-2675. (360)753-3860. E-mail: info@arts.wa.gov. Web site: www.arts.wa.gov

West Virginia Commission on the Arts, The Cultural Center, Capitol Complex, 1900 Kanawha Blvd. E., Charleston WV 25305-0300. (304)558-0220. Web site: www.wvculture.org/arts

Wisconsin Arts Board, 101 E. Wilson St., 1st Floor, Madison WI 53702. (608)266-0190. E-mail: artsboard@arts.state.wi.us. Web site: www.arts.state.wi.us

Wyoming Arts Council, 2320 Capitol Ave., Cheyenne WY 82002. (307)777-7742. E-mail: ebratt@state.wy.us. Web site: http://wyoarts.state.wy.us

CANADIAN PROVINCES ARTS AGENCIES

Alberta Foundation for the Arts, 10708-105 Ave., Edmonton AB T5H 0A1. (780)427-9968. Web site: www.affta.ab.ca/index.shtml

British Columbia Arts Council, P.O. Box 9819, Stn. Prov. Govt., Victoria BC V8W 9W3. (250)356-1718. E-mail: BCArtsCouncil@gov.bc.ca. Web site: www.bcartscouncil.ca

The Canada Council for the Arts, 350 Albert St., P.O. Box 1047, Ottawa ON K1P 5V8. (613)566-4414 or (800)263-5588 (within Canada). Web site: www.canadacouncil.ca

Manitoba Arts Council, 525-93 Lombard Ave., Winnipeg MB R3B 3B1. (204)945-2237 or (866)994-2787 (in Manitoba). E-mail: info@artscouncil.mb.ca. Web site: www.artscouncil.mb.ca

New Brunswick Arts Board (NBAB), 634 Queen St., Suite 300, Fredericton NB E3B 1C2. (506)444-4444 or (866)460-2787. Web site: www.artsnb.ca

Newfoundland & Labrador Arts Council, P.O. Box 98, St. John's NL A1C 5H5. (709)726-2212 or (866)726-2212. E-mail: nlacmail@nfld.net. Web site: www.nlac.nf.ca

Nova Scotia Department of Tourism, Culture, and Heritage, Culture Division, 1800 Argyle St., Suite 601, P.O. Box 456, Halifax NS B3J 2R5. (902)424-4510. E-mail: cultaffs@ gov.ns.ca. Web site: www.gov.ns.ca/dtc/culture

Ontario Arts Council, 151 Bloor St. W., 5th Floor, Toronto ON M5S 1T6. (416)961-1660 or (800)387-0058 (in Ontario). E-mail: info@arts.on.ca. Web site: www.arts.on.ca

Prince Edward Island Council of the Arts, 115 Richmond St., Charlottetown PE C1A 1H7. (902)368-4410 or (888)734-2784. E-mail: info@peiartscouncil.com. Web site: www. peiartscouncil.com

Québec Council for Arts & Literature, 79 boul. René-Lévesque Est, 3e étage, Québec QC G1R 5N5. (418)643-1707 or (800)897-1707. E-mail: info@calq.gouv.qc.ca. Web site: www.calq. gouv.qc.ca

The Saskatchewan Arts Board, 2135 Broad St., Regina SK S4P 1Y6. (306)787-4056 or (800)667-7526 (Saskatchewan only). E-mail: sab@artsboard.sk.ca. Web site: www. artsboard.sk.ca

Yukon Arts Funding Program, Cultural Services Branch, Dept. of Tourism & Culture, Government of Yukon, Box 2703 (L-3), Whitehorse YT Y1A 2C6. (867)667-8589 or (800)661-0408 (in Yukon). E-mail: arts@gov.yk.ca. Web site: www.tc.gov. yk.ca/216.html

Publications of Interest

Knowledge about the music industry is essential for both creative and business success. Staying informed requires keeping up with constantly changing information. Updates on the evolving trends in the music business are available to you in the form of music magazines, music trade papers and books. There is a publication aimed at almost every type of musician, songwriter and music fan, from the most technical knowledge of amplification systems to gossip about your favorite singer. These publications can enlighten and inspire you and provide information vital in helping you become a more well-rounded, educated, and, ultimately, successful musical artist.

This section lists all types of magazines and books you may find interesting. From songwriters' newsletters and glossy music magazines to tip sheets and how-to books, there should be something listed here that you'll enjoy and benefit from.

PERIODICALS

Allegheny Music Works, 1611 Menoher Blvd., Johnstown PA 15905. (814)255-4007. Website: www.alleghenymusicworks.com. Monthly tip sheet.

Alternative Press, 1305 West 80th Street, Suite 2F, Cleveland OH 44102-1996. (216)631-1510. Email: subscriptions@altpress.com. Website: http://altpress. com. *Reviews, news, and features for alternative and indie music fans.*

American Songwriter Magazine, 50 Music Square W., Suite 604, Nashville TN 37203-3227. (615)321-6096. E-mail: info@americansongwriter.com. Website: www. americansongwriter.com. *Bimonthly publication for and about songwriters.*

Back Stage East, 770 Broadway, 4th Floor, New York NY 10003. (646)654-5700.

Back Stage West, 5055 Wilshire Blvd., Los Angeles CA 90036. (323)525-2358 or (800)745-8922. Website: www.backstage.com. *Weekly East and West Coast performing artist trade papers.*

Bass Player, P.O. Box 57324, Boulder CO 80323-7324. (800)234-1831. E-mail: bassplayer@ neodata.com. Website: www.bassplayer.com. *Monthly magazine for bass players with lessons, interviews, articles, and transcriptions.*

Billboard, 1515 Broadway, New York NY 10036. (800)745-8922. E-mail: bbstore@ billboard.com. Website: www.billboard.com. *Weekly industry trade magazine.*

Canadian Musician, 23 Hannover Dr., Suite 7, St. Catharines ON L2W 1A3 Canada. (877)746-4692. Website: www.canadianmusician.com. *Bimonthly publication for amateur and professional Canadian musicians.*

Chart, 200-41 Britain St., Toronto ON M5A 1R7 Canada. (416)363-3101. E-mail: chart@ chartnet.com. Website: www.chartattack.com. *Monthly magazine covering the Canadian and international music scenes.*

CMJ New Music Report/CMJ New Music Monthly, 151 W. 25th St., 12 Floor, New York NY 10001. (917)606-1908. Website: www.cmj.com. Weekly college radio and alternative music tip sheet.

Country Line Magazine, 16150 S. IH-35, Buda TX 78610. (512)295-8400. E-mail: editor@ countrylinemagazine.com. Website: www.countrylinemagazine.com. *Monthly Texas-only country music cowboy and lifestyle magazine.*

Daily Variety, 5700 Wilshire Blvd., Suite 120, Los Angeles CA 90036. (323)857-6600. Website: www.variety.com. *Daily entertainment trade newspaper.*

Entertainment Law & Finance, New York Law Publishing Co., 345 Park Ave. S., 8th Floor, New York NY 10010. (212)545-6174. *Monthly newsletter covering music industry contracts, lawsuit filings, court rulings and legislation.*

Exclaim!, 7-B Pleasant Blvd., Suite 966, Toronto ON M4T 1K2 Canada. (416)535-9735. E-mail: exclaim@exclaim.ca. Website: http://exclaim.ca. *Canadian music monthly covering all genres of non-mainstream music.*

Fast Forward, Disc Makers, 7905 N. Rt. 130, Pennsauken NJ 08110-1402. (800)468-9353. Website: www.discmakers.com/music/ffwd. *Quarterly newsletter featuring companies and products for performing and recording artists in the independent music industry.*

Guitar Player, 1601 W. 23rd St., Suite 200, Lawrence KS 60046-0127. (800)289-9839. Website: www.guitarplayer.com. *Monthly guitar magazine with transcriptions, columns, and interviews, including occasional articles on songwriting.*

Jazztimes, 8737 Colesville Rd., 9th Floor, Silver Spring MD 20910-3921. (301)588-4114. Website: www.jazztimes.com. *10 issues/year magazine covering the American jazz scene.*

Music Business International Magazine, 460 Park Ave., S. of 9th, New York NY 10116. (212)378-0406. *Bimonthly magazine for senior executives in the music industry.*

Music Connection Magazine, 16130 Ventura Blvd., Suite 540, Encino CA 91436. (818)795-0101. E-mail: contactMC@musicconnection.com. Website: www.musicconnection.com. *Biweekly music industry trade publication.*

Music Morsels, P.O. Box 2760, Acworth GA 30102. (678)445-0006. Fax: (678)494-9269. E-mail: SergeEnt@aol.com. Website: www.serge.org/musicmorsels.htm. *Monthly songwriting publication.*

Music Row Magazine, 1231 17th Ave. S, Nashville TN 37212. (615)321-3617. E-mail: info@musicrow.com. Website: www.musicrow.com. *Biweekly Nashville industry publication.*

Offbeat Magazine, OffBeat Publications, 421 Frenchman St., Suite 200, New Orleans LA 70116. (504)944-4300. E-mail: offbeat@offbeat.com. Website: www.offbeat.com. *Monthly magazine covering Louisiana music and artists.*

The Performing Songwriter, P.O. Box 40931, Nashville TN 37204. (800)883-7664. E-mail: order@performingsongwriter.com. Website: www.performingsongwriter.com *Bimonthly songwriters' magazine.*

Radio and Records, 2049 Century Park East, 41st Floor, Los Angeles CA 90067. (310)553-4330. Fax: (310)203-9763. E-mail: subscribe@radioandrecords.com. Website: www.radioandrecords.com. *Weekly newspaper covering the radio and record industries.*

Radir, Radio Mall, 2412 Unity Ave. N., Dept. WEB, Minneapolis MN 55422. (800)759-4561. E-mail: info@bbhsoftware.com. Website: www.bbhsoftware.com. *Quarterly radio station database on disk.*

Sing Out!, P.O. Box 5460, Bethlehem PA 18015. (888)SING-OUT. Fax: (610)865-5129. E-mail: info@singout.org. Website: www.singout.org. *Quarterly folk music magazine.*

Songcasting, 15445 Ventura Blvd. #260, Sherman Oaks CA 91403. (818)377-4084. *Monthly tip sheet.*

Songlink International, 23 Belsize Crescent, London NW3 5QY England. Website: www.songlink.com.10 issues/year newsletter including details of recording artists looking for songs; contact details for industry sources; also news and features on the music business.

Variety, 5700 Wilshire Blvd., Suite 120, Los Angeles CA 90036. (323)857-6600. Fax: (323)857-0494. Website: www.variety.com. *Weekly entertainment trade newspaper.*

Words and Music, 41 Valleybrook Dr., Don Mills ON M3B 2S6 Canada. (416)445-8700. Website: www.socan.ca. *Monthly songwriters' magazine.*

BOOKS & DIRECTORIES

101 Songwriting Wrongs & How to Right Them, by Pat & Pete Luboff, Writer's Digest Books, 4700 E. Galbraith Rd., Cincinnati OH 45236. (800)448-0915. Website: www. writersdigest.com.

The A&R Registry, by Ritch Esra, SRS Publishing, 7510 Sunset Blvd. #1041, Los Angeles CA 90046-3418. (800)377-7411 or (800)552-7411. E-mail: musicregistry@compuserve. com.

The Billboard Guide to Music Publicity, revised edition, by Jim Pettigrew, Jr., Billboard Books, 1695 Oak St., Lakewood NJ 08701. (800)344-7119.

Breakin' Into Nashville, by Jennifer Ember Pierce, Madison Books, University Press of America, 4501 Forbes Rd., Suite 200, Lanham MD 20706. (800)462-6420.

CMJ Directory, 151 W. 25th St., 12th Floor, New York NY 10001. (917)606-1908. Website: www.cmj.com.

The Craft and Business of Songwriting, by John Braheny, Writer's Digest Books, 4700 E. Galbraith Rd., Cincinnati OH 45236. (800)448-0915. Website: www.writersdigest. com.

The Craft of Lyric Writing, by Sheila Davis, Writer's Digest Books, 4700 E. Galbraith Rd., Cincinnati OH 45236. (800)448-0915. Website: www.writersdigest.com.

Disc Makers, by Jason Ojalvo, Disc Makers, 7905 N. Rt. 130, Pennsauken NJ 08110. (800)468-9353. E-mail: discman@discmakers.com. Website: www.discmakers.com.

Hollywood Creative Directory, 3000 W. Olympic Blvd. #2525, Santa Monica CA 90404. (800)815-0503. Website: www.hcdonline.com. Lists producers in film and TV.

The Hollywood Reporter, 5055 Wilshire Blvd., Los Angeles CA 90036. (323)525-2150. Website: www.hollywoodreporter.com.

How to Get Somewhere in the Music Business from Nowhere with Nothing, by Mary Dawson, CQK Books, fico CQK Music Group, 2221 Justin Rd., Suite 119-142, Flower Mound TX 75028. (972)317-2720. Fax: (972)317-4737. Website: www. FromNowhereWithNothing.com.

How to Promote Your Music Successfully on the Internet, by David Nevue, Midnight Rain Productions, P.O. Box 21831, Eugene OR 97402. Website: www.rainmusic. com.

How to Make It in the New Music Business: Lessons, Tips, and Inspirations from Music's Biggest and Best, by Robert Wolff, Billboard Books. Website: www. billboard.com.

How You Can Break Into the Music Business, by Marty Garrett, Lonesome Wind Corporation, P.O. Box 2143, Broken Arrow OK 74013-2143. (800)210-4416.

Louisiana Music Directory, OffBeat, Inc., 421 Frenchmen St., Suite 200, New Orleans LA 70116. (504)944-4300. Website: www.offbeat.com.

Lydian Chromatic Concept of Tonal Organization, Volume One: The Art and Science of Tonal Gravity, by George Russell, Concept Publishing Company, 258 Harvard St., #296, Brookline MA 02446-2904. E-mail: lydconcept@aol.com. Website: www. lydianchromaticconcept.com.

Melody in Songwriting, by Jack Perricone, Berklee Press, 1140 Boylston St., Boston MA 02215. (617)747-2146. E-mail: info@berkleepress.com. Website: www.berkleepress. com.

Music Attorney Legal & Business Affairs Registry, by Ritch Esra and Steve Trumbull, SRS Publishing, 7510 Sunset Blvd. #1041, Los Angeles CA 90046-3418. (800)552-7411. E-mail: musicregistry@compuserve.com or srspubl@aol.com.

The Music Business Registry, by Ritch Esra, SRS Publishing, 7510 Sunset Blvd. #1041, Los Angeles CA 90046-3418. (800)552-7411. E-mail: musicregistry@compuserve. com or srspu bl@aol.com. Website: www.musicregistry.com

Music Directory Canada, seventh edition, Norris-Whitney Communications Inc., 23 Hannover Dr., Suite 7, St. Catherines ON L2W 1A3 Canada. (877)RING-NWC. E-mail: mail@nor.com. Website: http://nor.com

Music Law: How to Run Your Band's Business, by Richard Stin, Nolo Press, 950 Parker St., Berkeley CA 94710-9867. (510)549-1976. Website: www.nolo.com

Music, Money and Success: The Insider's Guide to the Music Industry, by Jeffrey Brabec and Todd Brabec, Schirmer Books, 1633 Broadway, New York NY 10019.

The Music Publisher Registry, by Ritch Esra, SRS Publishing, 7510 Sunset Blvd. #1041, Los Angeles CA 90046-3418. (800)552-7411. E-mail: musicregistry@compuserve. com or srspubl@aol.com.

Music Publishing: A Songwriter's Guide, revised edition, by Randy Poe, Writer's Digest Books, 4700 E. Galbraith Rd., Cincinnati OH 45236. (800)448-0915. Website: www. writersdigest.com

The Musician's Guide to Making & Selling Your Own CDs & Cassettes, by Jana Stanfield, Writer's Digest Books, 4700 E. Galbraith Rd., Cincinnati OH 45236. (800)448-0915. Website: www.writersdigest.com

Musicians' Phone Book, The Los Angeles Music Industry Directory, Get Yourself Some Publishing, 28336 Simsalido Ave., Canyon Country CA 91351. (805)299-2405. E-mail: mpb@earthlink.net. Website: www.musiciansphonebook.com

Nashville Music Business Directory, by Mark Dreyer, NMBD Publishing, 9 Music Square S., Suite 210, Nashville TN 37203. (615)826-4141. E-mail: nmbd@nashvilleconnection. com. Website: www.nashvilleconnection.com

Nashville's Unwritten Rules: Inside the Business of the Country Music Machine, by Dan Daley, Overlook Press, One Overlook Dr., Woodstock NY 12498. (845)679-6838. E-mail: overlook@netstep.net.

National Directory of Independent Record Distributors, P.O. Box 452063, Lake Mary FL 32795-2063. (407)834-8555. E-mail: info@songwriterproducts.com. Website: www. songwriterproducts.com

The Official Country Music Directory, ICMA Music Directory, P.O. Box 271238, Nashville TN 37227.

Performance Magazine Guides, 1203 Lake St., Suite 200, Fort Worth TX 76102-4504. (817)338-9444. E-mail: sales@performancemagazine.com. Website: www. performancemagazine.com

Radio Stations of America: A National Directory, P.O. Box 452063, Lake Mary FL 32795-2063. (407)834-8555. E-mail: info@songwriterproducts.com. Website: www. songwriterproducts.com

The Real Deal—How to Get Signed to a Record Label from A to Z, by Daylle Deanna Schwartz, Billboard Books, 1695 Oak St., Lakewood NJ 08701. (800)344-7119.

Recording Industry Sourcebook, Music Books Plus, P.O. Box 670, 240 Portage Rd., Lewiston NY 14092. (800)265-8481. Website: www.musicbooksplus.com

Reharmonization Techniques, by Randy Felts, Berklee Press, 1140 Boylston St., Boston MA 02215. (617)747-2146. E-mail: info@berkleepress.com. Website: www.berkleepress. com

The Songwriters Idea Book, by Sheila Davis, Writer's Digest Books, 4700 E. Galbraith Rd., Cincinnati OH 45236. (800)448-0915. Website: www.writersdigest.com

Songwriter's Market Guide to Song & Demo Submission Formats, Writer's Digest

Books, 4700 E. Galbraith Rd., Cincinnati OH 45236. (800)448-0915. Website: www. writersdigest.com

Songwriter's Playground—Innovative Exercises in Creative Songwriting, by Barbara L. Jordan, Creative Music Marketing, 1085 Commonwealth Ave., Suite 323, Boston MA 02215. (617)926-8766.

The Songwriter's Workshop: Harmony, by Jimmy Kachulis, Berklee Press, 1140 Boylston St., Boston MA 02215. (617)747-2146. E-mail: info@berkleepress.com. Website: www.berkleepress.com

The Songwriter's Workshop: Melody, by Jimmy Kachulis, Berklee Press, 1140 Boylston St., Boston MA 02215. (617)747-2146. E-mail: info@berkleepress.com. Website: www. berkleepress.com

Songwriting and the Creative Process, by Steve Gillette, Sing Out! Publications, P.O. Box 5640, Bethlehem PA 18015-0253. (888)SING-OUT. E-mail: singout@libertynet. org. Website: www.singout.org/sopubs.html

Songwriting: Essential Guide to Lyric Form and Structure, by Pat Pattison, Berklee Press, 1140 Boylston St., Boston MA 02215. (617)747-2146. E-mail: info@berkleepress.com. Website: www.www.berkleepress.com

Songwriting: Essential Guide to Rhyming, by Pat Pattison, Berklee Press, 1140 Boylston St., Boston MA 02215. (617)747-2146. E-mail: info@berkleepress.com. Website: www.berkleepress.com

The Songwriting Sourcebook: How to Turn Chords Into Great Songs, by Rikky Rooksby, Backbeat Books, 600 Harrison St., San Francisco CA 94107. (415)947-6615. E-mail: books@musicplayer.com. Website: www.backbeatbooks.com

The Soul of the Writer, by Susan Tucker with Linda Lee Strother, Journey Publishing, P.O. Box 92411, Nashville TN 37209. (615)952-4894. Website: www.journeypublishing. com

Successful Lyric Writing, by Sheila Davis, Writer's Digest Books, 4700 E. Galbraith Rd., Cincinnati OH 45236. (800)448-0915. Website: www.writersdigest.com

This Business of Music Marketing and Promotion, by Tad Lathrop and Jim Pettigrew, Jr., Billboard Books, Watson-Guptill Publications, 770 Broadway, New York NY 10003. E-mail: info@watsonguptill.com.

Tim Sweeney's Guide to Releasing Independent Records, by Tim Sweeney, TSA Books, 31805 Highway 79 S., Temecula CA 92592. (909)303-9506. E-mail: info@tsamusic. com. Website: www.tsamusic.com

Tim Sweeney's Guide to Succeeding at Music Conventions, by Tim Sweeney, TSA Books, 31805 Highway 79 S., Temecula CA 92592. (909)303-9506. Website: www.tsamusic.com

Texas Music Industry Directory, Texas Music Office, Office of the Governor, P.O. Box 13246, Austin TX 78711. (512)463-6666. E-mail: music@governor.state.tx.us. Website: www.governor.state.tx.us/music

Tunesmith: Inside the Art of Songwriting, by Jimmy Webb, Hyperion, 77 W. 66th St., 11th Floor, New York NY 10023. (800)759-0190.

Volunteer Lawyers for the Arts Guide to Copyright for Musicians and Composers, One E. 53rd St., 6th Floor, New York NY 10022. (212)319-2787.

Writing Better Lyrics, by Pat Pattison, Writer's Digest Books, 4700 E. Galbraith Rd., Cincinnati OH 45236. (800)448-0915. Website: www.writersdigest.com

Writing Music for Hit Songs, by Jai Josefs, Schirmer Trade Books, 257 Park Ave. S., New York NY 10010. (212)254-2100.

The Yellow Pages of Rock, The Album Network, 120 N. Victory Blvd., Burbank CA 91502. (800)222-4382. Fax: (818)955-9048. E-mail: ypinfo@yprock.com.

Websites of Interest

The Internet provides a wealth of information for songwriters and performers, and the number of sites devoted to music grows each day. Below is a list of websites that can offer you information, links to other music sites, contact with other songwriters, and places to showcase your songs. Due to the dynamic nature of the online world, this is certainly not a comprehensive list, but it gives you a place to start on your Internet journey to search for opportunities to get your music heard.

About.com Musicians' Exchange http://musicians.about.com/
Site features headlines and articles of interest to independent musicians and songwriters, as well as links and label profiles.

Absolute Punk www.absolutepunk.net
Searchable online community focusing on punk and rock music, including news, including reviews, articles and interviews; forums to discuss music and pop culture.

American Music Center www.amc.net
Classical and jazz archives. Includes a list of organizations and contacts for composers.

American Society of Composers, Authors and Publishers (ASCAP) www.ascap.com
Database of works in ASCAP's repertoire. Includes performer, songwriter, and publisher information as well as membership information and industry news.

American Songwriter Magazine Homepage www.americansongwriter.com
This is the official homepage for *American Songwriter Magazine*. Features an online article archive, e-mail newsletter, and links.

Backstage Commerce www.backstagecommerce.com
Provides secure online support for the sale of music goods for independent artists.

Bathtub Music www.bathtubmusic.com
Online distributor of independent music; receives commission on any sales made.

Beaird Music Group Demos www.beairdmusicgroup.com
Nashville demo service which offers a variety of demo packages.

Billboard.com www.billboard.com
Industry news and searchable online database of music companies by subscription.

The Blues Foundation www.blues.org
Nonprofit organization located in Memphis, TN; website contains information on the foundation, membership, and events.

Broadcast Music, Inc. (BMI) www.bmi.com
Offers lists of song titles, writers, and publishers of the BMI repertoire. Includes membership information and general information on songwriting and licensing.

The Buzz Factor www.thebuzzfactor.com
Website offers free tips on the music marketing and self-promotion ideas.

Buzznet www.buzznet.com
Searchable networking and news site featuring music and pop culture; photos, videos, concert reviews, more.

CDBABY www.cdbaby.com
An online CD store dedicated to the sales of independent music.

CDFreedom www.cdfreedom.com
An online CD store for independent musicians.

Cadenza www.cadenza.org
Online resource for contemporary and classical music and musicians, including methods of contacting other musicians.

Center for the Promotion of Contemporary Composers (CPCC) www.under.org/cpcc
Website for CPCC, an internet-based service organization for composers.

Chorus America www.chorusamerica.org
The website for Chorus America, a national organization for professional and volunteer choruses. Includes job listings and professional development information.

Finetune www.finetune.com
Internet Radio/streaming audio. User can create personalized channels and playlists online.

Film Music Network www.filmmusicworld.com or www.filmmusic.net
Network of links, news, and job-listings within the film music world.

Fourfront Media and Music www.knab.com
Site offers information on product development, promotion, publicity, and performance.

Garageband www.garageband.com
Online music hosting site where independent musicians can post music and profiles which can be critiqued by listeners.

Get Signed www.getsigned.com
Interviews with musicians, songwriters, and industry veterands, how-to business

information, and more.

Government Liaison Services www.trademarkinfo.com
An intellectual property research firm. Offers a variety of trademark searches.

Guitar Nine Records www.guitar9.com
Offers articles on songwriting, music theory, guitar techniques, etc.

Google www.google.com
Online search engine can be used to look up music, information, lyrics.

Harmony Central www.harmony-central.com
Online community for musicians with in-depth reviews and discussions.

Harry Fox Agency www.harryfox.com
Offers a comprehensive FAQ about licensing songs for use in recording, performance, and film.

iLike www.ilike.com
Music networking site. Signed and unsigned artists can sign up for free artists' page and upload songs and events. Works with other social networks such as www.facebook.com.

Independent Distribution Network www.idnmusic.com
Website of independent bands distributing their music with advice on everything from starting a band to finding labels.

Independent Songwriter Web Magazine http://www.independentsongwriter.com/
Independent music reviews, classifieds, message board and chat sessions.

Indie-Music.com http://indie-music.com/
Website of how-to articles, record label directory, links to musicians and venue listings.

Jazz Corner www.jazzcorner.com
Portal for the websites of jazz musicians and organizations. Includes the jazz video share, jukebox, and the "Speakeasy" bulletin board.

Just Plain Folks www.jpfolks.com or www.justplainfolks.org
Website for songwriting organization featuring messageboards, lyric feedback forums, member profiles and music, contact listings, chapter homepages, and more.

Last.fm http://www.last.fm/
Music tracking and social networking site.

Li'l Hank's Guide for Songwriters in L.A. www.halsguide.com
Website for songwriters with information on clubs, publishers, books, etc. Links to other songwriting sites.

Live365 http://www.live365.com/index.live
Internet radio/audio stream search engine.

Livejournal www.livejournal.com

Resources

Social networking community using open source technology; music communities provide news, interviews, and reviews.

Los Angeles Goes Underground http://lagu.somaweb.org/
Website dedicated to underground rock bands from Los Angeles and Hollywood.

Lyrical Line www.lyricalline.com
Offers places to upload original songs for critique or exposure, industry news and more.

Lyric Ideas www.lyricideas.com
Offers songwriting prompts, themes, and creative techniques for songwriting.

Lyricist http://www.lyricist.com/
Site offers advice, tips, and events in the music industry.

MI2N (the Music Industry News Network) www.mi2n.com
Offers news on happenings in the music industry and career postings.

The Muse's Muse http://www.musesmuse.com/
Classifieds, catalog of music samples, songwriting articles, newsletter, and chat room.

MOG http://mog.com/
Internet radio/streaming audio. Contains music news and concert reviews, personalized recommendations.

Music Books Plus www.musicbooksplus.com
Online bookstore dedicated to music books on every music-related topic, plus a free newsletter.

Music Publishers Association http://www.mpa.org/
Ofers directories for music publishers and imprints, copyright resource center and information on the organization.

Music Yellow Pages http://www.musicyellowpages.com/
Listings of music-related businesses.

MySpace www.myspace.com
Social networking site featuring music web pages for musicians and songwriters.

Nashville Songwriters Association International (NSAI) www.nashvillesongwriters.com
Official NSAI homepage. Offers news, links, online registration and message board for members.

National Association of Composers USA (NACUSA) www.music-usa.org/nacusa
A nonprofit organization devoted to the promotion and performance of American concert hall music.

National Music Publishers Association www.nmpa.org
Organization's online site filled with information about copyright, legislation, and other concerns of the music publishing world.

Online Rock http://www.onlinerock.com/
> Range of membership options including a free option, offers webpage services, articles, chat rooms, links, and more.

Opera America http://www.operaamerica.org/
> Website of Opera America features information on advocacy and awareness programs, publications, conference schedules, and more.

Outersound www.outersound.com
> Information on educating yourself in the music industry and a list of music magazines to advertise in or get reviewed by.

Pandora www.pandora.com
> A site created by the founders of the Music Genome Project; a searchable music radio/streaming audio site.

Performer Mag www.performermag.com
> Offers articles, music industry news, classifieds and reviews.

Performing Songwriter Magazine Homepage www.performingsongwriter.com
> Official homepage for the magazine features articles and links.

Pitchfork www.pitchforkmedia.com
> Offers Indie news, reviews, media, and features.

Public Domain Music http://www.pdinfo.com/
> Articles on public domain works and copyright including public domain song lists, research sources, tips and FAQ's.

PUMP Audio http://www.pumpaudio.com/
> License music for film and television on a non-exclusive basis. No submission fees, rights retained by songwriter.

Purevolume www.purevolume.com
> Music hosting site with searchable database of songs by signed and unsigned artists. Musicians and songwriters can upload songs and events.

The Recording Project http://www.recordingproject.com/
> Online community for musicians and recording artists, every level welcome.

Record Producer.com www.record-producer.com
> Extensive site dedicated to audio engineering and record production. Offers a free newsletter, online instruction, and e-bookson various aspects of record production and audio engineering.

Rhythm Net www.rhythmnet.com
> Online CD store for independent musicians.

Rock and Roll Hall of Fame + Museum http://www.rockhall.com/
> Website for the Rock and Roll Hall of Fame and Museum, including events listings, visitor info, and more.

SESAC Inc. www.sesac.com

Resources

Website for performing rights organization with songwriter profiles, industry news updates, licensing information, and links to other sites.

SingerSongwriter www.singersongwriter.ws
Resources for singer-songwriters, including an extensive list, featured resources and lists of radio stations organized geographically.

Slacker www.slacker.com
Internet Radio/streaming audio. User can create personalized channels and playlists online.

Soma FM www.somafm.com
Internet underground/alternative radio with commercial-free broadcasting from San Francisco.

Song Catalog www.songcatalog.com
Online song catalog database for licensing.

Songlink www.songlink.com
Offers opportunities to pitch songs to music publishers for specific recording projects and industry news.

SongRamp www.songramp.com
Online songrwriting organization with message boards, blogs, news, and streaming music channels. Offers variety of membership packages.

SongsAlive! www.songsalive.org
Online songwriters organization and community.

Songwriter 101 www.songwriter101.com
Offers articles, industry news, and message boards.

Songwriter's Guild of America (SGA) www.songwritersguild.com
Industry news, member services information, newsletters, contract reviews, and more.

Songwriter's Resource Network www.songwritersresourcenetwork.com
News and education resource for songwriters, lyricists, and composers.

SongwriterUniverse www.songwriteruniverse.com
In-depth articles, business information, education and recommended reading.

SoundPedia http://soundpedia.com
Internet Radio/streaming audio. User can create personalized channels and playlists online.

The Songwriting Education Resource www.craftofsongwriting.com
An educational website for songwriters. Offers discussion boards, articles, and links.

Sonic Bids www.sonicbids.com
Features an online press kit with photos, bio, music samples, date calendar. Free trial period first month for artists/bands to sign up, newsletter.

StarPolish www.starpolish.com

Features articles and interviews on the music industry.

SummerSongs Songwriting Camps www.summersongs.com

Information about songwriting camps, staff, and online registration.

TAXI www.taxi.com

Independent A&R vehicle that shops demos to A&R professionals.

United States Copyright Office http://www.copyright.gov

Homepage for the US Copyright office. Offers information on registering songs.

The Velvet Rope www.velvetrope.com

Famous/infamous online music industry message board.

Weirdo Music www.weirdomusic.com

Online music magazine with articles, reviews, downloads, and links to Internet Radio shows.

Yahoo! http://new.music.yahoo.com/

Search engine with radio station guide, music industry news, and listings.

YouTube www.youtube.com

Social networking site which hosts audiovisual content. Searchable database provides links to music videos, interviews and more.

Glossary

A cappella. Choral singing without accompaniment.

AAA form. A song form in which every verse has the same melody; often used for songs that tell a story.

AABA, ABAB. A commonly used song pattern consisting of two verses, a bridge and a verse, or a repeated pattern of verse and bridge, where the verses are musically the same.

A&R Director. Record company executive in charge of the Artists and Repertoire Department who is responsible for finding and developing new artists and matching songs with artists.

A/C. Adult contemporary music.

Advance. Money paid to the songwriter or recording artist, which is then recouped before regular royalty payment begins. Sometimes called ``up front'' money, advances are deducted from royalties.

AFIM. Association for Independent Music (formerly NAIRD). Organization for independent record companies, distributors, retailers, manufacturers, etc.

AFM. American Federation of Musicians. A union for musicians and arrangers.

AFTRA. American Federation of Television and Radio Artists. A union for performers.

AIMP. Association of Independent Music Publishers.

Airplay. The radio broadcast of a recording.

AOR. Album-Oriented Rock. A radio format that primarily plays selections from rock albums as opposed to hit singles.

Arrangement. An adaptation of a composition for a recording or performance, with consideration for the melody, harmony, instrumentation, tempo, style, etc.

ASCAP. American Society of Composers, Authors and Publishers. A performing rights society. (See the Organizations section.)

Assignment. Transfer of rights of a song from writer to publisher.

Audio Visual Index (AVI). A database containing title and production information for cue sheets which are available from a performing rights organization. Currently, BMI, ASCAP, SOCAN, PRS, APRA and SACEM contribute their cue sheet listings to the AVI.

Audiovisual. Refers to presentations that use audio backup for visual material.

Background music. Music used that creates mood and supports the spoken dialogue of a radio program or visual action of an audiovisual work. Not feature or theme music.

b&w. Black and white.

Bed. Prerecorded music used as background material in commercials. In rap music, often refers to the sampled and looped drums and music over which the rapper performs.

Black box. Theater without fixed stage or seating arrangements, capable of a variety of formations. Usually a small space, often attached to a major theater complex, used for workshops or experimental works calling for small casts and limited sets.

BMI. Broadcast Music, Inc. A performing rights society. (See the Organizations section.)

Booking agent. Person who schedules performances for entertainers.

Bootlegging. Unauthorized recording and selling of a song.

Business manager. Person who handles the financial aspects of artistic careers.

Buzz. Attention an act generates through the media and word of mouth.

b/w. Backed with. Usually refers to the B-side of a single.

C&W. Country and western.

Catalog. The collected songs of one writer, or all songs handled by one publisher.

CD. Compact Disc (see below).

CD-R. A recordable CD.

Resources

CD-ROM. Compact Disc-Read Only Memory. A computer information storage medium capable of holding enormous amounts of data. Information on a CD-ROM cannot be deleted. A computer user must have a CD-ROM drive to access a CD-ROM.

Chamber music. Any music suitable for performance in a small audience area or chamber.

Chamber orchestra. A miniature orchestra usually containing one instrument per part.

Chart. The written arrangement of a song.

Charts. The trade magazines' lists of the best-selling records.

CHR. Comtemporary Hit Radio. Top 40 pop music.

Collaboration. Two or more artists, writers, etc., working together on a single project; for instance, a playwright and a songwriter creating a musical together.

Compact disc. A small disc (about 4.7 inches in diameter) holding digitally encoded music that is read by a laser beam in a CD player.

Composers. The men and women who create musical compositions for motion pictures and other audio visual works, or the creators of classical music composition.

Co-publish. Two or more parties own publishing rights to the same song.

Copyright. The exclusive legal right giving the creator of a work the power to control the publishing, reproduction and selling of the work. Although a song is technically copyrighted at the time it is written, the best legal protection of that copyright comes through registering the copyright with the Library of Congress.

Copyright infringement. Unauthorized use of a copyrighted song or portions thereof.

Cover recording. A new version of a previously recorded song.

Crossover. A song that becomes popular in two or more musical categories (e.g., country and pop).

Cut. Any finished recording; a selection from a LP. Also to record.

DAT. Digital Audio Tape. A professional and consumer audio cassette format for recording and playing back digitally-encoded material. DAT cassettes are approximately one-third smaller than conventional audio cassettes.

DCC. Digital Compact Cassette. A consumer audio cassette format for recording and playing back digitally-encoded tape. DCC tapes are the same size as analog cassettes.

Demo. A recording of a song submitted as a demonstration of a writer's or artist's skills.

Derivative work. A work derived from another work, such as a translation, musical arrangement, sound recording, or motion picture version.

Distributor. Wholesale marketing agent responsible for getting records from manufacturers to retailers.

Donut. A jingle with singing at the beginning and end and instrumental background in the middle. Ad copy is recorded over the middle section.

E-mail. Electronic mail. Computer address where a company or individual can be reached via modem.

Engineer. A specially-trained individual who operates recording studio equipment.

Enhanced CD. General term for an audio CD that also contains multimedia computer information. It is playable in both standard CD players and CD-ROM drives.

EP. Extended play record or cassette containing more selections than a standard single, but fewer than a standard album.

EPK. Electronic press kit. Usually contains photos, sound files, bio information, reviews, tour dates, etc. posted online. Sonicbids.com is a popular EPK hosting Web site.

Final mix. The art of combining all the various sounds that take place during the recording session into a two-track stereo or mono tape. Reflects the total product and all of the energies and talents the artist, producer and engineer have put into the project.

Fly space. The area above a stage from which set pieces are lowered and raised during a performance.

Folio. A softcover collection of printed music prepared for sale.

Following. A fan base committed to going to gigs and buying albums.

Foreign rights societies. Performing rights societies other than domestic which have reciprocal agreements with ASCAP and BMI for the collection of royalties accrued by foreign radio and television airplay and other public performance of the writer members of the above groups.

Harry Fox Agency. Organization that collects mechanical royalties.

Grammy. Music industry awards presented by the National Academy of Recording Arts and Sciences.

Hip-hop. A dance oriented musical style derived from a combination of disco, rap and R&B.

Hit. A song or record that achieves top 40 status.

Hook. A memorable ``catch'' phrase or melody line that is repeated in a song.

House. Dance music created by remixing samples from other songs.

Hypertext. Words or groups of words in an electronic document that are linked to other text, such as a definition or a related document. Hypertext can also be linked to illustrations.

Indie. An independent record label, music publisher or producer.

Infringement. A violation of the exclusive rights granted by the copyright law to a copyright owner.

Internet. A worldwide network of computers that offers access to a wide variety of electronic resources.

ips. Inches per second; a speed designation for tape recording.

IRC. International reply coupon, necessary for the return of materials sent out of the country. Available at most post offices.

Jingle. Usually a short verse set to music designed as a commercial message.

Lead sheet. Written version (melody, chord symbols and lyric) of a song.

Leader. Plastic (non-recordable) tape at the beginning and between songs for ease in selection.

Libretto. The text of an opera or any long choral work. The booklet containing such text.

Listing. Block of information in this book about a specific company.

LP. Designation for long-playing record played at 331/3 rpm.

Lyric sheet. A typed or written copy of a song's lyrics.

Market. A potential song or music buyer; also a demographic division of the record-buying public.

Master. Edited and mixed tape used in the production of records; the best or original copy of a recording from which copies are made.

MD. MiniDisc. A 2.5 inch disk for recording and playing back digitally-encoded music.

Mechanical right. The right to profit from the physical reproduction of a song.

Mechanical royalty. Money earned from record, tape and CD sales.

MIDI. Musical instrument digital interface. Universal standard interface that allows musical instruments to communicate with each other and computers.

Mini Disc. (See MD above.)

Mix. To blend a multi-track recording into the desired balance of sound, usually to a 2-track stereo master.

Modem. MOdulator/DEModulator. A computer device used to send data from one computer to another via telephone line.

MOR. Middle of the road. Easy-listening popular music.

MP3. File format of a relatively small size that stores audio files on a computer. Music saved in a MP3 format can be played only with a MP3 player (which can be downloaded onto a computer).

Ms. Manuscript.

Multimedia. Computers and software capable of integrating text, sound, photographic-quality images, animation and video.

Music bed. (See *Bed* above.)

Music jobber. A wholesale distributor of printed music.

Music library. A business that purchases canned music, which can then be bought by producers of radio and TV commercials, films, videos and audiovisual productions to use however they wish.

Music publisher. A company that evaluates songs for commercial potential, finds artists to record them, finds other uses (such as TV or film) for the songs, collects income generated by the songs and protects copyrights from infringement.

Music Row. An area of Nashville, TN, encompassing Sixteenth, Seventeeth and Eighteenth avenues where most of the major publishing houses, recording studios, mastering labs, songwriters, singers, promoters, etc. practice their trade.

NARAS. National Academy of Recording Arts and Sciences.

The National Academy of Songwriters (NAS). The largest U.S. songwriters' association. (See the Organizations section.)

Needle-drop. Refers to a type of music library. A needledrop music library is a licensed library that allows producers to borrow music on a rate schedule. The price depends on how the music will be used.

Network. A group of computers electronically linked to share information and resources.

NMPA. National Music Publishers Association.

One-off. A deal between songwriter and publisher which includes only one song or project at a time. No future involvement is implicated. Many times a single song contract accompanies a one-off deal.

One-stop. A wholesale distributor of who sells small quantities of records to ``mom and pop'' record stores, retailers and jukebox operators.

Operetta. Light, humorous, satiric plot or poem, set to cheerful light music with occasional spoken dialogue.

Overdub. To record an additional part (vocal or instrumental) onto a basic multi-track recording.

Parody. A satirical imitation of a literary or musical work. Permission from the owner of the copyright is generally required before commercial exploitation of a parody.

Payola. Dishonest payment to broadcasters in exchange for airplay.

Performing rights. A specific right granted by U.S. copyright law protecting a composition from being publicly performed without the owner's permission.

Performing rights organization. An organization that collects income from the public performance of songs written by its members and then proportionally distributes this income to the individual copyright holder based on the number of performances of each song.

Personal manager. A person who represents artists to develop and enhance their careers. Personal managers may negotiate contracts, hire and dismiss other agencies and personnel relating to the artist's career, review material, help with artist promotions and perform many services. Piracy. The unauthorized reproduction and selling of printed or recorded music.

Pitch. To attempt to solicit interest for a song by audition.

Playlist. List of songs a radio station will play.

Points. A negotiable percentage paid to producers and artists for records sold.

Producer. Person who supervises every aspect of a recording project.

Production company. Company specializing in producing jingle packages for advertising agencies. May also refer to companies specializing in audiovisual programs.

Professional manager. Member of a music publisher's staff who screens submitted material and tries to get the company's catalog of songs recorded.

Proscenium. Permanent architectural arch in a theater that separates the stage from the audience.

Public domain. Any composition with an expired, lapsed or invalid copyright, and therefore belonging to everyone.

Purchase license. Fee paid for music used from a stock music library.

Query. A letter of inquiry to an industry professional soliciting his interest.

R&B. Rhythm and blues.

Rack Jobber. Distributors who lease floor space from department stores and put in racks of albums.

Rate. The percentage of royalty as specified by contract.

Release. Any record issued by a record company.

Residuals. In advertising or television, payments to singers and musicians for use of a performance.

RIAA. Recording Industry Association of America.

Royalty. Percentage of money earned from the sale of records or use of a song.

RPM. Revolutions per minute. Refers to phonograph turntable speed.

SAE. Self-addressed envelope (with no postage attached).

SASE. Self-addressed stamped envelope.

SATB. The abbreviation for parts in choral music, meaning Soprano, Alto, Tenor and Bass.

Score. A complete arrangement of all the notes and parts of a composition (vocal or instrumental) written out on staves. A full score, or orchestral score, depicts every orchestral part on a separate staff and is used by a conductor.

Self-contained. A band or recording act that writes all their own material.

SESAC. A performing rights organization, originally the Society of European Stage Authors and Composers. (See the Organizations section.)

SFX. Sound effects.

Shop. To pitch songs to a number of companies or publishers.

Single. 45 rpm record with only one song per side. A 12£ single refers to a long version of one song on a 12£ disc, usually used for dance music.

Ska. Fast tempo dance music influenced primarily by reggae and punk, usually featuring horns, saxophone and bass.

SOCAN. Society of Composers, Authors and Music Publishers of Canada. A Canadian performing rights organization. (See the Organizations section.)

Solicited. Songs or materials that have been requested.

Song plugger. A songwriter representative whose main responsibility is promoting uncut songs to music publishers, record companies, artists and producers.

Song shark. Person who deals with songwriters deceptively for his own profit.

SoundScan. A company that collates the register tapes of reporting stores to track the actual number of albums sold at the retail level.

Soundtrack. The audio, including music and narration, of a film, videotape or audiovisual program.

Space stage. Open stage that features lighting and, perhaps, projected scenery.

Split publishing. To divide publishing rights between two or more publishers.

Staff songwriter. A songwriter who has an exclusive agreement with a publisher.

Statutory royalty rate. The maximum payment for mechanical rights guaranteed by law that a record company may pay the songwriter and his publisher for each record or tape sold.

Subpublishing. Certain rights granted by a U.S. publisher to a foreign publisher in exchange for promoting the U.S. catalog in his territory.

Synchronization. Technique of timing a musical soundtrack to action on film or video.

Take. Either an attempt to record a vocal or instrument part, or an acceptable recording of a performance.

Tejano. A musical form begun in the late 1970s by regional bands in south Texas, its style reflects a blended Mexican-American culture. Incorporates elements of rock, country, R&B and jazz, and often features accordion and 12-string guitar.

Thrust stage. Stage with audience on three sides and a stagehouse or wall on the fourth side.

Top 40. The first 40 songs on the pop music charts at any given time. Also refers to a style of music which emulates that heard on the current top 40.

Track. Divisions of a recording tape (e.g., 24-track tape) that can be individually recorded in the studio, then mixed into a finished master.

Trades. Publications covering the music industry.

12-Single. A 12-inch record containing one or more remixes of a song, originally intended for dance club play.

Unsolicited. Songs or materials that were not requested and are not expected.

Vocal score. An arrangement of vocal music detailing all vocal parts, and condensing all accompanying instrumental music into one piano part.

Website. An address on the World Wide Web that can be accessed by computer modem. It may contain text, graphics and sound.

Wing space. The offstage area surrounding the playing stage in a theater, unseen by the audience, where sets and props are hidden, actors wait for cues, and stagehands prepare to chance sets.

World music. A general music category which includes most musical forms originating outside the U.S. and Europe, including reggae and calypso. World music finds its roots primarily in the Caribbean, Latin America, Africa and the south Pacific.

World Wide Web (WWW). An Internet resource that utilizes hypertext to access information. It also supports formatted text, illustrations and sounds, depending on the user's computer capabilities.

Category Indexes

The Category Indexes are a good place to begin searching for a market. They break down the listings by section (music publishers, record companies, etc.) and by the type of music they are interested in. For example, if you write country songs, and are looking for a publisher to pitch them, go to the Music Publishers heading and then check the companies listed under the Country subheading. The music categories cover a wide range of variations within each genre, so be sure to read each listing thoroughly to make sure your own unique take on that genre is a good match. Some listings do not appear in these indexes because they did not cite a specific preference. Listings that were very specific, or whose music descriptions don't quite fit into these categories also do not appear. (Category listings for **Music Publishers** begin on this page, **Record Companies** on page 381, **Record Producers** on page 391 and **Managers & Booking Agents** begin on page 402.)

Alternative (also modern rock, punk, college rock, new wave, hardcore, new music, industrial, ska, indie rock, garage, etc.)

Category Index

Dance (also house, hi-NRG, disco, club, rave, techno, trip-hop, trance, etc.

Folk (also acoustic, Celtic, etc.)

Instrumental (also background music, musical scores, etc.)

Jazz (also fusion, bebop, swing, etc.)

Rock (also, rockabiliy, AOR, rock'n' roll, etc.)

World Music (also reggae, ethnic, calypso, international, world beat, etc.)

RECORD COMPANIES
Adult Contemporary (also easy listening, middle of the road, AAA, ballads, etc.)

Alternative (also modern rock, punk, college rock, new wave, hardcore, new music, industrial, ska, indie rock, garage, etc.)

Blues

Children's

Dance (also house, hi-NRG, disco, club, rave, techno, trip-hop, trance, etc.

Instrumental (also background music, musical scores, etc.)

Folk (also acoustic, Celtic, etc.)

Jazz (also fusion, bebop, swing, etc.)

Category Index

Rap (also hip-hop, bass, etc.)

Religious (also gospel, sacred, Christian, church, hymns, praise, inspirational, worship, etc.)

Rock (also, rockabiliy, AOR, rock'n' roll, etc.)

World Music (also reggae, ethnic, calypso, international, world beat, etc.)

RECORD PRODUCERS
Adult Contemporary (also easy listening, middle of the road, AAA, ballads, etc.)

Alternative (also modern rock, punk, college rock, new wave, hardcore, new music, industrial, ska, indie rock, garage, etc.)

Blues

Children's

Classical (also opera, chamber music, serious music, choral, etc.)

Country (also western, C&W, bluegrass, cowboy songs, western swing, honky-tonk, etc.)

Dance (also house, hi-NRG, disco, club, rave, techno, trip-hop, trance, etc.

Folk (also acoustic, Celtic, etc.)

Category Index

Rock (also, rockabiliy, AOR, rock'n' roll, etc.)

World Music (also reggae, ethnic, calypso, international, world beat, etc.)

MANAGERS & BOOKING AGENTS
Adult Contemporary (also easy listening, middle of the road, AAA, ballads, etc.)

Alternative (also modern rock, punk, college rock, new wave, hardcore, new music, industrial, ska, indie rock, garage, etc.)

Blues

Children's

Dance (also house, hi-NRG, disco, club, rave, techno, trip-hop, trance, etc.)

Metal (also thrash, grindcore, heavy metal, etc.)

New Age (also ambient)

Novelty (also comedy, humor, etc.)

Rap (also hip-hop, bass, etc.)

Religious (also gospel, sacred, Christian, church, hymns, praise, inspirational, worship, etc.)

Rock (also, rockabiliy, AOR, rock'n' roll, etc.)

Rock

World Music (also reggae, ethnic, calypso, international, world beat, etc.)

Openness to Submissions Index

Use this index to find companies open to your level of experience. It is recommended to use this index in conjunction with the Category Indexes found on page 370. Once you have compiled a list of companies open to your experience and music, read the information in these listings, paying close attention to the **How to Contact** subhead. (Also see A Sample Listing Decoded on page 12.)

☑ PREFERS EXPERIENCED, BUT OPEN TO BEGINNERS

Manager Booking Agents

Openness Index

Film & TV Index

This index lists companies who place music in motion picture and TV shows (excluding commercials). To learn more about their film/TV experience, read the information under **Film & TV** in their Listings. It is recommended to use this index in conjunction with the Openness to Submissions Index beginning on page 413.

Geographic Index

This Geographic Index will help you locate companies by state as well as those in countries outside the U.S. It is recommended to use this index in conjunction with the Openness to Submissions Index on page 413. Once you find the names of companies in this index you are interested in, check the listings within each section for addresses, phone numbers, contact names and submission details.

General Index

General Index